RESCUE
BOARD

RESCUE
BOARD

*The Untold Story of America's Efforts
to Save the Jews of Europe*

REBECCA
ERBELDING

DOUBLEDAY
New York · London · Toronto
Sydney · Auckland

www.doubleday.com

DOUBLEDAY and the portrayal of an anchor with a dolphin are
registered trademarks of Penguin Random House LLC.

Grateful acknowledgment is made to HarperCollins Publishers for permission to reprint
an excerpt of "The World: Hope" from *New and Collected Poems: 1931–2001*
by Czeslaw Milosz, copyright © 1988, 1991, 1995, 2001 by
Czeslaw Milosz Royalties, Inc. Reprinted by permission of HarperCollins Publishers.

Pages 347–48 constitute an extension of this copyright page.

Book design by Michael Collica
Jacket design by Michael J. Windsor
Jacket images: photo of third meeting of the Board of Directors of the War
Refugee Board in the office of Secretary of State Cordell Hull courtesy of
Franklin D. Roosevelt Library; map © Encyclopaedia Britannica / UIG /
Universal Images Group / Getty Images; texture © Here / Shutterstock

Library of Congress Cataloging-in-Publication Data
Names: Erbelding, Rebecca, author.
Title: Rescue Board : the untold story of America's efforts to save the Jews
of Europe / Rebecca Erbelding.
Description: First edition. | New York : Doubleday, [2018]
Identifiers: LCCN 2017039969 (print) | LCCN 2017040279 (ebook) |
ISBN 9780385542517 (hardcover) | 9780385542524 (ebook)
Subjects: LCSH: World War, 1939–1945—Refugees. | United States. War Refugee
Board. | World War, 1939–1945—Jews—Rescue—Europe. | United
States—Politics and government—1933–1945. | BISAC: HISTORY / Holocaust. |
HISTORY / United States / 20th Century. | HISTORY / Europe / Western.
Classification: LCC D809.U5 (ebook) | LCC D809.U5 E73 2015 (print) |
DDC 940.53/145—c23
LC record available at https://lccn.loc.gov/2017039969

MANUFACTURED IN THE UNITED STATES OF AMERICA

1 3 5 7 9 10 8 6 4 2

First Edition

For Ron
8

Some people say we should not trust our eyes,
That there is nothing, just a seeming,
These are the ones who have no hope.
They think that the moment we turn away,
The world, behind our backs, ceases to exist,
As if snatched up by the hands of thieves.

—CZESŁAW MIŁOSZ, from the poem "Hope" (1943),
published in his 1945 collection *Ocalenie* ("Rescue")

Contents

RESCUE BOARD

Prologue

France, August 1942

THE BUSES THAT TOOK the children away arrived first. The sun beat down, and the loveliness of August in Provence—the olive groves green and gray, the newly harvested wheat fields still golden—stood in stark contrast to the tile factory, a looming brick structure enclosed by barbed wire. Within, more than fifteen hundred people waited for the end to begin.

Nearly seventy children, some just toddlers, were gathered in the factory's dusty courtyard as two large buses pulled up. Their parents did not know where the children would go, only that it would not be to Poland. The Jewish organizations working inside Les Milles—the name of this makeshift concentration camp—had negotiated with the French government to exempt the children from deportation. With the hours growing short before the first train was to leave, the time had come to say good-bye. Grasping tiny faces and stroking hair, mothers and fathers gave frantic good-bye kisses and cried, *"Gut sein"*—"Be good"—before the buses rolled away. Some of the parents screamed and collapsed.

Roswell McClelland watched off to the side, pacing and smoking. A twenty-eight-year-old Californian, Ross was one of only a few dozen Allied aid workers permitted in the concentration camps, mostly representatives of pacifist churches. He and his wife, Marjorie, both worked for the American Friends Service Committee (AFSC), a Quaker organization. Because the AFSC had fed hundreds of thousands of German children after World War I, the Nazis and their

French collaborators allowed them entry into the camps to distribute food and clothing while forcing other Americans out of occupied and collaborationist territory. And now, the AFSC found itself in a position none of the staff ever imagined: splitting up families, likely forever, in a heartbreaking attempt to save the lives of the children. As he watched the fathers and mothers wail, Ross tried not to get emotional. Though none of the other aid workers knew, Marjorie was pregnant with their first child. What kind of a world, he wondered, separates parents from their children?

Other prisoners in Les Milles, also watching the scene, had sent their children out of the camp sooner. Relief workers—including Ross and Marjorie—secreted the kids to orphanages run by the Oeuvre de Secours aux Enfants, a children's aid organization. As the war dragged on, some of those children would go into hiding with non-Jewish families; others would try to sneak over the border to Switzerland or to Spain; and others would be arrested and deported east like their parents before them. Several hundred children, whose mothers and fathers signed away all parental rights, had already left for America to be placed with new families. A group of fifty children from France had departed nearly three months earlier; their first letters from America would not arrive in time to reach their parents in Les Milles.

It was Monday, August 10, 1942, the beginning of the deportation of foreign Jews from southern France toward Drancy, a transit camp outside Paris. From Drancy, the prisoners would take a longer train ride toward an uncertain fate in Nazi-occupied Poland.

Ross had his suspicions of what awaited the prisoners of Les Milles. He had just returned to Provence after an emergency trip to Vichy, the capital of Nazi-collaborationist France, where he and a group of colleagues had managed to meet with Pierre Laval, the head of the authoritarian government. They implored Laval to cancel the deportations. McClelland impressed upon him that the Germans wanted to "exterminate these people." Laval scoffed. The accusation was preposterous, a fiction. The French were assisting the Nazis in removing troublemaking foreign Jews from France, and the prisoners were going to special ethnic reservations in southern Poland where they could live and work together. Besides, Laval added, if the United States loved the Jews so much, why didn't McClelland's country accept them?

In fact, many of the prisoners at Les Milles had been collecting the documentation required to get a visa to the United States. But for most, the bureaucratic obstacles erected by both the American and the Vichy governments—not to mention the challenge and expense of reserving space on one of the few passenger ships still crossing the Atlantic—made immigration impossible. The AFSC's Refugee Division tried to assist thousands, including a significant percentage of the Les Milles prisoners, with their applications and paperwork. McClelland knew many of them—knew their families, knew how close they were to getting the all-important visas, knew them as individuals in a way bureaucracies couldn't.

In the weeks prior to the deportations, Vichy France canceled exit visas for refugees, the last official document a prisoner needed to be released from a camp prior to immigration. As a result, even those who received their U.S. visas could no longer leave. The AFSC protested and got reprieves for a few. But in October 1942, more than 270 letters alerting the recipients their U.S. visas had finally been approved were returned to the Marseille consulate, marked "undeliverable." At least seventeen of the letters were for prisoners deported from Les Milles in the early morning of August 11, 1942.

After the buses with the children drove away, McClelland and his colleague, Russell Ritchie, left for a few hours, returning in the middle of the afternoon with two prisoners from Hôtel Bompard, a Marseille hotel used as a holding center for women waiting for their American visas. Having learned that their husbands would soon be deported from Les Milles, the two women surrendered their children and resolved to join the deportations voluntarily. For the second time that day, Ross walked into a terrible scene in the courtyard. The prisoners were lined up—the seven hundred who had been at the camp for months, plus eight hundred whom the Vichy guards had collected from the countryside over the previous week—for a long roll call.

The commandant of Les Milles, Robert Maulavé, refused to choose the prisoners who would leave first, saving his energy to plead to higher officials for those he felt should be exempted entirely. There was no humane way to go about his work, so he did it alphabetically, *A* through *H*. The roll call consumed hours. From "Abenstern, Otto," a thirty-eight-year-old from Stuttgart, to "Hersch, Hermann," fifty-six, from Berlin, the names were shouted, and 262 prisoners learned, definitively, that they would be going. Eighteen-year-old Richard Greilsamer, the youngest, accompanied his parents. Blondine Weill, aged eighty, the oldest, probably volunteered herself to spare someone younger for a few more days or to stay with her daughter, Pauline Frank. At least six people on the list had almost made it to Cuba in 1939 on the *St. Louis,* before being turned back and finding temporary safety in France. Ludwig and Irma Bauer, from Berlin, their son already in the U.S. Army, would never learn that on the day of their deportation, officials across the ocean in Washington, D.C., finally approved their American immigration visas.

Guards in black uniforms with carbines slung over their shoulders directed the selected group to find their luggage in the massive piles of belongings. Many of the prisoners wore overcoats, even in the midday sun, fearful that if they took them off, the coats would be confiscated. Surely, they would need them wherever they were going. People fainted in the heat and were carried to the infirmary, but their names remained on the lists.

At around 6:00 in the evening, the prisoners, grouped by families, slowly climbed into the railcars as guards barked orders, ready to prevent resistance. The train tracks ran parallel to the factory, about three hundred yards away, in plain sight of the prisoners who remained. As the stragglers shouting their good-byes were escorted out of the camp, the heavy iron factory gate clanged shut.

Ross McClelland had spent the previous day gathering food packages to send with the prisoners. The AFSC collected condensed milk, sardines, soap, and sugar. A random assortment to be sure, but better than nothing. One of the Jewish organizations had provided galvanized pails to serve as public toilets, water containers, and ladles for dipping. For hours, Ross navigated the AFSC's little gray Simca truck between their nearby storerooms and the train. Though the transport would not leave until daybreak, the guards refused to open the car doors to refill the water or empty the waste pails. They did, however, inspect for razors, knives, and any other implement the prisoners might use to try to commit suicide or to mount an attack. The camp's doctor told Ross there had been at least three attempted suicides earlier in the evening. The AFSC workers used the inspections to get their supplies onto each car.

Most of the prisoners, exhausted, settled into the straw piled on the floor to sleep as the relief workers outside continued their distributions. Throughout the night, as Ross passed, checking things off his mental lists, prisoners would call out to him. Pulling themselves up to the bars, they dictated messages to families in the United States, pleading with him to telegraph loved ones so they wouldn't worry anymore. Fistfuls of sweaty francs were thrust out the windows toward him, meant for relatives or friends still in the camp, or simply *"Fuer die Quäkers!"* Ross recognized some by their voices; others, he could see only when a passing guard directed his flashlight onto a pale, startled face.

Just before midnight, a Jewish organization managed to secure crates of tomatoes and melons from nearby farms. These, too, were distributed into each railcar with the help of the gray truck's headlights, illuminating the dust in the air. The night became a blur of supply distribution, personal messages, and questions from the commandant: whether Ross knew of a particular prisoner, someone who claimed that a visa had arrived, or would soon, and that he or she should be exempted.

At one point, Maulavé, haggard in a crumpled linen suit and smoking a cigarette, called Ross over. An elderly Polish man, senile, but aware enough to want to save himself, presented a tattered red American passport. It had expired in the 1920s. Ross, if he wanted to, could claim the man on behalf of the United States, but another prisoner would replace him on the train. "What was there to reply," Ross wrote, "but 'no, include him,' in the vain hope that someone younger, with more of his life ahead of him, might be saved. One had no right to make such a decision, but made it anyway."

In the early morning hours, Ross felt light-headed and took a short break in the camp's kitchen with some other relief workers—a French Red Cross nurse, a rabbi with one of the Jewish organizations, and two members of one of the prisoner committees, still negotiating for the lives of their comrades. Some workers he didn't know sliced pieces of banana and fig pâté, wrapping them in bits of paper to pass through the bars of the train. Ross bit into a tomato, the juice dripping down, drank some black coffee, and ate some potato salad, before noticing sacks on the floor marked for men and women, full of toothbrushes, soap, and handkerchiefs. Another distribution.

He slept for a few hours in the camp and at first light walked back to the train. Now that he could see inside, Ross saw a friend. Richard Freund, a young violinist from Breslau, had taken charge of his rail-car, and Ross watched him advocate for his fellow prisoners, making sure they all had their supply allotments and persuading the guards to empty the buckets. Freund, who had a reputation for always staying cheerful despite the circumstances, smiled from the train at Ross, who remembered that he had argued with the younger man to take his dark red Amati violin on the trip. Richard had been imprisoned in the French camps for two years and seemed excited about the change. His fate might be terrible, but at least something was happening.

At 6:30 sharp, an engine appeared in the distance, billowing smoke and moving slowly toward the camp. It coupled to the railcars, and the train pulled away immediately. Ross stood in the dirt, surrounded by empty wooden crates and the smell of waste and sweat and straw, and watched silently until the prisoners' screams faded in the air and the train disappeared into the distance.

Two Wars

NAZI GERMANY FOUGHT TWO simultaneous wars: the military war against the Allies and the genocidal war against the Jews. It launched the first on September 1, 1939, riding roughshod over Poland and daring the British and French to protest. Americans argued for more than two years over whether to join the conflict, before the Japanese attack on Pearl Harbor ended the debate. The second war began in 1941 when a decade of racial and religious persecution morphed into a plan to annihilate the Nazis' innocent enemies. The U.S. government confirmed the ongoing mass murder in 1942, and for more than a year Americans—to the extent they were paying attention—debated how and whether to respond. Finally, in 1944, the United States began fighting the second war.

On a drizzly Sunday in the middle of January, John Pehle, a young assistant to the secretary of the Treasury, walked from his office to the White House at lunchtime, and when he emerged, the United States had entered the war against the Nazi extermination of European Jews. When the war in Europe ended seventeen months later, tens of thousands of people—Jewish and non-Jewish—were alive due to the outcome of Pehle's meeting: a new government agency, the War Refugee Board (WRB), had been born. Pehle and his colleagues never became famous and spent the rest of their lives hearing—and agreeing—that the United States should have done more to help save the Jews of Europe. At the same time, few people ever knew what the War Refugee Board had actually done.

—

The odds that day—January 16, 1944—were stacked against John Pehle.

President Franklin Roosevelt had the flu. Rumors flew around official Washington about his ill health, a topic of particular concern because the Democratic National Committee met that weekend to debate nominating him for an unprecedented fourth term. The president felt physically weak and postponed things he wasn't up to doing.

Pehle, a tall midwesterner with a deep voice and light brown hair already starting to recede, had never had an official White House meeting, even though he had worked in Washington for a decade, rising through the ranks at the Treasury Department. Since 1940, when he was just thirty-one, Pehle had overseen Foreign Funds Control, responsible for keeping billions of dollars out of the hands of America's enemies. With a staff of nearly fifteen hundred, Foreign Funds Control also supervised the small amounts of relief money sent from the United States into Europe. This did not exactly qualify Pehle, or any of his colleagues, as humanitarian aid specialists.

Many people, including military officials, believed the United States could only truly help the victims of the Nazis and their collaborators by winning the war as soon as possible. Everything else was a distraction and a diversion of resources. Pehle thought they could do more than just fight militarily, but would Roosevelt?

Most worryingly, Pehle's news would undoubtedly upset the president. His friends had been lying to him, and Pehle—a man Roosevelt couldn't have picked out of a lineup—had the proof. Pehle's plan—an incredibly risky one—was to argue that if the president did not act immediately and follow the Treasury Department's advice, his legacy as a defender of the downtrodden would be forever marred. Millions had already died, but millions of lives were still at stake. Pehle felt convinced that some could still be saved, but only if Roosevelt acted quickly.

Pehle entered the White House, stomped his shoes clean, hung up his hat and coat, still damp with wintry drizzle, and climbed the stairs to the president's private study. He readied himself for the most important meeting of his life.

—

In the summer of 1942, a year and a half before Pehle's meeting, news of the ongoing massacre of the Jews began to reach the United States. Most Americans had known that Nazi Germany made life impossible for Jews, but the idea of a systematic mass-murder plan seemed absurd. And even if it was true, what could Americans do about it? Helping refugees escape Europe had never been a priority for the American government or the American people. Bigger problems—the Great Depression, war in Europe, war in Asia—stole most Americans' focus. Restrictive immigration laws instituted in the 1920s hadn't been written to target German Jews—and were in place long before the refugee crisis began in the late 1930s—but as a result of these laws many thousands of people who might have been able to escape couldn't do so. They were still in Europe waiting for immigration visas when they were rounded up and murdered by the Nazis.

The doors to the United States began to close in the 1920s. The Johnson-Reed Act of 1924, which passed overwhelmingly with bipartisan support, was born from intense postwar isolationism and eugenic theories. The law capped the number of immigrants from outside the Western Hemisphere at about 154,000 people per year, a far cry from the more than 10 million who had arrived in the United States in the decade prior to World War I. The act also applied "national origins" quotas and categorized applicants based on country of birth, not country of residence or citizenship. The quotas severely restricted persons from southern and eastern Europe, who had formed the majority of the immigrant population in recent decades, and kept most Asian and African people out entirely. Countries with large populations of Jews, Slavs, and people thought to be racially undesirable, poorer, and harder to assimilate were specifically targeted. Great Britain had the largest quota, and Germany was second, with a cap of 25,957.

The 1924 law also moved power over immigration to the State Department. Though the Immigration and Naturalization Service (INS) stayed in the Labor Department until June 1940, applicants for immigration visas had to present all their paperwork—identification, financial records, medical exams—to State Department officers at designated consulates around the world. Immigrants received their visas before leaving Europe, so Ellis Island became merely a holding area for illegal or sick passengers. As ships steamed past the Statue of Liberty, those on board could wave with ease; the hardest part of the process was already over.

Then, in 1929, the Great Depression hit the United States and the world.

As had happened before and has happened since, politicians blamed immigration for exacerbating American economic problems. President Herbert Hoover instructed the State Department to strictly interpret an obscure clause from a 1917 law about people "likely to become a public charge." Visa applicants who did not have sufficient financial resources were no longer eligible, because one could not assume they would ever find employment in America. The year before Hoover's restriction, 25,957 German immigrants entered, completely filling the quota allotment. By 1933, the number had fallen to 1,324.

On March 4, 1933, when Franklin Roosevelt recited the oath of office, the front pages of major newspapers reported on his laundry list of New Deal legislation but also on increasing antisemitism in Nazi Germany, where a new chancellor, Adolf Hitler, had taken power five weeks earlier. Jews were being kicked out of their jobs, stores boycotted, books burned. In protest, tens of thousands of Americans marched in major cities around the country, held rallies, and began an anti-German boycott movement.

Roosevelt's State Department staff, still settling into the massive Department of State building just west of the White House, felt that diplomatic tensions were too fraught to make any formal protest. Germany owed American investors $2 billion in loans after World War I, and the new Nazi regime acted on whims. Germany was a sovereign nation, and anyway it was not a crime to persecute your own citizens.

From Berlin, the U.S. consul general George Messersmith sent a warning to his colleagues in Washington in June 1933: The persecution of the Jews "is one of the most serious and one of the saddest problems that has arisen in a civilized country in modern times . . . I personally can see no hope for the Jews in Germany for years to come and all those who can possibly get out of the country, will wish to do so."

In the first full year of Nazi control, fewer than 4,400 Germans had been granted U.S. immigrant visas, while 83,013 persons, mostly Jews, sat on the waiting list. The State Department loosened the "likely

to become a public charge" instruction and reminded consular officials to be sympathetic. Otherwise, the process stayed the same. The
United States had an immigration policy, but no refugee policy. Those
fleeing persecution had to qualify, with the same paperwork and under
the same strict rules as everyone else. Soon, Nazi persecution stopped
being front-page news, and most Americans stopped paying attention.

Five years later, on March 12, 1938, Nazi Germany annexed Austria
in a territorial grab known as the *Anschluss.* Hitler rode triumphantly
through Vienna, with swastika flags hanging from every building and
people lining the streets to cheer. There were 1,413 immigration spots
available under the Austrian quota each year, but the consulate had
been a sleepy one, issuing only an average of 15 per month prior to the
Nazis' arrival. In the next four months, 40,000 Austrians applied, the
vast majority of them Jews. Between 500 and 4,000 people waited in
the gardens outside the consulate every day for an appointment with
the small—and now frantic—State Department staff. Eight hundred
letters arrived every day, all needing responses. The desperate Jews of
Vienna were being evicted from their homes and constantly threatened with arrest and imprisonment in concentration camps. Suicide
grew increasingly common.

Though the State Department controlled the issuance of visas,
Congress determined immigration law and set the quotas. In the
spring of 1938, three Democrats, all representing parts of Brooklyn,
proposed bills to assist refugees. Samuel Dickstein wanted to carry
over unused quota slots from year to year, reassigning them to countries according to need; Emanuel Celler wanted to remove the "public charge" consideration entirely for those escaping persecution; and
Donald O'Toole thought that all physically and mentally healthy refugees should be granted visas. Hearings on their bills were scheduled
for April 20–22, 1938.

Before they could take place, Messersmith, now assistant secretary
of state, made the trip down Pennsylvania Avenue toward the Capitol at Celler's request. After the hearings had been scheduled, both
Messersmith and Celler had heard from frantic refugee advocates, all
warning that the bills were dangerous. They shouldn't hold any debate
regarding immigration, Messersmith warned the Jewish congressmen
gathered in Celler's office, not in committee and definitely not on the

House floor. Immigration was simply too unpopular, and any proposal to increase the quotas would likely result in laws to cut or end immigration entirely. It was better to keep quiet and keep the quotas as they were.

The congressmen listened and argued among themselves for a long time. All were hearing from constituents, many with Jewish family members in Germany. But they made a unanimous decision: Celler would pull his bill, and Representative Adolph Sabath of Illinois would tell Dickstein and O'Toole to do the same. No hearings, no debate. The Jewish members of Congress would not propose any new legislation to change the immigration laws. It was just too risky.

At the end of April, President Roosevelt instructed the State Department to combine the Austrian and German quotas. Though Austria no longer existed—the busy consulate found itself in Vienna, Germany—Austrians were eligible for one of the now 27,370 quota slots available to the German-born. To most Americans, that number seemed far too high. In a Roper poll, 67 percent of respondents felt that German, Austrian, and "political refugees" (non-Jews being persecuted by the Nazis) should be kept out entirely—never mind the quotas. The 1937 recession had reversed some of the New Deal economic gains, and unemployment in early 1938 shot back up to 19 percent. Many Americans were feeling sympathetic but not charitable.

To address the worsening crisis, President Roosevelt called for an international conference in Évian-les-Bains, France, in early July. Thirty-two countries participated, discussing ways to assist Jews still in Germany who wanted to immigrate. But when individual countries were asked about accepting refugees, most—including the United States—demurred. Only the Dominican Republic offered to take German Jews, though the invitation wasn't quite an altruistic one. General Rafael Trujillo, the Dominican dictator, had initiated a massacre of poor black Haitians less than a year earlier and specifically sought to bring white wealth into his country. Rich Jews would do just fine.

The Évian Conference did have one tangible result: the formation of the Intergovernmental Committee on Refugees (IGC). But its work streamlining emigration met with little success. At one point, George Rublee, the seventy-year-old American director of the IGC, wrote to the State Department, "With the exception of the United

States, which has maintained its quota, and the British Isles, which are admitting immigrants at a current months rate equal to the rate immigrants are being admitted to the United States, doors have been systematically closed everywhere to involuntary emigrants since the meeting at Évian." Though the Nazis officially encouraged emigration, they demanded refugees surrender the majority of their wealth and assets first, which meant many didn't have the money to be desirable immigrants.

On the evening of November 9–10, 1938, the Nazis instigated a violent pogrom known as *Kristallnacht*. The attacks and the subsequent mass arrest of Jewish men and boys received widespread press coverage in the United States—upwards of a month of front-page newspaper stories. Roosevelt condemned the violence, adding that he "could scarcely believe that such things could occur in a twentieth century civilization." The president recalled American ambassador Hugh Wilson from Berlin and announced he would extend the expiration on tourist visas for Germans—including many Jews—visiting the United States who did not feel safe returning home. But while a Gallup poll in the wake of *Kristallnacht* showed that 94 percent of Americans disapproved of the Nazi persecution of the Jews, this still did not translate into a public appetite for increasing the quotas.

Senator Robert Reynolds, a North Carolina Democrat, decided he would fix the immigration laws. In the six years since he had entered the Senate, Reynolds had grown more isolationist, racist, and admiring of Nazi Germany. In January 1939, the same month he started his own antisemitic newspaper, the *American Vindicator,* Reynolds introduced five bills in the Senate, all dealing with immigration. Two were particularly spiteful: immigration quotas should be cut by 90 percent, Reynolds argued, and moreover all immigration should cease for ten years or until unemployment fell to three million people. During Senate hearings on the bills, speakers testified that America was traditionally a country of exclusion, not acceptance.

A month after Reynolds, Senator Robert Wagner, a New York Democrat, and Congresswoman Edith Nourse Rogers, a Massachusetts Republican, introduced a very different piece of legislation. The Wagner-Rogers bill proposed allowing twenty thousand German refugee children to enter the United States above the quota. Carefully worded by sympathetic relief organizations, the bill originally found a lot of support, and hearings in April went well. Unsurprisingly, Robert Reynolds repeatedly gave oppositional speeches on the Senate floor and recruited patriotic organizations like the American Legion to register their disapproval. Finally, Reynolds found his trump card, proposing a tragic compromise. Wagner and Rogers could have their twenty thousand children, but only by merging their bill with one of his: to end *all* quota immigration for five years. Shaken, Robert Wagner pulled the bill from consideration. None of Reynolds's bills ever came up for a vote.

As prospects for the Wagner-Rogers bill began to sour, Americans learned of the plight of the *St. Louis,* a ship that had sailed from Hamburg carrying 937 mostly Jewish passengers and at the beginning of June sat in Havana harbor. Many of the refugees had hoped to stay in Cuba while waiting their turns for an American visa, but by the time the ship arrived, Havana had canceled their landing permits. Even though a prominent relief organization, the American Jewish Joint Distribution Committee (JDC), offered to make substantial financial guarantees for the passengers, Cuban officials refused to permit 907 of them to disembark. The United States would not take them either. Allowing them to enter the United States would set a precedent—that a group of refugees could board a ship, create an emergency, and jump the quota line. Instead, American diplomats worked with the JDC staff to persuade France, the Netherlands, Belgium, and Great Britain to each admit a share of the passengers. The *St. Louis* refugees threw a party on board, thrilled no one would be forced to return to Germany.

The JDC, founded in 1914 to distribute aid to Jewish communities abroad, was not alone in trying to help refugees. Hundreds of organizations, large and small, local and international, expanded to assist refugees in Europe struggling to emigrate. Some organizations, like the American Friends Service Committee (the Quakers), divided their efforts between relief work like food distribution and medical care—where a little money could help many people—and helping individual refugees, where a lot of money might only assist a few. Others, like the Unitarian Service Committee and the Hebrew Immigrant Aid Society (HIAS), had types of refugees they preferred to assist:

HIAS, like the JDC, was established to aid only Jews; the Unitarians preferred to aid people of some sort of renown. All of these organizations formed a loose network to prevent stepping on toes and duplicating efforts. Thanks to them, tens of thousands of refugees were able to escape.

On September 1, 1939, Nazi Germany attacked Poland by land and air, beginning a war that had seemed inevitable for months. American civilians fled the Continent, while American diplomats wrote from Warsaw, "Continuing examination of such immigrants as reach Warsaw in order avoid disappointing persons."

When Nazi Germany turned west and invaded Denmark, the Netherlands, Belgium, and France the following spring, German Jews who had sought safety in these countries in the 1930s—including most of the passengers on the *St. Louis*—now found themselves under Nazi rule again. Many fled south and tried to escape over the French border to Spain and Portugal or across the Mediterranean to Casablanca. American relief organizations tried to reunite families and provide small amounts of money, clothing, and food. The efforts were emotionally stressful. One relief worker wrote home, "Day after day, men and women just sat at my desk and sobbed. They are caught and crushed, and they know it."

Between July 1, 1938, and June 30, 1940, the United States filled nearly every German quota slot available. Of the 54,740 German immigrant visas legally allowed under American immigration law over those two years, the State Department issued 54,725. The vast majority of these immigrants were Jewish. Passengers on vessels bound for the United States were asked to classify themselves by race, and until 1943 "Hebrew" was an option. From 1938 to 1940, 100,131 self-identified "Hebrews" immigrated to the United States. Most were refugees escaping persecution, and this figure is undoubtedly low, because many people persecuted as Jews under Nazi racial laws did not consider themselves "Hebrew."

June 30, 1940, marked the end of the quota year; on July 1, a new year's allocation of quota slots became available. A few days earlier, a French-German armistice formally separated France into a Nazi-occupied zone in the north (which included Paris) and an unoccupied zone controlled by Nazi collaborators in the south, known as Vichy France. France had fallen in just six weeks. Americans saw its surrender as an unfathomable nightmare. The French army's 117 divisions had mobilized 5 million men. The American army at that time numbered 269,023.

To most Americans, only one explanation made sense: France must have been brought down from within—a fifth column of spies and saboteurs secretly working to ensure Nazi victory. Many made a connection between refugees seeking haven in the United States and spies wishing to do the country harm. So did the president. At a press conference in early June, Roosevelt told reporters,

> Now, of course, the refugee has got to be checked because, unfortunately, among the refugees there are some spies, as has been found in other countries. And not all of them are voluntary spies—it is rather a horrible story but in some of the other countries that refugees out of Germany have gone to, especially Jewish refugees, they have found a number of definitely proven spies . . . the refugee has left Germany and then has been told by the German Government, "You have got to conduct this particular spy work and if you don't make your reports regularly back to some definite agent in the country you are going to—we are frightfully sorry, but your old father and mother will be taken out and shot."

With fifth column hysteria sweeping the country, the State Department reexamined the procedures for screening refugees and issued new instructions to consular officers: "All applications for immigration visas must be examined with extreme care and during the present period of emergency no such visa should be issued if there is any doubt whatsoever concerning the alien." Many refugees would now be disqualified, and "quotas against which there is a heavy demand will be under issued," but national security had to come first. Immigration under the quotas of Nazi-occupied and collaborationist countries dropped 38 percent between 1940 and 1941, from 42,686 to 26,490.

Even after the fall of France, when Great Britain stood virtually alone in opposition to Nazi Germany, many Americans did not want to get involved in the war. Congress authorized the nation's first peacetime draft in September 1940 but mandated that none of the drafted boys would serve longer than a year, nor deploy outside the Western Hemisphere. In the absence of weaponry, many soldiers were trained using wooden sticks as guns. America was not mentally or physically equipped for war, and those opposing involvement wanted to defend the Americas, not save England. In the spring of 1941, Roosevelt and his allies struggled to pass Lend-Lease, even naming the bill "House Resolution 1776" to convince opponents that supplying Great Britain would not weaken American sovereignty. That September, Congress reauthorized the peacetime draft in a nail-biter: it passed by a single vote.

The job of refugee advocates only got harder. Additional State Department scrutiny demanded more coordination and, for many refugees, led to more heartbreak. Officials began enforcing a new "relatives rule" in June 1941, rendering applicants with immediate family still in Nazi-occupied territory ineligible for visas. At the end of that month, the State Department suddenly announced that all applications now had to be approved by Interdepartmental Visa Review boards in Washington, due to national security concerns. Marjorie McClelland, who would soon move with her husband, Ross, to work in southern France, wrote to the Quakers from Rome, "All immigration to the U.S. stopped on June 30, thereby robbing many people of their hopes ... Our office has served as a sort of mourning ground for these people. We can't do a thing in the world to change the situation ... and [it] almost breaks your heart." American consulates in occupied territory closed entirely in mid-July 1941, cutting off thousands from access to the only diplomatic personnel who could have granted them visas.

The only refugees who could still escape Europe were those who had already made it to ports in southern France, to Lisbon, or to Casablanca. The Atlantic remained a battleground as Nazi U-boats attacked ships indiscriminately, and America debated whether the country should participate in convoys delivering Lend-Lease supplies.

Fewer and fewer passenger ships made the crossing: in June 1939, 123 ships arrived in New York harbor from all over Europe; in June 1941, only 12 appeared, almost all from Lisbon.

Then, on a sunny Sunday morning in December, the Japanese attacked Pearl Harbor, bringing the United States into the war. For most Americans, the plight of European Jews slipped entirely from view.

Revelation

DURING WORLD WAR II, AMERICANS had no framework with which to understand the Nazis' attempted annihilation of European Jews, and no word—not "Holocaust," "Shoah," or, until December 1944, "genocide"—to understand the crime. To them, rumors of villages being wiped out seemed a particularly brutal component of the war, and in war civilians die. Americans knew that Nazi ideology always held a special hatred for the Jews, so isolated stories about Jews being murdered were fathomable. But an actual extermination plan was not. It took time to realize that such stories were not only different—separate from wartime propaganda about the cruelty of the enemy—but also true.

The disentangling of the two wars began in Geneva, Switzerland, in early August 1942, eight months after Pearl Harbor, while most of that country seemed to be on vacation. It was a Saturday morning, and the American vice-consul Howard Elting expected a quiet day. His boss was away like everyone else, and Elting likely planned to spend the day catching up on paperwork. Instead, that morning a young German Jew walked determinedly up to the iron double doors of the consulate at rue du Mont-Blanc 3—a beautiful old building just steps from the Rhône—and, taking some deep breaths, entered.

Elting had never met Gerhart Riegner, the representative of the World Jewish Congress (WJC) in Switzerland, and he made an unforgettable first impression. Riegner, just thirty, was "in great agitation." He had news, which he had heard indirectly from a prominent Ger-

man businessman. After spending nearly a week mulling it over, Riegner wanted to send a clarion call to the world.

The Nazis, Riegner told Elting, planned to exterminate the Jews.
After gathering them together in the east—presumably in Poland—the
Nazis would execute as many as four million people there, possibly
with prussic acid. The murders would "permanently settle the Jewish
question in Europe." Within a few months, Riegner said, it will all be
over.

Elting believed him. They discussed how unfathomable the news
seemed, but it also made recent reports of mass arrests—in Paris, Vienna,
Berlin, prisoners placed in train cars, disappearing into the east—make
sense. Roswell McClelland spent that same weekend making food
packages in Les Milles for the train that would leave two days later.

Riegner gave Elting a message to transmit to Washington, asking
the State Department to give the news to Stephen Wise. Wise, the
World Jewish Congress's head, one of the most famous rabbis in America, and a Roosevelt supporter, would certainly persuade the Allies to
act.

Elting immediately transmitted the cable to the American legation
in Bern. (At the time, some countries, like Switzerland, recognized
U.S. legations headed by ministers, while others had ambassador-led
embassies; the designations were virtually equivalent.) He added his
own paragraph to the end of the report: "My personal opinion is that
Riegner is a serious and balanced individual and that he would never
have come to the Consulate with the above report if he had not had
confidence in his informant's reliability and if he did not seriously
consider that the report might well contain an element of truth."

Minister Leland Harrison was not as convinced and added his own
postscript before forwarding Riegner's message to the United States:
"The report has earmarks of war rumor inspired by fear and what is
commonly understood to be the actually miserable condition of these
refugees." The situation was bad, Harrison thought, but not *that* bad.

When the cable reached the State Department's European desk
on Tuesday afternoon, no one found the news as convincing as Elting had. Paul Culbertson, the division's assistant chief, couldn't "see
any justification for them to have put this thing in a telegram." He
drafted a letter informing Wise, then crossed it all out. Elbridge Dur-

brow, Culbertson's counterpart at the Eastern European desk, was equally dismissive, but exposed the true source of State's reluctance. They should refuse to forward the message due to Harrison's hesitations, the far-fetched nature of the allegation, and "the impossibility of our being of any assistance if such action [the murder of the Jews] were taken." The Geneva consulate had to inform Riegner that due to the "unsubstantiated character of the information," his cable would not be delivered to Wise.

Riegner's telegram might have died there, and the first news of a Nazi plan to exterminate the Jews would have come another way, at another time.

But, as it happened, Gerhart Riegner also visited the British consulate.

His telegram arrived in New York, via London. The British Foreign Office, like the State Department, also debated forwarding it, but the World Jewish Congress's representative in England happened to sit in Parliament. Getting caught keeping information from someone of his stature would be professional suicide. So at the end of August, the news of the Nazi plot finally reached Rabbi Wise.

Like Riegner, Stephen Wise agonized for a few days before steeling himself to contact the State Department, specifically Undersecretary of State Sumner Welles. The rabbi had no idea that a duplicate message was already there, lost in a pile of papers on some desk, somewhere on the third floor.

Undersecretary Sumner Welles was a model diplomat: independently wealthy, highly educated, impeccably connected—he had been a page at Franklin and Eleanor's wedding—an aristocrat in an office that deeply valued such things. Welles often acted as a surrogate for the president, which is exactly why Stephen Wise needed him.

Wise forwarded the text of Riegner's cable and apologized for bothering Welles, explaining that the dire information demanded the intrusion. Welles called the next day, September 3, and promised to investigate Riegner's report, asking the rabbi to postpone any public announcements until the State Department had confirmation. Then Welles left town on vacation. It would be late September, six weeks after Riegner walked into the Geneva consulate, before the State Department finally began to investigate whether the shocking news could be true.

Two months later, two days before Thanksgiving, Sumner Welles, wearing a bespoke double-breasted suit, his light eyes darkened and face grave, ushered Stephen Wise and his son, James Waterman Wise, into the undersecretary's office at the State Department. The three men sat down, and Welles picked up a small stack of papers with red seals on them. "Gentlemen, I hold in my hands documents which have come to me from our legation in Bern. I regret to tell you, Dr. Wise, that these confirm and justify your deepest fears."

To investigate, Welles had sent "triple priority"–level messages to Roosevelt's representative at the Vatican, Myron Taylor, and to Minister Leland Harrison in Bern, asking for more information. Taylor first responded that the Vatican had only heard rumors of "severe measures against non-Aryans" but later forwarded a report from Warsaw forecasting "an early end to the extermination of Jews in Poland." Harrison, initially a skeptic, became a believer as he learned more. In October, Riegner and his colleague Richard Lichtheim presented a lengthy report with statistics and witness testimony, which Harrison scanned in silence as the men sat uncomfortably. He asked a few questions about their sources, but he was convinced. Consul General Paul Squire in Geneva got confirmation from a German informant, nicknamed Frank, who claimed that the extermination order included both Jews and Poles, and secured a sworn statement from a Red Cross official about a Nazi proclamation ordering territories to be free from Jews.

Wise already believed in Riegner's information, but it still shocked him to hear Welles's confirmation and to feel so powerless to stop the murders despite being just steps from the Oval Office. No account of the meeting between Wise and Welles exists in the State Department's records, but Wise always claimed that the undersecretary urged him to publicize the information. The government wouldn't do it, but the rabbi certainly could.

Wise hurriedly called a small press conference before boarding a train from Union Station back to New York. None of the major newspapers had a reporter present, relying on the Associated Press for the story. Wise announced that the Nazis had murdered two million Jews and that he had State Department confirmation of the extermination plan. Most of Wise's additional information, though, came from unofficial sources. Some of it was wrong: Wise claimed that the Nazis were injecting air bubbles into the bloodstream of the victims and using corpses to make war-vital commodities, neither of which was accurate. But the gist of the news was true and devastating.

Jewish communities called for a international day of mourning. On December 2, 1942, thousands of people fasted and prayed for their loved ones who had been enveloped into the Nazis' murderous shadow. Six days later, five Jewish men in similar dark chesterfield coats entered the White House for a meeting with the president. Wise had made the appointment, which began with the Orthodox rabbi Israel Rosenberg giving a benediction over the president, who seemed visibly moved. The men presented a petition, asking Roosevelt to warn the Nazis against committing atrocities, to appoint a commission to investigate the crimes, and to "take such action as will strike fear into the hearts of the enemies of civilization and at the same time bring hope and faith to their victims." Roosevelt acknowledged the veracity of the reports and the difficulty of rescue, agreeing to issue a statement of warning and protest. But then his attention wandered onto the topic of political problems in North Africa.

Around the time the confused Jewish leaders listened politely to Roosevelt opine, officials in the State Department's European Division complained. Wise needed to "call off, or at least to tone down, the present worldwide publicity campaign," one official wrote in a memo. Another grumbled that a public declaration condemning the atrocities would force "governments of the United Nations [to] expose themselves to increased pressure from all sides to do something more specific in order to aid these people." He recommended removing any language that might give the impression that mass murder was actually occurring.

Certainly not all State Department officials felt this way, but a small group, centered on the European and Visa Divisions, had wearied of what they perceived as the constant and impossible demands from refugee organizations and advocates. This group believed nothing could stop the Nazis from murdering the Jews except military victory, and any diversions from that effort were dangerous. These officials would spend 1943 trying to deflect protests and convince agitators that the State Department had done everything it could to help the Jews.

Less than two weeks after Roosevelt met with the Jewish leaders, the United States, the Soviet Union, the United Kingdom, the French National Committee, and eight governments in exile (Belgium, Czechoslovakia, Greece, Luxembourg, the Netherlands, Norway, Poland, and Yugoslavia) signed a joint declaration denouncing Nazi mass murder. The text included explicit detail about the "bloody cruelties," noted that multiple sources had confirmed the information, and pledged to punish the perpetrators of "this bestial policy of cold-blooded extermination."

At this point, issuing a strongly worded warning seemed to be all the United States could do. On November 8, while Welles was still gathering information, British and American amphibious forces landed on the shores of Algeria and Morocco. Operation Torch, the plan to force the Nazis from North Africa and take back the Mediterranean, had begun. The ultimately successful landings exposed serious weaknesses in American training and military preparedness. The United States remained unready for the demands of this war. In retaliation, German forces swarmed south, occupying Vichy France. American diplomats, reporters, and relief workers, including the AFSC staff, were arrested and imprisoned in Nazi Germany. The United States had little leverage to demand their release.

At the moment the United States confirmed the Nazi plan to exterminate the Jews, the Americans had never been so far away.

3

John Pehle

JOHN PEHLE LIKED TO keep his desk clear. The Treasury Department staff was under standing order that all correspondence addressed to Secretary of the Treasury Henry Morgenthau Jr. needed an answer or acknowledgment within forty-eight hours. Nothing languished; nothing slipped through the cracks. Pehle's in-box stayed perpetually at zero.

Born in Minneapolis in 1909, John was Otto and Agnes Pehle's eldest son, the second of their four children. Like many Americans, the Pehles did not have deep roots in the United States. Otto had emigrated from Braunschweig, Germany, as a young teenager, while Agnes was the daughter of Swedish immigrants. The Pehle family spent most of John's childhood in Sioux Falls, South Dakota, and his teenage years in Omaha, where Otto worked in the oil industry. After earning an English degree from nearby Creighton College, John moved away to Yale for law school. There, he encountered two pivotal figures in his life: Professor Thurman Arnold, his mentor, and, on a blind date, Francha Elser, his future wife. Arnold was a pioneer of legal realism, a legal philosophy advocating that lawyers needed to identify and account for the personal and systemic biases, prejudices, and nuances that led to injustice. In a 1944 interview, Pehle credited Arnold with "influencing his general philosophy of government and law more than any other person" with whom he had come in contact.

Even before graduation in 1935, Pehle moved to Washington to join other legal realists at the Treasury Department, bringing his new wife along. Francha came from a vastly different background from John's: a woman getting an expensive Yale studio art degree during the Depression gives a hint of her family's social status. Her father had been a professor at Cornell Medical School, and Francha enjoyed a comfortable lifestyle. She loved dancing, painting, and fashion. She made John laugh, and they settled into a happy life in Washington—living first in the Virginia suburbs, then at their log cabin house in Maryland, which had served as a tearoom during the Wilson administration. There John planted big beds of asparagus in their large backyard, and Francha, with the help of household staff, cared for their son, John junior, born in 1939, and planned for a new baby, due in the late summer of 1943.

John Pehle thrived at Treasury, where young workers were trusted with vast responsibilities. At just thirty, he was promoted to become an assistant to the secretary, and in 1940 he became the head of the new Foreign Funds Control department. He and his staff froze $8 billion in accounts and assets associated with foreign individuals, corporations, and governments, all to deprive the enemy of any benefit to their war effort. Foreign Funds was economically fighting the war long before Pearl Harbor and by early 1942 controlled the resources of more than thirty-five countries, including almost all of continental Europe and much of Asia. Sometimes the job could be exciting—Treasury employees spiriting gold bullion out of the Philippines by submarine—but mostly it was just careful detective work and lots of form letters.

June 25, 1943, was a swampy, sweltering Friday in the middle of a Washington heat wave. The fans ran full blast as government workers, maintaining formality in suits and ties, sweated, smoked, and cursed. Pehle's office was on the fifth floor of the brick Sloane building, a furniture store with Treasury Department offices above, an outpost three blocks from the main headquarters. The heat and noise radiated up from the corner below, and Pehle added the smoke from his ever-present pipe to the heavy air.

At some point that day, Bernard Meltzer contacted Pehle with a proposal that would ultimately change his life. Meltzer, Foreign Funds Control's State Department liaison, was passing along an idea the

World Jewish Congress received from its Geneva representative, a man called Gerhart Riegner. Riegner thought he could save the lives of Jews trapped in Romania and France, but to do it, he needed the support of the American government, Treasury in particular.

Pehle would not have recognized Riegner's name or known of his role in notifying the Allies of the ongoing extermination of the Jews. If Pehle knew anything about Nazi atrocities at all, it was confined to what he read in newspapers and magazines. It's hard to say whether he believed what he heard or thought it might just be anti-Nazi propaganda; as of January 1943, fewer than half of Americans polled could imagine the Nazis had murdered two million Jews.

At first, Gerhart Riegner's proposal seemed similar to other requests coming into the Foreign Funds Control's offices that summer. Only four days earlier, Pehle had rejected a plea from the American Jewish Joint Distribution Committee to send money to a relief organization in Italy because "similar proposals which this Department has received have been consistently denied . . . it would be decidedly inconsistent with this Government's present position on such matters" to authorize the JDC's actions. It was the standard line, and Pehle's job to deliver it. But Riegner's request was different.

Riegner had cabled his appeal to the World Jewish Congress in mid-April 1943, and American diplomats in Switzerland met with him several times over the next two months to go over all the details. By late June, Bernard Meltzer felt ready to send Riegner's proposal over for Pehle's review.

Because Foreign Funds Control monitored international financial transactions, Pehle's office had to approve any relief money sent into Europe. Organizations had to obtain a U.S. government license, basically an official permission slip. Treasury staff issued licenses only after they were satisfied the transaction would not hurt the war effort. Licenses were highly technical, spelling out a specific amount of money, exactly what it could be used for, and all the rules and regulations the relief workers had to follow. Licenses were also very hard to get, especially in 1943, due to the war's uncertain outcome and the lack of practical rescue plans.

Riegner wanted to send relief into both Romania and France. Jews deported to Transnistria, a desolate area between the Bug and the Dniester Rivers in southern Romania, desperately needed clothing. With a license, Riegner thought he could secure a loan to buy and distribute some before the weather grew cold again. Riegner proposed that if the World Jewish Congress deposited money in a bank account in Switzerland or in the United States, he could show the local lenders that the money had arrived, payable to them after the war. That way, Riegner wasn't technically sending any money into enemy territory.

Riegner also realized he could save lives by helping children in hiding in France to escape over the border to Spain or Switzerland. This plan was a bit more complicated, because he would need to send French currency into France, and the Swiss banks wouldn't exchange any money for him. But if he could find someone in Switzerland who had French francs, he could exchange the money privately.

Nervous about two different funding proposals, Minister Leland Harrison wrote from Switzerland that the money would be impossible to monitor, so some of it might end up in enemy hands. Plus, Riegner needed to communicate with people in Nazi-occupied territory, something an American organization's representative was forbidden to do. Pehle was well aware of the challenges. These were exactly the reasons most licenses were denied, why the standard line read, "Current prohibitions against financial or commercial arrangements with enemy territory cannot be relaxed."

Pehle met Dr. Nahum Goldmann and James Waterman Wise of the World Jewish Congress on July 1 and doubted he could ever approve Riegner's plans. The two men gave him the impression that the Romanian money would really be used to bribe officials with $170,000 to permit the escape of seventy thousand refugees. A ransom scheme, Pehle wrote, was "very troublesome."

After Meltzer shared a cable confirming that the Red Cross would be involved in Riegner's project in Romania—this was no ransom scheme—Pehle came around. He decided that "Treasury's approval can be obtained in view of the humanitarian considerations involved provided that the scheme proved to be workable and no foreign exchange is made available to occupied territories during the war." Meltzer, mildly annoyed, pointed out that Pehle's yes had a lot of caveats. In particular, how could they know Riegner's scheme was workable before he tried it? Pehle honestly still wasn't sure but took a deep breath and finally told Meltzer that as long as money wasn't sent into enemy territory, Treasury would approve the license.

Pehle stressed that Treasury's approval—for now—could only be for the evacuation plans, helping children in hiding in France to escape over the mountains to Spain or Switzerland or assisting refugees in Romania to get to Palestine, nothing resembling ransom schemes. The purchase of relief goods intended for enemy territory would have to wait until Treasury had more details. Meltzer wrote in his memo of their conversation, "This can undoubtedly be worked out as soon as the scheme becomes a little more concrete."

Bernard Meltzer was unlike most of his colleagues at the State Department. He was Jewish, first of all, in his late twenties, and the son of Russian immigrants. Meltzer held law degrees from the University of Chicago and Harvard. He was, according to the dean of the University of Chicago Law School, "too independent a cuss to be a government clerk."

His independence certainly stood out at State. The State Department was built on bureaucracy. While the rest of Washington hurried, forever changed first by the New Deal and now by the war, the State Department stayed largely aloof and unaffected, still a club of Harvard and Groton graduates who enjoyed the same gossip at the same parties with the same people, no matter where they were in the world. As one 1942 critic put it, the State Department remained steeped in a "faded and moth-eaten tradition of Victorian diplomacy . . . a tradition of rules, of amorality within the prescribed bounds of international law." Even architecture set the State Department apart: the offices were just to the west of the White House in an elaborate building with tiers and a mansard roof, a mix of white and purple gray, all pediment and ornament and portico. The building looked fussy, a relic from another time—just like most of the men who worked there.

Assistant Secretary of State Breckinridge Long—who went by "Breckinridge" or "Breck" rather than his given name, Samuel—fit in well. He came from a distinguished family and had a Princeton education and a stable of pedigreed racehorses. He had been a third assistant secretary of state in the Wilson administration, befriending the then assistant secretary of the navy, Franklin Roosevelt. He raised funds for Roosevelt's election and was rewarded with an ambassadorship, remaining in Mussolini's Italy until 1936, when he resigned, supposedly for health reasons but also, possibly, because he held a too-friendly view of Italy's invasion of Ethiopia. Roosevelt called again in September 1939 at the outbreak of war, and Long joined the State Department to head a section called Special War Problems, which—much to his dismay—included the oversight of the Visa Division and with it matters related to refugees.

Over his nearly four years at the State Department, Long had gathered a staff of like-minded men, united in the prewar years by their concern over spies and saboteurs sneaking into the United States, and after Pearl Harbor by their desire to remain focused on winning the war, not on what they considered humanitarian diversions. They were constantly suspicious of the Jewish organizations advocating relief and rescue. In September 1942, at the same time Welles began to investigate Riegner's news, State Department officers read an extensive report from the Office of Censorship that identified many of the Jewish relief organizations, including the World Jewish Congress, as "tricky, deceitful, and absolutely unreliable. Those charged with the national security cannot afford under any circumstances to predicate their actions upon any representations or statements made by any of these groups."

R. Borden Reams, a member of Breckinridge Long's staff, didn't care that Treasury supported the Riegner plan. Even as its supposed refugee expert, Reams was responsible for some of the most odious opinions captured in State Department memos. He had called Riegner's August 1942 telegram "fantastic[al]." He had been a voice advocating for Stephen Wise to "call off, or at least tone down his present worldwide publicity campaign about 'mass murders'" and had debated whether the December 1942 Allied declaration actually had to acknowledge the Nazi extermination plot. Unsurprisingly, he didn't think Riegner's license was a good idea. It had no chance of success, he reiterated again and again to Meltzer, and therefore State should not approve transmitting any funds, even if the money would sit in blocked accounts in Switzerland. Besides, he claimed, "negotiations with the various governments on refugee evacuation were proceeding and . . . success might be prejudiced" if Nazi-collaborating officials saw an opportunity to receive bribes from Riegner instead.

Reams knew better than anyone that the supposed negotiations were hardly proceeding. Months earlier, he had opened a conference between British and American delegates to discuss refugee concerns at the posh Horizons resort on the north shores of Bermuda. In the wake of the December 1942 declaration, there had been enough public pressure advocating some sort of Allied response to the murder of the Jews—rallies, letters, even a star-studded spectacle titled *We Will Never Die* told largely from the perspective of the dead, which sold out Madison Square Garden twice and toured throughout the country—that the American and British governments had to show some action. Long had suggested a conference in Bermuda, a British territory where press could be controlled—a clear indication that the meetings were primarily a public relations gesture.

None of the State Department–selected American delegates (Representative Sol Bloom, Senator Scott Lucas, and Princeton University president Harold Dodds) knew anything about refugee policy, and all had been given explicit instructions. If they forgot these instructions, Reams stayed in Bermuda to remind them. They could not pledge any American money for relief, promise any food or clothing shipments, or propose bringing refugees to the United States. They should push for a meeting of the Intergovernmental Committee, the international organization established after the Évian Conference in 1938 that had not formally met for three and a half years. And they should definitely feel free to remind the British that Congress had no plans to expand the American immigration quotas, which were already "the most liberal of any nation in the world."

Even to outsiders, it was obvious that the conference would accomplish very little. Freda Kirchwey, the editor of the *Nation,* wrote that it represented "nothing but a series of excuses for the failure of the British and American governments to do anything effective to rescue the victims of Hitler's terror who still remain alive." The *Washington Post* complained in an editorial, "Hitler's mass executioners will not wait while the delegates at Bermuda carry on their exploratory consultations, arrange for committees and subcommittees, pile up mountains of statistics and do nothing."

The *Washington Post* was right. The executioners were not waiting. Just as the delegates were settling into the beachside resort forty-three hundred miles away, Nazi troops and police entered the Warsaw ghetto to round up almost all the seventy thousand remaining inhabitants for the gas chambers in Treblinka and Majdanek. The Nazis planned for a quick action—no more than three days to force everyone on trains. Instead, brave Jewish underground fighters coordinated a guerrilla uprising, using makeshift weapons to hold off the Nazis for nearly a month. Americans read about the battles in Warsaw as the delegates in Bermuda gave bland quotations to the few journalists permitted there. By the time the *We Will Never Die* pageant reached the Hollywood Bowl in July, the show included a new portion: "The Hymn of the Ghetto."

On the last full day of the Bermuda Conference, the delegates released a joint statement, just to say that the discussions would remain confidential.

The same group that had staged *We Will Never Die* issued a full-page newspaper ad in the *New York Times:* "To 5,000,000 Jews in the Nazi Death-Trap Bermuda Was a Cruel Mockery! Wretched, doomed victims of Hitler's tyranny! . . . You have cherished an illusion. Your hopes have been in vain. Bermuda was not the dawn of a new era, an era of humanity and compassion, of transmitting pity into deed. Bermuda was a mockery, and a cruel jest."

The State Department swatted away the criticism, and Breckinridge Long argued internally that they merely had a public relations problem. If these Jewish groups only knew about all the department's work on behalf of refugees, they would stop complaining.

Reams's opposition temporarily tabled Riegner's license. Pehle's approval was not enough, because ultimately the State Department controlled official cable traffic to Switzerland. Any orders sent to the Bern legation had to go through it.

Time slipped away. At the end of July, Harrison sent sober news from Bern: Riegner had seen figures bandied about in the press speculating that four million Jews were trapped in Europe. In reality, Riegner wrote, nearly four million had already been murdered.

Stephen Wise was unaware that the State Department had intentionally delayed Riegner's license. But something held it up, and he knew just what to do. The rabbi ventured to the White House on July 22 expressly to get President Roosevelt's endorsement for Riegner's plan. Afterward, in his letter of thanks to Roosevelt, whom he affectionately called "Chief," Wise reiterated how the rescue work would save lives "without, I repeat, one penny falling into the hands of enemy representatives." Wise pointedly sent copies to the Treasury and State Departments, making sure they knew Roosevelt supported Riegner's project.

Meltzer seized the moment, excited to see a way around Reams. Theorizing how Riegner's plan could work, Meltzer optimistically concluded, "It would appear that, unless there is some countervailing foreign policy objection, the Department should endorse, rather than veto the proposal." Meltzer's memo sat on Cordell Hull's desk, with no license sent to Bern.

At a morning Treasury meeting on August 5, Randolph Paul spoke up. A cheerful-looking man in his mid-fifties, Paul was Morgenthau's hardworking general counsel, a tax expert, and signatory of many memos to his boss about the battles between the State and the Treasury Departments over the Riegner license. State still sat on the approvals, Paul told Morgenthau: "There are certain elements in the State Department, which you may well imagine, are opposed to it." Morgenthau sarcastically retorted, "I can't imagine," as his staff knowingly laughed.

That day, Morgenthau called State to complain that it was "discourteous" of it to needlessly delay Riegner's license. Hull responded that it would be sent, personally adding, "Any view that this would make funds available to the enemy is not correct." Hull's note amounted to a deliberate reproach to Reams and the other staff still arguing internally that Riegner's plan would harm the war effort.

Things were looking promising. After nearly four months, it seemed as though Riegner could soon begin his rescue efforts.

In mid-August, a shock reverberated through the State Department. Assistant Secretary Adolf Berle walked into Sumner Welles's dusty, sunlit office to find his friend dictating his resignation letter and packing up boxes. Certain rumors about Welles were going to get

out soon, and he had "best get away," to lie low at his second home in
Bar Harbor, Maine. He had suffered a minor heart attack the previous
weekend, just from the stress of it all.

Welles's sudden resignation stemmed from an incident that had
taken place several years earlier. Back in September 1940, during a long
ride on the presidential train after the funeral of a former Speaker of
the House, he had drunkenly and unsuccessfully propositioned two
male African American rail porters. The FBI quietly investigated, but
the incident had been pretty well covered up until the summer of 1943,
when Hull pieced enough gossip together. It was time for Welles to go,
Hull decided, and with him any humanitarian checks on Breckinridge
Long and his staff.

Long struggled to temper his ambition after Welles's departure, even
as he carefully cut and pasted speculative articles about his possible
promotion to undersecretary into his diary. In light of the distraction,
Treasury took over the Riegner matter, drafting last-minute questions
that State Department staff sent to Switzerland without edits. By early
September, Treasury had readied the license and thought that State
had already transmitted it to Riegner.

As State and Treasury argued back and forth that summer, John Pehle
became convinced that something more had to be done for the Jews
of Europe.

Pehle watched Meltzer get so frustrated with his colleagues at State
that he resigned to take a naval commission, promising to tell Treasury everything as soon as he left. With Meltzer and Welles both gone,
Treasury had very few sympathetic friends at the State Department
anymore. Soon, any rescue plans would undoubtedly find even greater
resistance than the Riegner license had.

Meanwhile, Pehle was learning more about the facts on the ground
in Europe. Besides Hungary, which wasn't occupied by the Nazis
and where Jews were still relatively safe, the largest remaining Jewish
populations were in Romania, France, and Transnistria. Exactly where
Riegner wanted to help people.

From Swiss cables, Pehle learned about the deteriorating conditions in France. In one, a YMCA relief worker in Geneva wrote,

"Nearly 4000 children, between ages of 2 and 14 have been deported since autumn 1942 through Paris to unrevealed destination locked in windowless box cars 60 to 1 car without a single adult escort, without food, water, hygienic provisions." About 6,000 additional children had been abandoned in France, their parents deported before them.

Pehle stayed up late those nights, smoking his pipe and drinking scotch and sodas. At some point, two months after Meltzer had first approached him about Riegner's license, Pehle began to understand that these atrocities—these horrific, unfathomable, gruesome crimes—were both real and separate from the conventional military war. There is a big difference between the knowledge that millions of Jews were being murdered—which the American public learned in November 1942—and actual understanding and belief. The numbers were so big, the crime so incomprehensible. But that summer something clicked for him, and by the end of August John Pehle believed that it was the role of the U.S. government to try to save the Jews of Europe, and his personal responsibility as the director of Foreign Funds Control to do all he could to help. With the Riegner license successfully off his desk—so he thought—he was ready to completely revise the way Treasury looked at rescue and relief going forward.

State Department Hubris

On Wednesday, October 6, 1943, a little after noon, more than four hundred rabbis gathered at Union Station in Washington, D.C., most arriving on the morning trains from New York, Philadelphia, and Baltimore, but some coming from as far away as Cleveland. It was three days before Yom Kippur, the Day of Atonement, the holiest day of the Jewish calendar. Trailed by nearly a hundred reporters and well-wishers, the rabbis marched toward the U.S. Capitol, where a small group broke off to meet with Vice President Henry Wallace in his chambers. They all gathered again on the Senate steps—the rabbis, the reporters, Wallace, and a group of congressional leadership and Jewish congressmen. Rabbi Eliezer Silver, the president of the Union of Orthodox Rabbis, read their petition aloud, pleading for the establishment of an agency to rescue European Jews. Rabbi Wolf Gold appealed to God to help Roosevelt "save the remnant of the people of the book, the people of Israel," and for swift peace. The rabbis marched the twenty-two blocks to the Lincoln Memorial, where they prayed again and sang "The Star-Spangled Banner." Then the group split up. A small delegation headed to the White House, where they met with one of Roosevelt's aides, while most boarded streetcars past the Treasury building's granite columns, up Sixteenth Street to Ohev Sholom, the national synagogue.

Peter Bergson and his Emergency Committee to Save the Jewish People of Europe had organized the march to raise public awareness and governmental attention on the murder of the Jews. Bergson and his friends, collectively known as the Bergson Boys (because his committee frequently changed names, but the personalities stayed the same), had originally come to the United States to lobby for the formation of a Jewish army under Allied command. They gathered a mainly non-Jewish following, cultivating celebrities and politicians to their various causes. After reading about Wise's November 1942 press conference, Bergson, a twenty-seven-year-old Palestinian Jew with a pointed face and small mustache, refocused the group to lobby for rescue, as loudly as possible. It placed full-page ads in prominent newspapers, including the "Cruel Mockery" Bermuda ad, and actively raised funds with coupons at the bottom of ads, worded to leave sympathetic non-Jews with the idea that their donations would go toward humanitarian aid. It sent the *We Will Never Die* pageant around the country and held the Emergency Conference to Save the Jews of Europe in New York City in July 1943, featuring prominent speakers like Herbert Hoover and Dorothy Parker. The conference led to the Emergency Committee, which pushed for action, including for the United States to create an official agency to save the Jews.

The Bergson Boys did not work well with the other Jewish organizations. In fact, as the rabbis marched on October 6, Stephen Wise and Nahum Goldmann convened in Breckinridge Long's office, mainly to complain about Bergson and express their hope that the State Department would ignore his committee. Part of this antipathy was due to Bergson's affiliation with the Irgun—the militant wing of Revisionist Zionism that used violence and terrorism to oppose the British mandate of Palestine—but mainly because the man was arrogant and disruptive.

Bergson didn't like them either. He believed that American Jews like Wise and Goldmann didn't speak for the victims of Nazi persecution, but he did. The victims were "Hebrews" like him, Jews with greater allegiance to a hypothetical Hebrew nation than to any national identities. He believed his committee was the only group that spoke for the Jews of Europe and Palestine, the only one with the moral authority to plead for action on their behalf. Bergson's presumption infuriated established Jewish organizations.

The Emergency Committee also disliked the State Department, which it identified as an impediment to rescue. The committee's monthly magazine, the *Answer,* paired an account of the rabbis' march

with a cartoon of two State Department employees, both lazily reading the society pages of Washington newspapers. One passes a report
to the other titled "100,000 Jews Killed Monthly by Nazis." The cartoon's caption reads, "Refer to Committee 3, Investigation Subcom-
mittee 6, Section 8B, for consideration." Bergson began plotting to force
the State Department, specifically Long, to answer for its inaction.

The Treasury Department didn't associate with the Emergency
Committee in any way—after hearing Bergson's pitch in early August,
one staff member dismissed it as "nothing special"—but Bergson's
frustrations with State were certainly shared.

Pehle, still believing that Riegner's license had been sent to Switzerland and now convinced of the role he could play in rescue work,
decided to use his power over Foreign Funds to streamline aid.

He started by completely revising the Treasury Department's standard policy involving humanitarian cases. Pehle briefed Morgenthau
on the plight of Jewish children in France and emphasized that the
children could be evacuated if funds were available for the effort. But
one of the limitations was "the Government's blanket prohibition of
financial transactions involving trade or communication with persons
in enemy territory."

The standard line had to change, especially because "we have now
had sufficient experience in administering our trading with the enemy
controls to be able to permit certain well defined groups to conduct limited types of relief operations in enemy territory." Treasury
couldn't ignore safeguards—blocked bank accounts, verifications that
lenders were reputable, measures to prevent money from reaching the
enemy—but Morgenthau agreed to the dramatic liberalization of Foreign Funds policy.

Pehle also took the opportunity to assist the American Jewish
Joint Distribution Committee with some of its projects. He reversed
an earlier rejection of a JDC license to send relief money into Shanghai. Thousands of European Jews who had escaped there were starving,
and the JDC had not been able to send any money for four months.
Pehle authorized $40,000 per month, which could be repaid to lend-
ers after the war.

He also rushed a new request through the system. In early September, the JDC asked permission to send Saly Mayer, its representative in

Switzerland, $100,000 per month for the next six months—many multiples of the $25,000 the World Jewish Congress wanted for Riegner. Within two weeks, Pehle personally shepherded the project through all the necessary permissions and expanded it to allow for even more money, all without issuing a formal license for fear that Long's staff might notice and get in the way.

But Gerhart Riegner was still waiting.

In mid-September, Harrison cabled to ask about the project's status: Had all the Treasury cables in August asking last-minute questions about the planned efforts in Romania and France meant that the paperwork was ready? Long's staff was paying attention again after the Welles drama, and their excuses for still not issuing the license grew more blatant as the weeks passed.

Even after all the back-and-forth negotiations over the summer, James Keeley, head of Special Projects at State, wrote a new memo arguing the United States should refuse to participate in Riegner's projects. Keeley gave a tired retread of Reams's complaints, but with a new twist. First, he reminded his colleagues that Treasury's policies had changed—implying State needed to guide its Treasury friends toward safer ground. Then, without a trace of shame or apology, Keeley expressed his concern that Riegner might set a precedent: other organizations might also want to send relief money overseas. "Are we now prepared to do the same for them? If not, have we an unanswerable reason for continuing to refuse their requests? We shall no doubt need it." State sat on the license.

Morgenthau spoke directly to Hull, who again agreed the license should be sent. State called Morgenthau immediately to confirm the transmission to Switzerland. Yet they did not send any license for nearly two more weeks.

When the text of the license finally arrived in late September, Harrison consulted his British counterparts in Bern. They disapproved of Riegner's plan, because the "type of adventurers who would undoubtedly participate, suggests to me that no means can be devised which would prevent the scheme from giving rise to grave abuse." Because the British didn't like it, Harrison withheld the license. No one told the Treasury Department for yet another two weeks. Pehle, furious, demanded that Harrison be ordered to issue the license despite British objection.

It was now October 25. The rabbis had marched three weeks prior. More than six months had passed since Gerhart Riegner first wrote from Switzerland about his relief ideas. Roosevelt and Wise had agreed on them almost four months earlier. Possibilities for rescue changed every day, as the military war did. Escape doors opened and closed, but fewer people were alive to go through them. When Riegner first made his request in April, the Allies were trying to take Tunisia; by October, they were almost halfway up Italy.

And yet the State Department still debated internally whether to issue Riegner's license. Reams repeated to anyone who would listen that he did "not believe we can or should accede to the desire of Treasury . . . this proposal is objectionable." An entire office refused to initial a cable draft about the plan because it wasn't "in accordance with procedure." Breckinridge Long, to his credit, endorsed the idea, not wanting State to be criticized later, and it helped that the president had already approved.

The problem landed on the desk of a handsome man with prematurely white hair, an easy smile, and no experience in diplomacy. Edward Stettinius Jr. had been appointed the new undersecretary of state.

Stettinius, like many of his new State Department colleagues, came from a wealthy family. He rose through the ranks at General Motors before moving to U.S. Steel, becoming chairman of the board in 1938. When war broke out, Stettinius turned into a "dollar-a-year" man— a rich American who basically volunteered as a government executive for a $1 federal salary, first chairing the War Resources Board before becoming the administrator of Lend-Lease. Stettinius prized forward momentum—unlike most of his new colleagues.

In ego-bruising fashion, Breckinridge Long learned from his secretary that he would not be promoted, after she heard about Stettinius on the radio. Hull claimed he hadn't had a chance to tell Long in person.

Upon his arrival at State in early October, Stettinius immediately requested a briefing about refugee matters. He must have wanted to know whether all the public criticism of his staff was valid, but Stettinius had another motive: his close friend Oscar Cox had been working on refugee matters, too. The two men had worked together on Lend-Lease—Stettinius as boss, and Cox, a dark-haired young father, as his general counsel and the "brains behind" the operation. They shared an extraordinarily close friendship—the Coxes' Dalmatian puppy, a gift from Stettinius, bore the name Admiral Stett—and Stettinius took Cox's ideas very seriously.

In June 1943, Oscar Cox, intensely troubled by news of the ongoing massacre of the Jews, had drafted a proposal for a new committee that would consult with State, Treasury, and the Lend-Lease office on the "resettlement, transportation, maintenance, rehabilitation, and eventual return of refugees." The idea resembled the Emergency Committee's plan, which it began to push after its conference in July. Cox had made the rounds with his plan, but with little success. One of Morgenthau's assistants doubted a committee could be funded through donations, so Cox retreated to figure out whether Lend-Lease money could be used.

Stettinius's requested briefing on refugee matters was defensive and depressing. R. Borden Reams couldn't conceal his perpetual disdain from his new boss and used the briefing to complain about all the "extreme measures" the Jewish organizations were pushing. His report included a warning of "the danger" that the German government might release a large group of Jewish refugees for the Allies to deal with.

After the briefing, Stettinius shared the latest version of Cox's plan with his staff. They dismissed it as unnecessary and redundant, given the Intergovernmental Committee's work and the efforts of several other committees, neglecting to add that these groups were mostly defunct. Cox kept editing.

Despite his staff's complaints about the Riegner license, on October 26 Edward Stettinius cabled Leland Harrison, informing him that Treasury wanted it issued over British objections. The cable had obviously been written by a State Department employee, who used Stettinius's inexperience to sneak in an important phrase at the end: "You should, of course, comply with the Treasury Department's desires." Harrison understood the code. This was not an order—he didn't work for the Treasury Department, after all, and the British still objected—so Harrison didn't issue the license. Three weeks passed, and, consistent with a now well-established pattern, no one informed Pehle.

By November 23, John Pehle had grown tired of waiting. He had just gotten his hands on Harrison's request for clarification on Stettinius's October 26 order—a cable State had received almost a week earlier and had, somehow, forgotten to share with Foreign Funds Control. It was time for Secretary Morgenthau to act.

Henry Morgenthau Jr., a longtime neighbor and close friend of President Roosevelt's, had been secretary of the Treasury since 1934. His wife, Elinor, was one of Eleanor Roosevelt's dearest friends, and the couples often socialized in Washington and at home in Hyde Park. Morgenthau was in his early fifties, balding, with round glasses that neatly fit over his small dark eyes.

Like Hull, Morgenthau did not come to his position with a great deal of experience. Rather than working on financial matters, he had worked with agriculture policy prior to his appointment and oversaw his apple farm, Fishkill. Unlike Hull, Morgenthau was a talented administrator with a loyal staff—New Dealers, drawn to Washington for the opportunity to make a difference, highly educated, younger, and motivated.

Early in his tenure, a reporter had asked Morgenthau how he planned to use his new power. He responded, "Enthusiastically." Under Morgenthau's supervision, the Treasury Department transitioned from an agency dealing with the Great Depression to an agency funding the American—and, arguably, the entire—war effort. He facilitated the new Social Security program, completely changed the income tax structure, and organized war bond drives. Treasury staff prided themselves on working diligently and collaboratively, saving the government money at every step, and doing the most good for the most people.

In dealing with refugee matters, though, Morgenthau felt the tension between his own humanitarian impulses and his role as Treasury secretary. His father, Henry senior, had been the American ambassador to the Ottoman Empire at the end of World War I, reporting to the Wilson administration on the Armenian genocide. Now in power himself, Morgenthau knew that as the only Jewish member of Roosevelt's cabinet he was always carefully scrutinized for his actions. He did not want to subject his friend and boss to antisemitic attacks for supposedly prioritizing "Jewish" interests above "American" interests.

Morgenthau believed in a collaborative environment and kept excellent records. He held a morning staff meeting at 9:30, which could last more than an hour. His undersecretary, assistant secretaries, and invited guests would sit in a circle, Morgenthau sometimes behind his long, shiny, dark desk, flanked by the American and Treasury secretary's flags, with a portrait of Lincoln's Treasury secretary, Salmon P. Chase, keeping watch over them all. Morgenthau kept his desk clean, save for a blotter, a few papers, his phone, a fountain pen stand, an ashtray (usually full), and a box of cigarettes (always Camels). His longtime secretary, Henrietta Klotz—blond, Jewish, and religious while her boss was not—sat in on the meetings, though she didn't need to take notes. A long-established habit of having almost all of his meetings and phone calls either recorded or transcribed by a stenographer means that the Treasury staff's frustration and resentment toward the State Department still exists in their own words.

At 2:45 p.m. on Tuesday, November 23, Pehle and other Foreign Funds staff updated Morgenthau on their troubles over the Riegner license. Hearing their litany of objections and delayed cables, Morgenthau responded, "Gentlemen, I can say on the record that I am delighted at your motives . . . Unfortunately you are up against a successive generation of people like those in the State Department who don't like to do this kind of thing . . . Don't think you are going to be able to nail anybody in the State Department to the cross."

Treasury staff prepared a three-page memo to Hull for Morgenthau's signature, laying out the long history of the Riegner license. Their report, delivered to the State Department the next day, concluded, "I fully appreciate that some delays are inherent in handling these problems by cable. However, it is hard to understand the delays that have occurred in this case over the relatively simple matter of get-

ting our Minister in Switzerland to issue a license at my direction and
with your concurrence."

In true State Department fashion, nearly two more weeks passed
before the Treasury Department received Hull's response. Whoever
wrote Hull's letter was—as Morgenthau put it—"nobody's fool" and
had rebutted Treasury, point by point. The delays were actually the
fault of *Treasury,* the State Department staff argued, which had not
approved the license until the end of September. (It was really July.)
Morgenthau was putting poor Leland Harrison in a terrible position,
asking him to ignore the established procedure of consulting British
allies and to guarantee the money would not fall into enemy hands,
which Harrison simply could not do. While claiming to be sympathetic, "the Department, on the other hand, cannot accept responsibility for putting into operation a plan to which are attached conditions
which our Mission, in light of information available to it, states are
impractical."

Pehle and his friends fumed. With Morgenthau away at Fishkill,
they took several weeks revising their rebuttal. While they didn't want
to provoke Hull by calling his staff liars, his "conclusions . . . are predi-
cated upon his incomplete knowledge of the facts." Furthermore, the
secretary of state had contradicted himself, because he had agreed with
Morgenthau back in August that the money would not fall into enemy
hands. The frustrated Treasury staff worried about descending into a
war of memos—back and forth, with no end in sight, more delays, and
never convincing State of anything.

Two things happened, both out of the Treasury Department's control,
to break this cycle.

The first was the release of Breckinridge Long's congressional testimony on Friday, December 10. Back in November, congressmen who
supported Peter Bergson and his Emergency Committee had introduced identical resolutions urging Roosevelt to create "a commission
of diplomatic, economic, and military experts to formulate and effec-
tuate a plan of immediate action designed to save the surviving Jewish
people of Europe from extinction at the hands of Nazi Germany." The
Senate Foreign Affairs Committee passed it unanimously, while Rep-

resentative Sol Bloom, who headed the House Committee on Foreign Affairs, called for hearings.

The day after Thanksgiving, Breckinridge Long testified for four hours in closed session about the refugee and quota challenges that had haunted his tenure at the State Department. He discussed the Bermuda Conference negotiations and reminded the congressmen of the existence of the Intergovernmental Committee, which had finally met in August. He also revealed that the United States had taken in 580,000 refugees since 1933.

Long's testimony was so well received—one co-sponsor on Bergson's bill even commented that the State Department had "an excellent record and one which you and this country should be proud of"—that Long decided to print his testimony and release it to the public himself. Good publicity would counteract Bergson's ads and convince the public that a commission wouldn't be necessary.

It's hard to understand how the State Department could possibly have thought that 580,000 refugees had entered the country. The Immigration and Naturalization Service published yearly immigration statistics, which were then mined by the American Jewish Committee to identify the number of "Hebrew" arrivals. These numbers were public and published and clearly showed refugee immigration at just one-third of the number Breckinridge Long claimed in his testimony.

Congressman Emanuel Celler, a constant advocate for refugees, quickly wrote a press release pointing out Long's errors. Celler hit hard: "His statement drips with sympathy for the persecuted Jews, but the tears he sheds are crocodile . . . The tempest-tossed get little comfort from men like Breckinridge Long." As soon as newspapers picked up Celler's attack, Long's testimony crumbled quickly.

At first, Breckinridge Long had no idea what to do, writing to one of his staff, "They ask the question where we got the figure 580,000. We ought to be able to answer that." State Department officials had guessed a similar number in memos all year, and Long had a habit of adding a question mark in the margin but hadn't bothered to check on a real number before testifying. Long, in his diary, blamed everyone but himself: "The radical press, always prone to attack me, and the Jewish press have turned their barrage against me and made life

somewhat uncomfortable . . . They have to have somebody to attack . . .
Otherwise they would have no publicity. So for the time being I am
the bull's eye." Just when the Treasury Department needed him to be,
Long was vulnerable.

The second crucial development arrived a week after the release of
Long's testimony: a cable from London. Treasury had asked the British
to remove their objection to the Riegner license, and on December 17
their response finally arrived. London agreed to consider Treasury's
request but had other "grave objections" that had nothing to do with
financial matters or money falling into the hands of the enemy.

When he finally read the message, John Pehle thought it was a
"strong, shocking thing."

Great Britain, America's most trusted ally, was "concerned with the
difficulties of disposing of any considerable number of Jews should
they be rescued from enemy occupied territory . . . it is likely to prove
almost if not quite impossible to deal with anything like the number
of 70,000 refugees whose rescue is envisaged by the Riegner plan. For
this reason they are reluctant to agree to any approval being expressed
even of the preliminary financial arrangements."

Though Treasury didn't know it, the British were echoing the arguments Reams had made to Stettinius several months earlier: if we rescue the Jews, we must deal with them, and we don't want to do that.

Randolph Paul expressed his relief at being "away from all this
smoke screen now; we are into the real issue." Josiah DuBois, Foreign
Funds Control's resident firebrand, was livid: "Mr. Secretary, the only
question we have in our mind, I think, is the bull has to be taken by
the horns in dealing with this Jewish issue, and get this thing out of
the State Department into some agency's hands that is willing to deal
with it frontally. For instance, take the complaint, 'What are we going
to do with the Jews?—we let them die because we don't know what to
do with them.'"

Paul quietly added, "We are speaking as citizens, now."

Morgenthau immediately called the State Department to request a
meeting with Cordell Hull for first thing Monday morning.

The team gathered Sunday afternoon, their only day off in a six-day
wartime workweek, in order to plot. Oscar Cox joined them, explaining the most recent iteration of his plan, one in which Morgenthau,

Stettinius, and Leo Crowley of the Foreign Economic Administration would act in concert, with their relief activities financed through Lend-Lease. Cox suggested using the State Department's inevitable objections to establishing a committee to make the British into "a straw man, because their attitude is basically not different than the attitude of the people who have been working on this thing. And you can get these people out . . . if you really want to do it." One Treasury staff member enthused, "Oscar has a whale of a good plan, but he has to have an excuse to get it to the President. We have the excuse to get it to the President."

Ready for their showdown, on Monday morning, December 20, Morgenthau, Pehle, Paul, and Cox walked past the White House to the Department of State. The news that day was depressing: the *Washington Post* reported that the Fifth Army had taken San Pietro, just south of Monte Cassino, finally breaking the Germans' winter line, but had suffered heavy losses. A cold front moved into Washington, and for many families wondering whether a telegram would come for them, it would be another dark and gloomy Christmas. For the Treasury Department staff, their battles with the State Department were no longer just about Riegner's license. Their fight was now over the values the United States—and the new United Nations as a whole—would actually represent.

Hull and Long had also been busy over the weekend in anticipation of Morgenthau's demands. With the criticism of his testimony ringing in his ears, Long was desperate to prove his detractors wrong and save his job. On Saturday afternoon, as soon as he heard Morgenthau had requested a Monday morning meeting, Long preempted Treasury's complaints by finally sending Riegner's license to Switzerland, ordering Leland Harrison to issue it over British objection. That same day, Hull cabled his "astonishment" at London's cable about refugees, which was "incompatible with the policy of the United States Government." He instructed Ambassador John Winant to meet with the British immediately to find out what had happened. Now the Treasury staff would have no need to complain.

After their meeting at the State Department, the Treasury staff returned to their offices in great moods. Hull and Long were clearly scared, Morgenthau was sure of it. "From the time I called the State

Department and said that I wanted to have an appointment with
Mr. Hull—from that time on something must have happened
damned fast . . . When I walked in there Monday morning, the decks
were clear." Long had even pulled Morgenthau aside to confide that
the real problem at the State Department had been Bernard Meltzer, State's troublemaking and antisemitic former staff member. The
accusation—revealing that Long did not know Meltzer was Jewish or
that Treasury knew of Meltzer's support for the license—was laugh-
able. Morgenthau cheerfully responded that the rumor was *Long* was
the antisemite.

When his staff tried to turn to practical issues—wanting to remove
refugee matters from the State Department—Morgenthau was not
ready: "Excuse me just one moment. This is the biggest victory that
has happened on this front this year, and I am not going to let you
couple of old owls sit there and say, 'Yes, this is good, but what about
tomorrow?'"

The Treasury Department had gotten everything it wanted. The
secretary of state had rebuked the British, horrified at their fear of setting a precedent of rescue—a fear Hull's own staff had echoed. Breckinridge Long, publicly humiliated and personally vulnerable, had
finally ordered Leland Harrison to issue Riegner's license. Riegner
would, finally, eight months after his first proposal, have funding for
his projects. And Morgenthau got to call Breckinridge Long an antisemite to his face.

But John Pehle and his friends were not satisfied. If their experiences with the State Department had taught them anything, it was
that these problems would continue until someone else took charge of
rescue and relief projects. Morgenthau just needed more persuading
to go to Roosevelt and make their demands. And they had a plan. They
were about to drop a bombshell.

5

On the Acquiescence of This Government

JOSIAH DUBOIS HAD THE smoking gun. A prodigy who had graduated from the University of Pennsylvania at eighteen, DuBois worked as chief counsel to Foreign Funds Control. One of the youngest of Morgenthau's senior staff, he had a reputation as a firebrand: passionate, articulate, and unafraid, especially when discussing aid for people under Nazi control. His four younger brothers were all fighting in the war, and one of them, Louis, had been shot down in October 1943 and interned as a prisoner of war in Germany. DuBois held a military deferment as an essential government employee and felt an extra responsibility to fight from Washington.

In early December, while researching the history of the Riegner license for one of the Treasury Department's memos to Hull, DuBois had gotten a copy of Riegner's original April 20 cable, laying out his proposal for the first time. The cover letter attached to the cable, though, struck DuBois as unusual. After explaining he had not been transmitting messages coming from "R" (Riegner), Minister Leland Harrison in Bern asked that this message "not (repeat not) be subjected to the restriction imposed by your 354, February 10." The "354" was a cable number; every message, sent and received, had a unique number. DuBois didn't have a cable numbered 354, and when he called the State Department, it wouldn't give him a copy. Suspicious.

DuBois persisted and, with the assistance of a State Department friend, Donald Hiss (the brother of the future accused spy Alger), snuck into State's massive file room. There, the two men found a copy of 354.

The State Department had sent cable 354 to Harrison on February 10, 1943, around the time Breckinridge Long and the British were debating how to respond to the first public demands for rescue. The language was vague, which is probably how the State Department staff got Sumner Welles to initial it for transmission. But the cable clearly rebuked Harrison for sending certain messages: "With regard to reports submitted to you for transmission to private persons in the United States, it is suggested that such reports in the future should not be accepted unless extraordinary circumstances make such action advisable."

Cable 354 was marked as a response to "Your 482." Cable 482 had to be an example of the kind of information the State Department didn't want the Bern legation to send. DuBois and Hiss located cable 482, a long report by Gerhart Riegner intended for Stephen Wise, detailing atrocities in Poland and Romania. DuBois took notes on a small index card: "6000 Jews killed Poland daily; 130,000 R. Jews deported Transnistria; about 60,000 dead of the deported." Riegner gave the report to the Bern legation in January, and the State Department in Washington had forwarded it to Wise. Then, with cable 354, it had ordered Harrison to stop transmitting Riegner's reports. Until April 20, when Harrison requested the restriction be removed, he had been forbidden to send Riegner's information about the murder of Jews to the United States.

So there it was, a conspiracy laid out in bureaucratic cables. The Treasury Department now had more than enough reason to go to Roosevelt and demand that refugee matters be removed from State Department control. Because it couldn't admit DuBois had sneaked into the State Department, it needed to obtain official copies of cables 354 and 482 another way.

At the end of the December 20 meeting at the State Department, probably before telling Long he was an antisemite, Morgenthau innocently asked for a copy of cable 354, claiming that his staff had seen a reference to it but didn't have the cable. Blindsided, Long agreed to have his new assistant bring a copy to the Treasury Department by the end of the day.

Of course, it wasn't going to be that easy. William Riegelman, Long's assistant, brought a paraphrased copy of 354 to Treasury that afternoon. The young lawyer whom Long had hired was overconfident, indiscreet . . . and Henry Morgenthau's second cousin.

Morgenthau hadn't known Riegelman now worked for Long, and Riegelman seemed to be the only person who thought his new boss wasn't aware of the relation. (Morgenthau smirked and said, "In the first place, in his application he gives me as reference and he thinks that they don't know who he is.") In a hastily called meeting, Pehle and his colleagues seemed both flabbergasted and deeply suspicious of what Long might be plotting. Morgenthau thought Long was playing a "cheap trick," particularly because Riegelman bragged to Pehle's assistant that he had written the Riegner license himself. Clearly, Long planned to deflect Treasury's criticism using Morgenthau's cousin as a shield.

While debating how to deal with the introduction of Riegelman into an already complicated situation, the Treasury staff also had to address the problem of the cable. The paraphrased cable 354 Riegelman had brought them was missing the reference to "Your 482." Without that notation, there was no way to link the two cables together and no way to prove State's deception. They couldn't ask for a copy of 482 without giving away that they had already seen it. Riegelman made it clear that Long had paraphrased the cable himself, which meant that Long had deliberately erased the linkage, in a blatant attempt to cover his tracks. This time, another Treasury staff member, Ansel Luxford, played the spy, walking over to the State Department and feigning confusion about the paraphrased cable. He pestered Breckinridge Long into showing him the original cable text, giving Luxford an excuse to ask for a new copy—and a copy of 482. The file rooms were closed for the day, Long responded. Riegelman would bring them over on Tuesday.

When a copy of 482 hadn't arrived by 11:00 a.m., Luxford called Riegelman, who had five people looking for the missing cable. Riegelman explained, "Acheson's assistant, Hiss, had requested it and according to one of the girls in his office, he showed it to someone in the Treasury." Much to DuBois's relief, that incriminating tidbit went over Riegelman's head. Eventually, he found and delivered the cables. By the end of the day, Treasury finally, officially, had the full texts of 354 and 482. Now it had to decide what to do.

The Treasury staff presented a report of their findings to Morgenthau on December 23. In part, it read, "To put it bluntly, Mr. Secretary, it appears that certain responsible officials of this Government were so fearful that this Government might act to save the Jews of Europe if the gruesome facts relating to Hitler's plans to exterminate them became known, that they . . . attempted to suppress the facts . . . We leave it for your judgment whether this action made such officials the accomplices of Hitler in this program and whether or not these officials are not war criminals in every sense of the term." Leaving for Fishkill for the holidays, Morgenthau asked his staff to incorporate cables 354 and 482—and Long's attempt to cover his tracks—into something Hull couldn't possibly ignore or refute.

When Morgenthau returned on New Year's Eve 1943, his staff told him they didn't want to go to Hull again. DuBois had tried to draft a new memo, but every day counted, and the Treasury staff didn't believe Hull had any control over his staff. It was time to go directly to President Roosevelt, and Pehle, DuBois, and Luxford were working on something that would convince Morgenthau they were right.

Over the next few weeks, as the Treasury staff wrote and rewrote their arguments for Morgenthau, they kept finding more evidence of the importance of wresting control of refugee matters from the State Department. In early January, Pehle heard that Saly Mayer, the JDC's representative in Switzerland, was having trouble with his relief funds. In late summer, with the State Department staff distracted by Welles's resignation, Pehle had given Mayer official permission to undertake relief work but had not issued a formal license. Now Harrison was giving Mayer a hard time. So Pehle, confident that a very vulnerable Long would not refuse him, quickly drafted a license for Mayer and sent it to the State Department for transmission to Bern. Pehle learned the next afternoon that it had not yet been sent. Morgenthau demanded Riegelman send it by sunset, which would be at 5:31 p.m. exactly, "and no damn fooling." It didn't go out until the next morning, and only after Riegelman added a cover letter, warning Harrison that there might be a conflict between the JDC and the World Jewish Congress over currency exchange—a concern neither Riegner nor Mayer nor the Treasury Department had expressed. When Pehle complained, Riegelman retorted, "State felt that it is a better judge than [Treasury] of operations in the field."

Pehle called Riegelman to his office, trying to stay calm and ensuring a stenographer transcribed the discussion. Pehle was "very, very disturbed" that Riegelman had added warnings to the license. If he ever did that again, Treasury would refuse to work with him. Riegelman, again sharing too much, fought back: "Mr. Pehle, I want to ask you something: Don't you agree the Department of State has the right to send any telegrams to its missions it wants?" After all, Hull had approved Riegelman's cover letter. Pehle made the younger man repeat himself. Yes, Riegelman confirmed, Hull had agreed to the warning attached to the cable, knowing that Treasury had not. "That is what the Treasury is complaining about and feels very strongly about," Pehle replied. The conflict between the State and the Treasury Departments would continue boiling until Roosevelt himself weighed in.

Finally, on January 13, 1944, the group gathered at 11:00 a.m. in Morgenthau's office to present their arguments. They began by distributing an eighteen-page document with an astonishing title: "Report to the Secretary on the Acquiescence of This Government in the Murder of the Jews." The report bore Randolph Paul's signature but had been initially drafted by Josiah DuBois with collaborative edits and additions by Pehle and Luxford. The secretary quite liked the title, though he learned little new information since the late-December briefing; the staff had even copied wholesale some material they had originally written for Hull. The report was long, detailed, and full of impassioned talking points, intended to persuade Morgenthau to go straight to the president. On the first page, the Treasury staff implored, "Unless remedial steps of a drastic nature are taken, and taken immediately, I am certain that no effective action will be taken by this Government to prevent the complete extermination of the Jews in German controlled Europe, and that this Government will have to share for all time responsibility for this extermination." The memo concluded by borrowing a line from Emanuel Celler's condemnation of Long: "If men of the temperament and philosophy of Long continue in control of immigration administration, we may as well take down that plaque from the Statue of Liberty and black out the 'lamp beside the golden door.'"

Heading out of town for a war bonds drive speech, Morgenthau set up a staff meeting two days later, on a Saturday morning, inviting Oscar Cox and two of Roosevelt's top aides, Samuel Rosenman and Ben Cohen, to help them prepare for the president. When Morgenthau called with the invitation, Rosenman expressed concern that if the meeting leaked to the press, Morgenthau would be attacked for inviting three Jews. Morgenthau reassured him but was privately incredulous that Rosenman was worried about optics. Cox and several friends spent part of Friday working on final versions of a draft executive order and press release announcing a new agency, the project that Cox had been revising for seven months. It was time to marry Cox's plan with the Treasury's evidence.

Promptly at 9:30 a.m. on Saturday, January 15, 1944, the group met in Treasury secretary Henry Morgenthau Jr.'s office.

Before reviewing the new "Personal Report to the President"— a shorter version of the "Acquiescence" memo, still with all the facts but toned-down rhetoric—Pehle informed his colleagues of a puzzling new development. William Riegelman had spoken with Pehle's assistant, Florence Hodel, about a new idea he just had: a committee of State, Treasury, and Foreign Economic Administration staff tasked with refugee matters, under the direction of Howard Travers of the Visa Division. Riegelman had come to the same conclusion as Oscar Cox had in June, the Emergency Committee to Save the Jewish People of Europe had in July, and the Senate Foreign Affairs Committee had in December. The time for a relief and rescue agency had arrived, and the Treasury Department had to get its plan out first.

Pehle read the "Personal Report to the President" aloud: "One of the greatest crimes in history, the slaughter of the Jewish people in Europe, is continuing unabated. This government has, for a long time, maintained that its policy is to work out programs to save those Jews of Europe who could be saved. You are probably not as familiar as I with the utter failure of certain officials in our State Department, who are charged with actually carrying out this policy, to take any effective action . . . We have talked; we have sympathized; we have expressed our horror; the time to act is long past due." Ansel Luxford read a draft executive order establishing the "War Refugee Board." According to the final version of Cox's plan, the WRB would consist of the secretary of state, the secretary of the Treasury, and the foreign economic administrator (Hull, Morgenthau, and Crowley) and would be tasked with providing relief and finding safe haven for refugees. Cox envisioned the board could accept private contributions, appoint overseas attachés with diplomatic status, and work through both existing government facilities and private relief organizations.

They debated whether Morgenthau should approach Hull first as a courtesy. Some feared Hull would immediately run to the president to cover for his staff, and the whole bureaucratic quagmire would continue, with lives being lost daily. Morgenthau openly admitted there was a 90 percent chance Roosevelt would just tell him to figure things out with Hull. But the Treasury Department had to try.

Morgenthau finally called the White House to schedule time with the president the next day. With the meeting on the books and paperwork ready, the conversation drifted to daydreaming about the executive director of the new War Refugee Board. Ansel Luxford suggested John Pehle, who wasn't in the room to hear it. Morgenthau agreed. "I dreamed of that, too. I have been thinking about nothing else, but the question is whether I want to give him up." Morgenthau decided to have Pehle and Randolph Paul accompany him to the meeting with the president. Ben Cohen reiterated the need for an executive order and a full-time director, using words that would have resonated with Roosevelt: "We want a new deal."

The next morning, John Pehle woke up next to his wife, Francha, at their log cabin home surrounded by trees in Bethesda, Maryland. He kissed his two sons, John junior and five-month-old Stephen. He soberly put on a dark suit, long coat, and homburg hat and went to the office. The lives of thousands, maybe even millions, depended on his ability to convince the president that "the time to act is long past due."

Henry Morgenthau, Randolph Paul, and John Pehle climbed the center staircase to the second floor of the White House. They assembled in the Oval Study, the president's private office next to his bedroom, where large windows overlooked the Washington Monument. The room was cream colored with bright red carpet and cluttered with personality: naval paintings all over the walls, donkey toys all over the ornate wooden Resolute desk, and a lion-skin rug on the floor. Roosevelt was quite ill, and the meeting with the Treasury staff at 12:45 p.m. was his first of the day. Pehle had never been there before, and it was a very personal, intimate space for an uncomfortable conversation.

Morgenthau began, probably with some of the same lines he rehearsed the day before: "There are the facts, Mr. President, the most shocking thing I have found since I have been in Washington. Here we find ourselves aiding and abetting Hitler. How can we at this very late date try to make up for lost time?"

Morgenthau asked Pehle to recount everything they had discovered. It was a complicated story, but Pehle had been practicing this moment for the last twenty-four hours. He explained his team's detective work, emphasizing the ways Breckinridge Long and the State Department staff had obstructed rescue. Pehle quickly distilled the details of Riegner's license and the drama surrounding cables 354 and 482 into something Roosevelt would understand, growing more forceful as he saw the president following attentively.

When Pehle stopped to breathe, Roosevelt airily picked up the draft executive order announcing the establishment of the War Refugee Board. He skimmed it, then commented simply: Stimson should be on this, not Crowley. The substitution of Secretary of War Henry Stimson, instead of the foreign economic administrator Leo Crowley, would tie the WRB's humanitarian work directly to military operations.

There was no debate. As it turned out, Roosevelt needed no convincing. He, too, believed that more should be done and in fact had some ideas of his own. Jews were getting out of Bulgaria through Turkey, or at least he heard that doors were still open, but if Turkey entered the war, they might close. And perhaps Jews could get over the borders into Spain or Switzerland. Roosevelt had even already spoken with Stettinius about setting up offices in North Africa, Italy, Portugal, Spain, and Turkey to assist Jews.

The Treasury staff had come prepared, but the president didn't need to hear much. With the congressional "Rescue Resolutions" still pending, Roosevelt's preemptive action no doubt solved several problems for him, both publicly and within his own administration. The president would issue the executive order establishing the War Refugee Board, finally announcing an American policy of rescue and relief.

The only part of the presentation Roosevelt disagreed with related to his old friend Breckinridge Long. As Pehle delicately reported in a memo after the meeting, "The President seemed disinclined to believe that Long wanted to stop effective action from being taken." Instead, Roosevelt made excuses for Long, specifically that he had "soured on the situation" during the period of spy hysteria when some refugees had been "bad." (Morgenthau disputed Roosevelt's memory of Nazi saboteurs disguised as refugees, and they agreed to disagree.)

The meeting—which Pehle reported as only twenty minutes and Paul remembered as forty-five—broke up when Eleanor Roosevelt leaned in to remind the president that his lunch of roasted duck would soon be overcooked. Roosevelt never read Treasury's memo and didn't keep the copy the staff had presented to him.

Nazi Germany had an official government policy of murdering Jews. Now, for the first time, an Allied country had an official government policy to save them. In that moment, the United States joined the second war.

At the same time, the decision to create the War Refugee Board raised a host of new questions. Who would lead it? What would it do? How did it fit within the myriad existing rescue and relief organizations? The eyes of all the relief groups in the United States and all the families with loved ones somewhere in Nazi territory—maybe dead, maybe alive, but somewhere—would be on the WRB. The Nazis, too, would be sizing up their new foe and plotting ways to thwart any rescue plans. The military war would twist and turn, territories lost and gained on both sides, and all of it out of the new board's control. It was a daunting task, and in January 1944, after Roosevelt agreed to issue the executive order announcing a new policy, no one knew what to do next. What would this War Refugee Board really be?

A War Refugee Board

Henry Morgenthau didn't even return to his office before spreading the news, excitedly using the White House phones to ask Samuel Rosenman and Edward Stettinius—another of Roosevelt's suggestions, because he thought the undersecretary of state would be a more "sympathetic" liaison than Hull—to meet that evening.

When Stettinius arrived at Morgenthau's Massachusetts Avenue home, he made a stunning announcement—as if the day hadn't been momentous enough. After Pehle finished relaying the Treasury Department's findings to Stettinius, who was hearing everything for the first time, the undersecretary was horrified but not surprised. That's why Long is no longer in charge of the Visa Division or Special War Problems, Stettinius informed them.

A State Department reorganization, in the works for several months, had finally gone into effect the day before. After more than four years of service, Breckinridge Long had been officially removed from immigration and refugee matters and assigned to "Congressional Relations." The move wasn't advertised as a demotion, but clearly was. The Treasury staff knew that changes were coming but had not heard the details—and certainly not Long's reassignment.

But Roosevelt *had* known and, even after listening to Pehle and Morgenthau describe Long's obstruction, did not inform them. The president could easily have urged Treasury to work with Assistant Secretary Adolf Berle, Long's replacement. But he hadn't. Instead, he simply mentioned that in the State Department reorganization, no one appeared to be responsible for rescue plans. The new War Refugee Board, the president agreed, would fill the gap. Before the night ended, both Stettinius and Rosenman agreed that Pehle should be the acting director of the new organization.

Pehle left Morgenthau's and went home; Ansel Luxford and Josiah DuBois came over soon after, the house electric with their excitement. They smoked and drank, pausing only to add Roosevelt's requested edits to the paperwork so Pehle could triumphantly deliver the final copies to Rosenman before the president's Monday morning briefing. The men worked and celebrated long into the night.

Unbeknownst to his staff, Henry Morgenthau called the White House later that night, ostensibly about a war bonds speech but also to make sure his relationship with the president had survived the day intact. Roosevelt joked with him, and, relieved, Morgenthau decided that the meeting "left no unfavorable reaction in his mind about myself which is encouraging. I was very serious when I saw him ... and he didn't seem to like it too much ... I hope he will see the thing through."

The next morning, awake and ready early, Pehle waited for the Treasury Department car to pick him up and deliver him to the White House. With wartime gas and rubber rationing, which made tires a valuable commodity, the Treasury Department maintained a small fleet of cars used only for important occasions. Even Pehle, as an assistant to the secretary, had to specially request one to take him to the White House; he normally drove carpool in his British Austin. Minutes ticking by, Pehle peered out his front window.

The car never showed up. Pehle scrambled and miraculously made it on time to meet Rosenman to hand off the documents. He called Morgenthau and, after confirming that he had sobered up after his night of celebration, informed his boss of the car trouble. Morgenthau, livid, made a personal call to the Treasury garage to demand a report, "and I'm not going to take any God-damned excuse either."

Even though Pehle delivered the new documents to the White House, Roosevelt didn't issue the executive order or publicly announce the formation of the new War Refugee Board until the following Saturday. He didn't even look at the new drafts for a few days, waiting on a response from Cordell Hull. The secretary of state muttered a halfhearted endorsement of the WRB—it was a fait accompli after all—and Rosenman reassured Hull that the president wanted Stettinius to be the liaison on behalf of his department. Hull's name would remain on the official announcement and paperwork.

Even though Hull and Stettinius both knew about the War Refugee Board, neither of them told anyone on the State Department staff. Adolf Berle, the new supervisor of the Visa Division, determined not to repeat Long's mistakes, indicated that he wanted to investigate refugee problems. Stettinius sent him an old report to review but made no mention of the pending executive order.

The president's delay gave Pehle a week—a quiet but busy one—in which to plan. He moved his personal office out of Sloane, settling into a third-floor office in the west wing of Treasury, right near Morgenthau. He kept his office simple, placing his big desk in front of the window overlooking the White House and a smaller table right up against the window, keeping papers within arm's reach. He tacked just a few pictures on the wall and used the two overhead art deco chandeliers rather than desk lamps. It wasn't the typical suite befitting an assistant to the secretary by any means, but the Treasury Department was so crowded that the eventual War Refugee Board staff spread throughout the building, taking whatever office spaces they could grab.

The core team formed quickly, Pehle mainly gathering up friends he trusted and knew would be sympathetic to the project. Josiah DuBois really wanted to participate and finagled an assignment as the WRB's general counsel, but he soon wasn't involved in day-to-day operations.

But Florence Hodel was. She was thirty-six, with light eyes, wavy hair, a steely gaze, and a law degree from Cornell, where she had been the only woman on the editorial staff of the law quarterly. Her husband, Christopher Wagner, an emotionally abusive alcoholic, coordinated military supplies for the U.S. Army in England. Perhaps due to the volatile state of her marriage or possibly to her own liberalism, Hodel, who had always been the breadwinner of the couple, preferred her maiden name. Even though Treasury was one of the more progressive government agencies, she was still subjected to constant misogyny. One staff member remembered Hodel merely as "Pehle's girl Friday," and her responsibilities included supervision of the War Refugee Board's filing system. As a result, Hodel knew the inner workings of the War Refugee Board better than anyone—and good thing, because she would basically be in charge of it before the end of the war.

Pehle also recruited Joseph Friedman, a longtime Treasury employee from Ohio, recently returned from helping to establish Ecuador's central bank, and Lawrence Lesser, a former district attorney from New York, who had previously prepared criminal trials for Foreign Funds violators. Ward Stewart became the WRB's administrative director, handling employment, supplies, and financial matters. Hodel, Friedman, Lesser, and Stewart were all appointed assistant executive directors of the War Refugee Board and were all pulled from inside the Treasury Department.

Pehle hired another old friend from a bit farther away: James "Jim" Mann, a State Department employee at the Buenos Aires embassy and Pehle's former assistant. Pehle persuaded Stettinius to recall Mann to Washington. After his return to the United States, Mann assisted with cable communications at the State Department. He brought his biting wit and Kentucky drawl to the WRB's meetings, as well as his keen observations of goings-on at State.

Albert Abrahamson (who also went by "Jim"), the sixth and final assistant executive director, was an outsider to Treasury but contributed much-needed experience with refugee matters. In civilian life, he had been an economics professor at Bowdoin College, but his reputation as a negotiator meant he spent little time teaching anymore. Though a Republican, he had administered the Works Progress Administration in Maine in the 1930s, headed the National Refugee Service, and been an erstwhile agent with the Office of Strategic Services (OSS, precursor to the CIA). He supervised the WRB's research team.

The idealistic War Refugee Board senior staff were all in their thirties. Most had immigrant parents: Pehle, Friedman, and Lesser were children of German immigrants, Hodel was descended from French-speaking Swiss immigrants, Abrahamson's Polish immigrant parents spoke Yiddish at home. None were from old money or high society, but they were passionate and dedicated and made an excellent team.

Pehle cobbled the board's general staff together the same way—mainly from inside Treasury, with some outside specialists in various areas: public relations, psychological warfare, food distribution. Though the Bureau of the Budget limited the staff to twenty-five (later thirty), Pehle worked around the restriction by simply detailing people to the board—keeping them officially in their old jobs but working for the WRB full-time. Pehle himself was never counted among the twenty-five, because the Treasury Department detailed and paid him. In reality, there were sometimes as many as sixty staff members, including secretaries and overseas personnel, working for the War Refugee Board.

They still needed a permanent leader, and plenty of people had opinions on the matter. Roosevelt agreed that Pehle could be the temporary acting director but told Morgenthau, "You can't have your cake and eat it, too ... You have to have a name." At meetings, the staff debated various options, generally people who weren't Jewish but prominent enough to show the administration took the new rescue policy seriously.

Most suggestions were rejected immediately. Joseph Chamberlain "has a foot and a half in the grave and the other half on a banana peel"; James McDonald is "not a very strong man"; Sumner Welles "would be a little bit crazy." The suggestion of the labor leader Phil Murray elicited an "Oh God" from Edward Stettinius, and Morgenthau had to reassure him that "Phil wouldn't touch it." The journalist Dorothy Thompson, the only woman considered, was "too emotional." They discussed Hamilton Fish Armstrong, Clarence Darrow, and Al Smith, all dismissed out of hand, along with a host of Roosevelt administration officials. They spent a lot of time weighing the possibility of the former presidential candidate Wendell Willkie; Morgenthau thought Roosevelt would like the idea, and one Treasury staffer thought he would be even better than Pehle (Pehle responded with a sarcastic "Thanks"). But the Willkie idea went nowhere. Even Roosevelt's favored candidate, the University of North Carolina president, Frank Graham, who traveled to the White House to discuss the job, found his name struck from the list immediately afterward.

After considering dozens of names, Morgenthau concluded, "It really gets down to Pehle or Pehle." John Pehle embodied the qualifications—a "tough son of a bitch," knowledgeable, fair, respected by the relief organizations—and, in the absence of another candidate, was the best choice they had. Pehle would be their guy, at least for now.

On January 22, 1944, almost a week after the White House meeting, President Roosevelt signed Executive Order 9417 and released the text to the public. The order gave the impression that the War Refugee Board was the logical continuation of American policy, instead of the complete change it represented. The order began, "Whereas it is the policy of this Government to take all measures within its power to rescue the victims of enemy oppression," but of course this was the first time America had any policy at all to address mass murder. The new War Refugee Board, Roosevelt announced, would develop plans for the rescue, maintenance, transportation, and relief of the victims of Nazism and, if possible, oversee safe havens for refugees who escaped Nazi occupation.

Public response was overwhelmingly positive, and Pehle watched as telegrams and letters poured in. An opinion column in the *El Paso Herald-Post* titled "Rescue the Refugees!" stated, "Rarely has the President made a more desirable and popular move than his appointment of the Secretaries of War, State and Treasury as a war refugee board to rescue as many as possible of Hitler's victims."

In his congratulatory cable to Roosevelt, Peter Bergson took credit for the WRB's creation in his typical flowery fashion: "Three years ago I came to these shores with my colleagues . . . We raised the cry of our tortured and forgotten people . . . the American people have heeded our cry and yesterday you, Mr. President, heeded them. By your action you have become to us a living symbol of Democracy."

Arthur Werner of Piqua, Ohio, gave voice to the hope many now placed in the new board. Mr. Werner explained in his letter that he had been imprisoned in Buchenwald after *Kristallnacht* in 1938 but was now "among those fortunate Jewish people, who after years of persecution and concentration camps found refuge and a real home in the blessed U.S.A." While he did not know the fate of his mother or any of his friends, Werner and his wife had found a welcoming community in Piqua. He enclosed a check for $10—the War Refugee Board's very first donation. Werner apologized that it wasn't a lot of money, but he hoped the new board could somehow use his contribution.

There were a few in the administration, however, who were troubled by the news—mostly people who thought the Allies were already
doing everything possible to assist refugees. Robert Pell, the State
Department liaison to the Intergovernmental Committee, wrote to
Myron Taylor, who served as FDR's representative to both the Vatican and the IGC, "It is not for me to comment on an order of the
President but at least we are relieved from any further responsibility."
He heard rumors that some countries would withdraw from the IGC
and the whole thing would shut down, because it appeared that the
United States planned to foot the bill on all rescue matters. Pell criticized the order for "singling out Jews for special attention," which
would undoubtedly increase antisemitism in the United States. But, if
that's really what the president wanted, the "Department will help as
post office and messenger boy on the understanding that all responsibility will rest with the [WRB] Director."

Ambassador John Winant complained from London that he had
not been informed in advance about the board. Herbert Emerson, the
British director of the IGC, fielded questions from reporters but had
no answers. Reflecting this irritation, Helen Kirkpatrick of the *Chicago Daily News* reported from London, "American, British and Allied
relief officials here appear to have been surprised and confused . . .
Setting up of another organization to overlap the intergovernmental
committee, UNRRA, and the Army will be a positive guarantee that
money will be wasted in Europe, in the view of experts."

The War Department staff argued over what to tell theater commanders about the new policies, with one colonel complaining, "I cannot see why the Army has anything to do with it whatsoever . . . We
should word the cable so that we let him [the commander] understand
that he is still running the show and his primary job is winning the
war . . . so that the theater commander doesn't have to do anything at
all if he doesn't feel that he should."

In his diary, Breckinridge Long just shrugged at the news: "The
Pres't has appointed a Refugee Board consisting of Sect State, Sect
War and Sect Treas.—they to appoint a director to save the refugees
in German control. And it is good news for me. The 'Director,' when
chosen, will take over. I am out of that anyhow . . . What they can do
[that] I have not done I can not imagine. However they can try."

—

Pehle was determined to try everything, quickly and efficiently, and had boundless energy. Within two days of his meeting in the White House—while the WRB was still a secret—he and his team had already met with representatives from the United Nations Relief and Rehabilitation Administration (UNRRA), the JDC, the American Jewish Congress (AJC), and the International Red Cross. The WRB briefed George Warren, a sympathetic refugee expert who soon went to work with Jim Mann at the State Department. Everyone promised complete discretion. The final version of the executive order—at Hull's insistence—stipulated the WRB would "cooperate with all existing and future international organizations." With UNRRA, cooperation was easy: the man in charge there, the former New York governor Herbert Lehman, happened to be Morgenthau's uncle by marriage. UNRRA's mandate involved caring for refugees once they reached Allied-occupied territory and planning for their eventual repatriation, but UNRRA did not actively try to rescue people. The WRB antici-pated very little jurisdictional overlap.

The Intergovernmental Committee on Refugees, however, had a very similar mandate to the board, supposedly to assist refugees fleeing Nazi occupation. The twenty-nine member nations met infrequently, holding long meetings to dither over word choices and theoretical responsibilities. The IGC represented everything Pehle wanted to avoid with his agency, and he wasn't alone in thinking so. Roosevelt's adviser Sam Rosenman asked Morgenthau, "Now where does that leave this Committee that hasn't done a darned thing . . . I hope that they'll say that this is the end of the Committee because that Committee's a joke." Many people, like Pell and Taylor, believed the WRB announcement might lead the IGC to close. Few of the member nations would protest if the United States now wanted to take physical and financial responsibility for, potentially, millions of people.

In fact, few countries were willing to help the new War Refugee Board at all. Less than a week after the board's creation, Pehle and his staff drafted a cable to all the American diplomatic missions abroad, instructing them to inform their host countries of America's new policy of rescue and asking about the treatment of refugees—and possibilities for action—in their region.

The State Department staff, true to form, rewrote the cable extensively, so Josiah DuBois and Joseph Friedman arrived at the State Department to fight about it. They waited as secretaries typed copies of State's preferred text, listening to Howard Travers, the director of the Visa Division, complain about what a "terrible headache" refugee matters were. DuBois immediately noticed a change in the cable: the State Department instructed its staff abroad to use their own discretion, only sending refugee-related suggestions if they deemed the ideas in harmony with Roosevelt's policy. This, Travers argued, would prevent "time that would be wasted in sending messages containing perfectly silly and futile suggestions." DuBois protested, his memories of the State Department suppression of cable 482 still fresh. The War Refugee Board wanted to hear *every* suggestion and didn't want diplomats to decide what was silly or futile. Travers sighed and told DuBois and Friedman that he "could not see why the question of communications was any business of the Treasury Department ... the [State] Department itself would never have sent this kind of cable."

To put a stop to his staff's behavior, Edward Stettinius invited John Pehle over to the State Department, called the directors of all the relevant divisions together, and ordered them to cooperate with the War Refugee Board, forcing each person to verbally acknowledge the instruction in front of Pehle. Stettinius confided in Morgenthau that "as a Christian and as a believer in human beings" he was determined to see the War Refugee Board succeed.

Despite Travers's reservations, the cables went out on January 25 and 26. Hull complained the message had cost $10,000 to send; it was three pages long, coded "brown" (meaning strictly confidential), and sent to dozens of American embassies and legations worldwide, announcing America's new policy.

Responses trickled in throughout February, and with a few exceptions most were negative. The Foreign Service staff largely reported that their countries could not take increased immigration, especially if the refugees were Jewish.

In Central and South America, diplomats reported a fear that any Jewish immigration would increase antisemitism, partly on racial and religious grounds, but also because, as an American diplomat in La Paz put it, of "a resentment that Jewish immigrants . . . have competed with established Bolivian merchants." Tegucigalpa reported a population of 185 Jewish refugees in Honduras, with no desire for more: "It is unlikely that the immigration of other races incompatible with the mass of the present population (Spanish-Indian) would be permitted." The few countries willing to consider further immigration preferred farmers rather than merchants or other professionals. Mexico had an agreement with the Polish government in exile to accept 28,000 Polish refugees and offered to take Spanish Republicans stuck in North Africa, but neither of these groups was Jewish.

The impoverished island nation of Haiti, however, expressed enthusiastic support. On January 31, only four days after receiving the State Department's cable about the War Refugee Board, Minister John Campbell White reported that Haiti's president, Élie Lescot, offered $10,000 from the state lottery, the proceeds of a movie about Lescot's visit to the United States, and income from a new stamp surcharge on international parcels. Eleven days later, Lescot gave White $500 from the ticket sales and informed him Haiti had created its own refugee committee. He hoped Haiti's contribution, "small though it be, will help a little to ease the misery of those persons who are the pitiable victims of a horrible war brought on by madmen thirsting for domination."

In North Africa and the Middle East, where the Allies could potentially open refugee camps relatively near Europe, responses ranged from caution to dismissal. Minister James Moose in Jidda (now Jeddah), Saudi Arabia, reported sardonically that the instructions had no application to his country, for "in the past two years one Jew is known to have come to Saudi Arabia . . . due to a misconception of where Jidda is on his part, and to ignorance on the part of the Saudi officials that he was a Jew." Baghdad refused to let Jewish refugees even cross Iraqi territory. Egypt was willing to take refugees (and was already home to thousands from the Balkans, living in British camps), but they had to be repatriated immediately after the war.

Palestine would seem to be the ideal solution. In 1917, the British government had announced support for Palestine as a Jewish homeland, and after World War I the League of Nations granted Great

Britain the mandate to govern Palestine, with the Jewish Agency as the recognized Zionist leadership. The Jewish population rose from 55,000 to more than 400,000. But in 1939, to appease Arab unrest, the British issued the White Paper, limiting entrance to a final 75,000 Jews bearing "Palestine certificates" over a five-year period before closing the doors to Jews entirely. Though congressional resolutions called on the British to allow further Jewish immigration, the War Refugee Board decided not to take a public stance or to pin its hopes on Palestine as its answer.

In Asia and Europe, even nations affiliated with the Allied cause—including Intergovernmental Committee members—expressed their opinions frankly. Australia "is not interested in taking any initiative looking toward admittance of refugees, or in rescuing or assisting them"; its membership on the IGC was "partly a fear of appearing to be disinterested in the humanitarian side of the question." Recent epidemics and famine ruled India out. Afghanistan had a similar problem: "The willingness of the Afghan Government to admit qualified Europeans is probably exceeded by the reluctance of such persons to come ... living conditions ... are hard." The American consulate at Chengdu found it difficult to determine Chinese policy, because so few refugees attempted to come, and it did not know Japanese policy in the occupied areas, like Shanghai. Yunnan reported a growing scorn for Jews, though there were only about twenty German Jews in the province and most Chinese had never met one.

The Jews of Norway had either been deported to Poland or escaped to Sweden; though "there are no special obstacles apart from the measures adopted by the Nazi regime," clearly that was enough to exclude the possibility of Norway as a refuge. Ireland thought scarcity of food and transportation might prove an obstacle, though, with some financial help, it could accept five hundred Jewish refugee children. Iceland had no restrictions on Jewish immigration and had no visa requirements, but "since Iceland has never been approached ... it has not been in a position to 'cooperate' in their entry."

When looking at all the responses, it was clear to Pehle—and, really, anyone reading through them—that the War Refugee Board would not find many willing collaborators. It would need to grease palms, lay on guilt trips, and, often, just act alone.

—

Then there was the question of what the War Refugee Board should actually do to save people. For John Pehle and his team, their job was understandably daunting and vague. Europe had been at war for more than four years, and the Nazis and their collaborators maintained total control over the territories they dominated. The members of the War Refugee Board had no secret lens into these areas, no intelligence save for what they were reading in newspapers and the few reports they received from other departments. Roosevelt had suggested helping refugees get into Spain or Switzerland—but how? Pehle had no personnel in occupied territory, no underground resistance workers, no idea where to put money (or if money made the most difference), and no way to truly ever measure success. So he turned to people who might have some ideas.

The State Department staff had rarely imagined relief agencies as potential collaborators. The Office of Censorship regarded Jewish groups in particular as suspicious, unwilling to act in America's best interests. The IGC did not allow Jewish organization representatives to speak at its meetings. John Pehle decided his War Refugee Board would be fundamentally different.

On February 8, John Pehle sent letters to ninety-four organizations soliciting suggestions. After describing the new WRB, the form letter explained that "the Board is not unmindful of the fact that private agencies, including yourselves, have for some time been active in seeking means to effect the relief and rescue of Jews and other minority groups . . . the Board would appreciate . . . a detailed statement in writing of such specific action as you believe the Board should take." Some of the relief agencies were large and well-known—the JDC received a letter, as did the World Jewish Congress—but Pehle also wrote to the Little House of St. Pantaleon in Ventnor, New Jersey, and to the Greek Fur Workers Union Local 70 in New York. In case they missed anyone, Pehle issued a press release asking any organization not contacted to write in. The board received dozens of responses.

One popular suggestion involved simply appealing to Germany, maybe through the Red Cross or the Vatican, to voluntarily release Jews. At least four organizations thought that the WRB should start by asking for children and the elderly, because the Nazis surely didn't need them for forced labor. Agudas Israel suggested offering an exchange for German military and civilian prisoners in the United States, while the Union of Orthodox Rabbis requested that any potential exchange privilege rabbis and scholars. Many thought the War Refugee Board should provide refugees with food packages, medical supplies, and documents identifying them as under the protection of an Allied government. If the Nazis were unwilling to release or exchange Jews, they could be smuggled to safety or saved with bribes, especially in Romania and Bulgaria. Multiple organizations highlighted the need for evacuation ships and for transit visas through Turkey.

Safe havens were crucial to success. Relief groups felt sure the board could persuade neutral nations to receive many more refugees if the United States would promise to remove them to designated camps in Allied territory. These guarantees would be more credible, of course, if Congress increased immigration to the United States and the British allowed for free Jewish entry into Palestine.

Many organizations urged psychological warfare—direct appeals to the German people and to those in Nazi-collaborating nations, through leaflets dropped from the sky or radio broadcasts in various languages, making American policy clear to the local population: anyone participating in Nazi crimes faced punishment after the war.

It was obvious to everyone—the relief organizations, the Roosevelt administration in general, and Pehle in particular—that total Allied victory remained the only way to stop the murder of Europe's Jews. The board's mandate stipulated that it could offer "all possible relief and assistance consistent with the successful prosecution of the war," and few of the suggestions involved any real diversion of war resources. Even those groups that urged the WRB to carry released refugees on army troopships made it clear that the ships would already be empty. The Allied armies were beginning, slowly and painfully, to gain ground on the eastern front and in Italy. Neutral nations now wanted to prove to the Allies—particularly the increasingly powerful United States—that they could be trusted. Nazi collaborators, watching the war's progress, might be increasingly amenable to bribes and deals. Any War Refugee Board success would be due to Pehle's willingness to partner with existing groups, to the board's creativity, and to the dawning international recognition that the United States would emerge from this war victorious and a superpower.

John Pehle had his team, a list of projects, and the backing of the U.S. president. It was time to get to work.

Getting Started

J OHN PEHLE ARRIVED HOME from work in the early evening on Saturday, January 22, to a predinner phone call. When he picked up, a woman who had found Pehle in the phone book asked him bluntly, "Are you Jewish?" "No," Pehle replied, startled. "Why," she demanded, "are you doing this?" Pehle later remembered the call as evidence of a specific strain of public opinion—one that thought the murder of the Jews was exclusively a Jewish problem. Non-Jews should not bother themselves with such matters, and neither should the American government.

Doubts about the War Refugee Board were natural. To some people—including the woman on the phone—the United States was already fighting a total war and should not worry about a distracting humanitarian crisis, especially one that involved Jews. Years of toothless bureaucracy left others cynical. They had seen too many announcements about aid for refugees that never materialized or had limited success—the Évian Conference, the President's Advisory Committee on Political Refugees, the Bermuda Conference, the IGC—to believe that the War Refugee Board would be anything new.

John Pehle wanted to get something done immediately. He wanted to show the supporters and the skeptics that the WRB was different from the organizations that came before, and maybe prove to himself that he could handle the daunting challenges ahead. He had to channel the Treasury Department's months of righteous anger into tangible results while showing the outside world that his new agency wasn't just a token.

Pehle was determined to use the tools of bureaucracy—administration, government communications, and official diplomacy—to speed rescue rather than thwart it. His fight was not merely with unsympathetic administration colleagues but with intangibles. Time, distance, the war, and the limits of imagination all conspired against him. Europe was in perpetual shadow. The staff of the War Refugee Board never had a clear picture of the true situation in occupied lands. Even relief groups with overseas representatives mainly got their news from the underground: bits of intelligence smuggled into neutral areas, rarely verified and often weeks old. Such information had to go through the local American consulate, which would encode the text and forward it to Washington. There, the message was decoded, paraphrased, reviewed by the State Department European desk (and often by the Office of Censorship), then typed and mailed to the intended recipient. The whole process took at least a week—usually much longer—and the cable transmission cost between twenty and twenty-five cents per word, when the Sunday newspaper cost a dime. Just when every word mattered, precious details were lost.

The board staff could only make informed guesses: who was where, what they needed, how the WRB could help. They were a group of government bureaucrats in their thirties, tasked with saving the lives of people they had never met, in lands most of them had never seen, facing perils they could scarcely comprehend.

On the War Refugee Board's very first day, John Pehle used his newly granted power to completely change the American government's relief licenses. For years, Pehle had been responsible for keeping money out of the hands of America's enemies, his staff meticulously investigating any whiff of illicit financial dealings. It was time for that to change.

Earlier in the week, before he knew anything about the WRB, Assistant Secretary of State Adolf Berle invited two rabbis into his office. Representatives of Orthodox relief groups, the men begged for permission to send $100,000 to Switzerland. The underground movement in Poland would use the money to help Jews escape over the border to relative safety in Hungary. Berle, already showing that he was very different from Long, sympathized with the rabbis, agreeing to facilitate their license and even attempting to secure a favorable currency exchange rate with the Swiss government. (It is worth noting that this plan involved four times the money the World Jewish Congress had requested for Riegner and, unlike Riegner's plan, definitely involved sending money into enemy territory for resistance groups.) As soon as Pehle received the license for his approval, only a few hours after the president announced the War Refugee Board, he tore it all up and wrote a new one.

The new license text—like the ones recently issued for Riegner and for Saly Mayer—stated that the relief workers could borrow money using blocked bank accounts and could exchange currency in neutral countries. But Pehle added a third option: if the relief worker had difficulty, he could simply send money into occupied territory. Because there was no way to supervise any financial transactions in Nazi areas, Pehle effectively stated that relief workers no longer needed to worry about money falling into the hands of the enemy. Rescuing people was more important.

Pehle immediately rewrote Riegner's and Mayer's licenses to also include the new permissions. Riegner, receiving the updated license, responded, "I appreciate highly the liberal spirit which has motivated the amendment," and reported his first currency transaction the same day.

Pehle also quickly arranged for another $100,000, this time for the International Red Cross, ending another multi-month State Department delay. Back in September 1943, with Riegner's license still in limbo, the World Jewish Congress approached the State Department with a second proposal. Ten million dollars, raised by the American and British Jewish communities, would allow the Red Cross to buy and distribute medicine and food for the still-surviving Jewish population of Nazi-occupied Europe—depending, of course, on the whims of the Nazis. Breckinridge Long agreed in theory but decided the transaction needed Intergovernmental Committee approval. As one of the Treasury staff put it, Long gave the World Jewish Congress one of his typical "run-arounds . . . Long first tossed it into the waste-paper basket; namely, the Intergovernmental committee."

The Red Cross was eager for the financial assistance. But, true to form, the IGC casually debated; over the next four months, it solicited specific plans from the Red Cross, decided that the IGC would need to approve each project individually, considered what supplies could be sent through the ongoing Allied blockade, and dithered over where the money would come from. By early January 1944, the Red Cross had scaled back its request to 300,000 Swiss francs ($100,000), just to have some small amount of money on hand if any new opportunities to actually send food and medicine to Jews arose. Long finally claimed the State Department had no money to contribute after all, and the President's Emergency Fund, under Roosevelt's personal control, was empty. (The Treasury staff investigated and figured out the fund actually had about $80 million.) If the World Jewish Congress still wanted to continue, Long suggested, perhaps Congress would consider an official appropriation for the project.

Morgenthau's staff found the delays unacceptable. The State Department "could get it with a snap of their fingers," one staff member grumbled. "By the time you got an appropriation, this whole thing would be over."

During the quiet week between the White House meeting and the announcement of the War Refugee Board, Florence Hodel, Josiah DuBois, Joseph Friedman, and Lawrence Lesser met with American Jewish Congress representatives. (The AJC was part of the World Jewish Congress, also based in New York, and headed by Stephen Wise.) Florence Hodel took notes as the staff received a frank briefing on the fate of various Jewish communities. She scribbled, "Greece: There is no problem here, since the Jewish community here has been wiped out." The Red Cross plan was still in limbo, and that organization, perhaps the best situated to help Jews in occupied territory, desperately needed money. Most important, "with the changing military situation in Europe we [the WRB] face an accelerated tempo in the extermination program of the Germans. For this reason, time is of the essence and efforts must be made at once with no red tape if any lives are to be saved."

John Pehle sent a cable through the State Department to the International Red Cross in Switzerland, asking for an update on how and where it thought it could help people. He ended the cable definitively:

"We are prepared to see that funds are available at once." He didn't wait for a reply.

Before the Red Cross even acknowledged the letter, Pehle gathered its money. With the WRB's own budget in limbo, Pehle called Moses Leavitt, the executive director of the American Jewish Joint Distribution Committee, the largest philanthropic Jewish organization in the United States, which acted as the financial backers of most American relief organizations—Jewish and non-Jewish—assisting Jews in Europe. (The World Jewish Congress had far fewer resources, and a strong rivalry existed between the two groups, over both money and operations: the JDC was committed to working within the law, and the WJC wasn't.) Pehle trusted Leavitt explicitly, even soliciting him to teach a crash course on relief work. Leavitt immediately granted $100,000 for the project.

On February 8, after the International Red Cross's president, Max Huber, acknowledged the WRB's questions and promised a swift reply, Pehle sent the text of a new cable to the State Department for transmission to Switzerland: "The necessary funds for this project are being made available to you immediately . . . You are being requested to keep the War Refugee Board fully informed of the action which you take, as well as to indicate to the Board what other assistance is needed to carry out this and similar operations."

Less than three weeks after the War Refugee Board opened—but five months after the World Jewish Congress proposed the project to Breckinridge Long—the Red Cross would have its money. Huber wrote to "convey to the War Refugee Board the expression of our deep gratitude . . . for several months past our most urgent concern has been to draw the attention of Allied authorities to the almost tragic condition of various categories of civilians in Europe." With the War Refugee Board taking over, the IGC officially dropped its consideration of the project.

Pehle's frustration with the State Department and Intergovernmental Committee peaked in those first weeks of the WRB, not just because of the delays in aiding the Red Cross. The IGC's very existence cost the board more than $200,000.

The WRB's own funding was an unresolved question. Along with the "Personal Report to the President" and the draft executive order, Pehle had brought a draft memo to the White House meeting authorizing that the new agency would be funded out of the President's Emergency Fund. He left the allocation blank so Roosevelt could fill in whatever number he wanted (though Treasury staff made sure "million dollars" was typed in). At Roosevelt's direction, someone wrote "one" into the blank space.

One million dollars would not be nearly enough to fund the relief and rescue projects Pehle and his team envisioned. But alternative options were limited: either fund-raising directly from the public or soliciting Congress for an appropriation. The JDC, which raised money through the massive United Jewish Appeal yearly fund-raising drive, didn't want to compete with the U.S. government for money for Jewish rescue, worried that "this might cause chaos in the field of fundraising."

Pehle didn't want a fund-raising campaign, either. And he reiterated over and over that the War Refugee Board could not depend on government money for its activities. Congressional action took far too long. Instead, he felt the War Refugee Board should support the JDC, the World Jewish Congress, the Quakers, and all other relief organizations already working in Europe. These groups already had extensive networks and ongoing projects, so the WRB could help the most by making sure nothing got in their way. Pehle's staff would be red-tape cutters, cable senders, diplomatic liaisons, project supporters, and negotiators, but they would not be funders.

Pehle planned to use the WRB's $1 million mainly for administrative expenses, such as staff salaries for the people who weren't on assignment from other departments and the cost of sending cables overseas. He reserved half the money for clandestine operations, any projects that relief organizations shouldn't fund or couldn't know about.

Pehle also had access to secret money that never showed up on any of the WRB's accounting logs. After a dinner party held in Pehle's honor in mid-February, Morris Ernst, a prominent lawyer and co-founder of the American Civil Liberties Union, offered $100,000, a sum put together by Ernst's friends in support of the WRB. Ernst "was at the moment not in the least concerned with anything but saving life" and told Pehle he could draw on the money anytime.

The Intergovernmental Committee's budget, in contrast, dwarfed the board's. After the Bermuda Conference, the United States and Great Britain promised to split the cost of any relief projects the IGC sponsored. Less than a week after the WRB's creation, the State Department asked for a $5 million congressional appropriation for the IGC to fulfill American obligations to the organization until June 30, 1945. John Pehle only found out about the request because the confused budget director, having just dealt with the WRB's Emergency Fund allotment, sent State's paperwork to the Treasury Department to review. Pehle, understandably annoyed that he had not heard anything about this from the State Department, demanded the IGC's funding stop until he could review it.

Pehle got on the phone with Stettinius's aide but found out he was too late. The United States already owed the IGC's administrative allocation for February: £51,998 ($209,811.93), due immediately, with no time for congressional funds to come through. Pehle waited as long as he could, but by the end of February there were no other options. The IGC's money would have to come out of the War Refugee Board's budget. Out of the president's $1 million allotment, the board spent $228,792.36 in the month of February; 92 percent of that money went, infuriatingly, to the IGC.

Pehle also tried to speed up another longtime IGC project, but unlike the Red Cross money, where the War Refugee Board could act unilaterally, the number of interested parties limited his success. At the Bermuda Conference in April 1943, the British and American representatives had recommended evacuating refugees from Spain across the Mediterranean to a camp in North Africa, which might persuade the Spanish government to allow more refugees to cross the Pyrenees to safety. Four months after the conference, the Allies chose an abandoned military installation ten miles outside Casablanca, a camp alternately called Fedhala and Camp Maréchal Lyautey. Five months after that, when the War Refugee Board was created, the camp still hadn't opened.

Fedhala was bogged down by red tape: the British and the United States would fund the camp, located in territory controlled by the French Committee of National Liberation, which was concerned about security. The Allied military still partially controlled the area, so the Joint Chiefs had to be consulted. After the war, the IGC would repatriate the refugees in Fedhala, if any ever arrived, while the new UNRRA organization managed the camp itself. Despite a warning from an UNRRA staff member that Fedhala "in no way concerned us . . . we'd be smart in staying out of this," the War Refugee Board enthusiastically jumped into the fray.

The board's executive order contained an important provision: it could "appoint special attachés with diplomatic status . . . to be stationed abroad in places where it is likely that assistance can be rendered to war refugees." Eyes and ears on the ground, reporting back to Washington, became the WRB's most valuable tool. In Algiers, the eyes and ears belonged to Leonard Ackermann. Funny and artistic, Ackermann had joined the Treasury Department in 1942, just in time to be sent overseas. In early February, after seeing the announcement of the War Refugee Board, he wrote to his friend Lawrence Lesser to offer his help. It was a good thing Ackermann volunteered: before Lesser even opened the letter, Ackermann received the cable appointing him the War Refugee Board's representative in North Africa.

Ackermann wrote to Lesser, "I can see your fine Roman hand in this—always taking steps to see that I won't sit back on my feet and be my usual lethargic self. Seriously. However, I'm tickled pink. The job (even though I'm still somewhat confused as to what it entails) sounds interesting and I'm going to do my damndest to make it worth while."

While awaiting Pehle's instructions, Ackermann decided he would learn all about Fedhala. Moses Beckelman, an UNRRA social worker and the camp's first director, had already been to Spain to recruit refugees for the camp but found few willing to go. In fact, more than half the people he talked to actively opposed the idea. They had already escaped France and had no desire to go into French territory in North Africa. Waiting for liberation in Spain seemed like a better deal. Beckelman even tried to cancel the Fedhala project entirely: it cost too much money, took too much time, and was more trouble than he felt it would be worth. Overruled, he dutifully prepared an application form and posted advertisements in Spain for the camp. The French originally wanted six copies of each refugee application, with photographs and fingerprints, and would not tell Beckelman anything about their selection criteria. He didn't know whom to recruit.

In the War Refugee Board offices in Washington, Joseph Friedman knew he couldn't overtly pressure the French to be more lenient and decisive, so he found a private citizen to do it. He recruited Louis Dolivet, a former French resistance fighter turned leftist activist in New York, paying him $300 from Pehle's secret fund to write a message to a French official, pleading for him to speed the Fedhala decisions. John Pehle sent the text to Ackermann and asked him to type it out, put it in a sealed envelope, and deliver it, pretending he had received the letter directly from the United States and had no idea what it said.

The WRB's attempt at secret maneuvering, creative as it was, probably didn't matter. By the time Ackermann received the cable, the French had approved the Fedhala applications of 454 refugees living in Spain and later agreed to a total of about 700. Ackermann wanted to move the refugees out of Spain right away, but it was out of his control. Great Britain, responsible for providing the boats to carry the refugees, announced that none would be available until April. The bureaucracies involved had already invested nearly a year's work and at least $500,000 into the project, all to move 700 refugees, most of whom did not really want to leave Spain at all.

Even though the WRB was paying the IGC's bills and trying to make its projects successful, Myron Taylor, the IGC's American representative, angrily protested the board's very existence. The former chairman of U.S. Steel and one of the most famous industrialists in the United States, Taylor was known for his eponymous "Taylor Formula" to revitalize dying businesses. He had also introduced the clear address window in envelopes. Taylor had been Roosevelt's representative at the Évian Conference and at the IGC, though those meetings were so infrequent an embassy staffer in London generally appeared in his stead. Taylor also served as Roosevelt's personal emissary to Pope Pius XII and, managing to slip into Vatican City in September 1942, had investigated Riegner's telegram on the extermination of the Jews. Myron Taylor was an intimidating figure, tall, stern, twice the age of the War Refugee Board staff, and exponentially wealthier. The law library at Cornell, where Florence Hodel and James Mann had studied, had already been named for him.

Taylor was convinced the War Refugee Board trampled all over the IGC, which, he quickly reminded people, had also been Roosevelt's idea. He demanded a meeting with the new WRB staff, so they all obediently gathered on March 3 in Stettinius's office at the State Department along with several State employees. Taylor held court, explaining the history of the IGC and arguing that because the WRB shouldn't "make the other governments sore if we wanted to get any cooperation," the IGC must be consulted before the board did anything.

DuBois's memo about this meeting amounts to a written eye roll. He and Pehle felt not intimidated but bemused as Taylor and his State Department liaison, Robert Pell, evinced a complete lack of understanding. After Pehle described the board's plans related to psychological warfare—dropping leaflets and sending radio broadcasts into enemy territory to warn would-be perpetrators of postwar trial and punishment—Pell objected. He had been to Nazi Germany prior to the outbreak of war and seemed to remember Jewish leaders pleading with him not to draw attention to Nazi persecution, for fear it might increase. Surely, Pell argued, even though at least five years had passed and the Nazis had begun a campaign of mass murder, Jews would still not want the Allies to focus on their suffering.

Taylor questioned how the WRB's plans for Spain would interfere with the IGC's work there—until Breckinridge Long jumped in to alert Taylor that the IGC had no projects in Spain at all. DuBois gleefully wrote, "There followed a brief debate between Mr. Taylor and Mr. Long as to what the IGC had done if anything in connection with the evacuation of refugees to and from Spain." The War Refugee Board staff adamantly refused to seek IGC approval over any of their plans or delay any of their activities while waiting for Taylor to feel better.

Taylor, obviously dissatisfied by the WRB's cavalier attitude to his concerns, went straight to Roosevelt. He suggested the president command Pehle to travel to London at once "to clear up the uncertainties with the British Foreign Office and the Intergovernmental Committee." Roosevelt asked Morgenthau and Stettinius to just work everything out with Taylor by themselves.

The WRB might have been dismissive of him, but Myron Taylor did intimidate Edward Stettinius. Stettinius had succeeded the older man as chairman of U.S. Steel in 1938 and now, as undersecretary of state, certainly outranked him, but old hierarchies are hard to break. Stettinius managed to weasel out of having to meet with Taylor, leaving Morgenthau on his own. (The transcript of Stettinius's excuses ranks among the more unintentionally funny parts of Morgenthau's diaries: "I don't—no, the—it's just a matter of time . . . I'm—I'm not—I'm not trying to duck it. It's just a question of doing it and having the time to do it . . . I would think—I don't—I would think it would be an easy way, though, to—for you, so that you don't have to get in a lot of discussion about it—to just deal with it at a meeting of the Board. Don't you?") Morgenthau griped about it to his staff: "Stettinius would have to tell Myron Taylor to pipe down. 'Now, you didn't do anything for two years. To hell with you.' But club members don't talk like that."

Finally, Morgenthau hosted Myron Taylor in his home, making apologies for Stettinius when Taylor asked about his absence. Taylor agreed that the IGC's director, Sir Herbert Emerson, could come to Washington to meet with Pehle, instead of forcing the WRB director to leave for London. Emerson, a reasonable man, had sent Pehle a formal letter of support after the United States announced the new WRB, promising "the full co-operation of the Intergovernmental Committee in the pursuance of our common aims, and that any information or help I can give is at your disposal." Emerson traveled to Washington in April 1944. He and Pehle had perfectly pleasant meetings over lunch, held a joint press conference, and went their separate ways. The War Refugee Board remained completely independent. Taylor, satisfied that the problem he created had been solved, reported back to Roosevelt, "The two groups now find themselves in perfect harmony."

Through all of this, John Pehle paid little attention to Myron Taylor. He never considered going to London, and Morgenthau smoothed things over with Taylor without him. In the early days of the WRB, Pehle focused on proving his agency would not be thwarted by the obstacles—delays, funding, jurisdiction—that could have gotten in its way. With the IGC, Pehle succeeded. But some problems persisted, like the American ambassador to Spain, Carlton Hayes.

Hayes, a well-regarded professor of European nationalism at Columbia University and a devout Catholic, took on the difficult appointment of American ambassador to Franco's Spain in 1942. Generalissimo Francisco Franco preferred the Americans and British to the

Nazis, and the Nazis to the Soviets, so Spain had initially announced "non-belligerency" rather than neutrality. Hayes's main job was to give Spain no reason to side with the Axis powers. In the fall of 1943, however, rumors in the American press about Spanish loyalties led the State Department to demand an embargo of Spanish wolfram (tungsten) exports to Germany. By January 1944, Spain had not agreed to the embargo, so the State Department instructed Hayes to withhold American petroleum shipments. At the time the War Refugee Board came onto the scene, relations between the United States and Spain were at a low.

Pehle knew little of this. His War Refugee Board, concerned solely with rescue, sometimes inadvertently stumbled into ongoing diplomatic conflicts. Hayes, not a patient man, had no interest in explaining anything to the board, nor did he believe it could assist him with the refugee situation in Spain.

In some ways, Hayes was actually a year ahead of the WRB. In January 1943, seeing relief organizations in Spain competing over resources and refugees, Hayes had proposed some oversight: the formation of the Representation in Spain of American Relief Organizations. He appointed a director, twenty-seven-year-old David Blickenstaff, an American Friends Service Committee worker who, despite his youth, had more than five years' experience assisting refugees during the Spanish Civil War and in Vichy France, where he had been a colleague of the McClellands'. Blickenstaff took the money pooled from the various groups and divvied it up from an office adjacent to the American embassy, helping refugees with medical appointments, hot meals, language lessons, and sometimes just cash.

Hayes felt Blickenstaff's office was sufficient. When he received the State Department's initial cable about the creation of the WRB, he responded that it was not a good time to inform the Spanish Foreign Office. But it took ten days for Hayes's cable to reach Washington, and in the meantime Pehle had already sent another one, asking Spain to open WRB-financed refugee centers on the French border. Hayes, still polite, responded that Spain allowed refugees free entry, but any official announcement of this policy would only give the Nazis an excuse to tighten their border security on the French side. He concluded, "It is still my opinion that present political and economic crisis with

Spain is apt to have adverse effect on receptivity of Spanish Government even to proposals of purely humanitarian character."

Ever persistent, Pehle tried again. He cabled Madrid, asking to appoint Blickenstaff the WRB's representative in Spain. Hayes responded that everything was fine as is. So Pehle proposed James Saxon, a Treasury employee in North Africa, as the WRB's representative, if Hayes didn't want Blickenstaff to take the job. Hayes finally stopped being polite: "It has not yet been demonstrated to my satisfaction that the proposed program of the War Refugee Board without incurring risks which would outweigh the possible humanitarian benefits could make any substantial contribution toward the rescue of refugees." Hayes then refused to deliver a license to Samuel Sequerra, the JDC's representative in Barcelona, which would have granted him $100,000 to assist refugees crossing the mountains. Hayes questioned the Portuguese Sequerra's loyalty to the Allied cause and explained that all relief money had to go through Blickenstaff, ignoring the fact that two-thirds of Blickenstaff's budget also came from the JDC. The WRB, according to Hayes, could jeopardize all rescue efforts in Spain, and he would not do anything to assist until it was evident that "the War Refugee Board's efforts ... will result in fact in an increase in the number of such refugees." Hayes's demands were impossible: he wanted proof of positive results before allowing the WRB to attempt to save anyone.

Pehle, an incredibly even-tempered man, had reached his limit. In a memo to Morgenthau, he made a list of all the things Hayes refused to do: inform Spain of the new American policy, agree to a WRB representative, or give Sequerra his license. Pehle concluded, "Hayes has made life miserable ... The operations of the Board in Spain are completely paralyzed and we are losing practically the only opportunity we have at the moment for actually bringing people out of occupied territory." Morgenthau began to openly question whether Hayes should be removed as ambassador.

The War Refugee Board began working around Hayes, even attempting a move similar to the Fedhala letter. The board staff couldn't openly go to the Spanish embassy in Washington to ask for its government's cooperation—because Hayes would legitimately complain they were undermining his authority—so they got someone else to do it for them. At the end of April, Clarence Pickett, the director of the American Friends Service Committee, met with Josiah DuBois and then, no doubt completely coincidentally, gave the Spanish ambassador a memo requesting refugee reception centers for those crossing the border, a proposal identical to the WRB's. The JDC's European director, Joseph Schwartz, alerted Sequerra to his license, bypassing Hayes.

Despite Pehle's best attempts, Hayes continued to refuse any collaboration with the War Refugee Board, and the board couldn't seem to do a thing to fix the situation in Spain.

Pehle gained confidence on these early projects, despite his frustrations, and defined exactly what his new agency would be: one that worked quickly, eliminated red tape whenever possible, and looked for creative solutions to entrenched problems. He was now ready to get someone on the ground in neutral territory to see some results.

The board's completely untested, inexperienced, newest representative, Ira Hirschmann, was on his way to Turkey.

Hirschmann in Turkey

IRA HIRSCHMANN, A VICE president at Bloomingdale's and a pathological narcissist, would be the man responsible for the escape of seven thousand Jewish refugees to Palestine. A lifelong New Yorker, Hirschmann had worked in marketing and advertising for various department stores, but also, always, for himself. His appointment as the War Refugee Board's representative in Turkey came down to being in the right place at the right time and knowing how to take advantage of opportunities. And Hirschmann always knew how to take advantage of opportunities. "I may have a ripping story," he wrote to a *New York Times* reporter in February 1944, having arrived in Turkey only a few days earlier. "It may not be superfluous to keep in touch with me."

Ira Hirschmann was forty-two at the end of January 1944, when he boarded an army transport plane from New York to Miami to begin the long journey to Turkey, a country he had never visited and knew little about. A perpetual networker, he had assisted Fiorello La Guardia's mayoral campaign, founded a popular music appreciation society, and attended the Évian Conference as an observer. Though Jewish, he had never been heavily involved in Jewish philanthropy and wasn't particularly religious. He and his wife, Hortense Monath, a concert pianist, had no children and were going through a rough patch in their marriage, possibly due to his womanizing. Hirschmann eagerly awaited the adventure.

He had been planning the trip since September, originally at the behest of Peter Bergson's Emergency Committee to Save the Jewish People of Europe. Bergson had presented Hirschmann to Breckinridge

Long, asking for State Department assistance in getting him to Turkey to survey rescue possibilities. Long tried to convince the two men that Ambassador Laurence Steinhardt could act far more efficiently than a private citizen but, after Bergson wore him down, agreed to cable and see if the embassy would mind an American Jewish organization representative. Steinhardt thought it would be fine. So Hirschmann collected his vaccinations and took leave from Bloomingdale's in late January for a six-week exploratory trip to Turkey. His noncombatant identity photograph shows a smooth, confident man in a suit and tie (and always a white shirt; he abhorred colored ones), with dark, wavy hair, a full face, and a half smile. At some point during his preparations, he shed his affiliation with Bergson and the Emergency Committee.

Hirschmann became the War Refugee Board's very first overseas representative, appointed a few weeks before Leonard Ackermann, and produced its first significant international results. Pehle picked him, mainly, because Hirschmann was leaving for Turkey anyway, Oscar Cox had suggested they meet before the trip, and "he sounded very, very good." The entire WRB staff listened to Hirschmann falsely claim his trip came at Steinhardt's urging to be "clothed with some authority" so he could be more effective.

After twenty days' travel, Ira Hirschmann arrived in Turkey. The journey, initially delayed due to Hirschmann's "priority three" travel ranking as a private citizen, sped up after he bugged everyone he could think of—including Pehle, Long, and Morgenthau—to get a "priority two." Military planes ferried him from New York to Miami; to Puerto Rico; to Belém and then to Natal, Brazil; across the ocean to Accra; to Cairo; to Jerusalem; back to Cairo; and finally to Adana to board the train for a twenty-eight-hour ride to Ankara, where he arrived the evening of February 14, 1944.

Pehle's cable, formally naming Hirschmann the War Refugee Board's representative in Turkey, beat him by two days. He would be a special attaché, detailed to the American diplomatic mission in Turkey and responsible for carrying out Roosevelt's new rescue policy. He should maintain constant contact with Ambassador Steinhardt and with the WRB, aid the private relief agencies already working in Turkey, and develop his own plans for rescue and relief. Most crucially, Hirschmann was authorized to communicate with enemy territory, making him, according to a reporter friend, "the first and only United States citizen in Turkey to be allowed to disregard the Trading with the Enemy Act." Hirschmann stood at the ready, reporting to Pehle, "See possibilities for immediate action but tempo exasperatingly slow. Get ready for concrete cables from Ankara."

Ankara did not impress Hirschmann, or very many other visitors in the 1940s. The late president, Mustafa Kemal Atatürk, had selected the former headquarters of his resistance movement to be the new Turkish republic's capital in 1923, when there were only about thirty-five thousand residents. It was a planned city still being planned; Hirschmann claimed the tour of its few major streets did not take long, and it wasn't until 1940 that the American embassy reluctantly relocated there. In the days of the Ottoman Empire, the capital had been Constantinople (now Istanbul), a massive cosmopolitan city bustling with restaurants, theaters, and nightlife, all a full day's train ride away from Ankara. Food, clothing, and furniture were expensive and of poor quality in the new capital, and Americans were advised to bring everything, down to canned goods, from the United States.

Soon after his arrival, Hirschmann settled into an office on Atatürk Boulevard 243, on the main avenue bisecting the city, populated by most of the foreign embassies. At the end of a diplomatic luncheon held on his first day, he stayed behind at Steinhardt's residence in the hilly southern suburbs for a briefing on the refugee situation as seen from Turkey.

Turkey, a neutral country, straddled Europe and Asia, a frontier between Nazi-occupied and collaborating countries to the north and west, the Soviets to the east, and the morass of British and French and Arab areas in the Middle East. So, everyone was in Turkey—the Nazis, the Soviets, the Americans, all spying on each other, all trying to read the temperature of this newly secular, modernizing Muslim country. The American diplomatic presence spiked—from three Foreign Service officers in 1940 to eight by 1943, and an Office of War Information (OWI) staff of a hundred. The OSS branch in Istanbul, running intelligence and counterintelligence schemes, was large and indiscreet enough to have its own theme song, "Boo Boo Baby, I'm a Spy," played with a wink by Turkish musicians when a known American agent entered a nightclub. As in Spain, the United States, determined to keep Turkey from joining the Axis, strategically purchased Turkish resources at high prices to keep chrome, seed oil, minerals, mohair, and silks out of Nazi hands.

Ambassador Laurence Steinhardt oversaw the American embassy in Turkey. Though a political appointee, Steinhardt had already proven his talent as a diplomat, running the Moscow embassy during the tense years before the United States entered the war, while the Nazis and Soviets operated under a nonaggression pact, and then after the Nazi invasion in June 1941. Dark-haired and balding with bushy eyebrows, Steinhardt was himself Jewish and pleased to now have someone on his staff really focusing on the refugee problem.

When Hirschmann arrived, the question of aid to Jewish refugees remained a sensitive one in Turkey. A little more than two years earlier, in December 1941, an overcrowded boat, the *Struma,* had motored into Istanbul harbor carrying 781 Jewish refugees who had escaped from Romania. The Turkish government would not let them disembark, because London refused to grant Palestine certificates. For more than two months, the *Struma* sat, the refugees growing increasingly hungry and desperate, all within sight of the citizens of Istanbul. Finally, in late February, with the boat's engine ashore for repairs, the Turkish navy towed the *Struma* out into the Black Sea to drift. Within twenty-four hours, a submarine attacked, killing all passengers and crew save for one teenage boy. Since the *Struma,* no refugee boats had arrived in Istanbul.

The Turkish government was more willing to allow refugees to cross by land. In April 1943, it had granted permission for seventy children and five adult chaperones to travel by train from Istanbul to Aleppo, Syria, every ten days, later adding an additional nine "families" (loosely defined, about forty-five people in total) who could also pass through. A single train route stretched from Istanbul to Aleppo, and in at least one section of the track a maximum of nine trains could pass each day. The dilapidated transportation system was so taxed that the War Refugee Board in Washington discussed sending railcars to Turkey to help speed up the refugee evacuation process. In February 1944, though, the refugees were still largely theoretical. In all of 1943, only about eleven hundred had traversed Turkey, mainly Greek Jews who arrived in Izmir by wooden boat. For as long as the arrangement had been in place to transport a group of refugees every ten days from Istanbul, the plan had not worked. Not once.

By February 18, only a few days after arriving in Ankara, Hirschmann thought he had identified two problems: Bulgaria, and the complicated system of correspondence and lists. He dealt with Bulgaria first. Most of the refugees were coming from Hungary and Romania, but to get to Turkey, they first had to cross Bulgaria, which did not allow them through. Simply put, the door to freedom seemed locked from the inside. The United States and Great Britain had issued strong diplomatic protests in 1943 but held no sway over the Nazi-collaborating Bulgarian government. With the tide of the war turning against the Axis, Hirschmann decided that the Soviet Union, which had not yet declared war on Bulgaria, might have some influence America didn't.

Hirschmann met with the world-weary first secretary of the Russian embassy and a few days later with Sergey Vinogradov, the Soviet ambassador, asking them to pressure Bulgaria to open the doors. Relations between the two countries were less than cordial; we don't go to their parties, and they don't come to ours, First Secretary Sergei Mikhailov explained, smoking a cigarette, then lamented his years as a "captive" in Ankara. But if Hirschmann sent along the details, the Soviets would try.

While waiting for the results of Soviet intervention, Hirschmann tackled the complex process used to approve the hypothetical refugees prior to their arrival. In Istanbul, the Jewish Agency representative Chaim Barlas controlled the legal permission for Jews to enter Palestine. Even though the White Paper, limiting Jewish immigration to seventy-five thousand over five years, was technically set to expire in March 1944, there were still thirty-one thousand unissued certificates because so few Jews were able to escape during the war. Barlas, determined to issue as many of them as possible, compiled lists of names, dates of birth, and addresses, information he received from representatives in occupied territory. This list then took a circuitous route over thousands of miles—to the British authorities in Palestine; to London; to a British passport official in Istanbul; to the Turkish Foreign Office and the various ministries of the Turkish government; and finally to the Turkish consulates in Hungary, Romania, and Bulgaria. Nothing was automated. The list traveled by cable and mail, crossed countless desks to be checked by hand, and could get delayed or lost indefinitely. The people who had made it through all the stages of approval were then authorized to enter Palestine, if they could ever get out of Bulgaria and through Turkey and if they could still be found, three months after Barlas first wrote down their names.

As convoluted as the system was, the key to unlocking what Hirschmann called the "Bulgarian bottleneck" turned out to be frustratingly simple.

At a meeting with Barlas, Hirschmann learned that even though Bulgaria—and more important, Nazi Germany—wouldn't allow a wholesale evacuation of refugees through the country, they weren't hampering small groups, like the seventy-five children. Turkish transit visas were the real obstacle. With Hirschmann listening in, Barlas called the Turkish foreign minister, who declared he would not grant visas to enter Turkey until he had a letter from the British government confirming the refugees would receive Palestine certificates within twenty-four hours of reaching Istanbul. He had already asked for a letter several times and had not yet received one.

Hirschmann approached a British vice-consul who feigned ignorance about any letter, then called a few days later to say that he had found one, written a month earlier but never sent on to the Turkish Foreign Ministry. It had been sitting on a desk somewhere.

Secretly, six months earlier, the British government had decided to issue Palestine certificates to *any* Jewish refugee who reached Turkey and passed a security screening, even after the White Paper expired. Secretary of State Cordell Hull knew this, and so did Laurence Steinhardt, but the decision had not been publicized, because the British claimed that "secrecy is essential in the interests of the refugees themselves." No one had informed the Turkish government that the Jewish Agency would continue issuing certificates past March; no one broadcast the news that if refugees escaped to Turkey, they could get into Palestine. Hirschmann made sure the letter included the blanket authorization, and the Turkish government, now assured that the Jews would not stay in their country, proceeded to authorize the transit visas. Chaim Barlas also persuaded the British to allow him to authorize Palestine visas himself, without referring the list of names to Jerusalem or London—turning a three-month process into three weeks at most.

Less than ten days later, on March 4, the first group of children crossed the Turkish border near Edirne and arrived in Istanbul. Ninety other refugees had already arrived, including a group of young Jewish resistance fighters who had recently escaped from Poland to Hungary. Some had witnessed the loss of their entire families. With a few bureaucratic blips along the way, small groups continued to arrive for the next nine months. Hirschmann, in Ankara, seemed stunned by his own success, writing in his diary, "I really broke this bottleneck, but I do not know if the record will show it."

Hirschmann always saw himself as the hero of any story. He told Pehle not to pay attention to any press reports that didn't involve him, cabling, "It seems desirable that the board await my reports and those of the Embassy rather than be influenced by newspaper stories . . . it would be unwise to attach too much importance to the casual remarks of an individual government official." But Hirschmann had no problem publicizing his own efforts and successes. Just a day after admonishing Pehle—the same day he located the missing British letter—Hirschmann persuaded a BBC reporter to broadcast a summary of his work to London for retransmission into enemy territory, including details about the groups of refugees who had not yet arrived. It was an extraordinarily naive and egotistical move, but typical of Hirschmann. A few weeks later, the *New York Post* published "Palestine Door Opens to 5,000 Balkan Children," featuring a picture captioned "Ira Hirschmann, speeds aid for youngsters" and a breathless description of "nearly concluded" negotiations for the purchase of a boat.

Having solved the problem of refugees arriving by land, Hirschmann turned his attention to the sea. With a ship, hundreds of refugees could escape Romania and Bulgaria for Turkey in a single trip, so Hirschmann endeavored to find one.

First, he tried to borrow the *Nyassa,* a Portuguese ship the JDC had used to transport more than six hundred refugees from Cádiz,

Spain, to Haifa in late January (a move that made recruitment for Fed-hala more difficult, because refugees left in Spain were reminded of the prospect of Palestine). But even though the *Nyassa* flew a neutral flag, it couldn't get safe-conduct permissions, a constant problem during the war.

A cargo ship, the *Necat,* would cost $400,000 but once purchased outright could make many trips. The JDC offered to fund the purchase, and as an added inducement to the Turkish government Hirschmann vowed to donate the ship to the Turkish Red Crescent (part of the International Red Cross) once five thousand refugee children had arrived.

Hirschmann also set his sights on the *Vatan,* a fifty-year-old steam-powered cargo ship owned by a private Turkish company. The Jewish Agency thought between eight hundred and a thousand refugees could cram on board, but the Turkish government still insisted it had to approve even a single voyage. Hirschmann frantically cabled Pehle on February 18, asking the WRB to guarantee on behalf of the U.S. government that the ship would be fully replaced if damaged or destroyed. "The point," Hirschmann emphasized, "is that we must under all circumstances get a ship at once."

Pehle received Hirschmann's cable four days later, late on a Tuesday afternoon. By Thursday morning—after the request was cleared with the State Department, the War Shipping Administration, and Lend-Lease authorities—Hirschmann had his guarantees. The War Shipping Administration sent a representative from Cairo to Istanbul to give Hirschmann advice on reasonable payments and promises.

Hirschmann wrote in his diary, "The tone of the Wash. reply to my telegram was exactly right, giving me complete coverage on the boat." Steinhardt warned him not to let the War Refugee Board get too optimistic; things didn't move as fast in Turkey as they did in the United States. But when the board's guarantees arrived, Hirschmann was already in Istanbul ready to negotiate the terms of the *Vatan*'s lease.

Istanbul seemed to be a totally different world from Ankara, and Hirschmann was enthralled by it. "Water vivid emerald blue lashing shore, sun bright—air invigorating . . . Trip across the ferry from the Asiatic side memorable. Sea of Marmara, Bosphorus and Black Sea in distance. The boat plows thru Bosp and turns to the Old City on the hills, weather-beaten brown buildings, red roofs, spires, minarets, mosques, all rising from the sea."

Negotiations in Istanbul always included food and drink, another custom Hirschmann preferred. On February 29, Hirschmann and an American major stationed at the Istanbul consulate drove through the old city: "It was fascinating. Narrow, winding streets with myriads of small shops and stands outside; people and animals moving in and out of traffic in mobs." They boarded an old elevator and emerged in a small office, where a British colonel and a Turkish maritime expert poured them "the inevitable coffee" and told Hirschmann that negotiations for the *Vatan* were useless until the Turkish government agreed to the terms.

On March 15, ever searching for a better deal and annoyed by the bureaucracy involved with the other boats, Hirschmann decided he wanted the *Tari* instead.

The *Tari,* first of all, was a double-masted passenger steamship in excellent condition, no retrofitting required. Though the *Tari* normally carried nine hundred passengers, it could reasonably transport fifteen hundred for a short, uncomfortable, emergency trip. The Turkish Foreign Ministry offered the ship instead of the *Necat* or *Vatan* for a single voyage, with a promise of more if the United States could furnish an alternative ship for Turkey to use in the meantime. Though Hirschmann cautioned Pehle not to publicize his efforts because "their cooperation . . . would easily be lost to us by premature publicity," he also excitedly wrote to a friend, "I beg of you not to disclose this to one single person . . . that we now have a passenger ship, and I am off to Istanbul to make the necessary arrangements for its embarkation." The *Tari* waited in the harbor.

Three more days of meetings followed, which exhausted Hirschmann. "I was clear, quiet, firm and restrained. We are bargaining for the price. My tactics, which suffer from others, are still proving right . . . While debating with myself to decide which tact to pursue, mine or that recommended by others—I remembered the line of Emerson 'Follow your own star.' I did." He was so cranky at the end of one day's negotiation that he stopped the hotel's orchestra playing Schubert to inform the conductor that the horn and clarinet were playing incorrectly. ("All clarinets play too loud and too slow.")

Finally, everyone—the Turkish negotiators, Hirschmann, the war-shipping adviser, the Red Cross representative, and Barlas—came to an agreement.

Hirschmann immediately cabled Washington for permission to enter into a charter agreement ("What a race against time!") and for a guarantee that if the *Tari* were destroyed, the United States would provide a new passenger ship to the Turkish government. Turkey would not accept money or a cargo ship; it had to be an equally sized passenger vessel. Just as before, Pehle immediately persuaded the State Department and the War Shipping Administration to issue the guarantees, though the United States only offered to replace the shipping space, not to provide a passenger ship.

At the end of the negotiations, Hirschmann finally got to see his prize. In driving rain, a tough-looking Turkish sea captain whistled as he directed a tugboat out to the *Tari,* with Hirschmann peering out from his spot next to the boat's wheel. When they reached the ship, the War Refugee Board representative intrepidly climbed aboard, inspecting all the rooms, "even down the hatch to the wet hold." The ship would need rails on the stairs but otherwise matched exactly what they wanted.

The total cost for the *Tari*—about $160,000 for payment and insurance—was less than Hirschmann initially estimated, but the final charter paperwork was still onerous. Then, just as Steinhardt had predicted, the War Refugee Board in Washington grew impatient at how long the negotiations were taking. Though the *Tari* had been on the table for less than two weeks, John Pehle wrote several follow-ups directly to Steinhardt about the charter request. "The Board is deeply concerned with the turn which the negotiations for a Turkish vessel have taken," Pehle chided. "For more than two months you and Mr. Hirschmann have been carrying on painstaking negotiations . . . [the WRB] has immediately acceded to practically every condition . . . However up to now the Turkish Government has failed to make a boat available." The board would allocate the necessary money but invited Steinhardt to issue a threat: "If the impression were created in this country that the Turkish Government is not fully cooperating in the refugee rescue program there would undoubtedly be a reaction here quite unfavorable to Turkey."

Steinhardt was incredulous and angry. The Turkish government, he countered, had only six passenger vessels in its entire fleet. The United States refused to commit to replacing the *Tari* with a similar vessel if it was destroyed, so it clearly understood the value of such a ship. With all the Allied propaganda about how much shipping the United States could build—over a million and a half tons in a year—Steinhardt sympathized with the Turkish government, which couldn't understand what the trouble could be with promising to replace one measly passenger ship on the remote chance of an accident. The Turkish Foreign Office, Steinhardt raged, had rightfully grown "tired of the noisy protestations of the two richest countries on earth, which own or control practically all the shipping in the world, who stated that they wished to rescue refugees from the Balkans and were insisting that the Government of Turkey dedicate 16 per cent of its passenger fleet to the movement of refugees while unable or unwilling themselves to furnish a four thousand ton passenger ship and while posing as the saviors of refugees before the rest of the world."

John Pehle, chastened, made sure a passenger ship replacement would be available and the money would be ready. He never responded directly to Steinhardt's rant.

The final outstanding term of the *Tari* charter was a safe-conduct guarantee from Nazi Germany. The German ambassador Franz von Papen sent the request from Ankara to Berlin. Unbeknownst to Hirschmann, the Nazis immediately rejected it, and von Papen kept quiet, getting more and more pressure—from Turkey, from the Red Cross, from the German ambassadors in Switzerland and Romania, all spurred on by the War Refugee Board—to register support for safe-conduct for the *Tari*. At the end of April, Berlin informed von Papen that the request would be approved after all but then canceled the official written notification, right before it was to go to Ankara. For want of the Nazi permission to sail unmolested, the *Tari* sat in the harbor in Istanbul.

One of Hirschmann's favorite stories to tell, later in his life, had nothing to do with refugee boats. It was the tale of how he, Ira Hirschmann, rescued 50,000 Jews from Transnistria. Or was it 100,000? The story grew more and more dramatic each time he told it, personalities and details changed frequently, but the overall narrative stayed the same. Hirschmann bribed the Romanian minister Alexandru Cretzianu to order the Romanian government to save the Jews, and it did.

In his 1946 memoir, Hirschmann claimed that John Pehle, in their first and only meeting in Washington before his trip, solemnly brought him to a large wall map in the new WRB office and pointed to an area in former Ukraine between the Bug and the Dniester Rivers. "This is Transnistria, the notorious Death Valley . . . See what you can do about it," Pehle supposedly commanded. Hirschmann then wrote in a little notebook: "Transnistria: break it up." (In another telling, it was Morgenthau. Realistically, it probably never happened at all.)

Between 1941 and 1943, 147,000 Jews, mainly from nearby Bukovina and Bessarabia, were herded into Transnistria to await deportation to Poland, a deportation that never happened. Instead, the Jews starved, nearly 90,000 of them, and died of disease, which is why Riegner had spent most of 1943 trying to obtain a license to aid them. Transnistria was a miserable dumping ground for human beings, and only about 50,000 were left by the winter of 1944. "The advance of the Russian army almost on the borders of Romania endangers the lives of all 50,000 refugees in the concentration camps of Transnistria," Hirschmann wrote to Pehle on March 9. "Fear is expressed by refugees coming out of Romania that these people will become victims of a last minute sadistic purge by the retreating Romanians."

The next day, Hirschmann showed up an hour early at the home of an International Red Cross representative in Ankara, steeling himself for his first meeting with the Romanian minister Alexandru Cretzianu, an aristocratic career diplomat in his late forties. The meeting was awkward at first, neither man accustomed to meeting with the enemy, but they got along well and grew comfortable quickly. Hirschmann promised that the United States would reward humanitarian actions in the postwar reckonings, and Cretzianu confided that his government had recently decided to improve its treatment of Jews. Romania had just declared Transnistria an active military zone, so Cretzianu agreed to cable Bucharest, to guarantee the safety of Jewish refugees and, if possible, to begin to evacuate them.

A week later, the two men met again, this time in Istanbul, where

Hirschmann was beginning the *Tari* negotiations. Cretzianu showed Hirschmann a message announcing that the Transnistria evacuations had already begun. Hirschmann wrote in his diary, "This is a monumental achievement and I can hardly believe it. I predict that it will not be recorded that I did it. But I did as this record and Simond of the R. Cross will attest, and it is my finest hour."

Contemporary cables, memos, and his own diary bear out this version of the story: Hirschmann asked Cretzianu to cable his government, the Jews were evacuated from Transnistria, and Hirschmann believed it was all due to his personal intervention. The liberation was not sudden, though. Jews had been released slowly in small groups, beginning in the fall of 1943. On March 13, three days after the two men first met in Ankara, the Romanian government pulled out of Transnistria entirely, bringing the final 10,700 Jews still left in the area into Romania. At the same time, a Romanian emissary arrived in Cairo to meet with the British about switching sides and joining the Allies. Cretzianu had taken advantage of a timing coincidence, giving Hirschmann and the War Refugee Board the impression that Romania had taken a massive humanitarian action solely at their request.

The bribery Hirschmann recounted later in life is not in his diary, in any wartime documents, or in his 1946 memoir. But in subsequent memoirs and multiple oral histories, Ira Hirschmann claimed that he personally persuaded Cretzianu to make the request of his government by promising American passports for the diplomat and his family. In one telling, Hirschmann secretly returned to Washington and confided the bribe to Assistant Secretary of State Adolf Berle, who then supplied the passports. There is no evidence any of this ever happened; a Red Cross representative witnessed Hirschmann and Cretzianu's meetings, and Hirschmann had absolutely no authority to make such an offer. The Cretzianu family vehemently denied any bribe and in 1946, the former Romanian minister escaped to the United States via England, right before a new Soviet-controlled government sentenced him to a lifetime of forced labor. He would not become a U.S. citizen until the mid-1950s. If he already had an American passport, he never used it.

—

By late March, Hirschmann had broken the "Bulgarian bottleneck," had requested the liberation of Jews stuck in Transnistria, and had been incredibly busy, traveling from Ankara to Istanbul and back, meeting with diplomats and negotiating for ships. But he saw little visible proof of his success until March 30, when the *Milka* arrived and was almost turned back.

Three small Bulgarian boats sat in the harbor in Constanța, Romania. Only one, the *Bella Citta,* could be considered seaworthy and was supposed to take children to Istanbul but had no safe-conduct from Nazi Germany. Without a Red Cross flag (which could only be used for vessels with all permissions), the ship would be a target on the Black Sea.

One of the other boats, the *Milka,* flying the Bulgarian flag, disappeared from port in mid-March. Rumors flew that it was on its way to Istanbul, an illegal and extremely risky voyage on the wartime water. Barlas warned Hirschmann on March 20 that the *Milka* passengers were not "of the category for which I am authorized to approve immigration visas to Palestine." They were completely unscreened and had no entry or transit visas; no one in Istanbul even had a passenger list. Nine days later, the tiny 150-ton motor ship carrying 239 Jewish passengers rounded the Golden Horn. The Turkish government refused to let it land. Transportation to Aleppo, already at capacity, couldn't accommodate unexpected refugees, especially those who might be spies. Besides, as the Turkish foreign minister told Steinhardt, allowing the *Milka* could "open the flood gates."

Ambassador Steinhardt alerted the War Refugee Board, "It is the intention of the authorities of Turkey to refuse permission for the landing in Istanbul," and then he set to work, demanding Ankara allow the passengers to disembark. The British embassy, too, issued a strident protest. Finally, two days after reaching Istanbul, the refugees stepped onto Turkish soil. The Turkish government detached four freight cars from the train to Aleppo, replacing them with passenger cars for the *Milka* survivors, and Barlas obtained an exemption for their Palestine certificates.

In a report back to Jerusalem, Barlas reiterated the importance of the *Milka*'s arrival. "In this manner, for the first time since nearly two years, *olim* [immigrants] left the Balkans by sea for Palestine. This event aroused the greatest joy of the *Jishuf* [Jewish residents of Palestine] . . . I believe that I am correct to say that it may be regarded as a miracle that, in spite of the difficult situation in the Balkans and of the limited possibilities of transit, this number of *olim* was rescued and could be brought to safety in Palestine."

Ira Hirschmann publicly credited Steinhardt but in private reassured himself that the real victory was his. "Steinh. saved the situation. The Turks had balked and the refugees came thru . . . But I saved the group in the emergency. Much calling back and forth of newspapermen on this story. I have kept discreetly in the background pushing St. [Steinhardt] forward. The record will show some day that I did the pushing, prodding, and driving. I cannot act for an Ambassador, but I can direct—and see that the action is concluded."

The Turkish foreign minister's prediction that the *Milka* would "open the flood gates" came to pass almost immediately. On April 7, Hirschmann's last day in Turkey, the rickety *Maritza* landed in Istanbul, carrying 245 refugees, only 15 of whom had Turkish transit visas. Steinhardt again arranged for rail transport to Palestine.

Ira Hirschmann, having already extended his leave from Bloomingdale's once and unable to do so again, boarded a train in Ankara on April 8, 1944, for his journey back to civilian life in the United States. This time, the trip took only eight days with stops in Cairo (where he rode a camel, an "undulating animal who swells with dignity as he stretches his neck forward and growls ominously," and found the Sphinx "disappointing") and Algiers, where he conferred with Leonard Ackermann about the possibilities for rescue in Yugoslavia.

Even without Hirschmann's "pushing, prodding, and driving," ships continued to arrive in Istanbul, and Steinhardt secured permission for them to land, in such quick succession that soon the passengers could disembark as a matter of course. The *Bella Citta,* despite not having Nazi safe-conduct permission, brought 152 new arrivals on April 24. On May 1, the *Milka* brought another 272 refugees, and on May 17, 316 refugees arrived on a second voyage of the *Maritza.* The 561 passengers who made it to Istanbul on the *Maritza* in the spring of 1944 were incredibly lucky; the ship, known to be unseaworthy, capsized in a storm while returning to Romania.

In his report to Washington after the *Milka's* second arrival,

Steinhardt asked the War Refugee Board to "refrain from expressing publicly at this time our appreciation of Foreign Minister's action in allowing the continued transit to Palestine of Jew refugees arriving in Turkey illegally," because it might hamper Turkish relations with Arab countries. It was too late for such warnings. On April 11, the *New York Times* announced, "Steinhardt Helps 245 More Exiles," touting his success with the first group of *Maritza* refugees. Hirschmann, in Cairo on his way back to the United States, was quoted in the piece, hypothesizing that "it would be possible to establish a 'bridge of ships' from the Balkans over which the remaining communities of refugees might pass to safety."

Back in New York, Hirschmann slowly and reluctantly readjusted from a life of diplomacy to one of ad copy, from salvaging human beings to dealing with fabric remnants in the Bloomingdale's basement. His efforts produced the War Refugee Board's very first tangible results, the first people who left enemy territory and arrived in freedom largely due to the new American policy of rescue and relief. Hirschmann's involvement was far from over; within six weeks, he would return to Turkey, searching for a frightened man carrying a ransom offer for the lives of the remaining Hungarian Jews.

Warnings

JOHN PEHLE STOOD IN front of reporters for the first time as the acting director of the War Refugee Board on a mild Friday afternoon, February 4. It was two days after his thirty-fifth birthday. Ira Hirschmann was en route to Turkey, and though Pehle had spent the last two weeks gathering ideas, the press was eager for tangible successes. In a brief written statement, Pehle addressed any critics who questioned the board's potential:

> There has been some tendency for people to say that the task of the War Refugee Board is an impossible one, that it is too late to save more than a handful of Jews and other persecuted minorities in Europe from Nazi extermination; and that the Board at best will have to content itself with moral gestures.
>
> I do not share these views.
>
> I have been interested in this problem long enough to recognize the difficulties and to measure their magnitude. But what I have seen to date convinces me that Jews and other persecuted minorities can be saved if those charged with the task think they can be saved and are determined to drive toward that end.

What the gathered press didn't know is that only twenty minutes earlier, Pehle had been in the secretary's office in the southwest corner of the third floor of Treasury, listening to Morgenthau's warnings: "A lot of agencies start in Washington, and a lot of them have a lot of build-up . . . they go right up in the air and then come right down. So I would go very easy, John, in any publicity. Let your deeds speak for themselves, without promises, see?"

The advice was eminently sensible yet suddenly unnerving. To rescue anybody, Pehle had to convince the world that the U.S. government fully backed his War Refugee Board, yet Morgenthau was now telling him to avoid publicity, making promises, and raising expectations. Pehle believed the opposite to be true: press coverage could prove that despite the annoying "acting" appendage to his title, Pehle aimed to get things done.

Morgenthau clearly worried about the fate of the War Refugee Board, still in its infancy. Shaking his head about Pehle's decision to throw a press conference, Morgenthau lamented, "in view of the background on this thing, and the difficulty of getting your appointment," he personally wouldn't have called one.

Pehle's appointment hadn't been that difficult, actually, but Morgenthau was disconcerted by the trouble he encountered announcing it. For nearly two weeks after the January 16 meeting in the White House, a bland potpourri of mid-level bureaucrats, professors, and erstwhile politicians had been considered and quickly rejected for the WRB's directorship. Morgenthau persuaded the president to appoint Pehle until someone else could be found, then watched as Roosevelt repeatedly failed to make the announcement, finally deciding he didn't need to be involved after all. One of the president's secretaries told Morgenthau that he could issue a press release himself.

Confronted with the president's vacillation, Morgenthau was no doubt concerned that the president might have already lost interest in the War Refugee Board, or worse, perhaps it had merely been a favor to Morgenthau, a group to point to when anyone asked about American action to help the Jews.

The statement Pehle wrote for his press conference, then, was a direct challenge. If the president—or Morgenthau, or anyone— thought that the War Refugee Board would content itself with moral gestures, he was wrong. Not just because Pehle believed rescuing Jews was possible, but because he was going to try everything he could think of, in every way he could think of, to actually do it.

The very next day, Pehle set in motion his plan to persuade the president to tell the world, unequivocally, that America's new policy of rescue was for real.

On Saturday morning, Stettinius's office forwarded a letter from the British embassy to the War Refugee Board, which the State Department had begun to do with most refugee-related correspondence. The World Jewish Congress in London was pressuring for a new public declaration against Nazi atrocities, specifically one that referred to Jews, and the British wanted the United States to join in rejecting the request. The Foreign Office figured the December 1942 statement probably hadn't saved any lives, and any further statements might raise "hopes and expectations of far-reaching action whose fulfillment has in circumstances of war proved impossible."

Pehle let Josiah DuBois take a crack at the War Refugee Board's answer, because he had the most practice writing scathing reproaches. DuBois didn't disappoint. Pehle sent a cover letter justifying the response, pointing out that the WRB had to convince the rest of the world that "we mean business . . . The number of persons we can reasonably hope to rescue despite the attitude of our enemies obviously cannot be compared with the far greater number which might be saved from death by changing the attitude of enemy governments and particularly their functionaries and subordinates." A psychological warfare campaign—issuing forceful statements, dropping leaflets, broadcasting warnings—would be the WRB's best hope.

DuBois's proposed reply to the British embassy was appended to Pehle's polite and detailed explanation. After spelling out the purpose of the War Refugee Board (as if the British weren't aware), DuBois advised that the board was actively considering a strong new declaration specifically about the murder of the Jews. He summarily dismissed the British argument about the 1942 declaration; now that Germany and its satellites "know they have lost the war," the opportunity to save people was much greater.

At the end of the reply, DuBois was as blunt as a hammer: "Whether this Government will issue a declaration on Hitler's atrocities against the Jews depends on whether we feel that the issuance of such a declaration would help save some Jews from death."

The State Department promptly deleted DuBois's kicker and changed the draft to be more "friendly and courteous," because the European Division was "unable to understand how the plight of the Jew could be ameliorated through an argument with the British government."

The overall answer stood, however. Pehle and DuBois immediately got to work on a statement for the president.

Pehle laid out a twofold strategy for the War Refugee Board: persuade Nazis, and especially their collaborators, to stop killing, and take action to rescue those who could still be saved. At the heart of it, the board's plan was about leverage. DuBois's response highlighted a crucial difference between 1942 and 1944: the Allies were now winning the war. Axis-aligned governments could easily ignore Allied threats in 1942, when the Wehrmacht held most of Stalingrad and Nazi Germany reached the peak of its territorial control. By February 1944, however, the Red Army was entering prewar Poland, slowly but steadily chasing the Nazis west, as the Fifth Army drove them up the boot of Italy. The Axis feared the impending Allied invasion of France; it knew the attack was coming, but not when or where.

This new diplomatic advantage extended to the neutral nations—Portugal, Spain, Switzerland, Sweden, and Turkey. In 1942, these countries had no reason to liberalize their policies regarding Jewish refugees, and indeed most of the countries had declined to accept small groups of Jews with dubious nationality whom Nazi Germany had offered, effectively and knowingly condemning these people to death. With the tide of the war turning, however, common sense dictated more open cooperation with the Allies. If the United States suddenly cared about Jewish refugees, maybe it was time to pay attention and curry some favor. If Roosevelt said something, his words could not be ignored.

The draft declaration Pehle and DuBois wrote for the president began the same way as the "Acquiescence" memo had: "One of the blackest crimes in history, the systematic murder of the Jews of Europe, continues unabated." More than two million Jews had already been killed. Because young American men are fighting for "a world based upon freedom, equality, and justice . . . It is, therefore, fitting that we again proclaim our determination that none who participate in such acts of savagery shall go unpunished . . . All who knowingly take part in the deportation of Jews to their death in Poland are equally guilty with the executioner. All who share the guilt shall share the punishment." A person living in a Nazi-collaborating nation should "by his actions demonstrate to the world that in his heart he does not share these insane desires." The draft ended with a call for other nations to rally around "this righteous undertaking."

Promising a postwar reckoning was risky, because there was, at that time, no basis to prosecute criminals for the majority of atrocities. Legally speaking, the Axis powers could do anything they wanted to their own citizens, whom they deemed "political prisoners"; it was only illegal to mistreat Allied or neutral civilians and military. The Geneva Convention of 1929 codified the treatment of prisoners of war but applied only to the armed forces of belligerent countries and civilians of non-occupied countries who had taken up arms. Jews under Nazi occupation, therefore, were not prisoners of war, and the Red Cross could not intervene on their behalf—no food packages, no messages, no regulations on how they could be treated. The threat of war crimes trials over the murders of Reich Jews was pure hubris.

The declaration quickly made its way past the heads of the War Refugee Board. Morgenthau approved it immediately; Stettinius (acting for an absent Hull) got it on a Friday and sent his agreement on Monday. Pehle ventured across the Potomac to the newly opened Pentagon to secure the third and final signature. Finally, on March 6, Morgenthau asked Stettinius for a favor: Would he deliver the declaration to the White House himself? That way, Roosevelt could see that the State Department already approved, which might help move things along. Stettinius agreed and announced he would personally deliver the draft to Samuel Rosenman. Morgenthau, wanting to keep the text away from Roosevelt's overly cautious speechwriter, "hinted that I thought it might be better to do it some other way."

Morgenthau's instincts were right. When he visited the president the next morning, Morgenthau pointedly mentioned the board, Pehle's successes, and the cable to the embassies abroad, but Roosevelt hadn't heard anything about a declaration. After Morgenthau left, Roosevelt retrieved the draft from one of his secretaries, read it, and sent it to Rosenman to edit, supposedly commenting that it was "too much for the Jews" and should be broadened. Exactly what the WRB staff had hoped to avoid.

Morgenthau, given the unenviable job of reporting that the draft was under the knife, tried to remain a voice of reason as Pehle and DuBois paced and protested. "The declaration isn't much good" without explicit references to Jews, DuBois began to say, when Pehle interrupted: "I agree with that. Not only that, but if they are not willing to issue a declaration that pointedly refers to the atrocities, which doesn't take much courage in my estimation—it has been done before here. We don't talk much about it, but it was done in 1942. It was rather pointedly on the atrocities and a United Nations declaration on the Jews. It has been forgotten by now . . . It was never backed up by action, so it didn't do any good. But if he [Roosevelt] is shying away from merely saying, 'Look what is being done. It is going to be punished' . . . This will cause some trouble."

Morgenthau reminded them that he would not condone any plot to pressure the administration by leaking a story to the press: "I can't do things to undermine him. And you boys have to watch that, too."

"But it isn't against the President's interest; it is in his interest," Pehle complained. Morgenthau had no answer for him but forced Pehle to confirm out loud that he had understood the secretary's "little lecture." Don't get discouraged, but it was time to temper expectations.

Gritting his teeth, Pehle walked to Rosenman's office in the early evening, just as Washington grew dark and the streetlamps began to glow. Sitting in the West Wing, with Rosenman staring at him, the younger man read the edited draft. He took a deep breath and "explained . . . carefully why I felt that it was a mistake to weaken the declaration in the way that it had been weakened." It might not matter to Americans that the WRB's statement singled out the Jews for special attention, but "it was singularly important in Germany where the people were led to believe that this country was not concerned at all about the atrocities against the Jews who were not particularly regarded as human beings." After some argument—which Pehle tactfully called "discussion"—Rosenman finally blurted out, "I don't agree with you. Do you want me to say I agree with you when I don't?" He had already advised Roosevelt not to sign the declaration specifically because of its fierce condemnation of atrocities against Jews, because, he argued, antisemitism in the United States would intensify if Americans got the idea that the war was being fought on behalf of Jews.

Pehle requested a copy of Rosenman's redrafted declaration for Morgenthau and the board staff. When Rosenman balked, Pehle pulled rank. He was the acting executive director of the War Refugee Board, not just a Treasury employee, and would take responsibility for the security of the document. Rosenman "very reluctantly and only after he had first argued that he wanted to have the statement retyped" gave Pehle a copy, vowing to show his edits to the president in the morning. (Rosenman had also, under instruction from Roosevelt, changed the title, because the president issued "statements," not "declarations.")

"I read it to him, Mr. Secretary, word for word. I read it to him and made him listen to it . . . Instead of being a statement on the systematic murder of the Jews, it's now a statement on atrocities of all kinds which mentions the Jews among others." Pehle, still upset the next morning, burst into Morgenthau's office as soon as the secretary arrived. "The thing we were trying to bring home is that this country is opposed to the Hitler plan to exterminate the Jews. That is buried in this statement."

Morgenthau was less concerned. Rosenman had added a paragraph about the slaughter of civilians by the Nazis and Japanese, singling out Japanese atrocities against American soldiers for special mention. Three paragraphs in, Rosenman reverted to the WRB's initial text with some of his own edits: "In one of the blackest crimes of all history—begun by the Nazis in the day of peace and multiplied by them a hundred times in time of war—the wholesale systematic murder of the Jews of Europe goes on unabated every hour." He concluded with a more general vow to rescue "the victims of brutality of the Nazis and the Japs" and to aid the escape of Jews and all other victims "regardless of race or religion or color."

Morgenthau "would be delighted to see the President give this thing out. It's so much better than nothing . . . I would let it go. I don't think we can stop it." DuBois, uncharacteristically quiet throughout the discussion, finally commented that he didn't think it made any difference anymore; it didn't matter if such an ineffective draft went out or not.

By the late afternoon, Pehle resigned himself to Rosenman's version. He had spent the day visiting the State Department, where Stettinius agreed the whole thing had gone off the rails, but there was nothing they could do, "and he was not sure that any statement would be issued." Pehle also returned to the Pentagon, where Stimson, in a good mood that day, spent ten minutes reading the new draft, declared he felt it was stronger than before, then spent another half hour trying to boost Pehle's spirits with stories from previous administrations.

At the president's morning briefing, always held in his bedroom, Rosenman handed over a copy of the new draft for delivery at an upcoming press conference.

A week went by, and Pehle had not heard a single word about it. He asked Morgenthau to talk to the White House again; the WRB badly needed Roosevelt's words for its psychological warfare campaign, and "although some of us would have preferred the statement in its earlier form," the staff were eager to get it out. What was Roosevelt waiting for, or had he again changed his mind about a board-related request?

On Saturday, March 18, Morgenthau spent twenty minutes with the president and tentatively asked for an update on the atrocity statement. "I'll ask Sam where it stands," Roosevelt replied, accepting a new copy of the text, which Morgenthau brought him as a reminder. An hour later, Morgenthau called Rosenman to ask about the statement. "Well, my God—the last I saw of the thing, Henry, it was on his bed in the bedroom a week ago. I don't think he's done anything about it. It's probably in his basket."

Roosevelt thought Rosenman still had the text, while Rosenman had been sure the president was simply waiting for the right moment to issue the statement. It sat in his bedside basket for a week. It's possible that Roosevelt's physical deterioration might have contributed to his confusion. Beginning that night, the president would take his dinner in bed for the next three weeks, likely heeding medical advice, and ten days later would add a full-time cardiologist to his entourage.

There is no record of how Pehle and DuBois reacted when Morgenthau told them that the statement had simply gotten lost. It's possible he never told them.

After hanging up with Morgenthau, Rosenman immediately grabbed the text from Roosevelt's basket and sent a copy over to the British embassy—not to get approval, but strictly for its information. The British Foreign Office asked for a few days to consider the matter and decide whether to co-sign the statement or issue a simultaneous one of its own.

John Pehle waited—again, always—for all the factors outside the War Refugee Board's control to catch up. DuBois's retort to the British was now six weeks old, and each day that passed seemed a missed opportunity. In the case of the "Statement by the President" against atrocities, with special mention of the murder of the Jews, the delays ended up being fortuitous. While they were waiting for the British, Nazi Germany invaded Hungary.

News rarely traveled fast, and it took two days for the Allies to realize that Hungary was now an occupied country. Allen Dulles, head of the OSS in Switzerland, cabled the State Department on March 21, two days after the Nazis crossed the border. "All communications between Hungary and Switzerland interrupted for 48 hours and hence have no direct word regarding German coup. No news yet comes out of Germany." The American embassy in Lisbon wrote a memo summarizing all the rumors it was hearing from contacts in neutral countries: Ankara thought it was a formal occupation, Zurich wasn't sure, and Stockholm thought Hungary had declared war on Germany. In case it wasn't obvious, someone added a note to the bottom reading, "There is nothing official from any source."

The invasion caught the War Refugee Board by surprise, too. The very first license it had issued—the one Pehle used to proclaim that money could be sent into occupied territory as a last resort—helped refugees escape from Poland into relative safety in Hungary. In a memo written after one of the very first WRB meetings, Florence Hodel had written that Jews in Hungary "will remain safe unless there is a German invasion." Tens of thousands of Hungarian men had been forced into labor battalions during the war, but otherwise about 800,000 Jews had lived generally unmolested in Hungary, the largest and last intact Jewish community remaining in Axis Europe.

Immediately, the WRB sent messages to embassies abroad, asking them to work through the neutral countries to remind Hungary that any attempts to persecute or deport Jews "will be looked upon by this Government with the greatest disfavor" and taken into account after the war.

Pehle found Rosenman and told him the WRB would send over some new wording for the president's message, because "the military events in Hungary . . . in the last few days have certainly made the statement a timely one." The final text, only lightly edited by Rosenman, read, "As a result of the events of the last few days hundreds of thousands of Jews, who while living under persecution have at least found a haven from death in Hungary and the Balkans, are now threatened with annihilation as Hitler's forces descend more heavily upon these lands. That these innocent people, who have already survived a decade of Hitler's fury, should perish on the very eve of triumph over the barbarism which their persecution symbolizes, would be a major tragedy."

At his press conference on Friday, March 24, after conveying a message of friendship to the people of the Philippines, announcing the resignation of the alien-property custodian, and discussing the sale of Lend-Lease farm machinery, Roosevelt finally read the statement. He reiterated that both Stalin and Churchill had the text; the White House supplied copies to both embassies in advance of his announcement.

In the context of the statement, Roosevelt added that John W. Pehle had now been promoted to be the executive director of the WRB. The "acting" was gone, and he was now official.

Though it wasn't a declaration, wasn't solely about the Jews, and was part of a larger press conference, Roosevelt's statement still received a tremendous amount of attention. The front page of the *New York Times*, above the fold, announced, "Roosevelt Warns Germans on Jews: Says All Guilty Must Pay for Atrocities and Asks People to Assist Refugees." The paper called Roosevelt's statement an "unusual step" and reprinted the entire text on page 4, next to a photograph of John Pehle biting his pipe. To the *Stars and Stripes* ("Germans Warned Not to Persecute"), Roosevelt spoke "earnestly" and "sternly": "Observers considered the

President's mingled warning and appeal to ordinary Germans one of the most dramatic distinctions yet drawn by a United Nations leader between Nazi officials and the common man in the Reich."

Newspapers all over the Allied and neutral world covered the statement. *L'Écho d'Alger* published "Le président Roosevelt menace les criminels de guerre," while the Bari, Italy, *Gazzetta del Mezzogiorno* announced, "Roosevelt per l'aiuto alle vittime del nazismo," and Lisbon's *Diario de Noticias* proclaimed in a front-page editorial, "Yes, Mr. President." The British had already informed the BBC to report it "fully in all languages as a reaffirmation of the attitude of the United Nations . . . toward the Nazi and Japanese war crimes and atrocities." Less than a week later, the British foreign secretary Anthony Eden responded to a likely planted question about "whether . . . he has any statement to make" in the House of Commons. Noting Roosevelt's proclamation, he said the British "at once wholeheartedly associated themselves with the United States Government in this matter" and reiterated a call to prevent future persecutions.

The statement had been generalized and abstract prior to the invasion of Hungary. But by dint of timing, it also became the first strike in the War Refugee Board's quest to save the Jews of Hungary. It had an immediate emergency now: 800,000 lives were at stake. Pehle's push for publicity had paid off, and he felt so sure of the WRB's mission that his first proclamation as executive director bordered on the religious: "Let the people of the invaded countries heed the President's words; let them hide these people in their homes, in their barns, in their mines, quarries, and forests. We will find them and lead them to the havens prepared for them by the civilized peoples of the world."

10

Protective Papers

Over one million hungarian jews are crying for help! Let them, please not suffer the fate of the polish jews! Please, do not delay! Help!

I am an American citizen, but my parents and sister are in Hungary. Until now their lot has been bad, but now it seems there is no hope whatever for them . . . I fully realize that people are dying by the thousands and a few lives do not mean much, but to me these lives mean everything

I am turning to you in behalf of my mother and sister, both Hungarian citizens and living in Budapest, Hungary. Long before this I have tried at every possible agency and committee to help my people but was turned down, that nothing could be done. At least I had a little consolation that, even if life must be hard, it might be still endurable . . . But now I am terror stricken. What will become of them? Dear Sir, please tell me what can be done. Please, don't turn me away.

The letters were heartbreaking and arrived by the dozens. Americans, reading about the president's statement next to frightening articles about the sudden invasion of Hungary, homed in on John Pehle's name, and within days those with loved ones still in enemy territory began to write to the man they were sure could help.

The War Refugee Board staff kept all the letters and responded to each one. Most people received a personalized form letter, which always went out with John Pehle's signature: "I am sure you will understand that the task of the Board is so great that, of necessity, it cannot deal with problems limited to seeking out and rescuing any specific individuals . . . I assure you that everything in its power will be done to rescue and save the victims of enemy oppression who are in imminent danger of death."

John Pehle couldn't have agonized long over this difficult but necessary approach. He had no choice: the War Refugee Board couldn't locate and rescue specific individuals. The resources involved would have been enormous, and the undertaking very dangerous: sending relief workers into enemy territory to search for years-old addresses, hoping the owners still lived there, then spiriting those they found to safety, past thousands who also needed help. As one staff member later put it, the board decided to be in the wholesale rather than the retail business. The board would rescue the most people possible, rather than a selected few.

Physical rescue, for Hungarian Jews and those trapped in the interior of Nazi territory, was largely impossible. The people needing the most help were too far from the Allied armies and from the borders of neutral countries to escape in any great numbers. They clearly required protection where they were, so "rescue" became something more fluid and intangible.

At first, broadcast warnings seemed the most promising way to deter Nazi collaborators, who might be wavering about their commitment to a regime that seemed likely to lose the war. Roosevelt's statement had received worldwide attention. It played every hour for forty-eight hours straight on shortwave broadcasts in English and on fifty-one shows in the same span of time in German, including eleven recitations of the entire text. But Romania, Bulgaria, Poland, and Hungary somehow only heard it three times each, barely enough to penetrate and certainly not the mass reach the WRB staff had hoped. They had to have been satisfied, however, by the *Berliner Börsen-Zeitung,* which responded with "An Emotional Explosion in the White House," a derisive newspaper article long and antisemitic enough to prove the WRB had gotten under the skin of some Nazis.

But the WRB's psychological warfare campaign quickly began to ebb. Within a week of Roosevelt's statement, the Office of War Information had virtually ceased reporting it, because its broadcasts were meant for current news, though listeners were still reminded of the threat of postwar punishment. And after the president, there was nowhere to go but down. The WRB wrangled a host of prominent Hungarian American figures, sending their voices crackling across the wire, better angels pleading from afar to their former countrymen. None of the messages garnered much attention.

In Geneva, Switzerland, a lanky young man with dark hair and thoughtful eyes cut a March 23 article out of the Hungarian newspaper *Új Magyarság* and pasted it onto a blank sheet of paper. The article, which translated to "The Failure of the Office for European Refugees," announced that Roosevelt's new agency had made little progress and lacked money. Roswell McClelland noticed this particular article because it related to his new employer.

Ross was, in many ways, the perfect War Refugee Board attaché. After his mother died when he was a toddler, Ross was shuttled from his native California to various boarding schools in Europe, picking up German and French along the way. While in graduate school at Columbia, he met Marjorie Miles, a sunny blonde with a wicked sense of humor, who ran a nursery school in Harlem. Marjorie was a Quaker, while Ross later described himself as a "backsliding Presbyterian with Quaker sympathies." They married in November 1938, and soon after one of Marjorie's friends in the American Friends Service Committee learned of Ross's language skills. She recruited the couple to run the AFSC's Rome office, sweetening the pot by offering Ross a fellowship for his planned PhD in comparative literature. Ross, eager to delve into European archives, jumped at the chance, though the outbreak of war put an end to any scholarly ambitions. Instead, the couple proved themselves quite adept at relief work: both were meticulous, good-natured, and hardworking.

By early 1944, the McClellands had been in Switzerland for nearly a year and a half but in Europe since August 1940. After the American consulates closed in Rome in July 1941, rendering the country too dangerous and the opportunities to assist refugees too remote, they moved to southern France to join a larger AFSC delegation. Ross coordinated relief work in the internment camps, where he witnessed with horror the first deportations by train that took many of his refugee friends to their deaths at Auschwitz. Marjorie selected children for the United States Committee for the Care of European Children transports to America, forever separating them from imprisoned parents but saving their lives. In the fall of 1942, with Marjorie's pregnancy beginning to show, the AFSC asked the couple to take over its Geneva office, and the McClellands crossed the border. Their son, Barre, was born in January 1943, only a few months after Nazi Germany invaded Vichy France, capturing the remaining AFSC workers and interning them as prisoners of war. Geneva, in comparison, was a quiet post where the McClellands ran a distribution center out of their apartment, just steps from Geneva's oldest square, Place du Bourg-de-Four, providing clothing and small amounts of money to refugees already in the country. It was a perfectly nice place to do some good while waiting for the end of the war.

Pehle had just taken the "acting" helm of the board when he decided Ross would be his man in Switzerland. The head of the AFSC, Clarence Pickett, lamented the Quakers' loss, but Pehle didn't hesitate; the board had very few options for representatives in Switzerland, a country completely surrounded by enemy territory and without Treasury staff. The Americans living there had been confined for more than a year, no one getting in or out. Because the Quakers were known for honesty and industriousness—the WRB simultaneously and unsuccessfully tried to get Pickett, too, and David Blickenstaff for Spain—McClelland's job offer went by cable on February 13. Florence Hodel asked the AFSC for a picture of McClelland so the WRB staff could "meet" their new colleague.

After some soul-searching, Ross accepted in early March, writing to a friend, "This appointment had more the tone of a designation than an offer . . . One only wishes that such a board had existed in 1940, when the opportunities for saving people were far greater. Perhaps the frightful deportations of Jews from France during the summer of 1942 could have been, if not entirely avoided, at least considerably mitigated . . . I feel strongly, therefore, that even if the WRB has come at the eleventh hour one should go to work in an unstinting effort to make the most of the little time that remains." This was his chance to save the lives he couldn't save in France.

Due to some missing paperwork, the WRB didn't actually appoint McClelland until April 22, in the midst of a whirlwind week that included meet and greets with the IGC's director; Ira Hirschmann's triumphant return to Washington; and the miraculous news that Henry Morgenthau's son Robert had survived an enemy attack that had cleaved his naval destroyer in two. Having waited in limbo in Switzerland for two months, McClelland was eager to get started. Because the American legation was located in Bern, he commuted for most of the week, saying good-bye to little Barre and to Marjorie, who was pregnant with their second child, and boarding the train for the three-hour ride to the capital on Tuesday mornings, returning to Geneva on Friday evenings.

Switzerland served as a base for Jewish relief agency workers, some with close ties to resistance movements in enemy territory, including in Hungary, and McClelland's relationship with them—and the intelligence he gathered from them—would be pivotal for the War Refugee Board's plans.

In the first four months of 1944, the War Refugee Board had issued licenses worth almost $4 million, most for generic "relief and rescue," which gave the relief agencies flexibility. Nearly $3 million of that went to Switzerland, on behalf of eight different relief agencies. Pehle asked McClelland to meet with the agency workers for audits, because he had to ensure the representatives were following all the license rules. It was also an opportunity to gather ideas and see how the WRB could better assist people who had secret channels into occupied lands. Three of the workers, whose personalities reflected their organizations, stood out and would become McClelland's closest associates and the sources of his greatest frustrations.

Isaac Sternbuch, bearded with a lazy right eye, represented multiple agencies of the Orthodox community—the Vaad Hatzalah, the Union of Orthodox Rabbis, Agudas Israel, and HIJEFS (Schweizerischer Hilfsverein für jüdische Flüchtlinge im Ausland)—and had to deal with their many demands, none of which were straightforward. These groups understood the Nazi murder campaign differently than other refugee organizations: they saw a Nazi war against Judaism, rather than against Jews.

The Orthodox organizations emphasized aid and rescue for yeshi-

vas, rabbis, and religious leaders, targeting their efforts toward specific
individuals and small groups rather than toward a needy population
as a whole. Their leadership in New York never fully understood the
impossibility of targeted rescue and would send Sternbuch—and
McClelland—desperate pleas to find and rescue certain rabbis, deep
in enemy territory. They had little regard for the WRB's license rules;
when McClelland asked how he was spending his money, Sternbuch
confessed his colleagues wanted to open a children's home in Switzerland. Sternbuch knew this broke the terms of his license and apologetically drafted his own angry "response," which McClelland could
use when formally rejecting the request. The multiple sources of Sternbuch's projects and finances made close accounting impossible.

Saly Mayer, the JDC's representative, had fallen into his job the
same way McClelland had: his organization needed someone responsible, and he had been the head of the Swiss Federation of Jewish Communities. A middle-aged lace manufacturer in St. Gallen, Mayer was a
formal man, very precise and ponderous. The WRB trusted the JDC
more than any other Jewish organization, and eventually—though not
at first—McClelland's relationship with Mayer reflected that, too.

Like the WRB, the JDC operated on a "wholesale" basis, providing funds to assist the largest number of people possible. Through Saly
Mayer, the JDC funded most of the Jewish organizations still operat-
ing in enemy territory and some of the work of the International Red
Cross. Even though it sometimes paid a massive amount of money for
a relatively small number of people—like financing rescue boats from
Romania to Istanbul—these were exceptions. Mayer had the largest
budget of any relief worker by far but resisted an audit at first, considering McClelland's request "an affront to his integrity." Within a few
weeks, he came around, providing a breakdown of the $1,829,400 the
JDC had sent him between September 1943 and May 1944.

Gerhart Riegner was much more willing to share the details of his
operations—too willing, as it turned out. On April 28, Riegner sent a
written account of the World Jewish Congress's work in France to the
Bern legation's offices. After finally receiving his license, he had used
the money to evacuate children and young adults across the Spanish
border, to procure false identity papers, and to publish an underground
newspaper, though after the publisher was arrested, the paper went on

hiatus. Riegner also supported a Jewish resistance group's training and purchased their firearms, used for the "punishment of traitors." He added proudly, "Several traitors have already been destroyed for having denounced and sold Jews to the Germans." The Office of Censorship chastised the War Refugee Board for forwarding Riegner's audit to his bosses in New York, which "endangers national security" by sharing "information of possible military value" with the World Jewish Congress.

Gerhart Riegner also sent the War Refugee Board some of the first intelligence about Hungarian Jews, relaying the Nazi plan to quickly concentrate them together in makeshift ghettos. From him, the Bern legation would learn about economic deprivations, the new political personalities who had been installed in the Hungarian government, and where and in what numbers Jews were being collected together.

In early May 1944, John Pehle learned that deportations from Hungary to Nazi-occupied Poland had begun. Allen Dulles, head of the OSS in Switzerland, reported on May 18 that the Hungarian and German railway authorities planned to ship 300,000 Hungarian Jews to Poland; his well-sourced informant was the Hungarian minister in Bern.

Less than two months had passed since the Nazi invasion of Hungary, and German officials and Hungarian police had already forced Jews, their clothes sewn with still-bright yellow stars, onto cattle cars. In a span of fifty-six days between May 15 and July 9, more than 437,000 Hungarian Jews were deported, the vast majority to Auschwitz, most to their immediate deaths. Relief organizations pleaded for increased warnings broadcast into Hungary, for the Red Cross to send more representatives there, and for "protective papers" to be handed out to Hungarian Jews.

At the end of May, staff photographers at Auschwitz captured one day in the life of the camp, hoisting their equipment atop newly arrived trains to take in all the action. Several transports arrived that day, carrying entire communities. Women and children, blinking as they emerged from the darkened cattle cars, stared at the camera, daring the viewer to make eye contact and bear witness to what they still couldn't understand was happening to them. Men in three-piece suits, overcoats, and brimmed hats, bankers or mayors in any other context, were photographed for the last time, now remembered only for how they died. These photographs were discovered after liberation in an SS officers' barracks five hundred miles away, by a Holocaust survivor who immediately knew what she would see. The photographs proved the worst day of her life had not been a nightmare; they were of her town's arrival in Auschwitz and the day her family died. She, and they, were in them.

As the reports of the deportations increased, in number, detail, and desperation, relief agencies in the United States continued their call for warnings and protective papers, frantically unsure what else to do. The World Jewish Congress and Vaad Hatzalah got creative: maybe visas would allow specific Hungarian rabbis into Mauritius, or maybe money would give some rabbis and religious leaders the means to rescue themselves. The impossibility of the schemes demonstrates both the desperation and the incomprehensibility of the situation. McClelland tried gathering his own intelligence reports with the help of his assistant, a Hungarian refugee student named Laszlo Hamori, who acted as a liaison to underground groups. In late June, Hamori told McClelland that his own parents had disappeared.

Pehle and his staff received snippets of information from a variety of sources and tried to comprehend the crimes taking place thousands of miles away. The mistake-laden coding and decoding of still-slow cable traffic did not help, nor was there a master list of the proper spelling, location, or size of the concentration camps mentioned in any of the messages. For example, the World Jewish Congress asked for WRB help in transmitting relief packages for Czech nationals in the camps of "Oswierzim," "Bilenau," and "Ravenheim" (likely Auschwitz, Birkenau, and Ravensbrück). The board asked McClelland to see what he could figure out about a camp called "Dost or Tost." When the request reached him, decoding eliminated the spaces between the words, forcing McClelland to report back that he could find no information, not even a rough location, for "Dostortost." Multiple cables went back and forth for a month with questions about this most mysterious camp.

In early May, just weeks after beginning his work for the War Refugee Board, Roswell McClelland received a message from Sternbuch for his bosses at the Vaad in New York. "Assistance to those in Hungary is very difficult," it began. "We are trying various things, but with no feasible success to date. The situation is not clear yet. We have sent a courier again with 80 south-American passports."

Protective papers—passports; identity papers; certificates of citizenship, nationality, or protection that might exempt a bearer from persecution—were one of the few concrete options open to Pehle. It was a way to assist specific individuals in lieu of the impossible physical rescue. Jews with papers bearing the name of an Allied or neutral government could plausibly be considered "civilian internees" rather than "political prisoners," which would grant them status under the Geneva Convention. The Red Cross could intercede on their behalf, and they could be placed in special camps for Allied civilians, where treatment was (at least theoretically) regulated under international law. Any document that looked just legitimate enough for a perpetrator to worry about attacking the wrong person might be enough to save a life. In their responses to Pehle's request for advice, a few relief organizations had suggested the War Refugee Board distribute or coordinate protective documents, either those from Allied countries or more general documents like Nansen passports, which had been given to suddenly stateless White Russians after the Bolshevik Revolution. But Pehle had never really considered the power of the papers until April 6, 1944, right before the beginning of Passover.

On a windy day in the middle of a late-season cold front, Henry Morgenthau held a late-afternoon meeting in his office with representatives from the Union of Orthodox Rabbis, all rabbis themselves: Shabse Frankel; Abraham Kalmanowitz, the union's chief correspondent with the WRB; and Baruch Korff, their spokesman. The men needed Morgenthau's intervention to save Jews in the Vittel internment camp, including Frankel's parents and siblings.

Located in northeastern occupied France, Vittel held American and British citizens as well as Jews who had identity papers claiming citizenship in Haiti, Paraguay, Venezuela, Costa Rica, Peru, Chile, Ecuador, and Nicaragua. The State Department received periodic reports of life in Vittel from Red Cross and YMCA personnel, authorized to visit because of the presence of Allied prisoners. The American and British prisoners balked at their confinement but were otherwise waiting out the war in relative comfort. The February 1944 report included news of the recent Christmas Nativity play and of the newly reorganized camp library—now containing six thousand volumes—and a request for more rackets and balls, "necessary in order to play tennis as before."

For the Jewish prisoners on protective papers, however, Vittel was a dream compared with ghettos and concentration camps, and they worried it could be taken away at any moment. It was an open secret that the prisoners were not legally born or naturalized citizens of any Latin American country. Few, if any, spoke Spanish—and sometimes the Nazis checked—but they had purchased or been given legitimate or falsified papers in a last attempt to save their own lives. But the ploy only worked if the emperor continued to wear clothes—if everyone involved pretended the papers were real.

The War Refugee Board first learned about Vittel in February, when Lawrence Lesser, combing State Department files, discovered that the Jews there were in danger. Rumors were flying that both Paraguay and Peru had disavowed the validity of the documents issued in their names; when asked, Paraguay responded that the papers hadn't been canceled, but the consular officers who had issued them were "punished energetically." Switzerland, too, considered the papers illegally held—a serious matter, because the Swiss acted as protecting power for some of the Latin American countries and were responsible for protesting any maltreatment of their citizens. If they didn't officially consider the papers real, the Swiss wouldn't complain about what happened to the Jews who carried them. On February 21, John Pehle drafted a cable to the State Department, instructing the Bern legation to make sure Nazi Germany respected the Vittel prisoners' papers.

The State Department did not send Pehle's cable and did not inform him it hadn't. Nearly a month later, the War Refugee Board heard the Nazi administrators of Vittel were again beginning to question the papers' validity. In light of this information, and after discovering the State Department had not sent its first cable, Pehle drafted a second one, advising Switzerland that the United States considered these papers valid. The board also rushed messages to Latin America, requesting that each country likewise alert the Swiss that the protective papers issued in its name were real.

At the end of March, Isaac Sternbuch warned the Union of Orthodox Rabbis that 238 prisoners in Vittel had been isolated in preparation for their imminent deportation to Poland. Their only hope was for the Nazis to be forced to recognize their papers as valid and for the Allies to propose a prisoner exchange, the Jews for German civilians or military prisoners in the United States. Pehle immediately sent Sternbuch's cable to Kalmanowitz, and WRB staff weighed the logistics of an exchange. Two days later, Kalmanowitz, Frankel, and Korff were on the train from New York to Washington to enlist congressional support—which is how they got Morgenthau involved—vowing to complain to the press if they were not satisfied that all possible was being done for the Vittel prisoners.

Morgenthau, who canceled a doctor's appointment for the meeting, sympathized as the rabbis sat in his office and cried—"Now, look, you get upset and you get me upset"—but knew nothing about Vittel and needed to be brought up to speed. Pehle and DuBois informed him about their second cable to Bern, which, like the first, still languished unsent at the State Department. The State Department disagreed with asking for blanket protection, instead wanting the Bern legation to ask Switzerland to confirm the validity of specific prisoners' papers if Nazi Germany asked—assuming it asked prior to deporting the Jews. Rabbi Korff thought the delays were more insidious; he had heard the State Department believed the passports were really issued by Gestapo agents as some sort of trap. Pehle impatiently argued the United States could "pretty well force a Latin American country to refrain from revoking these things until after the war" and reminded Morgenthau the Nazis were not asking permission: "They are just starting to ship these people out. We are quibbling on this sort of thing while this goes on."

Morgenthau tried to reach Hull to demand a meeting that evening or, in lieu of that, threatened to call a full War Refugee Board meeting the next morning to clear up the cable dispute. After Morgenthau, Pehle, and DuBois thanked the departing rabbis, they commiserated about how people at the State Department, in Congress, and at the White House put on appearances but were not actually helping the board. Pehle was particularly frustrated by accusations that his own staff's stubbornness was responsible for the cable delays: the State Department "told them [the Rabbis] there were just a few words difference ... and we were just quibbling." "A few words make all the difference in the world," DuBois responded.

At 6:00 p.m., Morgenthau finally reached Hull by phone and described the rabbis' visit: "The poor fellows broke down and cried here in my office, and we had quite a time." The secretaries read the WRB's proposed cable together, and Hull didn't see the problem his staff had. When George Warren arrived forty-five minutes later to get a clean copy of the message, he refused to send it without explicit instructions from Hull, who had already left for the night. Morgenthau, his patience gone but the migraine he was supposed to be at the doctor's for quite present, called Hull's secretary while Warren sat in front of him, watching. "He's not questioning my word in my conversation with Mr. Hull, but he says he can't act until Mr. Hull gives him instructions," Morgenthau complained. "This thing has been delayed so long . . . I'm afraid I'm going to have to ask that it be read to Mr. Hull tonight . . . So that it could still, after all, if it goes out tonight, it will be in Switzerland tomorrow." Warren left with a copy of the draft, and Morgenthau finally got to go home.

Early the next morning, Pehle told Morgenthau that his living room phone had rung around ten o'clock the night before. It was George Warren with good news and bad news. Hull agreed to send the cable but wanted an internal State Department meeting to review the language one more time. A few minutes after Pehle had hung up, the phone rang again. This time it was Rabbi Korff excitedly celebrating the War Refugee Board's success. He had also just gotten off the phone with Warren, who told the rabbi the cable was being sent immediately with no changes. "So right in the space of two minutes they were giving them one side of the story and giving me another. That is where we stand." Pehle had told Korff he was being lied to; the rabbi declared that if he did not have proof the State Department had sent the cable by mid-morning, perhaps some publicity might help move things along. Morgenthau agreed: "I don't blame him. It is time a lot of people shouted from the housetops."

At 11:30 a.m., Morgenthau received confirmation the State Department sent the cable to Switzerland. He gathered Pehle, DuBois, and six other members of the WRB staff in his office to thank them. "Nothing has pleased me more than being able to get the State Department to send out this cable in regard to Camp Vittel. It just shows that if we put enough heat in the right place it can be done." Pehle thanked Morgenthau for "going to bat on this thing," and Morgenthau crowed that State Department staff would henceforth call him that " 'God-damned Jew.' It is a badge of honor."

After praising the War Refugee Board staff, Morgenthau acknowledged that it was likely a symbolic victory, over the State Department's delays and obstructions, not over the Nazis. It was almost certainly too late to save any prisoners deported from Vittel, including Rabbi Frankel's family. The board staff spent the next few months trying to find out more about the deportation—who was included and where they had been sent—and the board asked Latin American countries to demand the return of "their" prisoners, all to no avail. At least the State Department began to send the War Refugee Board's cables in record time—even keeping employees late if necessary. Pehle updated Morgenthau: "There is no question but that the situation has greatly changed for the better. Of course, we can't say how long this happy state of affairs will continue."

After the Vittel drama, the WRB staff seized on the idea of protective papers, which could be issued in large numbers without a lot of cost and could potentially save lives in enemy territory, particularly in Hungary. Unfortunately, it wasn't that easy. A sudden increase in the number of people claiming Allied citizenship could lead Nazi Germany and its collaborators to treat *all* such papers as illegitimate, including those of American citizens interned in places like Vittel.

But the War Refugee Board could at least ensure that papers already in circulation would be respected. Pehle wrote a message to the governments of Latin American countries asking them to insist that all people holding certificates be treated as verified Allied nationals who could be included in prisoner exchanges, giving Nazi Germany a material benefit to continue pretending the papers were real. The board also asked these countries to request a protecting power for Hungary. Protecting powers—a neutral nation that acted as a liaison between two countries at war, protecting those countries' citizens and property from the other—had to be designated between individual countries. Chile had already designated Switzerland as its protecting power in Germany, but if there were no Chilean nationals in Hungary, the country might not have designated a power there. Now there might be "Chileans" in Hungary needing protection.

Between 1941 and 1944, the number of "Salvadoran" Jews in Hungary jumped from zero into the thousands. There was an easy explanation, which involved no passenger ships from San Salvador: George Mandel-Mantello, a Jewish businessman from Romania, served as first secretary of El Salvador's Geneva consulate. Throughout the war, supported by Consul General José Castellanos, Mantello created thousands of nationality certificates, sending copies of them into enemy territory through neutral diplomatic couriers or via underground channels. After the invasion, Mantello began writing hundreds of certificates for Hungarian Jews, gathering names and photographs from loved ones who hoped their families were still alive to receive the documents. There was one significant problem, of which Roswell McClelland was all too aware: El Salvador did not have a protecting power in Hungary. No one stood behind these certificates. Jews in Switzerland began asking McClelland how to procure Salvadoran papers; in one week, he received at least five visitors inquiring about them. McClelland feared Mantello, in an attempt to save some, might be putting everyone holding a certificate at risk. Though the War Refugee Board sent multiple cables to El Salvador requesting it appoint a protecting power in Hungary, the Salvadoran government never did so. In Bern, the implications were clear, and McClelland had to explain to the relief worker Michel Banyai that the Swiss had no grounds to protest the deportation of his family, who held Salvadoran papers in Hungary.

In Washington, John Pehle and Lawrence Lesser tried their own protective paper schemes, with little success. In mid-April, they met with unofficial representatives from the Dominican Republic (including President Trujillo's eldest daughter) who offered blank Dominican papers for the War Refugee Board's distribution. Excited, Pehle and Lesser concocted a test to see if the papers would work. They compiled a list of fifteen Jewish families—including those of the Hungarian rabbi Joel Teitelbaum, the JDC worker Gertrude van Tijn, and the Warsaw ghetto educator Emanuel Ringelblum—from various parts of Europe. For their plan, the Dominican Foreign Office would send letters into Nazi territory stating these people were eligible for Dominican passports, issued as soon as they could appear at an embassy. Until then, the bearer of the letter should be treated as a Dominican citizen. If this experiment succeeded, Pehle heard that Trujillo might be willing to issue between three and four thousand passports, which could be sent through the underground into Hungary.

The State Department was much less enthused, and Assistant Secretary Adolf Berle drafted a watered-down letter. In his version, the letter would read that the recipient's application had been received by a Dominican embassy and would be reviewed once he or she reached neutral or Allied territory. Pehle stopped himself from sending his angry initial response, in which he called Berle's claim that such a letter could save lives "the most wishful of wishful thinking." Pehle rewrote a new, more forceful draft, emphasizing that the bearer would be under Dominican protection until he or she could reach a consulate. The State Department considered the scheme a "tawdry piece of business" but finally agreed to have Roswell McClelland send a short list, about two hundred names, to the Dominican chargé d'affaires in Bern and to try sending papers into Hungary through the underground. The plan never worked.

Pehle's final idea using protective papers temporarily upended the State Department's burdensome visa rules, which had delayed or prevented the escape of tens of thousands of European Jews before the war. In March, Pehle approached the State Department with an idea to reissue American visas to people who had been approved after July 1, 1941 (when the State Department's rules had changed), but who had been unable to emigrate prior to the outbreak of war. Berle argued each refugee would need to be examined again by a consular officer, so Pehle proposed Nazi Germany be informed, in the hopes it would allow potential immigrants to leave enemy territory to reach an American consulate. Pehle also advocated visas for anyone who qualified after July 1941 but had been unable to appear at a consulate in person prior to Pearl Harbor; for close relatives of American citizens; and for close relatives of anyone serving in the American military.

Finally, after weeks of calls and meetings, John Pehle wore the State Department down. Consular officers were instructed to reissue a visa to anyone who had been granted an American visa after July 1, 1941, provided he or she had been in enemy-occupied territory after the outbreak of war, passed a security screening, and still qualified for entry. The State Department agreed to compile lists of people who had been approved but never arrived in the United States. Soon after, the program expanded to include the spouse, parent, and unmarried children of American citizens and the spouse or children of resident aliens. Private citizens could apply with the Immigration and Naturalization Service on behalf of their family members. Every few days, the War Refugee Board sent compiled lists of names to Bern and Stockholm. The embassies there forwarded the lists to the Swiss and Swedish governments, asking for any protection these governments could provide, as well as an entry visa for anyone included who reached their borders.

While the War Refugee Board did not openly publicize this program, Lawrence Lesser called a meeting with relief organization representatives, who gathered at the Treasury Department offices in midtown Manhattan. Emphasizing that no one should mention this plan to the press—the World Jewish Congress quoted him as saying, "I will chop your head off if you do!"—Lesser outlined the details of the board's new program. Those who had already received visas would have them reissued. Those with loved ones in the United States would still need to undergo security checks and fill out applications. Still, the United States guaranteed they would be cared for and evacuated to safety. It was a rescue program, designed to get people out of the Nazis' grasp, and the representatives were cautioned to inform people that the plan did not mean their relatives, if located, could necessarily ever come to the United States.

Some representatives were skeptical. The American Friends Service Committee feared the plan might direct the Nazis to single out these individuals, putting them at risk. Still, some organizations must have informed their clients, because the INS quickly began to receive letters with the names, birth dates, and birthplaces of the people in Europe, their relationship to the petitioner in the United States, and their last known address. Over a seven-month span, the INS sent an average of twenty names a day to the War Refugee Board, which, in turn, forwarded lists via cable to Stockholm and Bern.

There is no evidence that the vast program ever assisted anyone. The number of people with the "last known address" as "deported to Poland," "Drancy," "Theresienstadt," or "Auschwitz" indicates that many of the petitioners had simply not given up hope.

The War Refugee Board sent warnings into enemy territory. It helped relief agencies send money, which was used for food, clothing, medicine, weapons, and bribes. It supported protective paper schemes, even persuading the State Department to reissue American visas. Yet none of it was certain. All was intangible; all were guesses. To all the people writing to Pehle, pleading for the lives of their loved ones, he could only respond by promising that the War Refugee Board was trying everything.

Blood for Goods

THE FLAGS SWAYED IN the slight breeze. Pigeons flocked to the parks; flowers lazily reached toward the sun. In the evening, a double rainbow would appear over the Capitol. It was a lovely early summer day, low humidity, mid-seventies, a clear sky. The weekend had been cold and drizzly, but the morning of Tuesday, June 6, 1944, was just about perfect in Washington, D.C., as tens of thousands of workers woke up and turned on their radios to hear that the long-awaited invasion of France had begun.

During the day, the subdued city saw no parades, no celebrating in the streets. Commuters quietly watched the new world go by, stepped into local churches for quick prayers, or chattered nervously to fellow passengers about what might happen next. D.C.'s public schools held ceremonies, kindergarteners waving small hand-drawn American flags, with "D-day" carefully lettered on the back. A citizenship ceremony at the courthouse held new meaning as the head of the D.C. Bar Association implored his new countrymen to think about the boys giving their lives that day for their freedom, too. Crowds gathered to read wire service updates posted on the *Washington Post*'s streetside bulletin board and pleaded with emerging reporters to share any new information. The invasion pushed the June 4 liberation of Rome to the newspaper's second page, where Roosevelt's radio address about Italy, delivered as the first planes carrying paratroopers took off from England, was reprinted in full. The president had reminded the anxious nation that "our Allied forces are posed for another strike at

Western Europe." No one listening had dared dream that the strike had already begun.

Henry Morgenthau Jr. had been awake for hours. As his staff piled into his office for the morning meeting, he teased the few who hadn't been up most of the night listening to the reports starting to come in. "I got the word at twelve-thirty, when the Germans first announced it . . . I knew—that was my trouble yesterday," Morgenthau confessed. He had spent Monday fiddling with his office radio, anxious in case they went early, and had refused to review some speech drafts, knowing they would all need to be revised after the invasion.

After about twenty minutes of jokes and gossip, Morgenthau redirected them to a topic "on the sorry side." It was John Pehle's turn. He needed to discuss the offer for one million Jews.

Nearly three weeks earlier, in the late afternoon of May 19, 1944, a clunky Junkers Ju 52 transport plane had landed in Istanbul. A fat-cheeked Hungarian man, carrying forged identity papers under a false name and without an entrance visa, walked down the stairs last. Because he lacked proper paperwork, the Turkish government placed him under house arrest at the historic Pera Palas hotel, where Chaim Barlas ran the Jewish Agency offices, near the American consulate in the cosmopolitan Taksim neighborhood. The man's real name was Joel Brand, and he was a member of the Zionist Relief and Rescue Committee in Budapest. The Nazis had sent him to Istanbul to present a ransom offer to the Allied governments, which they called *"Blut gegen Waren"*: "Blood for Goods."

This offer reached Pehle in a cable, which read at first like an update from Steinhardt about the persecution of Hungarian Jews. Around 200,000 were already centralized in camps. Deportations to Poland had begun, and the Jews of Budapest were undoubtedly under imminent threat. Then, in the final paragraph, Steinhardt wrote that a man named Joel Brand had just arrived with a proposal.

Adolf Eichmann, described as the Nazi "Commissioner for Jewish Affairs," promised to end the deportation and extermination of Jews in Axis-controlled areas and would allow Jews to leave Europe—a limited number to Palestine, but unlimited people through Spain and Portugal. In exchange, he wanted products that were difficult to obtain in Germany: two million cakes of soap, two hundred tons of cocoa, eight hundred tons of coffee, and two hundred tons of tea. Those goods would have to go through the blockade but would be relatively easy to gather. But Eichmann also wanted ten thousand trucks. For a whole host of reasons, particularly because a deal involving military vehicles would undoubtedly prolong the war, trucks were much harder.

Word of Brand's mission spread quickly in Istanbul. Barlas immediately sent the proposal to the British high commissioner in Jerusalem, adding a plea for Great Britain to do something: "The Jewish Agency fear that in light of past experience and of this fresh authentic information there cannot be the slightest doubt that fate of Hungarian Jews is sealed . . . They firmly hope that the magnitude and the seemingly fantastic character of the proposition will not deter the high allied authorities from undertaking a concerted and determined effort to save the greatest possible number."

At Steinhardt's request, the JDC's representative in Turkey, Reuben Resnik, interviewed Brand and prepared a report for the War Refugee Board, starting with the facts. Joel Brand was in his late thirties, married with two small children. He had helped found the Relief and Rescue Committee (also known as the Vaadat ha'Ezra ve'ha'Hatzalah, or Vaada), which, prior to the Nazi invasion, supported Jews escaping into Hungary. He spoke near-fluent English and tried to answer all questions posed to him honestly. He also visibly felt the burden of his mission.

Resnik explained the Nazi ransom scheme and gave his initial analysis. It could be a cover for an eventual peace proposal or designed to embarrass the Allies and expose their hypocrisy: condemning Nazi treatment of Jews, yet unwilling to care for large numbers of released prisoners. Maybe the Nazis were attempting to sow discord between the Soviet Union and the Western Allies—a reasonable theory because Brand indicated the Nazis promised not to use the ten thousand trucks on the western front but were silent about using them against the Red Army. But the scheme could also have exposed a split between various Nazi factions the Allies might be able to exploit.

Whatever Eichmann's motivation, Resnik, like Barlas, emphasized that the United States should try to negotiate: "Everyone with whom I have talked recognizes the impossibility of carrying out the proposals as they have been stated, but everyone believes that all should be done to continue exploration."

Joel Brand's mission was the first major proposal to reach the Allies, the first time the Nazis, watching the War Refugee Board, figured that if the Americans cared about the fate of the Jews, they might be willing to negotiate. Logically, the "Blood for Goods" ransom offer couldn't have been serious, or at least Eichmann harbored no illusions that the Western Allies might accept the trade. Cattle cars arrived in Auschwitz daily; the Nazis were not preserving the Hungarian Jews for possible exchange. But to the War Refugee Board, the possibility of one million lives was such tempting bait. Ransom *could* work, at least temporarily. Pehle knew that Jewish communities in Slovakia had pooled enough money to delay deportations three times already. Even if they could stall for time, the ploy might save lives.

Steinhardt's initial cable arrived in late May, and for nearly two weeks John Pehle waited to learn more. Finally, on June 5, the British embassy forwarded Barlas's initial report over to the Treasury Department, including a summary of its own. The War Refugee Board should not even think of taking this "sheer case of blackmail or political warfare" seriously. Great Britain refused any bargain designed to stave off Germany's defeat, nor could it care for a million released prisoners, which would undoubtedly force the Allies to call a temporary halt to the war. It did not want to be on the record as opposing any genuine proposals that merited real consideration, but this "monstrous bargain" was not one of them. The British hoped the United States agreed.

Actually, John Pehle didn't agree, and on the sunny morning of D-day, after briefing his colleagues, he concluded, "The best thing to do is to keep it alive." Morgenthau concurred and met with Pehle and DuBois the next day to brainstorm how to appease the British. Pehle, nervous about defying an ally, but more so about negotiating with the Gestapo without confiding in the Soviets, proposed dangling Ira Hirschmann as a lure.

Hirschmann had been back in America for six weeks. After a few days of adjustment—"Turkish cognac, women, mountains and diplomatic braid are difficult to shelve over night"—he took the train to Wash-

ington on April 17 to join Pehle for a press conference announcing the
WRB's successes in Turkey. Hirschmann detailed "his" rescue of Jews
from Transnistria; the electrifying effect the board's creation had on
refugees; a poor orphaned refugee boy Hirschmann had supposedly
wanted to adopt; and his hopes for the purchase of the *Tari,* which
merely needed German safe-conduct to sail.

Hirschmann reveled in the attention granted to him as a newly
arrived savior of Jews and made the rounds giving speeches. He wrote
to Steinhardt, without a hint of irony, "I have spoken before a number of groups 'off the record' as I did not wish to publicize myself further and I had made such an agreement with John Pehle and the State
Department. Among the meetings were The Foreign Policy Association, The Emergency Committee to Save the Jewish People of Europe,
The American Jewish Congress (Stephen Wise), The Hadassah, The
Palestine Lighthouse at which a thousand women attended, etc." Turkey, Hirschmann told the crowds, was an "observation tower into the
Balkans. It's a window. What we tried to do was to make a door of it."
He took thousands into his confidence and asked them to keep his
secrets.

Because much more work needed to be done in Turkey, Pehle persuaded Bloomingdale's to grant Ira Hirschmann another extended
leave. Hirschmann began planning his second trip, figuring he would
depart in mid-June and cross paths with Steinhardt, who planned to
return to the United States for vacation and consultation.

But the Joel Brand offer compressed the timeline. Hirschmann,
in Ohio for meetings about the new medium of television (which
he thought would be great for education but not advertising) and to
deliver a United Jewish Appeal speech, raced back to Washington. At
Hirschmann's request, Pehle drafted a letter for Roosevelt's signature,
commending Hirschmann's work and expressing confidence that he
would receive any cooperation needed. Pehle also gave him a $2,000
travel advance, confirmed his $25 per diem, and asked Morris Ernst to
pay a salary of $1,500 per month out of the secret fund, sent directly to
Hirschmann's secretary.

Meanwhile, the War Refugee Board could tell the Nazis that a special representative of the U.S. government was on his way. Though they
openly worried about Hirschmann's temperament—Pehle commented

"there are disturbing elements about Hirschmann"—Morgenthau approved the idea, adding that by the time the Combined Chiefs of Staff coordinated an Allied effort, the Hungarian Jews would be gone.

At the State Department, Edward Stettinius briefed the World Jewish Congress representative Nahum Goldmann on the ransom proposal. The men likewise agreed the United States should negotiate with the Nazis, though Goldmann cautioned that the Soviets "will learn about it . . . and, you know how touchy they are, they may be inclined to be suspicious."

Pehle drafted a cable of instruction to Steinhardt. The ambassador should make every effort to "convince the Germans that this Government is sufficiently concerned with the problem that it is willing to consider genuine proposals for the rescue and relief of Jews and other victims." Steinhardt should also inform the Soviet Union of the proposal; the State Department copied the American embassy in Moscow on the cable.

Ira Hirschmann spent a quiet train ride back to New York and a sleepless night pondering his new assignment. Had he been able to read some of the letters sent through the Hungarian underground to Switzerland, he might have panicked even more. In Budapest, the secret police had arrested and tortured Brand's wife and colleagues; some had been released, but not all. Ten thousand people were deported each day to Nazi-occupied Poland, but Jews in Budapest still hoped Brand would return and the Germans would set everyone free.

In the early morning of Sunday, June 11, Hirschmann boarded an army transport plane to return to Turkey. This time, it only took six days to reach Ankara, far fewer than the twenty it had taken the first time. He was delayed for two days in Casablanca—where he toured the still-empty Fedhala camp—then stopped in Algiers, Cairo, and Adana. Finally, Ira Hirschmann arrived in Ankara in the late afternoon of Saturday, June 17, and immediately went looking for Joel Brand, whom he could not find.

Hirschmann spent the next two days in a foul mood, in part because of some telegrams from home, probably from his wife, probably about their disintegrating marriage. He also expected a hero's welcome in the Turkish capital and was sorely disappointed. Though he and Steinhardt had been corresponding about the ambassador's future

in politics, Hirschmann felt resentful upon reaching Ankara. Steinhardt, Hirschmann wrote, "did not want me back" and "has not acted
especially well with me."

Reuben Resnik, however, received the brunt of Hirschmann's ire.
As soon as he discovered that Resnik had already met with Joel Brand,
Hirschmann decided the JDC representative "has worked nasty
intrigue in my absence and is obviously my enemy." That Resnik had
investigated the ransom proposal at Steinhardt's request only served as
evidence against both men. The grudges lasted months and seemed to
be largely one-sided.

Hirschmann was also frustrated to learn he could not interview
Joel Brand, whose mission entered its second month. Brand had disappeared. While Hirschmann had been stuck in Casablanca en route to
Turkey, Steinhardt had cabled Pehle, "Neither British Embassy nor we
are informed as to Brand's present whereabouts."

By June 19, Steinhardt learned that Brand, who had traveled to
Aleppo to meet with the Jewish Agency, was currently in solitary
confinement in Cairo, being relentlessly interrogated by British intelligence. Hirschmann finally conceded that the British would not
transfer their prisoner back to Ankara, so he packed his bags to return
to Egypt. His mood suddenly brightened; he was being sent on an
important mission to interview an agent of the enemy. In his diary, he
wrote, "I have the inside track as *the* government representative—and
I must use it with care and energy for my only purpose at heart—to
save others." His "delightful" June 21 flight featured "tasty food (relatively)." Hirschmann expressed sympathy for a sick passenger, wrote
of his desire to stay in North Africa despite the 118-degree heat, was
thrilled by a sandstorm, and playfully compared sand flies to planes
bombing him. There was a prestigious job to do, and Ira Hirschmann
was in his element.

Had he remained in Ankara for another day, Hirschmann would
likely never have interviewed Joel Brand. As he flew to Cairo, the
War Refugee Board received a message from the American embassy
in Moscow: the Soviet Union forbade "any conversations whatsoever
with the German government on the questions which the note from
the Embassy touched upon." As soon as the board received the news,
Pehle, his fears now justified, sent an immediate cable to Steinhardt:

"Please take no, repeat no, further action of any nature with respect to this matter pending further instructions."

But Pehle's plea was not forwarded to Cairo, where the British, disinclined to produce Joel Brand, suggested Hirschmann travel to London for joint meetings on the ransom offer instead. Hirschmann refused, brandishing his letter of support from Roosevelt. His instructions were not to go to London but to find and interview Joel Brand and brief Steinhardt on the proposal. The British finally gave in.

At 4:00 p.m. on June 22, less than two weeks after leaving Washington, Hirschmann was shown to a small house near the Nile, where he finally met the mysterious Nazi agent Joel Brand. Brand later described Hirschmann as "a somewhat conceited and pompous person . . . he promised a great deal," while Hirschmann saw Brand as a sympathetic figure, "forced by history to play a role for which he was ill prepared."

Hirschmann, clearly nervous, peppered Brand with questions, then interrupted the answers. Eventually, he relaxed and showed himself to be a deft interviewer, always probing for additional details. Brand admitted that he had no written list of Nazi demands, so everything was up for negotiation, though he thought goods would be valued more than money. Brand was also terrified for his family. He had not spoken with his wife in a month—he didn't know she had been arrested and tortured—but knew the Nazis "always take their revenge on others . . . I know what they are like." Because he hadn't returned to Hungary, the Nazis had no answer to their offer. "It is terrible for me with my family there—they will take it that I ran away." Hirschmann asked Brand to clarify. "They" were the Nazis.

Brand also recognized that the Germans would win the negotiations no matter what happened. They could obtain their desired goods or postwar immunity if the Allies accepted, but if the Allies stayed silent, there was an opportunity for, as Brand put it, "some big propaganda. To say that they wanted to set the Jews free and the Allies did not want it, so there was no other way but for them to kill them off."

In his report to Steinhardt, Hirschmann wrote that Brand saw the ransom offer as an act of desperation: "The fact that a high German officer tells to the Jew, Brand, 'We need things—go get them.' This, Brand said, appeared to him to be a great confession of weakness." The proposals were serious and the details easily negotiable. Hirschmann suggested persuading the British to keep the door open and let Brand remain in Cairo (rather than transporting him to London) so he could return to Hungary quickly. He also reminded the WRB of the need for secrecy and proposed a meeting between Nazi officials and American and British representatives in a neutral location.

Over the next two weeks, Ira Hirschmann almost died twice. One of the motors on his plane returning to Turkey failed immediately after takeoff. Though Hirschmann wrote very matter-of-factly in his diary, describing sweat dripping down the face of one passenger and a young Red Cross woman joking to break the tension, he was clearly terrified. To keep the plane high enough to land safely, the passengers threw bags of mail into the desert below, then crowded into the back to keep the plane's nose elevated. Eventually, with fire engines and Red Cross vehicles screaming toward them, they crashed into the sand.

Hirschmann spent an extra day in Egypt, rewriting his report and sleeping fitfully. By the time he returned to Ankara, he was seriously ill. Diagnosed with malaria, he had a fever that eventually hit 105 before it broke, and he spent the next week delirious and suffocating in his hotel room.

In London, the discussions surrounding the Brand offer progressed slowly, just as Henry Morgenthau had warned they would. On July 1, the British expressed their ongoing concerns to the War Refugee Board: so long as war matériel remained on the table, the Soviets wouldn't agree to anything, while "trading in concert with a Gestapo agent, Jewish blood against Allied goods, looked equally dangerous."

John Pehle considered the problem for about a week before sending a long cable to Moscow updating the Soviets. Pehle provided all the details about Brand and the offer, reiterated that no one was being deceived here, and implored the Soviets to recognize that dragging out negotiations could save lives.

On July 19, two months after Joel Brand arrived in Istanbul, the War Refugee Board staff was shocked to read the *New York Herald Tribune* headline "Nazis Reported in Bid to 'Spare' 400,000 Jews: London Hears of Huge Extortion Demand for Supplies by Allies." Secrecy was over: the British had unilaterally decided to publicize the ransom offer, effectively killing it. The article began, "The fate of perhaps 400,000 Hungarian Jews is currently being offered in barter by the Germans in what is probably the most monstrous blackmail attempt in history," and referred to the ten thousand trucks and a "prominent Hungarian Jew" as the messenger.

It's likely John Pehle saw the newspaper before the British cable reached him, rationalizing their decision in light of "fresh evidence which in our view compels us to take a different attitude . . . it would be highly dangerous to give even the appearance of a response to the Gestapo's suggestions. For we now have evidence that the Brand mission was intended as a cover for an approach to us or to the Americans on the question of a separate peace." The British also decided that Joel Brand, who had started a hunger strike a few days after his interview with Hirschmann, would remain in their custody in Cairo.

At face value, Joel Brand's mission was a failure. Pehle and Hirschmann had done all they could, but British nerves and the impossibility of Soviet consent doomed any deal.

The War Refugee Board decided that next time it would negotiate on its own, in secret.

Free Ports

A CACOPHONY OF MEMOS, MEETINGS, reports, and projects jumbled John Pehle's days. The War Refugee Board dealt with issues in dozens of countries at the same time, each navigating its own route through the war, each with its own relationship toward a Jewish community and to refugees, each weighing the possibilities differently. The ground shifted as the war did; projects that had started promisingly petered out, while other ideas raced to the fore when the board learned of an emergency or sensed a new opening. Everything overlapped, all the time.

Pehle led a staff of nearly sixty in the summer of 1944, many on temporary assignments from departments within Treasury, secretaries and clerks scrounging desks and typewriters from throughout the building. The assistant directors—Jim Abrahamson, Larry Lesser, Joe Friedman, and Florence Hodel—wrangled everyone, supervising the correspondence, the research, and the meetings with relief agencies, journalists, private citizens, foreign diplomats, and administration colleagues. Their dedication can be quantified: by the end of June, the WRB staff had facilitated nearly $5 million in licenses to sixteen different organizations for relief and rescue in eleven countries (and the ever-present "Nazi-occupied territory"). They had collected, written, and filed nearly six thousand cables, letters, newspaper clippings, reports, and memos. There is no record of any of them taking a vacation.

John Pehle signed his name to the War Refugee Board's weekly report on June 17, 1944, a looping *J* followed by a scratched "WPehle," his pen running out of ink at the end. It was a quick signature, fully legible thanks only to the name typed below it. The report, covering the board's activities between June 5 and June 10, 1944, ran to nineteen single-spaced pages, the longest update it would ever produce, delivered to the usual suspects—Stimson, Morgenthau, Hull, and their deputies; the Intergovernmental Committee; the Budget office; the OSS; and the White House. Weeks later, the reports might reach some of the WRB's representatives abroad by diplomatic courier. The topics in this particular report ran the gamut, from the International Red Cross's plan to stockpile food and clothing in Geneva to distribute in concentration camps, to the board's request that the Soviet Union publicly condemn the murder of Jews, to Ethiopia's lack of response to Pehle's questions about refugees there. For people in the WRB's inner circle, it was even longer: a separate cover sheet detailed the Joel Brand ransom offer, kept out of the main report "because of its extremely secret nature."

The biggest news in the report took up the first five pages. The WRB planned to open a refugee camp in the United States.

Three months earlier, on March 6, 1944, the same day John Pehle delivered his draft of the president's "declaration on atrocities" to the White House, Joe Friedman and Josiah DuBois had written up a plan to welcome refugees in the United States. In the declaration, Roosevelt would, they hoped, call "upon the free peoples of Europe to open their frontiers to the victims of oppression." But the text conspicuously failed to open U.S. borders to those victims, and other countries had already noticed the hypocritical disconnect. Nicaragua, in responding to the WRB's initial cable about refugees, had scoffed that it would "permit the entry of war refugees under the same conditions as the United States and in a number proportionate to the population of both countries." The Nazis, too, "must not be given the pretense of justification that the Allies, while speaking in horrified terms of the Nazi treatment of the Jews, never once offered to receive these people."

DuBois and Friedman acknowledged potential problems, including American opposition. Private citizens already sent letters warning the WRB, "There will be a great uprising in our country if all the Jews that want to come be sent here . . . The Jews are not wanted anywhere." For Roosevelt, welcoming refugees might be a hard sell in an election year. To make it more palatable, inside the administration and out, the War Refugee Board proposed treating the refugees like the thousands of German POWs already in the United States. Confining innocent people in internment camps wasn't ideal, but, the two men decided, "treating them as prisoners of war is better than letting them die." The camps would be temporary, and the refugees would agree to return to Europe after the war. In the report's conclusion, DuBois and Friedman evoked the ethos of America as a country of refuge: "In the hearts and minds of all people under Nazi domination and throughout the world such action might well have an effect tremendously favorable to our whole war effort and to our reputation as a nation which has always carried the torch in great undertakings."

Morgenthau loved the idea. But he couldn't decide whether Roosevelt would. Roosevelt had recently expressed his desire for Great Britain to publicly announce that anyone the War Refugee Board saved could go to Palestine. Refugee camps in the United States might put more pressure on Britain to keep the door to the Middle East open, or relieve it of the need to do so.

DuBois argued camps were imperative: "I am convinced, Mr. Secretary, that it is the heart of our whole program . . . We are approaching all other governments, asking them on humanitarian grounds to do something. We, ourselves, look like hypocrites." Morgenthau finally agreed that Pehle should collect a few more supporters in the administration, or "[Roosevelt] will think we are trying to put something over on him."

For nearly a month, John Pehle grew increasingly frustrated by the effort of trying to take this major step within the confines of a massive bureaucracy. Steps forward, steps back. Meetings, memos, revisions, repeat. Stettinius liked the idea offhand, but Stimson worried Roosevelt would be pressured to admit the refugees permanently. Rosenman agreed the atrocities statement and the camp requests should be kept separate "like ham and matzoth." At a formal War Refugee Board meeting in Hull's office, the secretaries finally all agreed Pehle could present the board's refugee camp proposal to Roosevelt. Energized by the reception of the president's now-public statement condemning mass murder, and his own promotion as the board's official executive director, Pehle drafted both a memo and an optimistic press release announcing refugee havens in the United States. The approach had worked the last time he saw the president, when the board was created. But Stimson got cold feet again and began arguing that the American people, who supported the current immigration quotas and "proportion of racial stocks," might feel they were being fooled into accepting an influx of immigrants. Steps back.

Pehle promised he would revise the plan but really just decided that if Stimson thought the American people objected to refugee camps, he would prove him wrong. Only two days after Stimson's complaints, Pehle gave a speech in Chicago titled "We, Too, Are Impatient." In his flat midwestern twang, Pehle drew the audience's attention to the phrase "temporary refuge" in the executive order establishing the WRB and emphasized the need to cut through red tape, because "this Board has no such time. This Board is concerned with what I call a simple and plain life-saving job." Its work could not be delayed by political squeamishness in the United States.

Back in Washington on April 5, Pehle opened his newspaper to read Samuel Grafton's syndicated column "I'd Rather Be Right." Pehle had met Grafton at Morris Ernst's dinner party in February, and the two men had clearly stayed in touch. In the column, Grafton explained "free ports" to his readers, places where goods were stored tax-free while importers waited to bring them into the country. The United States could provide similar space for refugees from Nazism, allowing them to enter outside immigration laws and returning them to their homelands after the war. Grafton made every argument DuBois and Friedman had, adding, "If we set up a system of refugee free ports, our fine new War Refugee Board can then properly appeal to other countries to do the same. If we do not go at least that far, the Board will be answered with a snicker should it make such requests of other lands."

Grafton's column slowly gained traction. In mid-April, Ira Hirschmann, who thought his Turkish exploits would get all the coverage at the press conference, grumbled afterward, "A reporter apparently was tipped off to ask the question about 'Free Ports' that got the headlines." In answering the reporter, Pehle carefully referred to Grafton's column and explained that many ideas were under active consideration, including free ports. One subsequent headline read, "Refugee Board Considers Plan for Free US Ports." Grafton rewrote his column for the radio, and Norman Jay turned his *Very Truly Yours* broadcast into an open letter to John Pehle, expressing his hope that with the establishment of free ports "America can heave a national sigh of relief as it forsakes the unnatural role it has played in barring refugees from its shores."

After a four-week propaganda campaign, Pehle reported to Morgenthau that the War Refugee Board's idea now had overwhelming public support. Representative John McCormack had entered Grafton's column into the *Congressional Record,* and a White House–sponsored Gallup poll revealed 70 percent of the respondents supported the plan. Even with public backing, getting Congress to act still seemed a long shot. McCormack had warned Pehle, "I am for this thing, but you let the President do this thing by Executive Order, then you see the wolves jump on him and the Congress takes action to vitiate what he has done." Pehle drafted a new memo laying out the president's options—an executive decision, or some kind of joint action with Congress—and got Hull, Stimson, and Morgenthau's approval. Then he awaited Roosevelt's arrival from South Carolina, where the president was purportedly fishing but really taking a monthlong doctor-mandated rest.

Less than a week after his return to the White House, Roosevelt met Pehle alone in the Oval Office. In a meeting lasting only about fifteen minutes, the president listened as Pehle summarized the board's proposal and the possibility of using a camp in Jerome, Arkansas, which would soon be vacated by Japanese American internees. Roosevelt seemed open to the idea, especially after flipping through all the newspaper clippings and letters of support Pehle collected, but he disliked the term "free port" and asked for alternatives. The president also explained that he needed an emergency, something involving fewer than a thousand refugees, so he could make a unilateral announcement and justify the decision to Congress. Pehle optimistically reported to Morgenthau that Roosevelt was "very, very favorably disposed toward the whole idea."

Pehle could have packaged any number of different situations, asking DuBois to write something dramatic to emphasize the direness of the chosen problem. But the crisis he found needed no packaging. It was a perfect, awful situation that the board could actually help alleviate. Pehle explained it to Morgenthau as "a real emergency" of "very vast proportions, and if something isn't done—just that many lives that won't be saved, that is all."

On May 11, the same day as Pehle's White House meeting, Leonard Ackermann had written Pehle a personal letter from Algiers, because government cables were never private and this message was highly confidential. He had been preparing for an upcoming trip to Italy and, while on a visit to Allied Force Headquarters in Algiers to review some documents, read a message about Yugoslav refugees. Thousands were still trying to escape to Italy, where the military would care for the refugees and funnel them to North Africa. Originally, the Allies had agreed to support 25,500 Yugoslav civilians in Egyptian camps, but these spots were filling up. Robert Murphy, Roosevelt's representative in Allied-occupied Italy, agreed with the British to expand the camps in Egypt, but the overall number of refugees under Allied protection was becoming a problem. So, he directed military officers in the Mediterranean to "discourage the evacuation of refugees" and "not to provide transportation to Yugoslav refugees" if the military encountered their boats on the open sea.

Ackermann protested vehemently, especially because he had just received word from Yugoslavia that partisan fighters there were willing to help Hungarian Jews escape to their territory. The Jews would need someplace to go, but now the Allied military was trying to stop the rickety wooden boats from crossing the Mediterranean. Ackermann quoted both the president's atrocity statement and the board's executive order at Murphy, arguing that the refusal to aid the refugees violated American policy. Murphy didn't budge, and Ackermann summarized his letter by telling Pehle that while refugees already in Italy were treated well, the people in charge openly opposed rescue "since it only makes their own burdens greater."

Murphy's instruction directly hampered the activities Ackermann and his new assistant, James Saxon, had been trying to encourage. In 1942, Saxon, a twenty-eight-year-old Treasury employee with an adventurous streak, had been responsible for burning millions of dollars to keep it out of the hands of the Japanese, before escaping Corregidor on a submarine carrying tons of gold and the president of the Philippines. He had now spent a year bored in North Africa and was pleased to be deputized into the War Refugee Board.

On a trip to Italy earlier in the spring, Saxon had learned that very few military officers knew or cared about America's new rescue policy. In meetings, they complained about the difficulties refugees created or joked that the War Refugee Board must want to move the entire population of Yugoslavia to Italy. In comparison, the Yugoslav partisans impressed Saxon, promising him that with more money they could bring people out to safety. Though one American general told Saxon the partisans were "congenital liars" and promised to oppose any WRB action to help them, Saxon handed off a money request to Ira Hirschmann, then on his way back to the United States from Turkey. The Yugoslav Refugee Committee in Bari, Italy, used $50,000 from Morris Ernst's secret fund to repair ships and aid in refugee transportation.

So while Roosevelt's War Refugee Board actively encouraged refugee evacuation programs, the Allied military was instructed to discourage them. Pehle received Ackermann's letter less than a week after his White House meeting. He had found his emergency.

Pehle immediately wrote a new report, reminding the president multiple times of his instruction to identify a problem that could provide political cover for establishing free ports. (Both Hull and Morgenthau coached Pehle to add in extra reminders, because "the important thing is to say two or three times in this thing, 'Mr. President, this is what you had in mind'" because Roosevelt tended to forget his own orders.) Pehle described the emergency: "The facilities for the care of refugees in southern Italy have become so overtaxed that the military authorities have taken steps actually to *discourage* the escape of further refugees to that area." He helpfully provided three draft documents: a message to Congress announcing the plan; a cable to Robert Murphy ordering him to arrange for the transportation of a thousand refugees from Italy to the United States; and a message to the secretaries of war, navy, interior, the Bureau of the Budget, and the director of the War Refugee Board, asking them to prepare a camp. Morgenthau gave Pehle's memo and the drafts to Roosevelt's secretary, who promised the president would take them with him when he left for Hyde Park that evening.

Then the War Refugee Board staff waited, just as they had with the statement on atrocities. A week passed, and Pehle heard nothing from the White House. Morgenthau thought the president might not have read it yet, or perhaps he simply wasn't ready to take any action.

To push the issue, Pehle and DuBois tried sneaking the topic of refugee camps into the May 26 cabinet meeting, asking Morgenthau to mention a supposed discussion between the War Refugee Board and the War Department over the critical situation for refugees in Italy and the need to find havens for them. Morgenthau admonished Pehle and DuBois for putting him in that position: "You people give me the damndest things to bring up! I am the catch-all for everything, and I have to do all these fights." The plan backfired: Roosevelt agreed the refugees should under no circumstances be sent back to Yugoslavia, but he proposed sending them to Sicily instead. Morgenthau "saw he wasn't ready to bring them over here yet . . . He isn't ready." They should not give up on the plan, "but his mind hasn't jelled on the thing . . . there is something, somewhere, that I think he is a little afraid of, that is all."

Morgenthau was wrong. Unbeknownst to the War Refugee Board, Roosevelt had already forwarded Pehle's memo and drafts to the State Department, asking for some minor edits. The State Department made the language even more forceful than Pehle had. The new text included a paragraph reading, "As the hour of the final defeat of the Hitlerite forces nears, the fury of their insane desire to wipe out the Jewish race in Europe continues undiminished. Knowing that they have lost the war, the Nazis are determined to complete their program of mass extermination." The board's draft had originally used the term "minority groups" rather than "Jewish race," but Edward Stettinius made the revision, because "the Jews are the only minority group which the Nazis are exterminating."

At his press conference on Tuesday, May 30—Decoration Day— Franklin Roosevelt surprised them all. Pehle excitedly called Morgenthau the next day to make sure the secretary had heard the news. Roosevelt had been asked about free ports, and he responded that he liked the idea but not the name and his administration was working on it. Lest Morgenthau think the president might have only been referring to overseas camps, Pehle had already checked the transcript, and "he clearly gave a good boost for the free ports."

Morgenthau and Pehle met with the president on June 1 in the early afternoon. Roosevelt was willing to bring a thousand refugees to the United States if Pehle could find a camp for them but would publicly emphasize that most refugees would be cared for elsewhere. Pehle presented Roosevelt with a list of synonyms for "free port," because the president had indicated his dislike for the phrase. After skimming the list, which included "Station of Safety (SOS)," "Liberation Camp," "Wartime Protection Depot," and "V-Camp," Roosevelt settled on "Emergency Refugee Shelter," because "it connoted the temporary character of the refugees' stay in the United States and also because the word 'shelter' is an honest word and that we won't be able to provide much more than shelter."

Assistant Secretary of War John McCloy arrived at Henry Morgenthau's house early the next morning. The two men often traveled to work together, and on the way they discussed abandoned army camps that could house refugees. At lunchtime, McCloy called to say that the War Refugee Board could have a camp; he just wasn't sure which one yet. Roosevelt clearly wanted to move quickly. At another press conference that morning, he "revealed that consideration is being given to the possible use of an army camp area no longer needed by the military as a temporary haven in this country for refugees." Morgenthau could only advise McCloy, "You better get it, that's all."

An hour later, they had it. Fort Ontario, in Oswego, New York, would become their emergency rescue shelter. As soon as he hung up with McCloy, Morgenthau called the White House to ask the secretary to inform the president that after "twenty-four hours and twenty minutes . . . the War Department has just notified me that they have room for a thousand refugees at Fort Ontario."

Morgenthau called Pehle into his office to show him Fort Ontario on the map, describing it as a nice place with "a good climate." Pehle pushed Morgenthau to ensure the draft message to Congress and draft cables reached the president's briefcase before Roosevelt left town that afternoon. When Morgenthau called his expectations unrealis-

Thirty-five-year-old John Pehle, newly appointed as the War Refugee Board's director, had no humanitarian relief experience but believed that the U.S. government could rescue Jews from Nazi persecution. March 1944.

After the *Kristallnacht* pogrom in Nazi Germany, Jews in Los Angeles protested the Nazis and expressed their support for increased aid to refugees. Circa November 1938.

Frustrated by the U.S. government's inaction, hundreds of Orthodox rabbis marched on the Capitol on October 6, 1943.

President Franklin Roosevelt, already seriously ill, campaigned for a fourth term with his good friend Treasury secretary Henry Morgenthau Jr. Morgenthau constantly worried his ambitious plans would annoy the president. November 1944.

Secretary of State Cordell Hull, Undersecretary Sumner Welles, and Assistant Secretary Breckinridge Long (left to right) at a meeting in Hull's office in 1942. Long and his staff were deeply suspicious of Jewish relief organizations and obstructed their efforts.

AMERICA'S LARGEST
ANGLO-JEWISH
WEEKLY

The Sentinel

DEVOTED TO
UNITY
IN JEWISH LIFE

Vol. CXXXIII, No. 4   Thursday, January 27, 1944   Price 10c per Copy—$4.00 a year

F. D. R. CREATES U.S. RESCUE BOARD

Roosevelt Announces Formation of War Refugee Board to Rescue Nazi Victims

Washington (JPS)—The formation of a War Refugee Board to undertake concrete action to rescue "the civilian victims of enemy savagery" was announced by President Roosevelt. Although the executive order which authorized the board did not mention the Jews specifically, the White House statement announcing the step placed the Jews on the top of the list of those whose rescue the new body is to effect.

The board is to consist of the Secretaries of State, the Treasury and War, and will have the services of a full-time paid executive. In addition, "the board, within the limits of funds which may be made available, may employ necessary personnel without regard for civil service laws and regulations." The board will co-operate with the Inter-governmental Refugee Committee and with the United Nations Relief and Rehabilitation Administration as well as with interested foreign governments.

"The personnel, supplies, facilities and services of the State, Treasury and War Departments" are to be util-

ministrative Council of the organization, declared that the President's action is "an important initial step in the direction of saving the remnants of European Jewry who are threatened with extermination in the path of the retreating Nazi hordes." He added that "it is the hope of American Jews that the new board set up by President Roosevelt will be given 'teeth' and the power to put into force a truly effective program on an international scale."

Claims Committee Policy "Puts Up No Defense"

New York (JPS) — The charge that the American Jewish Committee had "consciously" adopted a policy to "put up no defense" against anti-Semitic libels, in the "four crucial years of fascist expansion in this country, from 1937 to the summer of 1941," is made by Joseph Brainin, an editorial adviser of The Protestant, a monthly.

Writing in the January issue of the

FDR Praises Refugee Aid as Patriotic

New York (JPS) — In a letter read at the annual meeting of the National Refugee Service, President Roosevelt spoke with high praise of the agency's "outstanding service in this patriotic and human cause." The letter was addressed to William Rosenwald, retiring president of the organization.

Mr. Rosenwald reported that 260,000 refugees were admitted into the United States since 1933. He declared that "the Government showed its good will by issuing more than 500,000 visas to refugees. Actually, less than half of the total visas issued were used. Nevertheless, the very fact that they were granted affords evidence of the Government's hospitable policy."

Joseph E. Beck, executive director

of the organization, stated that "under a liberal interpretation of present laws, thousands of additional persons could have come into the country, and if there is a desire and will to give broad interpretation, these and other thousands may still be able to enter." He reported on the absorption of refugees in the war effort which led to a paring down of the agency's relief roll, pointed to the thousands that have entered the armed forces, and discussed a program for "the newcomers of the future," who will "require temporary relief and other economic assistance, at least for a minimal period."

Mr. Rosenwald was elected honorary president; Mr. Charles A. Riegelman, president; Richard S. Goldman, treasurer; Richard P. Limburg, assistant treasurer, and Stanley M. Isaacs, secretary. Prof. Joseph P. Chamberlain of Columbia University was re-elected chairman of the board of directors.

INTENSIFY DRIVE FOR FUNDS TO FIGHT POLIO IN COUNTY

A concentrated drive throughout the city and suburban towns will mark the closing days of the $500,000 fund-raising campaign of the Cook County

income. Persons stricken by polio are given medical and hospital care in private hospitals. Some of the epidemic cases are still being treated in these

Front page of the Chicago Jewish community newspaper *The Sentinel,* January 27, 1944, announcing the War Refugee Board, the official American response to the Holocaust.

Albert Abrahamson, Josiah DuBois, and John Pehle (left to right) meet in Pehle's office at the Treasury Department, March 1944. The staff juggled relief and rescue projects in dozens of countries.

Florence Hodel, the lone female assistant executive director of the WRB, ran the agency's daily operations in 1945. This portrait was taken in Los Angeles a few days before V-E Day. May 1945.

A secretary took this photo of Iver Olsen in his office in Stockholm, Sweden, and described him as "busy as a little bee." Olsen was a War Refugee Board representative, a Treasury attaché, and an OSS spy. September 1944.

As the representative of the American Jewish Joint Distribution Committee (JDC) in Switzerland, Saly Mayer had a large budget for relief and rescue. He also became entangled in ransom negotiations with the Nazis. Circa 1946.

Marjorie and Roswell McClelland in Rome in 1940. Four years later, while living in Switzerland and completely surrounded by Axis-occupied territory, Ross became the WRB's youngest representative, the only one who had witnessed Jews being deported.

Roswell McClelland was likely the first American to read details about killing operations at the Auschwitz-Birkenau death camp. As he read the reports, he calculated the number of Jews gassed there. Circa summer 1944.

The first group of Romanian children evacuated through Turkey arrives in Palestine in spring 1944, thanks to WRB representative Ira Hirschmann's success in breaking the "Bulgarian bottleneck."

Ira Hirschmann's identity paperwork while on his way to Turkey as a citizen noncombatant, issued January 27, 1944. Although he is listed as a member of the State Department's staff, he was actually an executive at Bloomingdale's department store.

Hundreds of Romanian and Bulgarian Jewish passengers hang off the sides of the *Selahattin,* the last refugee boat to reach Istanbul in 1944. Herbert Katzki, Hirschmann's partner in Turkey, sent this photograph to John Pehle. October 29, 1944.

The WRB spearheaded a propaganda campaign to draw public support for refugee camps in the United States. In early August 1944, 982 refugees arrived at the Fort Ontario emergency refugee shelter in Oswego, New York, the only group brought to the United States for humanitarian reasons.

Since the WRB could not place staff in Budapest directly, Sweden agreed to send businessman Raoul Wallenberg to rescue and provide relief for Hungarian Jews. This photo appears on Wallenberg's visa application. June 10, 1944.

After the Arrow Cross coup in Hungary in October 1944, Raoul Wallenberg frantically issued makeshift protective papers like these to save Jews from deportation. October 31, 1944.

A Holocaust survivor, recently liberated from Dachau, holds a Red Cross food package. The WRB sent 300,000 food packages from the United States and gave the International Red Cross the trucks, tires, and gasoline to deliver them to concentration camps in the final weeks of the war. April/May 1945.

tic, Pehle responded, "One reason these things go so far is that we ask unreasonable things, that is all. Of course they are unreasonable."

After a few minutes with Pehle, Morgenthau summoned the War Refugee Board staff and made a short speech: "I just wanted to tell you all how pleased I am at the way you people have been working so hard in the last month to take care of the refugees in this country, and you have actually accomplished that. I think you all ought to feel a personal satisfaction. As you know, it is very nice for America not to be high and mighty and tell the rest of the world what to do, and demonstrate themselves, and set an example. So I am very happy. I want to thank each and every one of you." After the group filed out, Pehle and DuBois remained. If the drafts weren't possible for the weekend, they would be ready when the president returned on Monday. Morgenthau was not worried at all about Roosevelt now: "He has had a mental block on this thing . . . Suddenly, it clears; he is satisfied; he goes overboard a hundred percent. I would let her ride."

On June 8, two days after D-day, and after briefing Ira Hirschmann on the Joel Brand ransom proposal, John Pehle met with Roosevelt again, who immediately asked how soon he could officially announce the new "Emergency Refugee Shelter." As soon as he wanted to, Pehle answered, and handed over all the draft memos. Roosevelt read them carefully, made a quick addition—for the refugees to receive medical exams—and signed them. He was particularly pleased with the selected location, one he remembered well from his days campaigning there, and declared, "Fort Ontario is my camp. I know the fort very well. It . . . is a very excellent place." He would announce the camp at his press conference the next day. Roosevelt was also interested to hear about the Nazi ransom offer, agreeing that negotiations should remain open.

At 11:15 a.m. on June 9, it was official. The United States would welcome a thousand refugees from the Mediterranean area to Fort Ontario in Oswego, New York. Pehle, who couldn't attend, had someone read him the press conference transcript over the phone. He then wrote a letter to Samuel Grafton: "I can't let this great day go by without thanking you for your Free Port pieces and for the support you obtained for us."

The "Message from the President of the United States Notifying the Congress That Arrangements Have Been Made to Care for
Approximately 1,000 Refugees in the United States" included a sentence that survived intact from Pehle's initial draft. It was an appropriate summary of the board's work and motivation for the trials ahead:
"In the face of this attitude of our enemies, we must not fail to take
full advantage of any opportunity, however limited, for the rescue of
Hitler's victims."

The War Refugee Board had its camp, but it did not yet have its thousand refugees. On June 19, Leonard Ackermann went to Italy to find
them.

The next two weeks were a blur of small towns, larger cities, dirt
roads, endless questions, and bedbugs so vicious that Ackermann
joked he deserved a Purple Heart. Thousands of refugees were spread
throughout Allied-occupied Italy—some in camps, but many not—
and Ackermann assembled a team of assistants immediately, because
the ship the War Department had arranged would leave in less than
a month. Ackermann traveled with Captain Lewis Korn, who had
been the assistant director of the Gila River War Relocation Center for Japanese Americans before reassignment to the Ferramonti
displaced persons camp in Italy. The two men planned a seven-day,
three-hundred-mile journey, which Ackermann called his "flying
motor tour," from Bari circling down the heel of Italy to Santa Maria
di Bagni, up to Taranto, and ending in Ferramonti. Sir Clifford
Heathcote-Smith, a British representative of the IGC, interviewed
refugees in Naples and Rome. Others headed north, to Salerno, Cam-
pagna, and Potenza.

The experience was, Ackermann later wrote to his family, "one of
the most interesting jobs that I have ever had." He tried fresh figs for
the first time, spent three days in the hospital with a suspected case of
appendicitis, and slept on straw and on the beach. Ackermann and
Korn collected three thousand names for the one thousand available
slots and interviewed hundreds of applicants, trying to answer all their
questions—mainly about whether the refugees could remain in the
United States after the war—and dealt with criticism from Zionist

groups that were encouraging refugees to wait for Palestine instead. While examining identity papers, Ackermann saw a German passport stamped with a red *J* for the first time. In his letters, he reminded his family that the people he met had been the lucky ones.

"It has been one of the most difficult and heartrending jobs that I have ever undertaken," Ackermann wrote to Pehle. "It was necessary in a number of cases to be hard and say 'no' where it would have been merciful and proper to say 'yes' . . . I only wish we could have taken more." Ackermann and Korn selected 778 refugees in the end, with half coming from either Santa Maria di Bagni or Ferramonti. They privileged those in refugee camps rather than those living freely and turned down Yugoslav partisans and men of military age to avoid criticism in America. The rest of the refugees mainly came from Rome, though Heathcote-Smith had not been as concerned with appearances and selected some young men. (He also created his own application forms, leaving a frustrated Ackermann to wait in line for five hours to call Rome for additional information about certain refugees.) In total, they identified 982 persons, mostly in family groups. Fourteen nationalities were represented, and 918 of the refugees were Jewish. Right before the *Henry Gibbins,* an army hospital ship, prepared to leave Italy for New York, a late addition joined the refugee roster: little Harry Maurer, quickly nicknamed "International Harry," was born in a jeep on the way to the dock.

Captain Korn accompanied the refugees to America, joined on the ship by Dr. Ruth Gruber, a representative from the Department of the Interior who had made it to Italy just before the ship sailed and became a constant advocate for the refugees. Aboard the *Henry Gibbins,* surrounded by wounded Allied soldiers, the refugees fought seasickness, then cautiously got to know one another. Gruber lugged a chalkboard out onto the deck and taught English, quickly assisted by some of the more able-bodied soldiers. The refugee children poked a wiggly dessert they soon learned was called Jell-O, and the adults, a few of whom had been professional entertainers before the war, put on a concert for their fellow passengers. The *Henry Gibbins* steamed into Hoboken on August 3, 1944. The refugees excitedly waved at the Statue of Liberty, disembarked, and were showered with delousing powder, which destroyed some of the clothes they had brought with them. They then boarded an overnight train, arriving at their new home in Oswego on August 5.

The War Refugee Board had little to do with Fort Ontario once the refugees arrived. For the next eighteen months, the War Relocation Authority took charge. The children attended the local public schools, started scout troops, and made friends with American classmates. The adults learned English and set up small businesses within the camp, catering to the other internees. The Justice Department denied all requests for overnight leave to reunite with family members who had immigrated before the war; the refugees had not legally entered the United States and were not free. John Pehle never visited Oswego nor met any of the refugees whose lives had been changed forever by his War Refugee Board.

Whether to Bomb,
Whether to Ransom

ROSWELL MCCLELLAND DIDN'T RECEIVE any of the War
Refugee Board's weekly reports in the busy summer of 1944. It
would be October before he read his first one; until then, he knew little
about the War Refugee Board beyond his own work and not much
more about the rest of the war, either. He learned about the establishment of Fort Ontario when the rest of the world did, after the War Refugee Board sent the announcement to embassies abroad. Likely due to
concerns over the secrecy of cable traffic, John Pehle never briefed him
on the Joel Brand ransom proposal. Like all Americans inside Switzerland, Ross speculated endlessly over the progress of the war beyond
what he could read in (often propagandistic) newspaper dispatches.

The plethora of relief agency workers, who all had contacts in
occupied territory, and the physical proximity of Switzerland to the
enemy meant that McClelland's days were filled with rumor, conjec-
ture, and detail, much more than he could transmit to Washington.
In the Treasury Department, John Pehle examined intelligence pouring in from the WRB's representatives abroad—including whatever
McClelland could send—plus reports and pleas from relief agencies
and ever-present war news. The War Refugee Board spent the equivalent of a clerk's yearly salary each month sending cables back and forth
to Europe (about $3,000), yet clear communication remained elusive.

Because the board acted as a conduit between relief organization
headquarters in America and their overseas workers, messages snaked
circuitously through the board's offices. Riegner would hand a message

off to McClelland, who would transmit it by cable to the WRB, which would mail it to the World Jewish Congress's New York offices, which then turned around and contacted the WRB to ask about whatever Riegner needed. The system seemed convoluted, but Pehle figured that any requests from overseas should have the approval of the relief agency's leadership, so even when messages explicitly stated, "Please contact the WRB," board staff forwarded them on without comment.

Ross McClelland forwarded one such cable on June 2, 1944, from Isaac Sternbuch to the Union of Orthodox Rabbis' offices in New York. The four-page message took eight days to reach the board's offices, arriving on June 10. Pehle mailed it to New York two days later, marking it "very confidential."

In the middle of the fourth paragraph on the second page—after urging more pressure to return the deported Vittel prisoners, for the Red Cross to visit Bergen-Belsen, and for more protective papers in Hungary—Sternbuch included a request that has come to dominate any discussion of the United States and the Holocaust: to bomb the rail lines near Munkács, Kaschau, and Prešov, the route to Auschwitz. "It is urgently requested . . . that airmail be sent to the towns," Sternbuch wrote; "15,000 Jews per day are deported to Poland over this route since May 15th . . . It is requested that you intervene and not miss another hour in this matter as this is one means of rescue."

McClelland noted the bombing suggestion before forwarding the message to Washington. Sternbuch shared copies of the original pleas from his underground contacts, along with an explanation of the codes they used ("Speditionkomplikation" meant the destruction of rail lines), but stated that these were just for McClelland's information because "the necessary steps, being most urgent, have already been made by Colonel Duti Jonge and by Mr. Jellinek of the English Embassy." A few days later, McClelland scribbled a note: "De Jonge [Alfred de Jonge, the American legation's military attaché] tells me Kashau-Presov RR line has been bombed—Sternbuch says no, at least not up to 2 days ago. I referred him to Mr. Jellinek of the British."

On June 18, Rabbi Jacob Rosenheim of Agudas Israel (a partner organization to the Union of Orthodox Rabbis) sent identical letters to Secretaries Hull, Morgenthau, and Stimson pleading for action "paralyzing the rail-road traffic from Hungary to Poland, especially by an aerial bombardment of the most important railway junctions of KASCHAU and PRESOV, through which the deportation-trains pass. By such a procedure, precious time would be won and thousands of human lives preserved."

A week later, on June 24, John Pehle spoke with Assistant Secretary of War John McCloy about Rosenheim's request, making it clear that he did not endorse the idea in any way. "I had several doubts about the matter," he dictated to his secretary after the conversation, "namely, 1) whether it would be appropriate to use military planes and personnel for this purpose; 2) whether it would be difficult to put the railroad line out of commission for a long enough period to do any good; and 3) even assuming that this railroad line were put out of commission for some period of time, whether it would help the Jews in Hungary." McCloy promised to look into the matter.

The final days of June and the first few of July saw a flurry of letters and opinions on the proposal. Just as Pehle spoke with McCloy, Roswell McClelland finished writing his own long cable, pulling together evidence from the Hungarian and Czech underground, from other relief organizations, and from his own research. To visualize the proposal, McClelland had even hired Frank Otten, a refugee architect, to draw a map of Hungary including the railroad lines to Poland.

McClelland began, "No doubt exists now that the majority of the Jewish population east of the Danube especially in northern, northeastern and eastern Hungary has been deported to Poland." He explained in detail the process of ghettoization and the period of deportation, which he believed to have lasted from May 15 to the middle of June, with twelve thousand people crammed each day into cattle cars for the two- or three-day trip to Auschwitz-Birkenau. He listed five railway stretches as possible targets, including between Kaschau (Košice) and Prešov. "It is urged by all sources of this information in Hungary and Slovakia that vital sections of these lines be bombed," he wrote, adding a noncommittal parenthetical: "I am not able to venture an opinion on the utility of this suggestion, which I submit as the proposal of these agencies."

When he received McClelland's cable five days later, Pehle sent a copy to McCloy, asking him to note the sections about bombing the railway lines.

While awaiting McCloy's response, Dr. Benjamin Akzin, a refugee lawyer who worked as a researcher for the WRB, sent his supervisor, Lawrence Lesser, a memo. Without hesitation, Akzin advocated for the wholesale destruction of Auschwitz and Birkenau. Though many prisoners would, of course, be killed in the process, "such Jews are doomed to death anyhow. The destruction of the camps would not change their fate, but it would serve as visible retribution on their murderers and it might save the lives of future victims." Allied failure to bomb, he believed, was "sheer misplaced sentimentality, far more cruel than a decision to destroy these centers."

The head of the World Jewish Congress's Rescue Department, A. Leon Kubowitzki, visited Lesser with the opposite opinion two days later. He could not recommend bombing the gas chambers and crematoriums from the sky, because "the first victims would be the Jews who are gathered in these camps, and such a bombing would be a welcome pretext for the Germans to assert that their Jewish victims have been massacred not by their killers, but by Allied bombings." Instead, the gas chambers should be destroyed from the ground using Russian paratroopers or the Polish underground.

On the Fourth of July, McCloy wrote to Pehle that although the humanitarian motives of the bombing appeal were appreciated, the War Department found the suggestion "impracticable." A bombing maneuver would necessitate "the diversion of considerable air support essential to the success of our forces now engaged in decisive operations and would in any case be of such very doubtful efficacy that it would not amount to a practical project."

John Pehle, still unconvinced that bombing the rail lines—or the camp itself—would aid the Jews of Hungary, and uncertain whether the action would violate the WRB's restriction not to divert military resources, dropped the matter.

In the early summer of 1944, the War Refugee Board staff, the War Department, and Jewish relief organizations in the United States knew very little about the mysterious Auschwitz-Birkenau camp. Though McClelland had spelled the camp names correctly in his cable, the State Department decoders rendered them as "Anachitz (Oswiecin) and Birke Nau" by the time the WRB got the message. Aerial photography of Birkenau, which the U.S. Army Air Force shot during the summer and fall of 1944 while performing reconnaissance on the Buna-Monowitz factories located five miles to the east, would not be discovered and analyzed until the late 1970s. Wartime documents frequently listed the camps separately with all variations of spelling, because the authors often did not know they were connected, nor that Auschwitz and Oświęcim (the Polish name for the nearby town) were the same place. In early July, Kubowitzki wrote that his colleagues were "shocked by Birkenau extermination. Were convinced Birkenau only labor camp." In Switzerland, Roswell McClelland received multiple letters from Isaac Sternbuch, who could not understand why the United States hadn't bombed "Treblinksi . . . Poniatow and Trawniki . . . [and] the well-known places of Oswieciem (Auschwitz), East-Prussia, where the Hungarian Jews are brought and killed by gas." Even if the camps had been spelled correctly, Sternbuch's advice would not have helped: Treblinka, Poniatowa, and Trawniki had all been destroyed by the Nazis in 1943, and the southernmost border of East Prussia was approximately 260 miles north of Auschwitz. Sternbuch felt that if McClelland "as mandatory of Mr. Roosevelt wired and demanded the bombing of these places, they would act quicklier in America."

Around the time he compiled his research about the deportations, Ross McClelland received specific and shocking descriptions of the inner workings of Auschwitz-Birkenau. In late June, Jaromír "Jean" Kopecký, the former Czech delegate to the League of Nations, handed him two reports written by unnamed prisoners who had escaped from Auschwitz, one by two Slovak Jews who had escaped in April after nearly two years there, and the other supposedly by a non-Jewish Polish officer, a major who had been imprisoned for eighteen months. McClelland received the reports in German, and they were extensive—twenty-seven and fifteen pages, respectively, the single-spaced typed text filled with minutiae including the dates and demographics of prisoner arrivals, specific names of prisoners and perpetrators, measurements of camp structures, hand-drawn maps, and sickening details of the process of prisoner arrival, selection, gassing, and the burning of corpses.

On July 6, McClelland sent a sixteen-page cable to the War Refugee Board, by far the longest he would ever send, distilling the information in the two reports. As with his message about deportations, Ross
carefully drafted, edited, reedited, and researched, basing his cable on
a summary he had asked Gerhart Riegner to prepare. He checked the
math contained in the reports, both by hand and with his calculator,
finally advising the WRB that between 1.5 and 1.75 million people had
already been murdered at Auschwitz. At the end of his introduction,
in which he stated plainly that the reports could not be dismissed as
hearsay, McClelland wrote, "For whatever use the WRB considers
it most effective, this report is submitted. When the facilities of the
mails permit, microfilm copies of the two reports in full will be sent."

By the time John Pehle read McClelland's cable, he had already
received two shorter versions of the two reports, a five-page summary
from the Czech government in exile in London and a three-page
cabled summary from Stockholm. Nothing in them affected Pehle's
ambivalence about bombing. In November, he would learn much
more about Auschwitz and change his mind.

Sternbuch's original June 2 cable, which first mentioned bombing the
rail lines to Auschwitz, had also included a "bitter" complaint from
the rabbi of Neutra in Slovakia, who begged for $1 million for his res-
cue work. At first, the Union of Orthodox Rabbis sprang into action
to raise this money, even before contacting the War Refugee Board
about bombing. It petitioned other relief organizations for their funds,
and the JDC asked Saly Mayer to meet with Sternbuch about it. Having sent $100,000 to Sternbuch for the rabbi of Neutra but unable to
gather the other $900,000, an Orthodox representative wrote to the
War Refugee Board on June 23 to "request your Board to designate
from funds under its control, whatever sums necessary to completely
exploit the existent rescue possibilities in these plans submitted." But
despite repeated requests, neither the War Refugee Board, nor Roswell
McClelland, nor even Isaac Sternbuch knew why the rabbi of Neutra
was pleading for so much money; no plans had ever been submitted.

In his cable updating the board, McClelland speculated that the
$1 million could be related to Joel Brand's ransom proposal—which

he had pieced together from rumors—or for the attempted rescue of Orthodox Jews. McClelland knew that the Jewish community of Budapest had already paid the Nazis a $200,000 down payment prior to Joel Brand's departure, and he assumed the subsequent deportations from Hungary were the fault of "over-zealous" Hungarians. The million-dollar request might be intended to deter future deportations. Sternbuch had also hypothesized the rabbi might have intended the money for Slovakia's Jews rather than Hungarian ransom.

Because no one knew for sure and more appeals for money arrived daily, McClelland, Sternbuch, and Mayer decided that Saly Mayer would be the hub for all relief and rescue money for Hungary. To assuage the Orthodox organizations, Mayer had agreed to dedicate all money he received from them to the rescue of the Orthodox community. Ross doubted that anyone would be able to escape Hungary but urged the WRB to plan in case the Nazis offered to release Jews. He also suggested the JDC send Saly Mayer at least $1 million for rescue work. The WRB immediately contacted the JDC, which agreed to come up with $1 million, even if it had to borrow it.

Placing Mayer in charge did not solve the overall confusion regarding relief requests, and on July 17 Ross McClelland was the last to learn of Sternbuch's new scheme. Sternbuch informed Ross that he had promised the Nazis monetary credit to purchase "tractors" in exchange for the lives of twelve hundred Jews who would be spared deportation to Poland. (McClelland thought the Joel Brand offer involved $2 million—not goods or trucks—and he didn't make the connection.) An exasperated McClelland wrote on the memo "First time I have heard of this!" Mayer refused to get involved and Sternbuch appealed to McClelland to intervene. Apparently, twelve hundred rabbis and important religious figures had left Bratislava by train on July 6 for Vienna. Sternbuch believed that if he deposited the money in a Nazi-controlled bank account for the cost of the tractors, the train would go to the Spanish border. Otherwise, the rabbis would go to their deaths in Poland. By the time McClelland learned of the deal, the train had been in limbo for nearly two weeks.

Sternbuch had already offered 1 million Swiss francs so the Nazis could purchase tractors, though neither he nor his organization had access to that amount of money. By the time he informed McClelland,

Sternbuch was hearing warnings through the underground about a deadline: the money within forty-eight hours, or the train would go to Poland. Mayer, ever logical, told McClelland he could not provide funds without knowing where the "1,200 holy men" on the train were, who controlled them, and the details of their journey. Most important, Mayer would not grant any money without a contract guaranteeing the rabbis' release.

Sternbuch couldn't provide any details beyond the payment demands. He couldn't confirm that anyone in the Jewish community beyond the Orthodox endorsed the deal, and he confessed that he wasn't even sure the information about the train was authentic. All Sternbuch had were copies of heartbreaking telegrams, some accusatory: "Are shaken by your irresponsible refusal . . . You bear the responsibility." McClelland, Sternbuch insisted, "must decide immediately . . . since it is too late to put the matter up to Washington. We do not wish to gamble with the lives of 1,200 people." The thirty-year-old War Refugee Board representative finally refused. There just wasn't enough information.

The day after McClelland first learned of Sternbuch's tractor scheme, the WRB in Washington found out about it too, when the Vaad Hatzalah Orthodox agency in New York called. In a telegram sent privately so McClelland wouldn't see it, Sternbuch had complained to his home office about Saly Mayer's stubbornness and asked his colleagues to pressure the War Refugee Board in Washington. McClelland, forced to explain the convoluted scheme to Pehle as he understood it, reported that he was still trying to figure out whether the train existed at all. He had been hounding Sternbuch for any details about this plan—and for that matter, about the rabbi of Neutra's intentions for the $1 million—but had never received clear answers. Instead, "Sternbuch decided recently to pass on to me rather incoherent and desperate appeals." Mayer also heard from his home office in New York: "Sternbuch claims that this group may still be rescued by repatriation if immediate action is taken, and that you have refused to assist in saving them . . . This situation is deeply disturbing to orthodox groups here, which are exerting great pressure on us." Though the War Refugee Board concurred with McClelland's assessment that there was not enough information to agree to the ransom, Ross still felt the need to defend both himself and the JDC representative: "Neither Saly Mayer nor myself have ever refused to grant serious consideration to any objective and acceptable proposal for effecting the rescue of endangered Jews in Hungary . . . Our primary concern has always been not 'It can not be done' but 'How can this be done.' In view of the contradictory and often unreliable nature of many of the proposals of Sternbuch, we have had to handle them with considerable circumspection."

Finally, in August, McClelland gleaned the truth. Sternbuch, through miscommunications and the urgency of coded pleas from Budapest, had conflated two different ransom negotiations. The money for tractors related, of course, to the Nazis' continued demand for trucks from the Joel Brand offer. The 1,200 rabbis and religious leaders were actually 1,690 Hungarian Jews, including rabbis, ransomed out of Budapest by Reszö Kasztner, one of Joel Brand's colleagues in the Vaada. Their train, which became known as the "Kasztner train," left Budapest on July 1 and arrived at the Bergen-Belsen concentration camp on July 8. The Hungarian Jews were there, and relatively safe, long before McClelland ever heard of the supposedly urgent plan.

The Nazis were clearly still willing to make a deal in Hungary. In early August, the War Refugee Board learned about a group of nearly fifty owners and associates of the Manfred Weiss factories in Budapest, one of the largest industrial concerns in Europe, who had landed unannounced in Lisbon in late June. They had turned everything over to the Hermann Göring Werke and paid 1.5 million Swiss francs to buy their own lives. The Weiss family would not meet with any American embassy staff in Lisbon to provide intelligence about Budapest. A few of the family members had been kept behind as Nazi captives to ensure their silence. But the Weiss group served as evidence that the Nazis wanted to eke out every bit of financial gain from their victims—"to pump out the necessary labor from the Jewry of Hungary and sell the balance of valueless human material against goods with value," as one Nazi told Kasztner.

On July 15, Kasztner asked which Allied representative could meet with the enemy. If Brand was not going to return to Hungary, someone else had to negotiate for him.

Joseph Schwartz, the JDC's European director, seemed the logical choice. Schwartz was, in the eyes of the Nazis, the head of an international Jewish conglomerate, and had both the power to make a deal and the money to pay for it. But the British and the State Department quashed the idea almost immediately. The British embassy stated definitively that the Allies should refuse any meetings. Pehle agreed at first, and the State Department cabled orders that Schwartz, as an American citizen, could not meet with any Nazi representatives. Schwartz had already arrived in Lisbon for the negotiations, but when he was briefed, the embassy wrote that he "reluctantly accepts Department's decision."

On August 11, Roswell McClelland picked up his pen and calmly drafted a cable to Washington. He had finally figured out what to do. Even though Joel Brand had failed to return to Budapest, the Jewish community remaining there—the last and largest in occupied Europe—had been collecting money, still trying to make a deal. On this basis, the Nazis were holding 17,290 persons whom they threatened to deport to Auschwitz: the Kasztner group of 1,690 at Bergen-Belsen; 15,000 the Gestapo were said to be keeping "on ice" in Austria; and 600 individuals in Budapest. The meeting with Schwartz was to make a deal for their fates.

Now, with the Allied refusals, the Nazis proposed to meet with Saly Mayer, a Swiss citizen, instead. They promised not to touch the 17,290 prisoners until after the meeting.

McClelland chose his language carefully and fully understood the ramifications of what he was writing: "Saly Mayer should be allowed to meet agents of the Gestapo . . . in an attempt to draw out negotiations and gain as much time as possible, without making commitments . . . In view of the rapidly changing military situation, any time gained is in favor of the endangered Jews."

John Pehle, thousands of miles away in Washington, concurred. Saly Mayer, whose whole experience with the JDC had centered on up-front, law-abiding, by-the-book relief work, nervously accepted the challenge. After the Brand debacle, they all agreed: this time, they would not tell Great Britain or the Soviet Union.

The Horthy Offer

O N JULY 19, 1944, THE *New York Times* printed an article on page 5 titled "Horthy Promises Not to Oust Jews." It was short—only two sentences long—but enough to get the board's attention. It read, in its entirety, "Admiral Nicholas Horthy, Regent of Hungary, has promised the International Red Cross Committee that no more Jews will be transported forcibly out of Hungary, it was learned today, and authorized the committee to direct evacuation of Jewish children to countries willing to receive them. A private informant said Admiral Horthy also authorized the committee to remove any Jews possessing visas to Palestine."

In Bern, someone handed Roswell McClelland a phone message from the Red Cross, a short, handwritten note in a mix of French and English containing a list of concessions the Hungarian government would make to its anti-Jewish policy. While waiting to verify the information, McClelland immediately cabled the WRB to alert it that rumors were flying; the board advised him of the *New York Times* article and asked him to confirm its veracity. The WRB also heard about the offer from London, Ankara, and the Vatican delegation in Washington.

After two anxious days, John Pehle finally received the details via Lisbon. Horthy was willing to concede to various demands. The Swedish government wanted all Jews with relatives or business connections in Sweden to be released to Sweden or Palestine. The Swiss sent a British demand for everyone with Palestine certificates to be released there.

The Swiss had also forwarded the WRB's requests to allow Red Cross access to camps and ghettos and for the release of all Jewish children under ten to go to Palestine. Admiral Horthy also officially suspended the deportations of Hungarian Jews, an order that had actually gone into effect ten days earlier in response to the international psychological warfare campaign—largely commissioned by the WRB—and the Allied bombings of Budapest. (The WRB didn't know it, but Horthy had also just read the Auschwitz reports for the first time.)

The War Refugee Board was hesitant to publicly confirm the new Hungarian offer—the Horthy offer, as it became known—until it figured out how to reply, especially with the leaking of the Joel Brand offer still stinging. But "the whole thing was charged with dynamite," Pehle told one of his staff, and within a matter of days the International Red Cross provided more details to the press. Jewish organizations began pressuring the WRB. Bergson's committee issued a statement calling for Palestine certificates for all Hungarian Jews and implying that the offer had come thanks to its efforts. Publicly, the board remained silent.

The clause at the end of the board's charge, to take all measures to rescue and relieve Nazi victims "consistent with the successful prosecution of the war," was an instruction few were ever tempted to ignore. The war moved quickly in the summer of 1944. Only ten weeks after storming the beaches of Normandy, Allied forces liberated Paris. Victory was not achieved, however, without sacrifice. Nearly fifty thousand American soldiers were killed in Europe between June and August 1944—husbands, sons, brothers, uncles, neighbors, teachers, high school crushes, friends, all gone. Everyone knew someone who lost a loved one. By summer's end, Herbert Lehman, the head of UNRRA, had lost his son Peter. Oscar Cox lost his younger brother, Ben. The former ambassador Joseph Kennedy lost his eldest son, Joe junior. Harry Hopkins's nineteen-year-old son, Stephen, died. Josiah DuBois's younger brother bided time in a German prisoner of war camp. Ambassador John Winant's eldest son and namesake remained the personal hostage of Nazi-SS chief Heinrich Himmler. All four of President Roosevelt's sons were in uniform, as were both of Vice President Wallace's and both of Henry Morgenthau's. As the press announced the new War Refugee Board on January 22, John Pehle's younger brother, Richard, a member of the 180th Infantry, had stormed ashore at Anzio.

Prioritizing the lives of European Jews over American soldiers, therefore, was a nonstarter. Many of the ideas that came across John Pehle's desk might save a few dozen here, a few hundred there, playing for time and keeping people alive until the liberating armies came. The sixteen million Americans in uniform and their Allied counterparts were undertaking the largest rescue effort, not the War Refugee Board, and the only guaranteed way to end the mass murder of Jews was total military victory in Europe. The first war always took precedence over the second.

Yet in July 1944, John Pehle prepared to take his largest gamble yet, one almost entirely forgotten now. If it had worked, the plan might have crossed the line, diverted war resources, and possibly prolonged the war. It also might have saved the lives of the remaining Jews of Hungary. All of them.

Hungary had always represented the War Refugee Board's best chance to save the most lives, the biggest potential return on investment. The WRB believed at least some portion of the population rejected the occupying forces, and there were still plenty of Hungarians who hadn't yet participated in any deportations or atrocities. Perhaps the board could convince those people that with Axis defeat looming on the horizon, becoming a war criminal wasn't the best idea.

Yet after Roosevelt's March 1944 condemnation of mass murder and the subsequent publicity, none of the political and religious figures the WRB recruited for its psychological warfare campaign garnered the same attention. By the end of May, the Office of War Information wasn't broadcasting anything about Nazi persecution, despite a reminder that deportations were beginning in Hungary. A spokesman claimed it was waiting for the WRB's "big guns." Pehle did his best. At his request, the archbishop of New York, Francis Cardinal Spellman, wrote a statement invoking the Hungarian hero Saint Stephen and expressing his shock "that a people with such profound Christian faith . . . would join in a hymn of hatred and willingly submit to the blood lust and brigandage of tyranny." The First Magyar Reformed

Church in New York City, on East Sixty-Ninth Street, invited five hundred Protestants, Jews, and Catholics to wear Star of David armbands during a special service of intercession, which the OWI recorded and played over the BBC into Hungary. Both the Senate Foreign Relations and the House Foreign Affairs Committees unanimously denounced the persecution of Hungarian Jews, as did Cordell Hull, who blasted the puppet Hungarian government, which "by its servile adoption of the worst features of the Nazi racial policy stands condemned before history."

Outside the United States, others joined in the board's appeal to conscience. The World Council of Churches in Geneva urged all Christians to remember they "dare not remain silent" in the face of such sin. The king of Sweden wrote a personal plea to Horthy, because, as a Stockholm newspaper declared, "all neutrality ceases to exist in face of these deliberate and cold blooded crimes against defenseless and innocent people." The War Refugee Board nudged the Vatican, and soon thereafter Pope Pius XII addressed an open telegram, asking Horthy to assist the "many unfortunate people who are suffering because of their race or nationality."

If the Hungarian leadership would not listen to the United States, an enemy combatant, perhaps they would listen to the neutral nations of Portugal, Spain, Turkey, Switzerland, and Sweden, all of which had diplomatic personnel on the ground in Budapest. Leveraging the stature of a superpower soon to be victorious in a world war, the War Refugee Board staff approached these countries for help.

Pehle reached out to Portugal first. Dr. Robert Dexter, a doltish and disagreeable Unitarian minister and aid worker, was the board's Lisbon representative, selected for the same reason Ira Hirschmann was chosen from Turkey: the board needed someone, and Pehle happened to meet Dexter. Had Pehle investigated Dexter, the WRB might have chosen differently. Dexter had been in Lisbon for most of the war (though he still spoke no Portuguese) and, once imbued with power as a representative of the American government, played favorites with the relief agencies to such an extent that one of the board's assistant executive directors, James Mann, had to fly to Portugal to negotiate a truce. Dexter spent his days, as Mann put it, fussing with the refugees in Lisbon, rather than opening rescue channels, and busily paraphrasing incoming and outgoing cables into incoherency.

The WRB, therefore, worked with the Lisbon embassy directly regarding Hungary. At the board's request, Portuguese officials promised to warn Hungary against deportations and to forward any information about the treatment of Jews. In late May, Pehle asked Portugal to increase its diplomatic presence in Budapest, because "the lives of 800,000 human beings in Hungary may well depend on the restraint that may result from the presence in that country of the largest possible number of foreign observers." But Ambassador R. Henry Norweb advised against the request. Two months earlier, after the Nazi invasion, the State Department had urged the Portuguese government to distance itself from the new Hungarian regime. To turn around and pressure it to send more staff, therefore, would be contradictory. For Pehle, Portugal was a dead end.

Due to Ambassador Carlton Hayes's intransigence, the War Refugee Board never had a representative in Spain. Hayes had refused to allow Pehle to appoint David Blickenstaff, and three other options Pehle proposed also fell through. Pehle's requests for the Spanish government to warn Hungary and to increase its diplomatic personnel were met with silence. Finally, in June, Hayes reported what he was sure would be good news: according to him, Spanish diplomats in Hungary reported that deportation rumors "happily far outstripped the actualities" and the Nazis seemed too preoccupied with waging war to be sidetracked by mass murder. He refused to forward the board's request for Spain to increase its diplomatic presence in Budapest. Pehle, fed up with the ambassador's antagonism, complained to Cordell Hull that because of Hayes the War Refugee Board had lost valuable time.

Over the summer, the War Refugee Board's contact with Spain improved dramatically, in part because Carlton Hayes wasn't there. Facing public accusations that he was hampering the board's relief efforts, the State Department recalled Hayes for consultation. (There's no direct evidence the board leaked its difficulties with Hayes to the press, but plenty of smoke. Hayes certainly blamed Pehle and loudly vented his frustration at him over several meetings.) Left in charge in Madrid, the American chargé d'affaires began forwarding all the WRB's bottled-up requests to the Spanish government officials who already knew what was coming. A wealthy businessman, Dannie Heineman—who happened to share a plane with James Mann, on his way to deal with Robert Dexter—snuck the Spanish Foreign Office a list of the WRB's requests even before the embassy began transmitting them.

The WRB had also—finally—managed to evacuate 573 refugees out of Spain and into Fedhala, fulfilling its promise to the Spanish government. The British, tasked with transporting the refugees by ship to North Africa, had announced four different sailing dates over a four-month period, only to cancel all of them. After the British claimed the ship for the planned June 7 voyage needed repairs and would not be available, Hayes griped that the Spanish government might soon re-imprison the refugees if they didn't leave soon. The real reason for the so-called repairs became clear when hundreds of Allied ships descended upon the beaches of Normandy.

Blickenstaff, forced to deal with the logistics of moving more than five hundred anxious and frustrated refugees, finally corralled them from all over Spain to Cádiz, an ancient port city on a narrow peninsula. On June 21, everyone gathered on the docks, where a boat waited, one obtained by a War Shipping Administration official once the United States finally stopped listening to British excuses. Blickenstaff's wife, Janine, stood off to the side by their car, patiently waiting for her promised week of vacation in southern Spain as soon as the refugees left.

At the last minute, the ship's captain called Blickenstaff over. His men had found lice on twenty-two of the refugees, and those passengers could not under any circumstances board his vessel. The infested few sat helplessly on the dock in a bureaucratic no-man's-land—according to their documents, they had already exited Spain—watching Blickenstaff argue on their behalf. Finally, defeated and exhausted, Blickenstaff arranged for delousing, then for the smaller group's passage on a French freighter leaving from Algeciras the following week. He found a bus and gasoline and, instead of his vacation, embarked on a fourteen-hour ride to Algeciras, only to have the mayor of the town refuse to allow them to stay in his city longer than twenty-four hours.

They returned to Cádiz, waited another week, boarded the bus again back to Algeciras, and finally left.

At Fedhala, the reunited refugees, comprising twenty-two nationalities (and some legally "stateless"), settled into stone buildings and canvas tents, trying to adjust to the windswept dirt and dust that invaded every crevice. The desolate camp, with its communal kitchens and makeshift cisterns created from metal trash cans, was a far cry from life in Spain, but it spelled safety, especially for the Sephardic Jews who had been released from Bergen-Belsen to join the transport. The refugees made the best of things. Some played chess, dominoes, or cards; others organized social events, opened schools, or worked in the carpentry shop to help UNRRA staff fix things around the camp.

Within weeks of their arrival, Moses Beckelman, the camp's director, suggested closing Fedhala entirely: it was a waste of money, and the refugees could be transferred to other camps in North Africa. Pehle insisted it stay open, writing that Beckelman's proposal "indicates that he is unaware of the Horthy offer." Closing the camp "might well prove tragic in its consequences, for in the eyes of the Hungarian Government it might easily throw open to question the sincerity of the British and American Governments' professed willingness to receive on United Nations' territory Jews and other victims of enemy oppression."

In their meetings in Washington, Fedhala was one of the only topics Pehle and Hayes agreed upon: it had to remain open, if only to receive any Jews released by Horthy or by Nazi Germany. After Hayes's return to Madrid in August, he reported on the progress made in his absence (and because of it): the Spanish were issuing even more letters of protection in Budapest, had warned the Hungarians against atrocities, and promised to issue Spanish entry visas to relatives of Americans, in case this would add any measure of protection.

Turkey was next. In early May 1944, before the War Refugee Board could make any request of its government to put pressure on Hungary, Ambassador Steinhardt had done some investigating on his own. After noticing that so few Hungarians were arriving on refugee boats, he asked the Turkish Foreign Office, which confided "that every Jew entering the Turk consulate in Budapest was arrested as soon as he left and transported to an unknown place." After the War Refugee Board made its formal appeal for intercession with Hungary's leadership, the Turkish government apologetically explained why it could not assist. First, at the request of the Allies, Turkey had decreased its sale of strategic war matériel to Hungary. Second, the Turkish government was hiding the deposed Hungarian prime minister, Miklós Kállay, and his family in its Budapest embassy. With the relationship between the two nations so fraught, Turkey felt unable to assist further.

Switzerland, as the American protecting power in Hungary, served as conduit for the WRB's many formal protests against deportations and atrocities. In addition, the WRB made the same requests of Switzerland as it had with the other neutrals, with mixed results. The Swiss Foreign Office passed along a great deal of information, both officially and in confidential meetings, about conditions on the ground in Budapest. But when Pehle asked Switzerland to increase its diplomatic presence there, the Foreign Office said no, for fear of violating the country's all-important neutrality. The Swiss Foreign Office felt the Nazis and Hungarians would view a diplomatic increase as a sign of pro-Allied espionage. The excuse was a good one, and Pehle didn't push back. The United States depended on Switzerland to remain neutral to maintain communication lines with the enemy and to protect American interests, property, and the thousands of American POWs held by the Axis forces.

Sweden had no such qualms. In late May 1944, after the War Refugee Board asked Sweden to pass along any information about the situation in Budapest, to warn Hungary, and to increase diplomatic representation, all three suggestions were immediately accepted. The Swedish Foreign Office provided the War Refugee Board with detailed reports from its Budapest legation, including demographic data, descriptions of new legal restrictions, and details of how and where Jews were being rounded up and sent to Auschwitz. Per Anger, a Swedish diplomat on leave from Budapest, described witnessing Hungarian police assisting in the deportations of Jews gathered in brickyards near Budapest; the War Refugee Board used this information to register another formal protest through Switzerland. The board even received a reminder that Sweden served as protecting power for Iran, and if the United States could persuade Tehran to make a formal request, Swedish diplomats would issue Iranian protective papers in Budapest.

Most of the WRB's information from Sweden came via its intrepid representative, Iver Olsen. Olsen, who had immigrated to the United States from Norway as a child, was a daring and mischievous guy with an easy smile, willing to take chances and disinclined to seek permission. He simply didn't have the time or desire to dither over details. To Pehle, Olsen held the three most important qualifications for a WRB representative: he was a Treasury employee, already in the right country, and a friend.

Olsen had arrived in Stockholm in December 1943 to serve as the legation's financial attaché, but this wasn't his only job. As an OSS spy, code-named Crispin (or the less interesting No. 799), Olsen monitored the movement of money and war matériel between Sweden and Nazi Germany. He officially added "War Refugee Board representative" to his list of duties in early April; to the OSS, he went to work for Garbo, its code name for the WRB.

After the board asked Sweden to increase diplomatic representation, it soon learned that a Swedish businessman, already planning a trip to Hungary, might be willing to act in that capacity. Olsen may have first met him in an elevator; Raoul Wallenberg's import company offices were a few floors above Olsen's at Strandvägen 7A, a prestigious address in the heart of Stockholm. Descended from a prominent banking family, Wallenberg was thirty-one, spoke fluent English—thanks to a University of Michigan education—and had already traveled several times to wartime Budapest for business. He was thoughtful, ambitious, a born organizer, and willing to take great personal risk. After an all-night dinner at the Grand Hotel in Saltsjöbaden, Wallenberg agreed to take the job.

The Swedish government planned to appoint him an attaché to the Budapest delegation. If the Hungarian government protested, the Swedish Foreign Office would refuse to recognize the newly arrived Hungarian chargé d'affaires in Stockholm. "In making this assignment," Ambassador Herschel Johnson wrote, Sweden "feels it has cooperated fully in lending all possible facilities for the furtherance of an American program . . . The newly designated attaché, Raoul Wallenberg, feels . . . that he, in effect, is carrying out a humanitarian mission in behalf of the War Refugee Board. Consequently he would like full instructions as to the line of activities he is authorized to carry out and assurances of adequate financial support for these activities so that he will be in a position to develop fully all local possibilities." Due to cable traffic delays, Johnson had to make this request four times before the board finally sent guidance for Wallenberg on July 7. By then, Wallenberg was already on his way to Budapest.

Wallenberg wasn't an American citizen or an official representative of the United States, so John Pehle wrote ambitious instructions, arranging $50,000 for his projects (out of the budget for the still-idle *Tari*). Wallenberg could offer bribes, "since money and favorable post-war conditions might motivate action," and should be creative, try to visit concentration camps, and establish partnerships with prominent Hungarians, with the Roman Catholic Church, and with the International Red Cross.

Though the WRB didn't know it, by the time Raoul Wallenberg arrived in Budapest on July 9, Horthy had already ordered the official end to mass deportations from Hungary. This certainly did not stop the persecution, nor the rounding up, internment, and deportation of smaller groups, and Budapest's Jews lived on edge, their fates up for negotiation between Horthy's government, the Nazis, and the Allies. Because Sweden, Switzerland, and the War Refugee Board had been demanding the release of children, those with Palestine certificates, and those with ties to Sweden, Horthy offered these groups first.

After learning the details of the Horthy offer in late July, John Pehle insisted that the United States immediately respond with unconditional acceptance. The Intergovernmental Committee leadership agreed that the Allies had to answer as quickly as possible but worried about gaining the approval of all thirty-two member countries and about financing any evacuations.

The British government, however, stalled. It obsessed over hypothetical havens for the Hungarian Jews who might be permitted to leave. Sure, those with Palestine certificates could go there, but if Hungary expanded the offer, other released Jews needed a place to go. On July 26, a week after the offer hit the press, the British embassy wrote it would consider three possibilities: the United States, Latin America, or Angola, if Portugal would give permission to use the colony. British territory was not an option, nor was Palestine. It wanted to coordinate any official response through the cumbersome IGC.

The International Red Cross, which had originally received the offer, began panicking at the long delays: Did the United States and Great Britain not realize that lives were at stake? Horthy could change his mind at any time, and the Nazis could blame the Allies for any further atrocities, because they had their chance to save people. By the end of July, neither the United States nor Great Britain had publicly acknowledged the offer, much less responded.

On July 29, ten days after the *New York Times* article announcing the offer, John Pehle sent draft text to Stettinius at the State Department. Horthy had issued a direct challenge to the Allies and the United States needed to give a forceful answer. Pehle wanted to "accept completely and unequivocally the Hungarian proposal without any limitation as to numbers." No IGC, no categories, no worrying about where to send people. Pehle attached a draft cable to Switzerland, asking the Red Cross to inform the Hungarian government that the United States "will arrange for the care of all Jews permitted to leave Hungary who reach neutral or United Nations' territory, and will find for such people havens of refuge where they may live in safety."

In short, the United States would offer to take *all* the Hungarian Jews, if Horthy would release them. Some could join the refugees at Fedhala, and Pehle would figure out destinations for the others later. At the time he wrote his response, more than 200,000 Jews remained, centered in Budapest, and moving them all to neutral territory would certainly divert military resources and possibly prolong the war, something John Pehle was expressly forbidden to do. Still he wanted them all.

The State Department informed the International Red Cross that America would officially deliver its answer no later than August 7. The British had until then to opt in.

The British embassy asked if the United States would consider delaying its response until August 11, because the War Cabinet wanted to discuss the matter. The War Refugee Board agreed, but the new deadline was firm, and the British had to accept the offer entirely. The United States would not budge and would not change the tone or substance of the answer. Perhaps unsurprisingly, the War Cabinet meeting could not arrive at a decision; some officials warned the offer might be "a plot by the Germans to break up the delicate political situation in the Near East by putting there thousands of people who are regarded by the local inhabitants of such places as being undesirable." Pehle didn't understand or care why the British would rather doom Hungarian Jews to death than upset the Arab populations of the Middle East. He held fast.

With one day left before the deadline, the British embassy in Washington announced it would accept the Horthy offer, but only after negotiating the language and terms. It reiterated strong reservations and emphasized that its ability to accommodate refugees was limited, counting on the United States not to force Britain into accepting more people than it wanted. Couldn't the Hungarian Jews go to havens in North Africa or Italy—under the guidance of the IGC, of course—or to Latin America? With some semblance of self-awareness, the British wrote, "It is not thought that reference to the Committee [the IGC] would be interpreted in Axis Europe as a delaying gesture."

On August 11, almost two years to the day after Gerhart Riegner appeared in his office, Howard Elting left the Geneva consulate to deliver the American response to the International Red Cross. The United States fully accepted Horthy's offer, all of it. Jews bearing protective papers could leave; Jewish children under the age of ten would go to Palestine; deportations would officially cease. Moreover, Ambassador Harrison sent a separate memo to the Red Cross to reiterate: "The Government of the United States . . . specifically repeats its assurance that arrangements will be made by it for the care of all Jews who in the present circumstances are allowed to leave Hungary." Though the proposal involved "substantial difficulties and responsibilities," the United States would figure out the bureaucratic details later. Whomever Horthy would release, the United States would care for.

Portugal, too, offered to take small groups, though it told the WRB it would be easier if no more than three hundred to four hundred people arrived at a time. It had already begun issuing visas to groups of Hungarian Jews, but the Germans were not permitting them to leave. Some had found refuge at the Portuguese embassy in Budapest. (In July 1944, the WRB helped two of these Jews, Vilmos and Jolie Gabor, escape Hungary. The Gabors' daughter Magda was having an affair with the Portuguese minister in Budapest, and another daughter, Sari—already married and living in Hollywood—asked the U.S.

government to intervene to help her parents so the affair wouldn't be revealed. Sari was known to the WRB by her married name, Mrs. Conrad Hilton, and to everyone else by her stage name, Zsa Zsa Gabor.)

Turkey already allowed Hungarian Jews to pass through the country, should any show up on a boat to Istanbul or on the border.

The Swiss also agreed to receive Hungarian Jews, provided the United States arrange for their maintenance and removal as soon as possible for havens elsewhere. They were serious about this: A few months later, a rumor spread in Bern that eight thousand Hungarian Jews were about to show up on the Swiss border. In a matter of days, the Swiss had a plan to deal with the entry of the refugees, and the United States had one to deal with the logistics of removing them. But the rumored eight thousand never arrived. In a memo to Ambassador Harrison, Ross McClelland wrote, "I do not ... see just what steps could be undertaken either by ourselves (other than continued propaganda pressure via the radio and leaflets) or by the Swiss to avert or mitigate this final and radical 'solving' of the so-called Jewish problem. From conversations I had this morning I have the feeling that the Swiss would be willing to do all they could through their Legation in Budapest if they knew exactly how to proceed."

The Swedes agreed wholeheartedly to protect and assist anyone, reminding the WRB that their legation already had more than fifteen thousand people under protection. Minister Johnson cabled the WRB that the "Swedish Legation in Budapest stands ready to aid all Jews who apply."

Josiah DuBois, who happened to be in London with Morgenthau for meetings, stayed behind to work with the British on a joint public declaration announcing Allied acceptance. Both the State Department and the British thought the final sentence of the board's proposed text, which read, "The United States is now awaiting information with regard to the concrete steps which the Hungarian Government will take to carry out its proposal," should be edited to "sound a little less like a dare to the Hungarians." Despite DuBois's protestations, the British also insisted on changing "arrangements for the care of all Jews" to "arrangements for the care of such Jews," clarifying that they would only accept responsibility for those who fell into the specific categories mentioned in Horthy's offer, not everyone. DuBois finally

relented but encouraged the WRB to still use "all Jews" when publicizing the joint declaration in the United States.

Though the WRB tentatively began planning for the care of any
Jews Horthy might release, no one was optimistic. In the same cable in
which he advocated for Saly Mayer's ransom negotiations, McClelland
observed that "in spite of preliminary reassuring news of an agreement
between the Hungarian Government and ICRC [International Committee of the Red Cross] to permit Jewish emigration to Palestine and
elsewhere . . . it now appears that ranking Gestapo agents . . . have no
intention of permitting them to emigrate freely." Ira Hirschmann, writing on August 12 that a rumored group of two thousand Hungarian
Jews had not yet arrived in Turkey, observed, "Information received
in Istanbul from reliable private sources indicates that although the
Hungarian Government has agreed to provide the necessary exit facilities, final authorization must be granted by the German military and
political organizations . . . such authorization has not until now been
granted."

By the beginning of September, it was obvious even to average
Americans that the Nazis were preventing any emigration from Hungary. A *New Republic* editorial on September 4 reminded readers that
saving the remaining Hungarian Jews "would depend on the consent
of the Nazis rather than of the Hungarian government . . . Proposals, at
this late date, to evacuate Jews from Hungary by way of available troop
ships and transport planes are unrealistic, since they do not take Nazi
opposition into account . . . It seems that the delivery of Hungary's
Jews will come through military liberation rather than evacuation."

Adrift

IN *SURVEY GRAPHIC* MAGAZINE'S September 1944 issue, John Pehle shared the story of a boy who had escaped certain death thanks to Ira Hirschmann's efforts in Turkey. Under the heading "The Human Hunted," young David's story tugged at readers' heartstrings. He had watched his parents die by Nazi firing squad in Warsaw, wandered in the woods for weeks, and hid with the help of a kindly Christian couple before being captured and sent to Transnistria. After Hirschmann saved the Jews there, David boarded a boat to Istanbul and, again thanks to Hirschmann, soon left for Palestine, arriving right before his thirteenth birthday.

As Ira Hirschmann told the story from the lectern at his April press conference—the one overshadowed by the free ports story—David's little sister had also died, trampled to death in Warsaw. David hid in a water barrel, snuck in and out of a concentration camp, and drifted for five years, until an underground guide physically carried him into Hungary. After meeting the boy in Istanbul, Hirschmann had wanted to adopt David and bring him to New York, but "the Zionists already had their eye on him—he's the kind of material they need in Palestine."

David never complained about the discrepancies in these stories, because David was fictional. "We invented that one," Pehle confessed privately to Morgenthau. When the *Milka* had arrived in Istanbul in March, Hirschmann was five hundred miles away in Ankara and never met any passengers on the only refugee ship to arrive during his stay. So to publicly demonstrate the WRB's impact, the staff invented "David," as well as "Leon and Ruth," who, according to an NBC radio interview with Pehle, had escaped by foot over the Pyrenees with only the clothes on their backs in the middle of winter and were waiting to leave for Fedhala.

Over the summer, the very real Fort Ontario and Fedhala refugees reached their new homes, behind fences and watched by guards. But in the two months since Hirschmann had arrived back in New York, the relief situation in Turkey had descended into chaos, and few refugees were arriving. The three ships that had crammed 1,224 refugee passengers on voyages to Istanbul in March, April, and May had been nowhere to be found in June, when only 233 persons, almost all from Bulgaria and Greece, reached Turkey. The "bridge of ships" remained a dream. Luckily, Pehle had already negotiated with Bloomingdale's to borrow Ira Hirschmann again.

Finally recovered from the life-threatening malaria he had contracted after interviewing Joel Brand in Cairo, Hirschmann spent his July 4 dinner taking stock of thirty-six-year-old Herbert Katzki, his new partner and the second WRB representative in Turkey. Pehle hired him to bring relief experience to Hirschmann's operation, because Katzki had worked for the JDC since 1936, and had witnessed the Nazi invasion of Paris in 1940. Katzki had fled south, working with refugees in Vichy France (where he crossed paths with McClelland) and Portugal. His extensive connections brought him to the attention of the OSS, so his work in Turkey also included some light espionage. Luckily, Hirschmann liked the clean-cut, straightforward Katzki, who was willing to stay in the background and let him take all the credit. The two men generally divided their workload—Katzki in Istanbul and Hirschmann in Ankara, each with a new American secretary by his side.

Dozens of relief agency workers, legitimate ones and play-actors, had descended on Turkey since Hirschmann left in April, squabbling among themselves and driving up the price of relief goods and potential refugee ships. Hirschmann characteristically took responsibility for the influx: "The enormous excitement created by my work here originally has sent representatives here from all over the world to claim credit." The Turkish Foreign Office complained, especially about newcomers who "grossly exaggerated their connections and importance."

Eri Jabotinsky, the Emergency Committee's representative (and son of the late Ze'ev Jabotinsky, the founder of Revisionist Zionism), had even held a press conference while en route to Turkey, claiming to be sent by the War Refugee Board. To deal with the problem, Hirschmann and Katzki formed a coordinating committee of relief representatives, which met Monday afternoons in Istanbul and mainly discussed boats: the vessels they knew were waiting in Constanța; the demographic makeup of the passengers; and whether organizations could independently charter boats for "their" refugees.

On Saturday, July 8, Ira Hirschmann sighted the *Kazbek* in the distance and two days later watched the refugees, between 739 and 761 of them (the count was never clear), carefully traverse the gangplank near Haydarpaşa terminal on the city's Asian shore, ready to immediately board a special train for Palestine. In his diary, Hirschmann wrote that "258 children are among those I had brought out of Transnistria. Spindle-legged, emaciated little orphans, carrying all their life's possessions in their skinny arms in a bundle. Large bellies, aged faces. Thus has Hitler wrought! . . . The sight of these children . . . is graven on my heart and will stay with me. It serves only to urge me to re-double my efforts." The *Kazbek,* for which the JDC paid nearly $150,000 (for both the ship's journey and the train to Palestine), was the only refugee ship to arrive in July.

The *Tari*—the big, beautiful ship Hirschmann had explored in the driving March rain—had still not sailed. Germany's refusal to grant safe-conduct was alternatively blamed on the Turkish reduction in chrome shipments to the Axis or, one Red Cross worker speculated, the fact that the passengers were ultimately destined for Palestine: "Germans consider Arabs their friends and have no intention of aiding Jewish immigration viewed with disfavor by the Arabs." With the Turkish government insisting on safe-conduct, Steinhardt refused to sign the charter, preventing the WRB from "a hemorrhage of 5,000 Turkish pounds daily" to rent a ship that couldn't sail. The *Tari* began making short commercial voyages, with the agreement that the ship would be called back to port if the German safe-conduct arrived. The Jewish Agency believed it never would; Ira Hirschmann had destroyed the *Tari* plan when he had gossiped about the ship to audiences of thousands in New York. The Red Cross agreed: the *Tari* had been "doomed by the excessive zeal of Mr. Hirschmann." The War Refugee Board moved on.

The long, low *Bardaland,* a single-steam-stack cargo ship bobbing in the waves, had distinct advantages over the *Tari.* The ship sailed under the flag of neutral Sweden and already had safe-conduct permissions from all the belligerent countries to transport Greek relief supplies. It was, Hirschmann thought, "a beauty in dock at Istanbul," and the Swedish government seemed amenable to diverting it from the normal Canada-to-Greece route in order to evacuate eight hundred to a thousand children from Constanța directly to Haifa. The *Bardaland* waited in Istanbul for more than a month as the WRB explored costs, logistics, and charters, debating whether the necessary passenger retrofitting could be accomplished in Istanbul harbor (the WRB's choice) or Egypt (Steinhardt's). Finally, the American legation in Stockholm reported with a sigh that the Germans were denying safe-conduct to the *Bardaland* after all and had "even expressed resentment at the Swedes' making the request." Warned that the empty ship would sail for Sweden unless the WRB intervened immediately, Pehle sent a frantic cable, but it arrived too late. The *Bardaland* was already gone.

The War Refugee Board wasn't the only customer in Turkey looking for ships. A trio of Orthodox representatives begged their American headquarters for $200,000 and put a down payment on a ship specifically meant for Orthodox passengers. Hirschmann gave his blessing for the plan, even though, as furious Jewish Agency representatives pointed out, Hirschmann had no control over the issuance of Palestine certificates. The ship never sailed.

Eri Jabotinsky concocted a plan to sneak a wooden boat up the Danube to rescue Jews from Budapest. When Hirschmann, who thought Jabotinsky a "sinister fool," pointed out that the boat was too tall and deep to navigate the river and would be in danger of hitting mines and that he seriously doubted that any Jews would be allowed to escape in this way, Jabotinsky responded that the *Taurus* would leave the first week of August. It didn't. The Emergency Committee reserved the boat but had no money to fund the trip.

On August 1, 1944, Burton Berry, the American consul general in Istanbul, made a major announcement: the next day, Turkey would break off diplomatic relations with Nazi Germany. Berry estimated a

50 percent chance that the Germans would begin retaliatory bombing, and the air attaché, a Texan, explained the Turkish military probably couldn't defend Istanbul for more than an hour. Herbert Katzki, with 2,000 lire in his pocket, broke through the crowds to buy flashlights, chocolate, cigarettes, and suitcases to transport confidential records. In both Istanbul and Ankara, the German diplomatic community of about twenty-five hundred people frantically packed, throwing their suitcases on the sidewalks to be hauled to the train station for the journey back to Nazi territory.

Amid the drama, it's unclear whether Hirschmann or Katzki knew what other members of the Ankara staff already did: On July 19 and 20, unidentified submarines had attacked two ships on the Black Sea. One coal ship, the *Kanarya,* was only half a mile from the Turkish coast, and, miraculously, the two torpedoes missed. The *Semsi-Bahri* wasn't as lucky: the sailing ship sank near the entrance to the Bosphorus.

After the *Kazbek*'s arrival in early July, Hirschmann had been waiting impatiently for others, all delayed, he thought, due to Romania's insistence on exit permits for all passengers or possibly the Turkish consul in Bucharest's demands for lists. Three Turkish boats—the *Morina, Mefkure,* and *Bülbül*—and one Greek boat—the *Smyrna*—were ready to sail from Constanța as soon as bureaucracy got out of the way. Chartered through the Jewish Agency and bankrolled by one of Saly Mayer's JDC licenses, they had no safe-conduct permissions.

On August 2, the day Turkey broke relations with Nazi Germany, Hirschmann learned that one of the small Turkish vessels, the *Bülbül,* had raised anchor in Constanța and was on its way to Turkey. He began arranging for food for the passengers' train trip to Palestine: eggs, cucumbers, olives, grapes, salami, watermelons. Soon he heard all three Turkish ships were on their way, but the rumors of their arrival in Istanbul kept changing: Katzki thought that one had appeared, then all three, then just one, and finally that the *Bülbül* safely arrived. Hirschmann sent Pehle a long cable, preemptively confirming that eleven hundred Jewish refugees—the "largest number of refugees which has ever arrived at one time from the Balkans"—were receiving food and medical attention. Hirschmann, and the rumors he was hearing, were all wrong.

It was nearly midnight on August 6, after an interminable day without any news at all, when Hirschmann, working late at the embassy during a blackout, received a phone call from Katzki in Istanbul. Katzki was using a telescope to peer up the Bosphorus through the pouring rain and thought he spotted something in the distance: maybe one of the refugee boats coming through the violent summer storm. The three boats had started together, but clearly something happened along the way. After many more phone calls, the news reached Hirschmann before sunrise: one of the boats had been torpedoed.

Upon leaving Constanța on the evening of August 3, the *Mefkure*, carrying 320 passengers, developed motor trouble almost immediately, and the *Morina* and *Bülbül* sailed far out of sight. After seven hours, the *Mefkure* left Romanian waters and the ship's escort turned back. Soon after, Captain Kâzim Turan realized they were not alone; over the next day, he monitored a large black object in the water slowly tracking the ship, which due to the mechanical problems only traveled at about five miles an hour.

A little after midnight on August 5, a rocket screamed over the mast of the *Mefkure;* then more rockets, incendiary bombs, and machine gun shots erupted from the submarine trailing the boat. A fire broke out. Captain Turan and his sailors panicked, abandoning the passengers and jumping onto a dinghy to escape. There was no one left in charge to shout instructions and no other life rafts. The vast majority of the *Mefkure* passengers—among them eighty Jewish orphaned children—died in the flames, or were shot in the water, or drowned.

The five survivors—an eight months pregnant Hungarian newlywed, her husband, two Polish men in their thirties, and a Romanian woman who couldn't swim—were carried by the currents toward the *Bülbül*, which also picked up the *Mefkure* crew's dinghy. The *Bülbül* had initially been far ahead but encountered its own mechanical difficulties and was nearby during the attack. The boat went dark to escape detection and made no attempt to save any *Mefkure* passengers until the submarine was long gone. The *Bülbül* then headed for the Bosphorus and Istanbul but was turned back by storms, docking in Port Igneada, a small Turkish port city near the Bulgarian border. The *Morina,* which had been waiting for the others at the mouth of the Bosphorus, arrived in Istanbul on August 9.

No one knew if the waters were safe to continue, so the *Bülbül* waited. Pressured by the JDC and the American embassy, the Turkish government began supplying food. Finally, rather than continue in dangerous waters, the passengers traveled over land on fifty oxcarts, walking and riding for sixty kilometers over the Yıldız (Istranca) Mountains to the small ancient town of Vize. There, they boarded trucks to the nearest major train station, forty kilometers away in Çerkezköy. They arrived in Istanbul the evening of August 14.

The attack on the *Mefkure* cast a pall over Istanbul, a city still bracing for bombings. For several days, Hirschmann believed a British naval intelligence report that the *Mefkure* had not been attacked at all but merely hit a rock. Katzki, however, interviewed Captain Turan and the five surviving passengers, all of whom clearly described a submarine and machine guns. John Pehle let Hirschmann decide whether the route from Constanța was now too dangerous: "We know that your decision will take into account the relative risk to the refugees if they remain in Bulgaria, Romania or Hungary as the case may be as contrasted with the risks of sea voyages."

Pehle took advantage of the propaganda opportunity. As the investigation into the *Mefkure* attack continued, he issued a press release to implore Americans, "If anyone had any doubts about the German attitude toward refugee rescue operations, or anticipated a lessening in the Nazi program of extermination, he now knows the ugly truth." (Pehle had no idea—and probably never learned—that a Soviet submarine, not a German one, had attacked the boat.) Pehle asked the Office of War Information to increase its psychological warfare campaign and asked Stettinius for a public statement declaring the United States would prosecute the *Mefkure* attackers after the war.

Ira Hirschmann was not a cautious man and, even before the dirty and weary *Mefkure* and *Bülbül* passengers arrived, pushed for the Bulgarian ships *Vita* and *Perin* to sail. The refugees could decide themselves whether they wanted to risk escape by sea. The Jewish Agency representatives cabled their counterparts in Bulgaria and Romania to proceed. Yet no more boats arrived in August or September.

Things began stabilizing in Istanbul. The German military did not target the city. Hirschmann continued prodding Romania and Bul-

garia to send refugees and for more concessions, even as these countries signaled interest in joining the Allies. During a meeting with the
Bulgarian minister in Turkey, Hirschmann threatened that the United
States wouldn't be satisfied until Bulgaria's "scandalous anti-Jewish
laws are completely revoked," promising American goodwill should
it comply. His unilateral display of diplomatic force resulted in a stern
cable (which he called a "stinger") from the State Department: "It is
assumed that you are aware of the fact that any discussions with Bulgarian or Romanian authorities must be strictly confined to questions
of relief of refugees . . . and must not enter into the field of the domestic affairs of these countries." Pehle followed up with Hirschmann in a
personal letter sent through pouch, because cables "leave much unsaid."
After thanking him for his work on the *Mefkure,* Pehle pointed out
that it's "not easy to separate the political from purely relief matters" and reminded Hirschmann that the WRB had no authority to
enter into any postwar commitments. Undeterred and unrepentant,
Hirschmann reported in his diary, "I get off my telegram on the
Bulgarian situation, it is coming to a head and I am *winning.* They
are *revoking* the anti-Jewish laws. What a victory! I have saved these
45,000 people from within their country, instead of without."

Romania switched sides, joining the Allies on August 23; two weeks
later, Bulgaria followed. With the Soviet military moving through
the Balkans, there were fewer pockets of refugees for Hirschmann
to save. Intent on a concrete achievement, he found a new pet project: a group of German immigrants living in Turkey, who, thanks to
the break in diplomatic ties, were now threatened with forced repatriation to Nazi Germany. Most were not Jewish but instead intellectual and political opponents of the Nazi regime and—perhaps most
important—included some of Hirschmann's personal friends. They
believed themselves to be at risk, Hirschmann argued to the Ankara
consulate staff, and therefore should be his responsibility. In a span of
four days in his diary, he recounted meeting a professor ("and by quick
action save him"), a woman ("I induce her to steps, no matter how
desperate, to remain"), "a pretty girl" ("They will *kill* her. I must help"),
and a man and wife ("we spirited [them] away and hid for the night").

Eventually, that project died, too. Turkey interned some Germans, while others returned to Germany or remained free. Hirschmann never made any approaches to the Turkish government, never reported the problem to Washington, and failed to mention it anywhere in his eighty-four-page final report. He did, however, write in his diary that upon encountering people whose lives he saved, he would magnanimously respond that the American people saved them, not he.

Hirschmann met with Ambassador Steinhardt in late August, impatient for a new assignment: "Ambass. Steinh ... reveals that I have made the best record for the War Ref. Bd, that the issue is now out of politics: that we should slow up. Also that some of my activity with the Enemy has been resented by the State Dept ... I sound him out on moving into Romania. He does not oppose it, but it will require pressure."

On September 1, Hirschmann formally cabled the War Refugee Board for permission to travel to Romania. He planned to investigate why no boats had sailed since the *Mefkure,* because moving Jews out of Romania could create space for Hungarians who might cross the border in the future.

Upon receiving Hirschmann's request, Joseph Friedman of the WRB staff authorized the trip but never transmitted the cable to Ankara. Ten days later, Friedman sent an enigmatic response: Hirschmann needed to wait, because "broader questions not relating to refugee matters are still pending clearance." Hirschmann grew bored with his many swimming and shopping trips, recognizing that the delays didn't bode well for the decisive WRB action in the Balkans he thought necessary. On September 20, when Hirschmann received Friedman's disappointing cable, he wrote to Pehle, "As the policy of the Board ... makes it clear that my activities are limited to the rescue of refugees ... I am of the opinion that the future opportunities for the rescue of refugees from Hungary through Turkey are so limited as to no longer require or justify my continued presence." The War Refugee Board formally recalled Ira Hirschmann on September 26; Herbert Katzki remained to oversee any board matters in Turkey.

Once Turkey ceased to be an active site of rescue, it had no place for Ira Hirschmann.

After waving good-bye to embassy staff who traveled to the airport to see him off, Hirschmann took an early morning flight to Palestine on October 4. While there, he played tourist with the prominent American rabbi Judah Magnes; paid his respects to Magnes's Zionist lobbying partner, the ailing Henrietta Szold; visited David Ben-Gurion (who Hirschmann, with an amazing lack of self-awareness, felt was "lacking the humility of a truly great man"); and, on October 7, reunited with someone he never thought he would see again: Joel Brand. In Hirschmann's room at the King David Hotel, Brand explained that he had undertaken two hunger strikes while in solitary confinement before the British had transferred him to a prison camp. He had only recently arrived in Jerusalem, after threatening to act "as an enemy of the British" should his internment continue. Brand felt the Allies could still accept his ransom offer; he vaguely knew of new ransom negotiations in Switzerland but didn't think Saly Mayer would be willing to make a deal. Hirschmann remained impressed with Brand but doubted he could be useful "since he is a marked man."

Leaving Palestine, Hirschmann hopped across North Africa one last time—from Cairo to Benghazi to Tripoli to Algiers to Casablanca. In Casablanca, he ran into Leonard Ackermann, who had also been recalled to the United States, because rescue opportunities in North Africa and Italy were now so limited. From Morocco, Hirschmann took a plane headed for Miami (or Bermuda, he wasn't sure) but got off during a fueling stop in the Azores to transfer to a flight bound for Newfoundland. He arrived in North America in the early hours of October 13.

Hirschmann spoke at a Treasury Department press conference while still acclimating to the new hemisphere. As with his April press conference, his triumphant reporting was overshadowed, this time by speculation over whether the slowing of Balkan emigration meant the War Refugee Board's work had concluded. Ready to return to Bloomingdale's, Hirschmann submitted his formal resignation to the board, writing, "In time of war, as I understand it, killing people seems to be the main job at hand. Through the Board I was privileged to undertake a job of saving people, instead of killing them. I wish to thank you for this broad and unique opportunity in the field of human welfare."

With that, Ira Hirschmann retired to civilian life. That life—at least in the short term—consisted largely of giving speeches about his accomplishments. Within a week of his return to the United States, Hirschmann began writing his triumphant memoirs about his time in Turkey.

Midnight Sun

In May 1944, the U.S. government, through the War Refugee Board, effectively laundered money for rescue work through the Goodyear Tire and Rubber Company. At Pehle's urging, staff at Goodyear Tire—no doubt astonished that the former head of Foreign Funds Control was making this request—agreed that if the board transferred $50,000 to their Akron, Ohio, headquarters, they would remit to Iver Olsen the equivalent in Swedish kronor from their factory in Norrköping, Sweden.

For much of the summer of 1944, Olsen focused on a hazardous plan to rescue refugees from Lithuania, Latvia, and Estonia by water. Accustomed to taking risks in his OSS work, he transferred that same adventurous spirit to his WRB projects. He would need "the most skillfully organized type of underground operations," because "the Baltic countries are now virtually sealed to everything." Olsen appointed three country-specific underground groups, all headed by former ambassadors and politicians who had found wartime refuge in Sweden. After a confidential discussion with a Swedish Foreign Office official, Olsen reported to Washington that the work would be very dangerous, but they might be able to rescue six hundred to seven hundred intellectual, racial, and political refugees from each country.

The War Refugee Board paid for the project directly out of its President's Emergency Fund allocation. Such a large deposit in a Swedish bank, however, would certainly draw suspicion, and the WRB wanted to avoid any impression that the United States was funding unregulated refugee entry. Even Swedish Jews, Olsen wrote, are "very interested in Jewish rescue and relief operations, so long as they do not involve bringing them into Sweden." So, John Pehle, who had experience trying to stop companies from sneaking money overseas, decided to spirit Olsen's funds past the Swedish government and people.

There are no references to the Goodyear Tire deal in the War Refugee Board's records, save for a mysterious $50,000 entry on the financial ledger; it's likely the relevant documents were destroyed to prevent a public scandal. But Henry Morgenthau received copies of much of the WRB's correspondence in a daily briefing folder, and the WRB staff forgot to purge his records, too. "This arrangement worked well," Olsen reported from Stockholm in a cable only found in Morgenthau's records, "and although not fool-proof, it is desirable from security point of view. At this time we do not recommend bank transfers as receipt of cable transfers of such size by individuals involved in operations unavoidably attract notice and suspicion."

Iver Olsen's work was a microcosm of all the WRB's overseas projects and full of constant adjustments and confusions. An infrequent correspondent, Olsen sent few cables to Washington but made up for it with weekly packets of Swedish newspaper clippings of interest to the WRB and monthly multipage letters directly to Pehle, informing him of all his board activities in Stockholm. The long hours didn't bother Olsen, who missed his wife, Mildred, and two young sons, Norbert and Iver junior, left behind in Washington. Already a chain-smoker, he started drinking heavily, building a necessary tolerance to conduct espionage in social settings, and out of loneliness. By June 1944, he had lost twenty pounds from his already slight frame.

Few relief agencies had designated representatives in Sweden, so Olsen rarely had to act as a conduit of correspondence or license money, though he still had a few headaches. In June, the Vaad Hatzalah sent $10,000 to its representative, Rabbi Wilhelm Wolbe, tasking him with the rescue of specific rabbis in the Baltic countries, particularly Lithuania. The assignment revealed a heartbreaking lack of comprehension: by the summer of 1944, more than 90 percent of the Jewish population in Lithuania had already been murdered. Olsen held out little hope the Vaad would be successful, writing that "Wolbe's comprehension of the urgency of this problem perhaps best may be suggested by the fact that the day after he received $10,000 for Lithuanian rescue operations, he went off on a month's vacation and I haven't seen him since." Even after Wolbe returned and explained to his colleagues that he could not even communicate with Lithuania, the Vaad never gave up, demanding the WRB—at the very least—locate five specific rabbis who had been deported from Kovno and arrange Swedish protective papers for them. Their pleas grew desperate: "Practically nothing done for the rescue of Lithuanian Jewry. Our committee is deeply perturbed. You are again urged to spare no expense to do everything to try to save everything listed in our cables and the greatest number possible in this group." The real problem, of course, was not Wolbe, the War Refugee Board, or the will to act. Nothing had been done because, in 1944, nothing could be done to save Lithuanian Jews.

Still, fewer relief agency representatives meant that Olsen's confidential negotiations could generally stay secret. At the end of June, three Nazis quietly approached him with a ransom offer: 2 million Swedish kronor (they later demanded material goods) for all the Jews left in Latvia. The Nazis guaranteed they would release at least two thousand people, which led John Pehle to insist Olsen ask for the current location of the other ninety-one thousand Latvian Jews. The Red Army's military advance into the Baltics killed any deal.

In August, Olsen invited Thomas von Kantzow, Hermann Göring's stepson and a Swedish citizen, to his Stockholm apartment for drinks. Olsen liked the younger man, the son by a first marriage of Göring's beloved late wife, Carin. Olsen implored von Kantzow, who frequently traveled to Germany, to pressure his stepfather to do what he could to ease the persecutions—with the reminder that when the war ended, Göring would be on trial for his life. "This chap seemed very impressed and said that he would press the matter with Göring to the best of his ability."

Olsen's other secret project, of course, was the Lithuanian, Latvian, and Estonian underground operation. After receiving approximately 209,000 Swedish kronor from Goodyear's Norrköping plant, he initially distributed 110,000 kronor ($26,400) for Estonian rescue, 55,000 kronor ($13,200) for Latvian rescue, and 35,000 kronor ($8,500) for Lithuanian rescue. Each group's leaders promised to keep detailed accounts and to turn over everything—boats, guns, ropes, motors—once their work was completed. They took advantage of the long Scandinavian summer nights to attempt the perilous business of evacuations.

The Latvian group's first trip turned back due to motor difficulties; on the second one, the crew miscalculated, landing in Latvia in broad daylight. The men miraculously managed to slip ashore unseen to establish contacts and bases. On their return, the motor had to be repaired four times in the middle of the Baltic Sea. Air raids over Latvia prevented their first attempted refugee retrieval; on the second try, the boat began taking on water, and the crew made it back to Sweden using only a sail and oars. By the end of August, the Latvian group had lost several workers—who had been either captured or shot—and at least one boat, which had to be abandoned at sea. But they had brought nearly two hundred anti-Nazi refugees to Sweden, including approximately sixty women and fifteen children.

One month later, that number jumped to almost four thousand, more than 50 percent of them women and children, but none of them Jewish. On some nights, as many as a dozen boats arrived on Gotland, an island off the Swedish coast, and it proved impossible to figure out which came as a result of the WRB's contribution and which came independently, now that the Red Army was liberating the country. Some boats sank, while others were captured by Germans and the refugees imprisoned, among them the president of the last Latvian Parliament, who was sent to a concentration camp in Germany. One boat ran out of fuel and drifted for six days before the tides finally drove it against the Swedish coast. Finally, Olsen called a halt to the rescue mission, in part out of fear the Nazis would take advantage of the confusion to send their collaborators to Sweden to escape Soviet imprisonment. Of the twenty-four crew employed in the WRB-funded rescue attempts, eight were dead or missing by the end. The Latvian group told Olsen "most refugees . . . would not have reached this country and would have perished at the hands of the occupation powers ravaging our country but for the generous aid given by the United States." They did not clarify whether the occupying powers in question were the Nazis or the Soviet Union.

The Estonian group had even worse luck than the Latvians on their first attempt: they entered a minefield and were promptly arrested and jailed by the Swedish marine police. In recounting the story, Olsen cheerfully reported to Pehle that "everything is now cleared up and they should be off in a couple of days." Olsen made secret arrangements with the Swedish General Staff (whose cooperation saved Olsen from "a few score years of imprisonment for espionage") to sneak away from Stockholm to a restricted zone on the Baltic coast, where the Estonians had set up headquarters. Olsen excitedly took rides in both of their boats—the open speedboat, which was later withdrawn from service after several crewmen suffered broken arms trying to control the wheel in rough seas, and a cabin cruiser, which was fired upon but fast enough to outrace the German submarines.

The Estonians ultimately rescued approximately 275 people and enabled 200–300 to escape on other boats—a lower number than Olsen would have liked, but they suffered from frequent fuel shortages, so Olsen made arrangements with Texaco to cover the price of fuel. Olsen also lamented the group's failure to rescue 300 French and Czech Jewish women imprisoned in Tallinn, who he indelicately assumed were "war whores." They had apparently made contact with the women, who were too frightened to risk escape, especially with Soviet liberation imminent. Many of the refugees who made it to Sweden were intellectuals affiliated with the Estonian National Committee, which had just declared war on the Soviet Union. Because Olsen believed the Nazis were also hunting for them, he did not complain.

Olsen preferred the Lithuanian group, particularly Dr. Algirdas Vokietaitis, a tall, handsome, former Kovno professor and resistance fighter responsible for the group's technical arrangements. He was, Olsen reported, "most certainly the cleverest operator in all three groups." In July, Vokietaitis disappeared into Lithuania to locate people in danger and arrange for their escape. When the boat returned the following week, he didn't show, and by the third week the crew learned that he had been captured and executed. Olsen was deeply affected by the news, calling Vokietaitis "my man . . . a hell of a fine, fearless fellow." In a letter to Pehle, Olsen brainstormed ways in which he might find and save the Lithuanian, in case he was still alive, but talked himself out of it: "Consequently, all I can do just now is to keep the boat going, with the hope he will show up." Olsen believed the loss of Vokietaitis marked the beginning of a great series of misfortunes for the Lithuanian group: at least five boats were captured or destroyed by German vessels, and 250 refugees and crew died or were missing. Only about 150 Lithuanian refugees made it to Sweden, none of them Jewish, before Olsen stopped the operation, mainly because "all the boats had been lost and losses were getting increasingly disproportionate to the number of persons rescued."

On September 29, 1944, Olsen cabled to Pehle that all the WRB-supported transports had ceased. The Red Army had moved into the Baltic countries, the summer light dimmed, and rescue became too dangerous.

A few weeks later, the Swedish Communist newspaper *Ny Dag* published a string of sensational articles. The first one, "Baltic Fascists in Large Numbers to Sweden; The Swedish Authorities and the American Legation as Organizers?," accused an unnamed American diplomat of spending 900,000 kronor to help pro-Nazi anti-Communists escape to Sweden. Minister Johnson claimed no one on his staff fit that description, which was technically true; Olsen had only spent 209,000 kronor, and no one knew whether any of the refugees were pro-Nazi, though Olsen had his suspicions. Johnson admitted to the board that at the very least the "charge that most of the Baltic refugees are anti-Soviet is probably true ... Most of them apparently found Soviet rule distasteful to them and would prefer to avoid a repetition of the experience."

Olsen's efforts in Norway and Denmark were smaller. He provided 7,500 kronor ($1,800) to a Danish student underground organization, which wasn't much money, but the students were "most happy to have an outlet to the free world." In September and October, the group transported sixty refugees to Sweden and brought twenty resistance fighters back to Denmark. They mostly carried weapons, Allied propaganda to secretly distribute to German soldiers, broadsides, and various publications to keep hope alive, ranging from Arne Troelsen-Terp's *From the Front in Denmark,* to Mary O'Hara's horse lover's novel *My Friend Flicka,* to a joke book called *Occupation Humor from Norway and Denmark.*

The American Relief for Norway group led a robust relief program for a while, funded through a WRB-facilitated $400,000 license. They supported resistance fighters' families, distributed money through the

Lutheran church, and helped more than a thousand Norwegian refugees flee into Sweden in September alone. In the fall, longer nights
made it easier and safer to escape over land, but the warmer clothing
needed to combat the cold was difficult to obtain in wartime. American Relief for Norway could not meet the demand, especially after
October, when the German military began retreating from Norway,
scorching everything in their wake and displacing thousands of Nor-
wegians. Olsen was forced to watch, helpless, as starvation threatened
his country of birth.

Olsen also served as the WRB's conduit to its new agent in Budapest,
Raoul Wallenberg. Wallenberg was, perhaps, the WRB's greatest secret:
even the Stockholm legation staff in Budapest did not know that he
was working for the Americans. Pehle never had direct communication with Wallenberg, and one of the only things he knew about the
man—that Wallenberg was half-Jewish—was an exaggeration Wallenberg frequently told. (He was, at most, one-sixteenth.) Pehle would
send messages to Stockholm, where either Olsen or Johnson passed
them to the Swedish Foreign Office for transmission to Wallenberg
in Budapest. The cable delays inherent in each stage of this process
meant that it took a month, on average, to receive any replies. Pehle
only knew whatever Wallenberg sent through Olsen's infrequent dispatches.

By the end of July, after only a few weeks in Budapest, Wallenberg
had already gathered a large and loyal staff, mainly of Hungarian Jews
under Swedish protection, and reported that he knew what to do. The
deportations seemed to have stopped, though Wallenberg thought
the situation was still quite bad in Hungary, and he wanted to create
a Swedish-protected refugee camp for a thousand people near Budapest. He still issued protective papers to any Hungarian Jews with any
relationship to Sweden and was hiding several prominent Hungarian
rabbis and religious leaders in his large rented offices. The board staff
thanked Wallenberg, asking for more information about his proposed
refugee camp. Olsen feared the Swedish Foreign Office felt that Wallenberg "jumped in with too big a splash." Still, he was "working like
hell and doing some good."

By September, Wallenberg had spent only 3,000 kronor of the 60,000 available to him, because the Hungarian Jewish community covered most of his expenses. While he had originally focused on issuing Swedish protective papers for those in danger—and had already granted five thousand of them—now that the danger of deportation had passed, Wallenberg moved on to relief projects, purchasing goods and distributing small amounts of money to needy people.

The board made several requests of Wallenberg—to find out information about an uprising in Slovakia, to assist relatives of Americans, and to investigate a ransom scheme involving a managing director of a General Electric subsidiary whom the Nazis were offering to release from Mauthausen in exchange for 1 million Swiss francs. The communication lag between question and answer—a month on average—rendered these requests useless. Wallenberg never responded to any of them.

Wallenberg, writing on October 12, felt he had nearly completed his rescue work. Jews with Swedish papers were exempted from building military fortifications outside the city, and he planned on moving them into homes designated for non-Jews. He was helping the Red Cross open a hospital and distributing clothing and other supplies. He wrote to the WRB, "When I arrived, the situation of the Jews was very bad . . . I think that [the Hungarian Jews] will have every reason to thank you for having initiated and supported the Swedish Jewish action the way you have in such a splendid manner." Wallenberg obtained a transit visa through Nazi Germany, planning to go home.

In early November, with the end of Baltic evacuations, a smooth Danish resistance project, and the Nazis retreating from Norway, a War Refugee Board representative seemed unnecessary in Stockholm. Olsen excitedly received word that the War Refugee Board agreed he could close his office.

Before the sun returned to the northern sky, he would have to open it again.

What Kind of Peace

JOHN, YOU ARE LOOKING for new worlds to conquer," Henry Morgenthau, constantly in big-picture mode, said to Pehle with a smile. It was late afternoon on Wednesday, August 23, and the war looked different than it had a few weeks prior—especially to Morgenthau, who had just seen it himself. His recent trip to London had included a detour to France, where the excited Treasury secretary beamed while setting foot on conquered territory. He had been allowed within five thousand feet of the front lines, where he reunited with his soldier-son Henry III and swiped a German helmet as a souvenir. (If Berlin radio broadcasts were to be believed, Morgenthau also stole the Bayeux Tapestry, an absurd and ironic claim that served only to remind the members of the SS that they had meant to steal it from the Louvre's vaults themselves.)

Morgenthau returned to America preoccupied by a potential crisis. (He wasn't objective enough to call it a scandal.) In early August, he had flown to London for meetings about opening financial channels to liberated French territory. While there, he maneuvered his way into discussions about managing a soon-to-be-defeated Germany. The Allied armies were moving fast, so a decisive plan for the conquered lands—whether to destroy factories or leave them operable, how to denazify the population, how to ration food, how to govern—took on accelerated importance. Morgenthau, convinced that the military instructions were both too vague and too lenient, had been pleased to hear Eisenhower say he would "treat them rough." But, to Morgenthau, the current plan seemed like "a nice WPA job" that allowed the Germans to retain enough economic strength to wage war again within a decade. To reassure him, the British foreign minister, Anthony Eden, shared the November 1943 Tehran Conference proceedings, during which Roosevelt, Churchill, and Stalin had agreed that Nazi Germany would be divided into occupation zones. Morgenthau, who had just read a State Department reparations proposal based on a unified Germany, had never heard of the partition agreement, a plan now ten months old.

Neither had Secretary of State Cordell Hull. When Morgenthau told him, Hull gasped. Roosevelt had apparently never shared the results of the Tehran Conference with the State Department. "I have asked and I have not been allowed to see them," Hull kept repeating. Morgenthau, in dictating the conversation afterward, was floored by the admission. "The sum and substance of this is that here a meeting takes place sometime last November in Tehran where these three men, Roosevelt, Churchill, and Stalin, agree to the dismemberment of Germany, and all these people go ahead and make studies without taking that into consideration and without implicit instructions. It is like telling an architect to build a house and not telling him where it should be built, how it should be built, or how many people it is to house." Now that he knew postwar Germany was a real problem—and that no one at State had prepared an acceptable plan—Morgenthau characteristically decided to take matters into his own hands. "I said to him, 'You know, Cordell . . . this isn't my responsibility, but I am doing this as an American citizen, and I am going to continue to do so, and I am going to stick my nose into it until I know it is all right.'"

A week later, Morgenthau learned that the secretary of war, Henry Stimson, hadn't even seen the president since June. Stimson hadn't explored any postwar policies, Morgenthau decided, and did not want to take the initiative to set up a committee to formulate a new, stricter treatment for Germany. Morgenthau, on the other hand, already had a plan for such a committee, envisioning that it could be headed—like the War Refugee Board—by Hull, Stimson, and Morgenthau. After Morgenthau shared the initial outline of his idea for a demilitarized, agricultural Germany, Stimson commented that an agricultural state could not support a large population and that Germans might have to be relocated. Morgenthau retorted, "Well, that is not nearly as bad as sending them to gas chambers."

John Pehle sent a confidential memo to Morgenthau proposing another group, this one within Treasury. The problems about "the kind of peace which the Allies are to impose upon Germany are as important and challenging as any with which the Treasury is concerned," he wrote. Morgenthau agreed. The other members of his staff were busy wrestling with the details of a new international financial system established at the Bretton Woods Conference in July. At the meeting on August 23, he instructed Pehle, who "just has a normal amount of work to do; he isn't overworked," to lead the committee.

As summer turned to fall, Pehle grew more involved in Treasury Department activities beyond the War Refugee Board, including revising a handbook for the Allied military on the surrender of Nazi bureaucrats and ghostwriting part of Morgenthau's book on postwar Germany, published in 1945 as *Germany Is Our Problem.* Pehle's new worlds now included the postwar one.

The night after he appointed Pehle to the postwar committee, Morgenthau attended a state dinner honoring Sveinn Björnsson, the first president of Iceland. Roosevelt offered a rambling toast, then Sveinn spoke. After he finished, Roosevelt lifted his glass again. "The President seemed to have completely forgotten that he had already toasted him, and did it all over again. Everybody was so stunned." Morgenthau returned to the White House the next morning for a visit, dictating later, "I really was shocked for the first time because he is a very sick man and seems to have wasted away." Yet when their conversation turned to the postwar world, Roosevelt reassured his chronically insecure old friend that they would continue to work together on the new United Nations. Morgenthau ended his dictation with "What will come out of it all I don't know."

Morgenthau hadn't been alone in England, and when his boss returned to the United States, Josiah DuBois stayed behind to negotiate with the British over the joint public statement on the Horthy offer. While in London, DuBois, like Morgenthau, picked up some very distressing information.

Even before the creation of the War Refugee Board, long before the Allied armies landed on the European mainland, the United States had vowed to hold war criminals accountable for their actions. In August 1944, Josiah DuBois discovered that these vows, and therefore the WRB's entire psychological warfare campaign, had all been built on sand.

International law, DuBois learned, defined "war crimes" as crimes perpetrated in war by one country against the citizens of an enemy country. But the term did not apply to domestic victims, so a country could technically murder its own citizens with impunity, as well as citizens of collaborating countries and stateless persons. In other words, the Allies had no legal grounds to try Axis leaders for crimes against German Jews, Hungarian Jews, or the Jews of any nation allied with Germany. The War Crimes Commission had been set up in London but was poorly funded, was sporadically staffed, had no guidance, and was wholly inadequate in the face of crimes of this type and scale.

Immediately upon DuBois's return, Pehle, who had already directed a member of his staff to investigate the history of war crimes prosecution, sent a memo to Edward Stettinius: "Needless to say, it would be a fearful miscarriage of justice if such war criminals were permitted to escape punishment for their inhuman crimes." Pehle attached the texts of the many public pledges that would be revealed as empty threats if the Allies couldn't hold trials. The State Department responded that the issue remained "very much on our minds." Though the War Refugee Board pestered the State Department five more times over the next three months, the War Crimes Commission never received instructions. In December, Joseph Friedman called the State Department for an update and learned, confidentially, that "State and War had not been able to find a legal theory to justify the punishment of Germans for killing German Jews." Pehle received another letter from Stettinius promising that his August memo remained under consideration.

Pehle decided the War Refugee Board needed a permanent representative in London. One of the WRB's assistant executive directors, James Mann, Pehle's bespectacled former aide with a Kentucky drawl, was already on the right side of the Atlantic and an easy choice. Mann had been on the Iberian Peninsula for about a month, in Lisbon cleaning up a conflict between the JDC and the World Jew-

ish Congress about the supervision of a few refugee children, and
in Madrid trying, one last time, to persuade Ambassador Hayes to
allow a WRB representative there. Only two days after Pehle finally
decided to just appoint Mann as the WRB's head of both Spain and
Portugal—Hayes (and Dexter) be damned—Paris's liberation effectively ended any WRB work in both countries. Mann was now free
to take up an office in London's Grosvenor Square, an area that Iver
Olsen, passing through on his way to Sweden in 1943, observed had
more American personnel than downtown Washington, D.C.

After arriving in London in late August, Mann discovered that the
WRB's ongoing conflicts with the British government were not just
over the care of any refugees the Nazis might release but also over all
licenses the WRB had been issuing to relief organizations. When, in
mid-September, the WRB issued a license for $150,000 for the French
Relief Fund, based in London, the British government froze the money,
claiming the license was an attempt "to undertake transactions con-
trary to laws and regulations of United Kingdom." In October, British members of the Special Committee on Relief—a joint American
and British group that approved Red Cross projects funded by Allied
donations—snuck into their proposals new language mandating that
any money intended for occupied territory needed approval of both
American and British officials. This new rule would give the British
government veto power over any War Refugee Board relief or rescue
licenses.

Unsurprisingly, the board disagreed. Joseph Friedman drafted a
stern and incredulous response: "It is clear that the British Government's view stems from what appears to be a basic disagreement with
the action being taken to implement this Government's policy to
save the lives of persons in enemy territory in imminent danger of
death . . . The fundamental question is not one of joint consultation . . .
but rather whether the British Government is prepared to adopt and
follow a refugee rescue policy similar to that of this Government." The
WRB received no reply.

As members of the Roosevelt administration, the War Refugee
Board staff felt confident in protesting the British stance on rescue
and on relief licenses, and Morgenthau remained determined to have

a say in postwar planning. But 1944 was an election year, and Roosevelt's health was a concern. For most of the summer, the Treasury staff remained cautiously optimistic about his reelection but began to worry in October as polls tightened and they faced the prospect of a new president, Governor Thomas Dewey. When Dewey issued a statement condemning the Nazis' "savage and unrestrained murders" and praising the State Department for promising postwar punishment, the WRB staff reassured themselves that at least the Allies—presuming they could find grounds to do it—would punish perpetrators no matter who won the American election.

Pehle was more troubled by Dewey's running mate, Governor John Bricker of Ohio, who attacked Roosevelt for ignoring immigration laws, pointing to the few military-aged men among the Fort Ontario group. In a speech, Bricker claimed, "Instead of the pale-faced children and frail women, the group consisted largely of men . . . I am not saying that this group was 'cleared with Sidney.' I do not know." (The phrase "cleared with Sidney" referred to the Jewish labor leader Sidney Hillman. During the 1944 campaign, the Republican Party used the phrase as a dog whistle, both to imply that Roosevelt deferred to leftist cronies and to stoke antisemitic prejudices.) In response, the board reminded the press that the governor had signed an appeal to Roosevelt back in May specifically endorsing the establishment of emergency refugee shelters.

Morgenthau saved his anger toward Dewey until just before the election. At a Chicago speech on November 4, Dewey blamed the Morgenthau Plan, calling for an agrarian postwar Germany—a summary of which had been leaked to the press in late September—for halting the war's progress. It was "just what the Nazi propagandists needed . . . It put fight back into the German Army; it stiffened the will of the German nation to resist. Almost overnight the headlong retreat of the Germans stopped . . . the blood of our fighting men is paying for this improvised meddling." Morgenthau was furious. After both Stimson and McCloy argued that refuting Dewey's attack would politicize the War Department, Morgenthau had a Treasury staff member circulate an editorial to various newspapers condemning the claim.

The Treasury's concerns faded on November 7. Though the popular vote was closer than any of Roosevelt's previous elections, the president won reelection handily, taking 432 electoral votes to Dewey's 99.

On Election Day 1944, General Dwight D. Eisenhower, supreme commander of the Allied forces in Europe, issued a new warning to the Germans. With the exception of Dewey's statement, the WRB had not been actively compiling psychological warfare statements for several months, but as the Allied armies prepared to cross into Nazi Germany, Pehle readied one for Eisenhower's signature:

> Germans! There are within your midst large numbers of persons in forced-labor battalions and in concentration camps . . . Without regard to their nationality and whether they are Jewish or otherwise, Germans, these are my orders: You shall disregard any order from whatever source, to molest, or otherwise harm or persecute any of these people. As the Allied armies, already firmly on German soil, advance, I shall expect to find these persons alive and unharmed. Severe penalties will be inflicted upon anyone who is responsible, directly or indirectly, in large measure or in small, for their mistreatment.

Eisenhower had approved the warning in mid-October but removed the word "Jewish." The phrase "whether they are Jewish or otherwise" became "without regard to their nationality or religious faith." Roosevelt endorsed the edited text on October 26, but the British government objected to "these are my orders: You shall," arguing that it was "unnecessarily provocative." Pehle, having waited over a month to issue the statement, agreed only because he did not want the warning delayed any further.

With Eisenhower commanding troops on German soil, the election over, WRB representatives coming home, and a new focus on war crimes trials and the management of postwar Germany, the War Refugee Board considered disbanding. In June 1944, the Senate had passed the Russell amendment as part of the Independent Offices Appropriations Bill. The new law stipulated that all agencies in existence for more than one year needed a congressional appropriation and could not be funded through the executive branch. Roosevelt couldn't continue to simply create agencies to fix problems and fund them indefinitely without Congress's input. The WRB faced two choices: it could approach the House of Representatives for a formal appropriation, or it could dissolve. It was legally required to decide by January 22, 1945.

At first, the board planned to shut down. In mid-September, one staff member had drafted an executive order terminating the board, while another tried to calculate reimbursement for unused vacation leave. But by the end of October, it was clear the war might not be over by Christmas after all, and the news out of Hungary worsened.

John Pehle appeared in front of the House Committee on Appropriations on November 20 to discuss House Document 70, requesting $150,000 for the War Refugee Board. The amount was somewhat arbitrary. The WRB had a healthy administrative budget, so the $150,000 was enough to warrant a congressional appropriation, but not so much—the WRB hoped—to need much debate. Most congressmen at the hearing praised the board's work, though Pehle deflected some questions from Congressman John Taber, who represented a district neighboring Oswego and Fort Ontario, over whether the board had bypassed American immigration laws. Finally, the chairman asked, "As a matter of fact, Mr. Pehle, considering the vast field involved and the millions of people affected, this appropriation of $150,000 is almost in the nature of a token expenditure?" Pehle answered, "We feel that way about it." The War Refugee Board would survive past January 21, 1945, with a $150,000 appropriation from Congress.

In New York, Ira Hirschmann read the November issue of the *National Jewish Monthly* with great interest. The cover featured his old boss John Pehle advertising an article, "The War Refugee Board—Success or Failure?" The writer acknowledged that much of the board's work remained secret but rendered his verdict in the subtitle: "Too Little and Too Late."

But the war was not over yet, and now neither was the WRB.

A Coup in Hungary

ROSWELL McCLELLAND MET WITH Saly Mayer every few days throughout August to prepare for Mayer's meeting with the Nazis to bargain for the Jews from the Kasztner train and any other Jews they might be inclined to offer up. Though Ross's initial impression had jibed with Mayer's stern and imperious reputation, the two men grew to trust each other. Mayer attended dinners at the McClellands' Geneva apartment, occasions that threw Marjorie McClelland into a panic about preparing sufficiently kosher meals for her religiously observant guest. Mayer had a difficult relationship with his own son, who was Ross's age, and might have transferred some of his affection to the American, whom he nicknamed "Hanukkah," no doubt a reference to Ross's skill at making small bits of aid last as long as possible. Before dinner, Mayer, always formally dressed, would bounce Ross's toddler son, Barre, on his knee, singing nursery rhymes. They saved serious talk for McClelland's office.

Saly Mayer, clearly intimidated by the prospect of bargaining with "Willies" (a nickname for the Nazis, after the *SS-Hauptsturmführer* Dieter Wisliceny, who had accepted ransom from the Slovak Jewish community in 1942), was determined to be ready. He made it clear he would be negotiating as a neutral Swiss citizen, not as an Allied representative of the JDC. He met with Swiss and Red Cross officials to ensure any Jews released could enter Switzerland. They approved, but with the unsurprising caveat that "any goods transaction (barter) with respect to such matters [is] to be entirely excluded." The War Refugee

Board responded likewise, in a cable that didn't arrive until after the first meeting: "Ransom transactions of the nature indicated by German authorities cannot be entered into or authorized. If it is felt that a meeting between Saly Mayer and the German authorities would have possible effect of gaining time the Board does not object to such a meeting."

Reszö Kasztner had been negotiating with the Nazis since they occupied Budapest in March. In late June, he paid approximately 7 million Swiss francs, the equivalent of about $1,000 per person, in exchange for the release of 1,684 Jews, among them prominent Hungarian rabbis and members of Kasztner's own family. This was the train that was sent to the Bergen-Belsen concentration camp rather than to freedom. The Nazis demanded further ransom to release them to Switzerland. Kasztner assured Mayer that the members of the Gestapo would liberate five hundred Jews from Bergen-Belsen just for meeting with them and "to show their good faith and their decent ways." The rest of the passengers, however, would remain in the camp, and Kasztner suggested Mayer proactively deposit 1 million Swiss francs in a bank against future negotiations.

The Swiss refused to allow Nazi negotiators to enter the country, and because Mayer understandably wouldn't enter Germany, the meeting took place halfway across the St. Margrethen bridge, on the Swiss-German border. In mid-morning on August 21, Kasztner and three SS officers led by *SS-Obersturmbannführer* Kurt Becher crossed from the German side of the Alter Rhein River. Saly Mayer, his lawyer, and a friend steeled themselves on the Swiss side, then approached. Standing in the middle of the bridge, the group spoke for several hours before taking a break, reconvening in the afternoon for further conversation.

Becher made it clear that *Reichsführer-SS* Heinrich Himmler knew and approved of the preliminary negotiations. As proof, he offered a confused group of 318 Hungarian Jewish men, women, and children, who had spent nearly two months in Bergen-Belsen before being gathered together and dumped on the Swiss border near Basel a few hours before the meeting.

In hastily typed notes, Mayer wrote, "There is no other option than the delivery of 10,000 trucks . . . Complete destruction or this offer."

Accustomed to using code words to communicate with the JDC in New York, Mayer began calling the negotiations "ARBA," the Hebrew word for "four." Becher, who became "Cup" for the English meaning of his name, worked directly for Himmler. He boasted sterling Nazi bona fides: SS-unit leader (likely tasked with killing partisans) and, more recently, Jewish property expropriator in Budapest, a process called Aryanization. Notably, Becher acquired the Manfred Weiss conglomerate in exchange for the lives of the owners and their families, who had mysteriously appeared in Lisbon in June. During their meeting on the bridge, Mayer had antagonized Becher by calling his proposed deal "Menschenhandel" (slave trade); the Nazi grew "visibly annoyed over this and tried to pretend it was a different thing." Still, Mayer wrote, the Nazis weren't ashamed. His notes include a direct quotation: "If we lose war, then at least Jews are no longer here."

The group agreed on a ten-day break, during which Mayer would find a way to prove American interest and Becher would prepare a list of goods the Nazis demanded in addition to the trucks. McClelland sent a lengthy cable to Pehle, asking for evidence that Mayer had $2 million at his disposal. The board agreed Mayer could claim he had the money, but he could make no financial or material commitments. Instead, he should pretend to be confused by Becher's list or raise specific questions about the quantity and types of goods the Nazis desired.

Mayer met with the ARBA negotiators in St. Margrethen again on September 3, 4, and 5, this time without Becher. Each night, he called McClelland to debrief. On the first day, the Nazis floated amounts as high as 100 million Swiss francs and claimed the release of the rest of Kasztner's group would cost 1.2 million Swiss francs (about $280,000), plus sheepskin and tractors. (Around this time, Pehle saw a *Life* magazine photograph of a tractor pulling German war supplies out of Paris and speculated that the Nazis wanted to use the tractors to retreat.) Mayer parried with an insistence on Red Cross supervision of all labor camps. After the second day, McClelland wrote in his notes, "US to be held responsible for what happens to Jews . . . Becher wants material. *No* means death." After the third day, he wrote, "What will ARBA offer in return?" then answered his own question: "Keep them alive."

McClelland did not update Washington again until September 16 and, even then, only sent a short cable commenting on the difficulty of the dealings. Mayer had attempted to stall, but "all time possible has now been gained and . . . in all probability the Gestapo has lost patience so that these negotiations can be considered as having lapsed, negotiations which after all were ultimately doomed to failure." McClelland's characteristic handwritten annotations on the cable are absent, and he clearly had no idea how to proceed.

Soon McClelland would add Slovakia to Mayer's long list of demands. On August 29, the Slovak underground, inspired by Romania's defection to the Allies, launched an uprising against Jozef Tiso's Nazi-collaborating regime. An independent nation allied with Germany, Slovakia had been the first unoccupied country to voluntarily deport its citizens, sending about fifty-seven thousand Jews to Nazi-occupied Poland in 1942. Two years later, with the uprising threatening his power, Tiso called on the newly created *Einsatzgruppe H* to swarm in, crush the partisans, and deport the remaining twenty-four thousand Jews.

Information about the uprising reached the United States almost immediately. Pehle hoped to be fast and proactive enough to prevent deportations and deployed the same tactics the board had tried in Hungary in the spring. The WRB urged the Swiss and Swedish governments and the International Red Cross to send strong warnings into Slovakia. It pressured the Vatican to intervene; after all, Slovakia was a Catholic country, and Tiso a Catholic priest. From Switzerland, Roswell McClelland immediately plugged into his underground channels, sending even more money across the border to aid Slovak partisans. Between July and September—just before and after the uprising—McClelland sent 950,000 Swiss francs (more than $220,000) into Slovakia. Pehle authorized the JDC to send $178,000 more.

The negotiations on the Swiss border resumed in late September, but it was more of the same. Mayer complained he couldn't select goods in Switzerland without a Nazi specialist, but the Swiss would undoubtedly refuse to grant that person an entrance visa. The Nazis promised to end the deportations of Slovakian Jews and to release the remaining Kasztner Jews from Bergen-Belsen. McClelland reported to the board, "By bluffing it has happily been possible to draw matters out another time although whole affair is becoming very strained."

In the meantime, the SS death squads of *Einsatzgruppe H* deported a majority of Slovakia's Jews. The rabbi of Neutra—who had demanded $1 million from Isaac Sternbuch—suddenly disappeared. Only a small group holding protective papers, including some Americans, remained but had been arrested and confined to a large estate in the famous Catholic pilgrimage village of Marianka. The United States had never recognized Slovakia as an independent country and therefore didn't have a protecting power to assist the American prisoners. Nazi Germany scornfully dismissed the War Refugee Board's warnings, responding that it "does not (repeat not) recognize the right of the U.S." to protest the deportations, and "in addition it considers the tone of these notes unacceptable, in particular the threat." In November, McClelland reported that the Marianka estate had almost certainly been abandoned, the prisoners deported to Auschwitz.

In Hungary, the stalled discussions took on new urgency. With Soviet troops at the border, Ferenc Szálasi, the leader of the fascist, pro-Nazi Arrow Cross Party, seized power in Budapest, forcing Admiral Horthy, who had been secretly negotiating an armistice, to resign. Within a day, the Arrow Cross mandated Jews once again wear the yellow star. Within two, Jews once again began to disappear.

Raoul Wallenberg, who only three days before the coup had dictated an optimistic message to the WRB and had been planning his trip home, updated the WRB again on October 22, his adrenaline evident. His Jewish staff had gone into hiding, and he still couldn't locate ten of them, who might have gotten caught up in the arrests. More than a thousand Jews had already been murdered, and Swedish protective papers probably couldn't save their bearers much longer.

As the situation deteriorated in Hungary, the War Refugee Board staff repeated the actions they had taken before, in Slovakia and also northern Italy, where, in the summer, Jews swept north by the retreating German army had been threatened with deportation. The WRB asked the Vatican to appeal to Hungarian Catholic principles; publicized the threat against Budapest's Jews; and protested through the Swiss Foreign Office, which warned the WRB to watch the tone of its "messages which are in the nature of threats to officials in Germany." But for the most part, the War Refugee Board waited. It had reason to be hopeful: by November 1, the *New York Times* was reporting that the Red Army was only twenty-four miles from Budapest. Pehle assumed the Jews would be liberated soon.

The ARBA ransom negotiations finally resumed on October 29. The Allies were fast approaching the German border, and Mayer expanded his list of demands to include the end of all extermination activities (and all actions "not directly related to normally accepted concept of a war effort") and the release of all Jews holding protective papers. He also expected Red Cross supervision in camps to ensure the terms of any agreement were fulfilled. In exchange, Mayer would place 20 million francs in an authorized account, which the Nazis could use on credit. When the Nazis demanded cash instead, Mayer claimed the money had to remain blocked until the ARBA negotiators provided their list of goods, which Mayer would then arrange for export.

With a deal nearly completed, Roswell McClelland didn't know what to do. The board had gained the time it wanted—for Kasztner's Jews, anyway—but clearly not enough. The war still raged; the Arrow Cross rounded Budapest's Jews up by the thousands, forcing them to march toward Germany. Even if the JDC were permitted to send actual funds, the American government would not allow exports of war matériel or commercial products to Nazi Germany. The charade had to end. On November 16, McClelland sent a long update to the WRB, concluding, "It is my considered opinion that SM should be instructed by WRB and JDC to discontinue negotiations as tactfully as possible. I personally fear that if bluff is carried too far before being broken off Nazis may effect reprisals on Jews out of anger."

McClelland kept a very important piece of information secret. He never told Pehle, and the only reference in his copious handwritten notes is a reminder not to tell Swiss police "I was at Savoy on Sun.

night." Later in his life, after others, including Kasztner, had written about the ARBA ransom scheme, McClelland would finally confess.

On Sunday, November 5, Roswell McClelland stepped off a train in Zurich. After disembarking, he walked toward the east side of Paradeplatz and entered the one-hundred-year-old white neo-classical Hotel Savoy Baur en Ville, nestled amid the various Swiss bank headquarters. He stopped at the bar to down two glasses of stiff brandy. A few minutes later, in a large conference room dominated by a green table with twenty empty seats, Saly Mayer presented Roswell McClelland, personal representative of President Roosevelt, to *SS-Obersturmbannführer* Kurt Becher, dressed in his crisp SS uniform. The opposing sides sat facing each other. Saly Mayer went on and on—McClelland later described Mayer as "a tremendous talker, he talked in great oblique circles"—even translating a Dorothy Thompson article in *Reader's Digest* about the coming German defeat, all to convince Becher that the United States wanted to negotiate. McClelland was there as proof.

The fact of the meeting, however, was more important than the message. In the midst of a world war, an American government representative held a top secret, unauthorized meeting with a high-ranking SS official to negotiate on humanitarian matters. McClelland and Mayer were playing with fire.

A few days later, in a personal letter addressed to "my dear and good friend Ross," Saly Mayer wrote, "With all happenings in this Arba-Barter Job of the past 6 months I have enough courage left to face all the unknown the future holds in store. You have been very good to me and I do thank you most heartily. There is at least one man who knows that I have left nothing undone to 'produce results' even if unorthodox methods had to be applied."

On November 18, Pehle responded to McClelland's pessimistic cable about ending negotiations. He confirmed that providing any money to the Nazis "cannot (repeat not) be supported by the Board in any way and further it is the Board's opinion that no (repeat no) funds from any source should be used to carry out such proposal." But he also gave McClelland an impossible instruction: keep the negotiations going. Pehle provided no suggestions as to how to prolong the ruse. Frustrated, McClelland scribbled on the side of the cable, "Without funds it cannot be continued." McClelland broke the news to Mayer that the meetings had to end.

In the early morning hours of December 7, the Nazis took 1,335 Jews, the rest of the original Kasztner group, by train from Bergen-Belsen and deposited them on the border near St. Margrethen. Despite McClelland's orders, Saly Mayer had kept negotiating.

Even without money, Mayer had managed to turn the conversation toward something he thought might be more palatable to the United States. In exchange for an end to mass killing, he proposed supplying concentration camps with food, clothing, and medicine to be distributed under Red Cross supervision. In effect, the Nazis would not have to expend any resources to keep Jews alive—though McClelland noted they had not been expending much anyway—and could claim after the war that they had performed "humanitarian acts" in allowing the supplies to reach the prisoners.

Becher had his own reasons to keep the negotiations going. Himmler wanted to maintain an outlet to the West in case he wanted to propose a separate peace, and Becher also thought that ARBA provided him an alibi as a good, helpful Nazi. Despite the Nazis' scornful rejection of the WRB's warnings of a postwar reckoning, the message had clearly sunk in. After Kasztner claimed Mayer had the money but would never pay so long as the rest of the Bergen-Belsen group remained imprisoned, the Jews arrived on the Swiss border.

Roswell McClelland hoped their release—for which multiple relief organizations claimed credit—might change Washington's mind about Mayer's proposal. McClelland was "personally skeptical that such a watered down proposal (from SS view point) will hold any great interest for Germans [but] certainly nothing has been lost in making it and a few more precious days have been gained." But the board once again said no.

Saly Mayer refused to give up. On December 28, he wrote his arguments: "There are two Nazi groups in the SS organization, of which one is for the preservation of the still existing Jews, the other for the extermination. It is our interest and intention to support the former against the latter. In order to do so, we have to make an offer." Having rejected the possibility of providing war matériel, "we have negotiated on the basis of sustaining the Jews in the hands of the Germans and Hungarians ... Our plan also has the advantage that it may be defended on ethical grounds" and doesn't break any of the JDC's rules or, he thought, American law.

McClelland sent Mayer's message to the War Refugee Board immediately. If the board would issue the license, the JDC would authorize 20 million Swiss francs, one-third of its entire 1944 budget. The money could only be used by the Red Cross and only under the joint signatures of Mayer and McClelland.

The War Refugee Board finally agreed in January. After informing the War Department and the British government—though not Moscow, because the State Department feared rousing Soviet suspicions—John Pehle issued license W-2402. The terms were, as McClelland joked to Mayer, "pretty binding for us both!"

Armed with the license, Saly Mayer finally, after stringing the Nazis along for more than five months on spit and promises, had something real with which to negotiate.

McClelland's Report

O N AN UNSEASONABLY WARM November 1 in Washington, Pehle was preoccupied with the future. He spent much of the day working on a report criticizing the British occupation plan, which, he thought, advocated too much freedom for a defeated German population. Morgenthau was busily planning a Treasury Department reorganization and rethinking the entire domestic economic system, which even his staff worried would be an overreach. With the noise of typing and low, whispered conversations around him, Pehle pulled a cover letter on "Legation of the United States of America" stationery out of a thick envelope that had just been handed to him. Three pages later, he saw Roswell McClelland's signature for the very first time. McClelland's Auschwitz report had finally arrived.

When the Seventh Army finally reached the border near Geneva in late September, Switzerland had been surrounded for nearly two years. Officially, American diplomats there had been trapped. A secret courier had been sneaking microfilm once a month from Bern to Lisbon and back, enabling the State Department to receive new cryptographic tools from Washington, but this ended in February 1944. Allen Dulles, head of the OSS in Switzerland, made one daily phone call to report on new intelligence. Letters and packages from home, mainly routed through Lisbon, took months to arrive, if they ever came at all. Any time-sensitive or confidential correspondence had to go through the code room, which sent nearly 9,000 cables to Washington in 1944—a huge increase from the 161 messages sent in 1939.

In his long July cable, McClelland had promised Pehle he would send the reports on the Auschwitz-Birkenau extermination camp "when the facilities of the mails permit." By the time they arrived, Pehle had forgotten about them entirely.

Ross McClelland spent a long time preparing the reports, months in fact. Whenever he had a spare moment, usually late at night in Bern while away from his family, he worked on them, translating the reports from German, then editing and revising by hand for clarity and effect. He covered pages of yellow notebook paper and light green scraps with his spidery handwriting, crossing out words, adding marginalia. He created paragraph indentations, deleted a drawing of a watchtower, and checked the math on the numerical estimates of the murdered. By the time he sent the reports to the War Refugee Board, McClelland knew the contents intimately.

He also understood what they meant on a personal level, in a way Pehle never could. In his cover letter, McClelland wrote, "While it is of course impossible to directly vouch for their complete authenticity, I have every reason to believe that they are, unfortunately, a true picture of the frightful happenings in these camps." The dates in which the Slovak escapees reported French Jews arriving at Auschwitz tracked with his own memories from that summer two years earlier, when he worked in Les Milles. He remembered back to the bright August morning when he watched his friends being taken away, and understood the end to their story.

On October 12, when a courier came to collect envelopes for the first diplomatic pouch in nearly two years, McClelland submitted his typed copies of the reports. That day, Nazi radio out of Berlin reported that rumors of mass executions at Auschwitz and Birkenau were "devoid of any foundation."

McClelland returned to Geneva the following night, and after a few hours' sleep Marjorie woke him up. At daybreak, they made it to the clinic, where Marjorie gave birth to their second son, Kirk Richard McClelland. Kirk was born with blue eyes and an inch of dark hair, entering the world before the doctor had time to take off his hat. A package of baby clothes Marjorie's family sent from Connecticut when their first son was born finally arrived just after the second.

The envelope in Pehle's hands, then, contained Roswell McClelland's first direct message to the War Refugee Board. McClelland had included three copies each of the two reports, totaling more than 150 pages. The testimonies—one written by two Slovak Jews who had been in Auschwitz from the 1942 deportations until their escape in April 1944, and one by a non-Jewish Polish major who had escaped separately—were nauseating in their details. Pehle was stunned by the pages of specifics: the cattle car trip to Auschwitz, the selection process, how the gas chambers worked, the typhus and dysentery outbreaks, the burning of corpses, all explained calmly and soberly. He had never read anything like it.

Pehle immediately gave a copy of the reports to Morgenthau's personal secretary, Henrietta Klotz, who took them home to read. She lost a night of sleep. At Morgenthau's regular morning meeting, Pehle already knew he wanted to publicize the contents. He wondered whether the Book-of-the-Month Club, popular nationwide, might publish the reports, "because this ought to be required reading for the people of the United States. I think it would do an awful lot of good."

While awaiting Morgenthau's feedback, the WRB's assistant executive director Florence Hodel made a list of ways in which the board might use the reports. It could simply release them to the press, publish them in some form, or add the information to the army manual for soldiers entering Germany. Maybe the board should begin a new psychological warfare campaign, dropping the testimonies in pamphlet form over enemy territory. Pehle took the liberty of sending a copy to the Book-of-the-Month Club editor to gauge his interest.

Pehle also considered approaching the War Department again about bombing Auschwitz. He had remained neutral about it over the summer as agency representatives, WRB staff members, and the Polish government in exile submitted variations of the request, from destroying the camp altogether to persuading the Soviet Union to send armed paratroopers. But, finally understanding the reality of Auschwitz, Pehle changed his mind. His November 8 letter to McCloy was direct and forceful. "Until now, despite pressure from many sources, I have been hesitant to urge the destruction of these camps by direct, military action. But I am convinced that the point has now been reached where such action is justifiable if it is deemed feasible by competent

military authorities. I strongly recommend that the War Department
give serious consideration to the possibility of destroying the execu-
tion chambers and crematories in Birkenau through direct bombing
action." Pehle stapled the letter to a copy of the Auschwitz reports.

McCloy responded ten days later, providing the same answer as
before but with more explanation. The necessary precision bombers
to target the gas chambers were not nearby and were needed elsewhere.
The War Department told Pehle it had "given careful consideration to
your suggestion" but concluded that bombing the camp was simply
too dangerous and success too uncertain. The WRB could not divert
resources, and McCloy reminded Pehle, "The positive solution to this
problem is the earliest possible victory over Germany, to which end
we should exert our entire means." He returned the reports without
comment, and, almost certainly, without reading them.

Neither man knew that on the very day Pehle read the reports,
Auschwitz's gas chambers shut down.

With "direct military action" still not a possibility, John Pehle
thought the War Department could help him in another way. In
late October, Sergeant Richard Paul of *Yank* magazine, a U.S. Army
publication for soldiers, had called to see if the board could help him
find an atrocity story for the December 1 issue. Paul, the son of the
now-retired Treasury official Randolph Paul (who had accompanied
Morgenthau and Pehle to the meeting urging Roosevelt to create the
WRB), wanted details from an official source. The Auschwitz reports
arrived at a perfect time. Pehle gave Paul copies and sat for an interview about the WRB's work and about Auschwitz, emphasizing that
however shocking the information might be, nothing had been exaggerated. "We on the War Refugee Board have been very skeptical. We
remembered too well the atrocity stories of the last war, many of which
apparently were untrue." The board was making the reports public "in
the firm conviction that they should be read and understood by all
Americans."

Pehle did some math: if the *Yank* article was slated for the December 1 issue, the WRB should therefore plan for nationwide publication
a few days earlier, on Sunday, November 26.

Paul's draft for *Yank,* however, was rejected by his New York edi-
tors, according to WRB's clearly incredulous press officer Virginia

Mannon: "Our reports were too Semitic and they had asked him to get a story from other sources . . . I told him. . . . that inasmuch as the whole Nazi extermination program was more than 90 percent Jewish, it was most unlikely that he could get any stories that did not deal principally with Jews." Sergeant Paul also had difficulties with the Pentagon in clearing the reports for overseas publication, because it was "'a hell of a hot story' and would have to move through the highest military channels for approval." If *Yank* didn't want to publish stories about Nazi atrocities against Jews—presumably fearing antisemitism among soldiers who might think they were being asked to risk their lives rescuing Jews—the WRB could not help.

The Book-of-the-Month Club passed, too. It had just published *Story of a Secret State,* the Polish resistance officer Jan Karski's book about wartime Poland and the Warsaw ghetto, and didn't want to burn its readers out on too many atrocity stories.

Undeterred, Pehle moved ahead with his plan to release the reports. After deleting some perpetrator and prisoner names, and debating but ultimately retaining stories of Jewish *kapos* attacking fellow prisoners, the board sent dozens of copies to journalists nationwide on Saturday, November 18, under the title "German Extermination Camps—Auschwitz and Birkenau." Pehle also provided copies for each of the congressmen at the House Appropriations Committee hearing about the WRB's funding. He pointedly failed to clear his decision with the War Department or any other government branch.

The newspaper copies came with a one-page cover note emphasizing that Americans should read and believe: "It is a fact beyond denial that the Germans have deliberately and systematically murdered millions of innocent civilians—Jews and Christians alike—all over Europe . . . So revolting and diabolical are the German atrocities that the minds of civilized people find it difficult to believe that they have actually taken place. But the governments of the United States and of other countries have evidence which clearly substantiates the facts." After explaining the board's general mission and informing readers that the two reports had been written independently, Pehle concluded, quoting McClelland, the "Board has every reason to believe that these reports present a true picture of the frightful happenings in these camps."

The WRB's phones rang ceaselessly as reporters in Reno, Chicago,

Flint, Miami, Philadelphia, Milwaukee, and other cities throughout the country prepared their front-page stories. They quoted extensively from the reports, shared copies with their editorial writers and cartoonists, and checked details, preparing for the story to hit on November 26.

But Elmer Davis, the Office of War Information's director and a former journalist himself, had not approved the text for public consumption. Pehle and two members of his staff were summoned to Davis's office on a Thursday afternoon, three days before publication day. Flanked by six members of the OWI staff, Davis strenuously objected to the WRB's unilateral decision to release the reports, an oversight that Pehle claimed was unintentional. Pehle later confided to Hirschmann, "We did run into some opposition . . . 'unfortunately' the opposition didn't develop until the story had been released to the press," adding the quotation marks to ensure Hirschmann caught his sarcasm.

Pehle and his staff sat through the verbal flogging as Davis and his people registered their objections. One believed it might result in bad press overseas. Another thought the reports were overdramatic, "concerned with a multiplicity of 'mean little things.'" They didn't like the fact that Pehle's cover note was, like all official WRB statements, written on "Executive Office of the President" letterhead. The timing of the release, coinciding with the sixth war bond drive, could be a problem. Perhaps the most baffling excuse was the OWI's belief that the reports might be false, created by Nazis or antisemites, because they described Jews being cruel to other Jews. By the time the WRB staff was released from the meeting, they could only laugh at the absurdity. Virginia Mannon, the board's press officer, wrote that "the whole meeting was pretty futile, since the release was a fait accompli . . . The enormity of the crimes which the WRB had perpetrated against the OWI was so great that Mr. Davis admitted there was practically nothing to be done at this late date."

After the meeting, Davis wrote again, asking the WRB to supplement its cover note to the press by releasing a public statement claiming the credibility of the reports rested with the unnamed men who wrote them. He reiterated that the prisoners might have escaped with the help of SS officers eager to place anti-Jewish stories in the press.

Pehle drafted a response, then didn't bother sending it. The WRB had no intention of throwing any doubt on the reports.

Despite OWI's concerns, the "German Extermination Camps" publication was certainly not the first report about massacres to appear in the press. A reader looking for information could find it, though atrocity stories were usually relegated—due to competition with war news and the fact that they were usually unverified—to the inside pages of the newspaper. After the liberation of the largely abandoned Majdanek concentration camp in July 1944, the Soviet Union had invited journalists to tour the camp. The ten million subscribers to *Life* magazine could read a description of the crematoriums and mass graves in a September article, "Sunday in Poland," while *PM,* a daily New York newspaper, printed a two-page spread including a life-sized photograph of a child's shoe the reporter had taken from the piles of victims' belongings discovered at the camp and brought home. The *New York Times* quoted Ambassador Averell Harriman in Moscow promising the crimes had not been exaggerated.

At long last, the excruciating details of the "German Extermination Camps" report hit newsstands throughout the country on November 26. The *Philadelphia Inquirer* proclaimed, "1,765,000 Jews Killed with Gas at German Camp," and called the report "the most incredibly shocking story of the war . . . For 58 horrifying pages of single-spaced, blood-curdling sentences, the report unfolded . . . By its very detail, the report fairly shouted 'this is the truth!'" Larger newspapers carried original reporting, mostly on the front pages. Nearly seventy others, large and small—the *Denver Post,* the *Wheeling News Register,* the *Texarkana Gazette,* the *Fargo Forum,* Boise's *Idaho Statesman,* the *Grand Rapids Herald*—carried Associated Press or International News Service dispatches. The articles were all lengthy, describing the horrific details of Auschwitz and the process of prisoner arrival, selection, and gassing. Louisville's *Courier-Journal* reprinted the text, almost in its entirety, in small font over a full newspaper page. Most articles began by noting that the shocking information, once thought to be just rumor, was now confirmed by an official government agency. "This time," wrote a *Topeka Capital* journalist, "apparently beyond the shadow of a doubt, the Germans have been carrying out mass murder and torture in a manner which will shame civilized mankind for generations to come."

In the days that followed, editorials appeared in papers from the *Miami News* to Maine's *Lewiston Gazette* to the Portland *Oregonian*. The editorials were strikingly similar. Most began with a reflection on past atrocity reports, usually World War I rumors of German brutality, before emphasizing that the "German Exterminations Camps" report had been verified by the War Refugee Board (specifically, by Hull, Stimson, and Morgenthau). The *Fall River Herald News* in Massachusetts titled its editorial "German Culture," writing, "Many Germans must have been infected with stench of the crematories and it is a stench that will remain with the Germans indefinitely. We do not know of anything they can do to remove it."

Pehle's decision to emphasize the veracity of the reports—and not to water them down with the OWI-suggested disclaimer—resulted in the nationwide publication, for the first time, of information about the Auschwitz-Birkenau extermination camp with the imprimatur of the United States.

Inevitably, new articles appeared about the need for postwar justice. One congressman reminded the *New York World-Telegram* that the list of "war guilty of the last war" had dwindled from nine hundred to twelve prior to any trials. The United States could not permit that to happen again, nor would Americans settle for anything less than unconditional surrender. The *Salt Lake Tribune*'s editorial board wrote, "It is time to silence the sob-sisters and apologists who are slyly beginning to quietly campaign for a soft peace and a pardon for 'a people led astray by inhuman or insane leaders.' Such pleas are insults to the intelligence of Americans and a betrayal of the men and women in uniforms exposing their lives and risking their reason in an effort to stop these atrocities and exterminate the rabid beasts and reptiles that are causing more sorrow and suffering in this age of enlightenment than was ever known in the world before." An editorial cartoon in the *Minneapolis Star-Journal* showed a Nazi holding a sign reading "Soft Peace for Germany" being crushed under the weight of hundreds of bricks labeled "Atrocity Stories." The cartoon was called "The Weight of Evidence."

The War Refugee Board staff was thrilled by the press reports. Virginia Mannon kept a running list of newspaper and editorial coverage as well as anecdotes, like how Mrs. Actin of Treasury's disbursement office stopped by to say her priest had talked about the reports in his Sunday sermon. She gleefully anticipated OWI's reaction to all the positive press: "I am almost coming to the modest conclusion that OWI might take a lesson from us on the atrocity stories ... Do you think we should heap coals of fire on OWI and offer them copies of the editorials to use overseas, as one of the gentlemen suggested that they might do? Or let them stew in their own juice?" In the margin, another WRB staffer scribbled, "Yes." Two OWI sources admitted the report was receiving excellent coverage in Great Britain and had even been entered in evidence at a war crimes trial in the liberated part of Poland. The army requested copies of the reports for its magazines—more vindication after the *Yank* rejection.

Thousands of American citizens wrote to the WRB in Washington asking for copies—for their fellow soldiers, their neighbors who didn't believe, their students, their church. University libraries wrote in, and professors asked for multiple sets to use as teaching tools. The France Forever organization asked for five thousand copies to distribute to its membership. Others wrote for more personal reasons, like Hugo Hecht of Cleveland, who wanted a copy because "many of my relatives and friends probably died there." The WRB staff sent copies to each person who made a request and made it clear they encouraged reprinting and distribution.

One week after the report's release, Gallup published the results of a poll about Nazi atrocities. A full 76 percent of Americans believed Germans had murdered many people in concentration camps, compared with only 12 percent who did not believe (and 12 percent who had no opinion). But despite the WRB's reporting that 1.7 million people had been killed in Auschwitz alone, most people still couldn't fathom the numbers. The largest plurality, 27 percent, estimated that fewer than 100,000 people had been killed. Only 12 percent believed the number to be more than 2 million. The *Washington Post* headline noted that most people had "underestimated," but "regardless of the number involved, the American people are fully prepared to believe atrocities have taken place."

That same issue of the *Washington Post* included an editorial prompted by the WRB report, describing the crimes at Auschwitz as "systematic and purposeful," deserving of a name greater than "atrocity." The editorial board proposed a new word, one coined by the Polish scholar and attorney Raphael Lemkin, who wanted this new category of crime to be adopted and prosecuted under international law. For the first time in a newspaper, Americans read the word "genocide."

War at Christmas

B ELIEVING THAT ALLIED VICTORY was imminent and that
the War Refugee Board's efforts would soon end, John Pehle privately reflected on the past ten months of his life and work. A letter
from his college English professor Father Francis Reilly "served the
useful purpose of stimulating my own thinking."

The priest had written to commend his former student's accomplishments and to sympathize with the problem he saw Pehle facing:
minorities with a persecution complex. "If 'their skirts were clean,' if
they 'set their houses in order' and 'keep within the spirit of the law'
their lot would be more to their liking,—but 'you cannot have your
cake and eat it.' Reformation must come from above and from within,"
Reilly wrote. The years they had known each other led him to presume
Pehle was a kindred spirit, someone who would smile in agreement
with these observations.

Pehle was, by nature, professional, guarded, and measured in his
thoughts and words. He kept no surviving diaries, never wrote a memoir, and later in life only hesitantly discussed his War Refugee Board
work with others. His response to Father Reilly is the most personal
and heartfelt thing Pehle ever wrote that survives in an archive:

> Maybe it is because I am young and optimistic that I find it
> impossible to be passively fatalistic about the plight of minori-
> ties. On the contrary I am profoundly troubled by the sense
> of complacency and inevitability that so frequently prevails

among my fellow-members of the majority when minorities are discussed. And it is shocking to see people persecuted and killed merely because they happen to belong to groups that are powerless to defend themselves. If I have reached any conclusion worthy of generalization on this matter, it is that individuals should be judged as individuals and not as members of groups ... Law violators, dirty skirts, cake-eaters and inferiority complexes—to borrow your own expressions—exist in all groups in pretty much the same proportions, so far as I can observe. I happen to resent them wherever they exist. But I resent equally the unfair condemnation, by the majority, of all members of a minority because of the sins of some of its members. And I have literally shuddered at the results of this attitude in Europe where millions have been slaughtered merely because they happen to share an ancient religion and cultural heritage. I consider myself fortunate to have been asked to serve our Government in conducting an emergency program of relief and rescue of the persecuted minorities of Europe. It has been a rewarding experience. It has given me a chance to reduce a shocking injustice if only by a minute amount. I wish I could do more.

John Pehle was the most unlikely of "woke" heroes. Until late 1943, just the year before, he had no humanitarian relief or rescue aspirations. He was a latecomer to this war, an ill-prepared general. He wasn't an activist, politician, or revolutionary but a white Protestant man from the Midwest, a straight-shooting Treasury Department federal employee with a homburg hat, two kids, and a house in suburbia. He collected pipes, bowled in a league with guys from the office, and spent his days manipulating bureaucratic tools—which, in less idealistic hands, led to red tape, delays, and complications—and harnessing them to save lives.

If Father Reilly responded to Pehle's firm rebuke, his letter does not survive in public records.

Two days after a nation's breakfasts got cold while Americans read about Auschwitz-Birkenau in their morning newspapers, John Pehle sat in Henry Morgenthau's office as his colleagues discussed his fate.

He listened quietly for at least thirty minutes as they debated what he should and ought to know and do and what sorts of responsibilities he would have, as if Pehle weren't right there in the room. He had no choice in the matter.

Faced with staffing gaps, and restructuring to anticipate postwar challenges, Morgenthau suddenly needed an assistant secretary in charge of the Surplus Property office in the Procurement Division, someone who could sell government assets, from clothes to film to vehicles, and could reconvert factories for postwar use. It would be a massive job, overseeing billions of dollars, with corruption a constant temptation. Morgenthau wanted no part of it. He had argued to Roosevelt that Surplus Property should be removed from Treasury entirely, but he lost that fight and now proposed the best option he could imagine. "Pehle has run a fifteen-hundred-man shop with great success. He is the only one here who has time, and who has had the administrative experience . . . And I think he should do it. We are in a mess." At lunch the day before, Pehle had begged off. He didn't want the job, but Morgenthau decided he needed someone "willing to say, 'I am a good soldier; I'll take it on until we can lick it.'" At the meeting, Pehle spoke up only when someone assumed he would have to resign from the War Refugee Board. "I won't shirk my responsibility. I think we have to think through the relationship between this and the War Refugee Board . . . I'd like to think that through, myself." Morgenthau gave him one night to worry, but the new assignment was nonnegotiable.

The next morning, Pehle reluctantly agreed to take over Surplus Property and Procurement. He wanted to stay with the War Refugee Board as well, to avoid public criticism and because he couldn't predict his replacement. It wasn't a good time to ask the War or State Department for help selecting a new director. Henry Stimson was annoyed Pehle hadn't notified the War Department prior to releasing the Auschwitz reports; he had read about them in the newspaper along with the rest of the country. John McCloy didn't recall seeing anything in advance either, even though Pehle had forwarded copies in early November with the bombing request.

The State Department was experiencing an even more volatile week than Treasury. The same day the Auschwitz reports hit newsstands, Cordell Hull, who had been in and out of the hospital all year, resigned after nearly twelve years as secretary of state. Assistant Secretaries Adolf Berle and Breckinridge Long also submitted their resignations, and Roosevelt nominated Edward Stettinius to head the State Department. Neither Stimson nor Stettinius was prepared to propose a new War Refugee Board director, though Stettinius wondered aloud whether his new State Department should officially assume the board's duties.

Now tasked with two jobs, Pehle tried to make the best of things, jokingly claiming Morgenthau's box seats at the upcoming Army-Navy football game as surplus property. The Treasury Department released a brief statement that, at Pehle's suggestion, barely mentioned the War Refugee Board. Political junkies could blink while reading the November 30 newspaper and miss the story entirely.

On Friday evening, December 1, a messenger knocked on the door of Otto and Agnes Pehle's home in Omaha. He handed them a telegram. Before that long night ended, through their tears, they telephoned their elder son in Washington to tell him he was now their only surviving son. Twenty-eight-year-old first lieutenant Richard C. Pehle of the First Battalion, 180th Infantry, Forty-Fifth Division, Seventh Army, had fallen in combat on October 24, on the last day of a three-week battle to liberate the small village of Frémifontaine, France, in the foothills of the Vosges Mountains. Despite a seven-year age gap, the Pehle brothers had been close. They looked similar, with twin widow's peaks, and both attended college at Creighton. John and Francha would soon change fifteen-month-old Stephen's name to honor John's little brother, an uncle the toddler would now never meet. Despite his grief, John Pehle returned to work on Monday. It had been a hell of a week, and the war that was supposed to be over by Christmas wasn't.

It was counterintuitive for the winter of 1944–1945 to be hard times for the War Refugee Board. Allied victory seemed certain, though no one knew when the end would come. The thousands of Jews emerging from hiding in liberated territory proved the Nazis would ultimately lose their second war, too. European Jews yet lived, though no one knew how many. Nazi control quickly constricted as American, British, and Soviet boys advanced from all directions. But instead of concluding with hope, the WRB's work wound down amid profound fear for the future.

On October 26, Ira Hirschmann gave the keynote address at a Metropolitan Zionist Fund event, raising money to support Palestine as a homeland for surviving European Jews. His speech, supposedly giving an insider's perspective, might have been different had he actually still been one. A cable from the American embassy in Jerusalem, sent two weeks earlier, arrived in Washington that day, containing potentially devastating news.

Though the White Paper had technically expired in March 1944, the Jewish Agency continued issuing Palestine entry certificates to all Jews who escaped to Istanbul. In October, the British decided the ad hoc arrangement had been in place too long and, without alerting Washington or the War Refugee Board, imposed new White Paper limits. Jewish immigration into Palestine would henceforth be restricted to 1,500 persons per month for the next six months (with a few exceptions), for an overall total of 10,300 new arrivals. Those quotas were further delineated, a razor segmenting the monthly portions. A maximum of 1,000 immigrants from Yemen, 900 from Italy, 200 from Turkey, 5,000 total from Romania and Bulgaria, and 3,200 children of any nationality could enter Palestine, in monthly percentages. There was no special dispensation for refugees escaping Nazism. When the WRB wrote to London for confirmation of the new restrictions, no one responded.

Once the quota news reached him, Herbert Katzki frantically contacted Pehle, raising important questions: What of the people in Budapest or Bergen-Belsen benefiting from protection because they held Palestine certificates—were these now canceled? Did the failure to include Hungary or Slovakia in the quota list mean that no one could emigrate from these countries? Did this kill the agreement with the Turkish government regarding ships from Romania and Bulgaria?

In Washington, the British embassy told the WRB that Palestine certificates held by Jews in concentration camps and in Hungary were still valid, and "while the bookkeeping is terribly confusing . . . the

British Government will regard the White Paper limitation as flexible." The WRB staff was not reassured.

After two months with no refugee boats arriving in Istanbul, the *Selahattin* docked in late October with 547 passengers, many literally hanging off the side of the small ship. Some Hungarian men, liberated from forced labor in the copper mines in Bor, Yugoslavia, disembarked still wearing prisoner uniforms. An additional 283 refugees crossed into Turkey by rail in late October and early November. The new restrictions, Katzki learned, were retroactive. Already, 830 certificates were gone.

Katzki then discovered another complication. The Turkish Foreign Office, also hoping to limit refugees, used the Allied realignment of Romania and Bulgaria as an excuse to unilaterally end transit permits for the so-called children's scheme—the 75 children and 10 adults allowed to enter Turkey every ten days. The day before the Foreign Office's announcement, 119 had arrived, and Katzki knew 70 more would reach the border soon.

Katzki alerted Ambassador Steinhardt, who, at a meeting with Turkish officials, "indicated clearly that any attempt to disturb the existing arrangements would prompt me to go straight to the Prime Minister for an explanation as to why the Turkish Government desired to no longer participate in the humanitarian act of helping us to rescue unfortunates." Steinhardt thought his protest worked, reassuring Katzki that the "children's scheme" would continue, because his "violent reaction has punctured these trial balloons." Katzki guessed the Turkish Foreign Office was feeling inconvenienced by so many new arrivals, between the children and the *Selahattin,* and feared being pulled into an Arab-Jewish conflict by facilitating the transit of refugees destined for Palestine. And with the new British-imposed quotas, the Turkish government had additional cause for concern: refugees might become stuck in Turkey, unable to enter Palestine.

Emigration slowed, and only two large groups arrived in Istanbul in December and January. The *Toros,* traveling from Constanţa with 908 passengers, showed up unexpectedly on December 5, the final refugee boat to arrive in 1944. The passengers were also the last to receive Palestine certificates upon arrival. The group—which included children repatriated from Transnistria, forced labor survivors, and Hungarian escapees—boarded trains for Palestine on December 7, using nearly two-thirds of the month's quota.

The other group, arriving in January, had been en route for six weeks. At the end of November, Soviet representatives in Stara Zagora, Bulgaria, detained more than six hundred people traveling over land from Romania. Though the group had exit and transit visas, the Soviets held them for over a month, interrogating each emigrant and, as a demonstration of control, removing anyone born in Soviet territory. On December 21, Katzki heard that the Soviets had finally released the remaining refugees, but this presented a new problem. The group had started their journey before the British government had formally voided the agreement that new arrivals in Turkey could receive Palestine certificates. Despite the extenuating circumstances, the British held firm, which meant that Turkish border agents detained the refugees, refusing entry visas for people who had no ultimate destination. Steinhardt made "energetic interventions," and finally, on December 31, the British relented. Katzki believed the Stara Zagora group would likely be the last to arrive.

There were few projects left for Katzki in Istanbul. On New Year's Day 1945, the Soviets finally rejected his proposal, carried over from Hirschmann, to survey Romanian relief needs. They considered Romania an active military zone, claimed the area already had a "Jewish representative" (though, despite repeated attempts, the WRB could not discern who that might be), and didn't want more Allied civilians entering the country. Though the board received many pleas to assist Romanian and Bulgarian Jews struggling to regain civil rights and property, the board had no jurisdiction there. It could approve relief licenses and forward lists of medical, food, and clothing needs to American organizations but couldn't intervene directly.

On January 19, Pehle recommended Katzki close the WRB offices in Turkey. The Istanbul consulate assumed custody of all board property—lamps, telephones, buzzers, a desk fan, and a safe. Katzki dismissed his messenger, canceled coal delivery, and prepared to return to America. In all of 1944, nearly seven thousand refugees escaped from Hungary, Romania, and Bulgaria to Istanbul and, from there, to Palestine.

The Red Army encircled Budapest. On December 6, the War Refugee Board sent its last communication to Raoul Wallenberg, a letter rather than a cable. Pehle, explaining the WRB had followed Wallenberg's efforts with keen interest, wrote, "I think that no one who has participated in this great task can escape some feeling of frustration in that, because of circumstances beyond our control, our efforts have not met with complete success. On the other hand, there have been measurable achievements in the face of obstacles which had to be encountered, and it is our conviction that you have made a very great personal contribution to the success which has been realized in these endeavors."

There is no evidence Wallenberg ever received Pehle's letter. On December 22, Wallenberg's final report, written two weeks earlier, arrived in Washington. Jews remained under dire threat. More than forty thousand people had been sent on forced marches in the cold and the rain toward Germany; many died on the roadside. Twenty thousand prisoners in labor battalions struggled to dig fortifications. Dysentery raced through the Jewish ghetto. After Wallenberg intervened, Jews holding protective documents were exempted from labor service, so more than fifteen thousand traumatized people returned to Budapest. He also managed to save two thousand people about to be deported, though the Nazis threatened force if he interfered again.

As the WRB read Wallenberg's report, the Red Army began the siege. The Spanish diplomatic corps fled Budapest, leaving Sweden in charge of more than three thousand Jews under Spanish protection. The Portuguese legation was gone. Before the end of the year, Stockholm lost the ability to communicate with its diplomats in Hungary. The Red Army made slow progress, neighborhood by neighborhood, as Budapest residents starved, froze, or were caught in cross fire. Nazi personnel, including Adolf Eichmann, escaped. The WRB heard no news from Budapest until late January. The first cable seemed reassuring: "Wallenberg is safe and sound in that part of Budapest occupied by Russians." Three months went by without another word.

From the west, the Allied armies continued a long, slow drive into the Reich, hampered by snow and lacking supplies and ammunition. On December 16, Germany launched a vicious surprise counteroffensive through the Ardennes forests, thrusting into liberated French and Belgian territory, creating a seventy-mile-wide, fifty-mile-deep bulge, thinning the Allied lines. The Nazis sought to recapture the port of Antwerp, thereby splitting and surrounding the Allied armies and perhaps forcing a separate peace. It did not work. The attack soon slowed, and by the time the Allies regained the lost ground at the beginning of February, approximately 19,000 Americans had been killed, 47,500 were wounded, and more than 23,000 were missing. More Americans died in the Battle of the Bulge than in any other battle during World War II.

On Saturday, December 23, WEAF in New York City aired a live, nationwide broadcast, "Christmas in Freedom," between 4:15 and 4:30 p.m. Dorothy Thompson opened the program, speaking from a New York studio, before the live feed switched to Oswego. Joseph Smart, the director of the Fort Ontario shelter, welcomed listeners to the festivities, where "men and women of many lands and many faiths are celebrating their first Christmas in America together." The all-refugee choir sang the Yugoslav carol "A King Is Born to Us," and "I Bring You Something New," sung in Czech. Smart then spoke to listeners on behalf of the shelter residents, who wished to give their thanks "for the hospitality and kindness America has shown them, and to wish every one of you a very joyous holiday season." The choir closed with "Silent Night," then, as the sun set, returned to their barracks, still surrounded by a fence topped with barbed wire.

Before he adjusted his radio to hear the program, John Pehle sent yet another request about war criminals to the State Department. Because Stettinius still hadn't addressed the WRB's August memo on postwar trials, Pehle urged the new secretary of state to issue another public statement guaranteeing justice: "In view of the fact that an unfortunate impression has been created that the United Nations have no real intention of punishing those guilty of crimes against stateless persons . . . a statement would be particularly effective if you were to declare specifically that in the eyes of this Government persons who commit crimes against Axis Jews are war criminals."

Stettinius finally answered in early January. A new warning was "inadvisable at the present juncture," but he promised the State Department staff wasn't ignoring the problem. Pehle sent Stettinius two draft warnings for Roosevelt, Churchill, and Stalin's consideration at the upcoming Yalta Conference, because a powerful warning from the

Allied leaders would be a positive deterrent against a final purge of Jews still in Axis territory. Stettinius promised to bring the drafts with him.

In the meantime, the War Crimes Commission in London imploded. The commission's British representative resigned, complaining that the British had never given him instructions. Two weeks later, the American representative, Herbert Pell, was fired when Congress refused to allocate funds for the commission, because some congressmen didn't believe that discussions about trials were necessary until after the war. The Allies still had no legal framework for punishing Axis war criminals for crimes against Jews.

At a January 12 Treasury meeting, Pehle announced that three groups in the past week had complained he spent too much time with Procurement and not enough on the War Refugee Board. The board needed a new director, especially because it might become "a cornerstone for a post-war agency in this field. You are not going to find a great many people who are going to follow this thing through."

That afternoon, Ansel Luxford and Josiah DuBois suggested Brigadier General William O'Dwyer. He was under consideration for several government jobs, so the WRB "will have to act fast." Pehle thought O'Dwyer a natural choice, but after a visit to Treasury, O'Dwyer wouldn't commit. Eight days later, Pehle called again. The nudge worked: William O'Dwyer would become the WRB's new director, so long as Morgenthau could get him released from the army.

On Saturday, January 27, two days after O'Dwyer accepted the job—and just as, unbeknownst to the WRB, Soviet troops liberated Auschwitz-Birkenau—John Pehle resigned. Morgenthau explained to Roosevelt that Pehle's resignation and O'Dwyer's appointment should be announced immediately and simultaneously to preclude any rumors or bad publicity. John Pehle cabled Herbert Katzki in Istanbul, Ross McClelland in Geneva, and Iver Olsen, who had just returned to Stockholm, to let them know personally. To Morgenthau, whom he still saw daily, Pehle sent a letter to preserve his sentiments in writing: "I cannot terminate my service as Executive Director of the War Refugee Board without expressing to you personally the satisfaction which I have derived from this task. As I know so well, the War Refugee Board would not have been established if it had not been for your courage and intense interest . . . I want to thank you on my behalf, as well as on behalf of the many people who have benefited from the Board's activities."

Pehle gave a copy to Lawrence Lesser, Josiah DuBois, Ansel Luxford, and Florence Hodel. The War Refugee Board staff dwindled. Albert Abrahamson and Virginia Mannon had left at the end of December, Joseph Friedman in mid-January. Lesser moved to Procurement with Pehle. Luxford and DuBois were busy with other Treasury projects and had never been involved in day-to-day WRB activities anyway. Of the six original assistant executive directors, only Florence Hodel remained at the WRB offices in Washington. Though Pehle kept the same office space, he was now gone too. Effective immediately, William O'Dwyer became the executive director of the War Refugee Board.

Prisoner Exchanges

WILLIAM O'DWYER HAD A reputation as a man who could get things done. His name had first bounced around the Treasury offices in January 1944, when Roosevelt wanted someone prominent to be the WRB's first director. Back then, the War Department wouldn't release him, but a year later General William O'Dwyer was the WRB's man.

O'Dwyer had emigrated from Ireland at twenty, with, according to the extensive lore surrounding him, only $23.35 in his pocket. Six years later, in 1916, he was an American citizen and a beat cop. Seven years after that, he graduated from Fordham University Law School. After working as a lawyer and local judge, O'Dwyer won the 1939 district attorney election in Kings County, New York, and became famous nationwide for smashing the Murder, Inc. organized crime syndicate. By 1942, he had lost most of his accent, and the New York City mayoral race to Fiorello La Guardia. O'Dwyer took leave from Kings County to join the military, but in his fifties and in the midst of a political career he was not meant for the front lines. He roamed New York and Washington, ping-ponging between various bureaucratic positions—inspecting, overseeing, advising. In 1944, after winning reelection as district attorney in absentia, the soon-to-be brigadier general O'Dwyer became the American representative to the Allied Control Commission in Italy. He continued inspecting, overseeing, and advising, but Italian recovery became such a turf war between London and Washington that O'Dwyer refused to return. The War

Refugee Board's offer, which moved him out of the army's grasp and into a prominent stateside appointment, came at the perfect moment.

Originally, Henry Morgenthau had breathed a sigh of relief at O'Dwyer's willingness to become the board's new executive director. But O'Dwyer quickly proved a disappointment.

John Pehle soon commiserated with Morgenthau: "We were both taken in. I was taken in, and you were, too." On February 2, 1945, less than a week after his resignation, Pehle outlined the sequence of events that led to O'Dwyer's appointment, just to record the exact ways in which the general had manipulated and deceived the Treasury Department staff.

Carefully noting that O'Dwyer had approved his biography for the WRB's press release, Pehle underlined the inclusion of "District Attorney for Kings County, New York on leave" and his "inactive status" with the War Department. Yet within two days, O'Dwyer told Florence Hodel he would be returning to Kings County to reassume his position. The War Refugee Board had successfully given him an excuse to get out of the army, but he didn't see the directorship as a full-time job. The press excitedly reported O'Dwyer's return to New York, because "the Refugee Board post can be held by Gen. O'Dwyer without interfering with his prosecutor's duties, it is believed."

On January 30, O'Dwyer, at lunch with Morgenthau, confirmed he planned to hold both jobs, figuring the War Refugee Board could have him three or four days a week. By early February, O'Dwyer's name had already appeared in the press as a potential New York City mayoral candidate for the fall election.

O'Dwyer held a press conference in mid-afternoon on January 31, admitting beforehand "there can be no discussion of the details of the work of the War Refugee Board"—he didn't know them—but he wanted "to make the acquaintance of the press." The new director answered some easy questions about the board's reach, speculated about the number of refugees trapped in enemy territory, and denied his mayoral ambitions. The *Philadelphia Inquirer*, in the article "O'Dwyer Shocks Capital by Modest Demeanor," mentioned a "beautiful blonde secretary sitting next to him whispering the customary answers. General O'Dwyer didn't listen to her once."

Florence Hodel was nobody's secretary and, according to the transcript, provided or confirmed the answers to any difficult questions. In the weeks and months to come, as O'Dwyer politicked and Pehle ducked in whenever he could spare a moment, no one worked harder or with more dedication than Florence Hodel. She was the only WRB staff member whose work spanned the entirety of the board's existence. She participated in Pehle's first meeting and shut the lights off at the end.

Florence Hodel was thirty-seven, the eldest of three sisters, all challenged by their parents to achieve more than most women of their era. Jacob Hodel, an accountant, had demanded his young daughters provide weekly logs of their expenditures before paying their ten-cent allowances; both Florence and her sister Ethel ended up at the Treasury Department. Hodel graduated from Wellesley and Cornell Law, before working for Legal Aid in New York City. In 1939, hearing that the Treasury Department offered good jobs for female lawyers, she made her way to Washington, working alongside James Mann in the general counsel's office and later on Pehle's Foreign Funds Control staff. Serious and quiet, Hodel was a private woman with tight lips and frizzy pulled-back hair. She had no children and lived alone after her estranged, alcoholic husband joined the army and left for England. At the creation of the War Refugee Board, Pehle immediately poached her and trusted her completely.

After January 1945, Florence Hodel largely ran the WRB office. She signed letters to the public, forwarded cables to relief organizations, and attended meetings with Morgenthau when O'Dwyer wasn't in town, and often when he was. "I didn't have to be [in the office]," O'Dwyer once told Morgenthau. "She was here." At a mid-February meeting, when Morgenthau complained about the confusing chain of command—Pehle still kept him advised of most WRB activities instead of O'Dwyer—Pehle reminded him, "Miss Hodel is doing a very good job. You can always rely on her for this stuff." Morgenthau responded, "I am heavily."

Halfway through O'Dwyer's press conference, a reporter asked whether the general would "take up the cudgels" on adding crimes against Axis nationals to the War Crimes Commission's charge. The general confirmed he would, but the WRB no longer needed to intervene. The lack of a congressional appropriation for the commission outraged the public, already furious from news of the recent Nazi massacre of American POWs in Malmédy, Belgium. Walter Winchell, on his January 28 radio program, blasted, "I declare now, in my opinion, the German war criminals may escape punishment, and that our own State Dept is largely at fault." Winchell blamed Stettinius and called on the American people "to stand by the graves of our murdered soldiers."

Unbeknownst to Morgenthau or the War Refugee Board staff, three cabinet members—Stettinius, Stimson, and Attorney General Francis Biddle—had already given Roosevelt a report on the intended punishment of war criminals. They proposed a military tribunal that would consider membership in criminal organizations (like the Gestapo) evidence for a guilty verdict and reaffirmed the November 1943 Moscow Declaration's plan to place the accused on trial where the crime had taken place. Most important, the trials would include "crimes against German nationals, stateless persons, and neutrals." A new American, British, and Soviet working group replaced the War Crimes Commission and began building criminal cases.

The State Department announced this new proposal in early February, responding to "persistent heckling by the press." Though it provided few details, the public fervor dissipated. The Yalta Conference ended without any new joint warning. Nevertheless, when Stettinius returned to the United States, the State Department publicly resolved to punish "those responsible for a government's crimes against its own nationals such as the Nazi regime's atrocities against Jews of German nationality."

As winter turned to spring, the War Refugee Board offices were filled with uncertainty. Relief organizations warned of a possible "sadistic orgy" of violence, a frantic massacre of all prisoners remaining in Nazi hands, and an attempted erasure of any evidence. Others worried the Nazis would simply abandon the camps, condemning inhabitants, still far behind enemy lines, to starve or freeze to death. In Bern, Roswell McClelland heard that surviving prisoners would be taken into the redoubt, a mountainous area of southern Germany where Nazi leadership could supposedly entrench for years, directing guerrilla resistance and holding prisoners for ransom. No one knew which rumors, if any, were true. As the Red Army crossed the prewar German border in the east, hundreds of thousands of German citizens fled in fear of rape and retribution. The American and British armies, recovering from the Battle of the Bulge, raced quickly toward Berlin.

Amid heightened anxiety, the War Refugee Board continued efforts to remove refugees from deep within enemy territory, even with liberation imminent. In 1944, most of the people who escaped with the assistance of the WRB had come from the edges of Nazi territory—France, Romania, Bulgaria, the Baltics—areas now either freed or under Soviet control. The released prisoners in the winter of 1944–1945, though, came from deep in the Reich, and for every life saved, the Nazis attempted to exact a price.

Prisoner exchanges were always complicated affairs, and the warring governments held few of them, mainly to swap each other's diplomats. All negotiations had to go through neutral intermediaries, and the dithering took time. A prisoner exchange scheduled for January 1945 took eight months of advance planning as the parties bargained over the multiple categories and rankings of prisoners available to be traded.

The lists gradually took shape. The Nazis identified 641 "Category A" prisoners in Bergen-Belsen, all actual Allied citizens, including 45 Americans, 267 Paraguayans, and 111 Ecuadorans. The WRB also received a list of "Category F" prisoners—Jews holding Latin American papers. With the support of the State Department, the board decided Swiss diplomats in Berlin would select 75 of these prisoners for the final list, which, it hoped, would prove to the Nazis that there was value in treating the identity papers as valid and protecting their bearers. The WRB's gamble took exchange slots away from legitimate Allied citizens, left in Nazi Germany for the duration of the war. But the WRB believed the possible benefit to thousands of Jews holding protective papers—in Bergen-Belsen, Hungary, and elsewhere—was worth the sacrifice.

The Bern legation also suggested a new "Category G" ranking, which included the immediate family members of resident aliens living in the United States. Though none of these people were included in the prisoner exchange, the Nazis were alerted that the United States considered them exchangeable in the future and therefore worthy of special consideration.

To keep its promise to Latin American countries that liberated Jews would not appear on their shores, the War Refugee Board planned for "Category F" prisoners to be transported to an UNRRA camp in Philippeville, Algeria. The JDC agreed to pay for food, clothing, and any other necessities.

On January 30, 1945, 826 prisoners arrived in Switzerland, including 150 prisoners holding "unverified" protective papers (rather than the 75 the WRB had requested). They were in sorry shape. Fourteen exchangees had to be hospitalized in Switzerland. Four more died in their first days of freedom. On February 8, the *Gripsholm* sailed from Marseille for the United States carrying sick and wounded soldiers, as well as the "legitimate" exchangees, while the rest were routed to Algeria.

The War Refugee Board's plan worked. After the exchange, the SS transferred some Bergen-Belsen prisoners holding protective papers to civilian internment camps. A Swiss inspection of the Liebenau camp noted new arrivals, who could now enjoy hot baths, food packages, a library, and educational courses. The Nazis now knew these people could be exchanged in the future.

Isaac Sternbuch, the Swiss representative of American Orthodox organizations, was also seeking creative ways to release Jews from concentration camps. In the fall of 1944, he had asked McClelland to inform the Union of Orthodox Rabbis that "Musy" was on his way to Berlin to fight for the Jews deported from Vittel six months earlier, particularly the brothers of Sternbuch's wife, Recha. Jean-Marie Musy, the former president of Switzerland, claimed to have the friendship of Heinrich Himmler, and Sternbuch trusted he would be a powerful ally. McClelland later annotated his copy of this cable with "Origin of the whole Musy affair."

When Musy returned in November, he had no news about the Vittel prisoners but claimed the Nazis would sell other prisoners to the Allies. Because the WRB was refusing to allow Saly Mayer to pay ransom, McClelland saw no reason to transmit Sternbuch's update to the Orthodox agencies in New York. So Sternbuch circumvented him, sending a commercial cable to the Vaad Hatzalah explaining that if it scraped together enough money, thousands of Jews would be rescued. Sternbuch reassured McClelland that Musy just wanted to enrich himself, so no official ransom payments to the Nazis would be necessary. Sternbuch had no problem with profiteering, so long as lives were saved. Neither Sternbuch nor the Vaad had any sense of discretion, so the Vaad began openly fund-raising to pay ransom as rumors flew throughout Switzerland and the United States about Sternbuch's plans.

Then, on February 2, Recha Sternbuch's two brothers, Jakob and Joseph Rottenberg, crossed the Swiss border, having been located and released, supposedly at Musy's request. They were proof, Sternbuch excitedly reported, that Musy's promise of a "first train" carrying twelve hundred people would soon come true. McClelland, though he felt the chances "highly doubtful," interrupted the Swiss Federal Police director's vacation to verify the hypothetical group would be allowed to enter the country. Musy requested 5 million francs in a Swiss bank account. Though McClelland warned Sternbuch that the War Refugee Board would not issue a license for direct ransom payments, Sternbuch "didn't want to make an issue of the money question at this point for fear of hurting M's feelings and perhaps jeopardizing the whole program of rescue." Ross McClelland felt morally conflicted. Musy might be able to use his connections to save people, but he wasn't remotely trustworthy. McClelland sat at his typewriter and tried writing a narrative of the entire story. As he reached the seventh page, Isaac Sternbuch called. The train had crossed the border.

The 1,210 prisoners, Jews released from the Theresienstadt (Terezin) camp in Czechoslovakia, were elderly—90 percent between sixty and eighty years old. They had apparently volunteered for the journey, though they hadn't known where they were going or that freedom would be at the other end of the trip. Stepping forward was a dangerous gamble in a concentration camp, but this group had gotten lucky. Sternbuch, understandably thrilled, saw the transport as proof Musy was a valuable collaborator and that his own risk taking and persistence had paid off. The Vaad held a press conference in New York to announce the arrival, rejoice, and weep. Sternbuch touted Musy's efforts in the Swiss press, which printed articles titled "Merci, M" and "Grâce à M. Musy."

Desperate to ensure that this transport really became the first of many, Sternbuch stressed the importance of a license so he could pay Musy promptly. Musy demanded money, but he—and, more important, the Nazis—also wanted positive press in the United States. During a meeting with Sternbuch, McClelland scribbled, "Musy would be very happy if some kind of a press statement (White House, WRB, etc.) that it is a very happy state of affairs when Germans relent and let the Jews out, Musy be mentioned as former Bundespresident."

A week passed after the first train arrived, but none followed. Musy blamed the WRB, because "there had been no favorable comment in the American press." Musy "must receive convincing evidence to show in Berlin that the press of the United States is commenting favorably [along the] lines of 'Nazis having finally seen the error of their ways and have now not only ceased exterminating the Jews but are releasing them as proof of their change of heart.'" Sternbuch and the Orthodox organizations immediately parroted Musy's complaints, because the lack of public praise for the Nazis "may jeopardize the future success of the whole rescue program."

In case the problem was money, the Vaad officially requested a license for $937,000 (the equivalent of 4 million Swiss francs, because Sternbuch found a lender with 1 million in Switzerland already) on February 14. The WRB proposed that the money could be placed in a joint bank account under Musy and McClelland's names. McClelland hated this idea. An informant had just leaked to the Bern legation that Musy "has been charged by Himmler to get in contact with the American government to learn the conditions of peace." McClelland didn't want his name linked with Musy's, particularly on a bank account of frozen ransom money. McClelland proposed opening a joint account with Sternbuch instead, though he wasn't thrilled with that idea either.

O'Dwyer refused to issue Sternbuch's license for direct ransom payments, even when the Vaad (falsely) claimed that a second transport sat just beyond the Swiss border, awaiting a deposit in Musy's account. O'Dwyer grew even more frustrated when he learned the Vaad had been plotting with Sternbuch through the Polish government in exile's diplomatic pouch, their messages circumventing the U.S. government's censorship rules. The Vaad finally, reluctantly, "under the circumstances," agreed to the WRB's offer: a joint account in McClelland and Sternbuch's names, with payments only permissible after signatures from both men.

Henry Morgenthau still worried. As the new license sat in the State Department awaiting clearance, Morgenthau met with John Pehle and Florence Hodel—O'Dwyer was in New York—and decided to forbid any ransom payments. He had caught wind of a forthcoming *Chicago Tribune* story, which he summarized as "Henry Morgenthau, the Jew, is dealing with Himmler to bring out Jews, and Jews only." Morgenthau raged, "If the thing goes wrong—and not only the future treatment of Jews in Europe is at stake but whole question of anti-Semitism in this country—and I think that the people who are largely to blame are these Orthodox Jews that have gone ahead and not told us. They haven't the money, and then they go ahead and want the money." Pehle wasn't angry but cautiously optimistic: "They are very persistent. As you know, they have been driving Miss Hodel and General O'Dwyer crazy, and they certainly added some gray hairs to my bald head, but they do get around . . . We have never wanted to stop it, because they get results. Is it risky? Sure it is risky; this whole thing is risky."

In a letter to the Vaad on February 28, 1945, O'Dwyer laid out the details of license W-2426, explicitly stating it had been the "unanimous decision of the Board that under no circumstances could this money be used for the payment of ransom," though the money could be used for "legitimate expenses" to care for released prisoners. Two weeks later, Vaad representatives ventured to the Treasury Department to protest the restrictions; Morgenthau conceded that McClelland and Sternbuch could purchase relief goods without prior approval from Washington. The next day, Rabbi Baruch Korff of the Vaad accosted O'Dwyer in the middle of Connecticut Avenue and demanded additional concessions. Morgenthau's secretary stopped answering Korff's calls. (After a long evening meeting with Vaad staff in early January over their bizarre and ultimately discarded proposal to use a Swedish ship to circumnavigate the globe and exchange Japanese prisoners in Peru for yeshiva students in Shanghai, Pehle commented, "One of the Rabbis said last night that there is a saying among them that you cannot compare the effect of a request made one hundred times with a request made one hundred and one times.")

In Switzerland, Sternbuch, reaching for an explanation after trains failed to arrive, decided that Saly Mayer had sabotaged Musy's efforts—an ironic claim, because the JDC was providing the $937,000 for Sternbuch's license. (The JDC and Vaad offices in New York made this deal, because "Sternbuch, rather than ask Mayer for funds, would rather die in his tracks.") At first, McClelland found the accusation funny, jokingly calling Mayer "you saboteur!" But the Vaad in New York believed Sternbuch, and the WRB asked McClelland to weigh in. The Vaad's accusation was "grossly and flagrantly incorrect," he wrote, "purposely interfering with Musy's activity in behalf of rescuing Jewish deportees is the furthest thing from Mr. Mayer's mind. Saly Mayer has already been the first to applaud the success of other groups and has never displayed Musy's tendency to 'monopolize' such rescue activities."

By early April, Sternbuch and Musy had aspirations beyond trains. Musy returned from Germany, where he had negotiated with Himmler and with *SS-Brigadeführer* Walter Schellenberg, the head of Reich foreign intelligence (whom Musy recommended the Americans hire after the war). Himmler remained open to negotiations, promising to surrender the concentration camps intact to the Allied military, to feed the prisoners and not evacuate them. In exchange, the *Reichsführer-SS* wanted assurances that there would be no "Negro occupation troops" in Germany and that camp guards would be treated as military POWs, rather than shot on the spot. After assuring Musy that the American military did not summarily execute guards, McClelland suggested that SS guards wear uniforms and not offer resistance, and asked about the size, demographics, and location of concentration camps. Musy claimed to need an official answer to the entire proposal immediately, but the War Refugee Board instructed McClelland to stall. He kept asking Musy for information about the location of camps and waited for them to be liberated.

Meanwhile, McClelland had to deal with the nearly three thousand prisoners freed through the Mayer-Becher and Sternbuch-Musy negotiations. The War Refugee Board had promised to find alternative havens for any Jews released into Switzerland, and the Swiss insisted it do so as soon as possible. McClelland planned to move the liberated prisoners to the UNRRA camp at Philippeville as soon as he could obtain transportation.

Moving the refugees to North Africa turned out to be just as complicated as the Fedhala evacuations a year earlier. Dealing with UNRRA, the French, the British, the military, and the refugees themselves was a bureaucratic nightmare, and people seemed to believe McClelland, as War Refugee Board representative, headed the whole operation. Despite what the barrage of letters, petitions, and angry refugees in his office presumed, nearly every aspect was out of his control. Though the largely Zionist Kasztner group wanted to go directly to Palestine—some had Palestine certificates already—the British government insisted on a security screening, which it claimed could only happen outside Switzerland. A Hungarian newspaper in New York published an open letter to the War Refugee Board on the front page, expressing its "stunning shock and a most painful amazement" upon learning the refugees would be evacuated to an intermediary location, adding, "We wonder if it would be possible for your Honorable Board to suspend and alter its decision so as to comply with the yearnings of these refugees." Josef Fischer, a leader of the Kasztner refugee group, argued that removing them from Switzerland was illegal, and threatened physical resistance. Saly Mayer received a "thoroughly hysterical" letter from the refugees with "SOS" printed diagonally across every page. McClelland confided to the British embassy in Bern, "I wish the military authorities in the Mediterranean area could get transportation organized so we could cut the whole matter short."

Repeatedly, McClelland explained that the decision belonged to the Swiss—or, in the case of Palestine, the British. Clearly exhausted, he bluntly told Fischer he was "personally very sorry that a solution to your problem which you find acceptable cannot be found. For me the matter remains the relatively simple one that the Swiss authorities do not seem desirous of keeping your people here and are accordingly availing themselves of previously given American and British guarantees to remove you from Swiss territory." To another refugee, he vented, "I do not imagine that you would have protested against being removed from Bergen-Belsen; and as a matter of fact your removal from Bergen-Belsen to Switzerland was based on the *certainly not harsh condition* that you also be removed from Switzerland . . . Would you not also be willing to admit that you were the objects of *favorable* discrimination when rescue efforts were centered upon your group to the exclusion of a great many other fellow sufferers in similar camps in Germany?" The complicated logistics meant that Kasztner and Musy Jews remained in Switzerland until after the war.

Iver Olsen had returned to Stockholm in the middle of January, much to his dismay, and O'Dwyer, with Pehle's agreement, asked him to remain as the War Refugee Board representative. For the most part, refugee matters had quieted in Sweden. The Lithuanian, Latvian, and Estonian rescue efforts had been over for months, though Olsen received the happy news that the Lithuanian resistance leader Algirdas Vokietaitis, rumored to have been executed, was alive in a concentration camp. But the days were long and dark, and in his absence Olsen's office had been moved more than a mile from the main legation building—a long, blustery walk along the water in the middle of a Swedish winter.

In mid-April, the staff of the Swedish legation in Budapest returned home to Stockholm. Though his hopeful mother and stepfather met the ship, Raoul Wallenberg was not among the passengers. Most of the diplomats, disembarking amid cheers, had spent the siege of Budapest hiding, along with the Swiss diplomatic corps, in the tunnels under Esterházy Palace. In March, a Swedish newspaper had printed an interview with a Hungarian Jew who had beaten the legation staff to Stockholm, announcing Wallenberg's heroism. Herschel Johnson proudly sent a copy of the article to Washington, but none of the War Refugee Board staff realized Wallenberg was missing until April. Finally, Olsen heard on the radio that he had been murdered, though the returning Budapest legation only knew that Wallenberg had disappeared after departing for the Russian lines to brief the Red Army on his activities.

We now know that Soviet intelligence arrested Wallenberg and sent him to Moscow, where—according to Soviet reports—he died of natural causes in 1947. The full details of his death—including whether a healthy thirty-four-year-old man really died of natural causes and exactly where and when he died—are still unknown. It is likely, however, that his ties to the War Refugee Board at least partly contributed to his arrest. Not long before Wallenberg was arrested, *Ny Dag,* the Swedish Communist newspaper, had accused the American legation of aiding the escape of pro-Nazi anti-Communists from the Baltics. And the Soviets could easily draw connections between Wallenberg and Iver Olsen, a known OSS agent. There is no evidence Wallenberg worked for the OSS himself, but as Cold War tensions ramped up, the Soviets drew their own conclusions.

The spring brought ransom negotiations to Stockholm, too, but Olsen tried to stay uninvolved, fearing they could be Nazi attempts to compromise the United States in the eyes of the Soviet Union.

In March, Felix Kersten, a friend of Himmler's, contacted the World Jewish Congress. Himmler still wanted positive press for the release of the Kasztner and Musy groups in Switzerland and was supposedly open to the idea of moving Jews to Red Cross–supervised camps. Kersten, whose conversations with Himmler coincided with Musy's, thought Himmler had already ordered camp commandants to improve conditions for Jews, and offered to arrange a meeting between the *Reichsführer-SS* and a Jewish representative.

In the final days of the war, Norbert Masur of Mosaika Församlingen, the local World Jewish Congress offices in Stockholm, traveled into the ruins of Berlin accompanied by Kersten. Upon his return, Masur reported to Olsen that he had met Himmler in the early morning hours of April 21, after the *Reichsführer-SS* returned from Hitler's birthday party. Himmler "appeared in top form" and criticized "the extent to which Allies had propagandized German atrocities," particularly in Bergen-Belsen and Buchenwald, which had already been liberated, because the camps "had been left intact to the Allies at his own command and that all he was getting in return was Allied horror stories." Himmler agreed to release fifty Norwegian prisoners and a thousand Jewish women from Ravensbrück to Sweden, to grant Red Cross access to the remaining camps, and to provide lists of Dutch Jews in Theresienstadt, though they could not be evacuated. Himmler also promised that no Jews would be shot, but "gave only a half promise" that Jews would not be moved from camp to camp. While in Germany, Masur witnessed columns of emaciated prisoners marching out of the Oranienburg concentration camp.

Musy, reporting what he had witnessed in Berlin, told McClelland that placards covered the city, all exhorting Germans to die rather than be carried off by the Red Army as slaves. The last-minute prisoner evacuations added to the general chaos of the end of the war as millions of people fled the approaching armies. The War Refugee Board could only work to keep concentration camp prisoners alive long enough to be liberated.

Packages

RED CROSS TRUCKS CAREENED down destroyed German streets, hitting rubble and breaking down. Aid workers pored over their maps, trying to guess routes that might not have been bombed. Sustained by American-donated gasoline and precious tires, the trucks carried tens of thousands of boxes of food and soap, which had been packed across the ocean months earlier, routed through liberated, neutral, and enemy countries, and bore no mark of the American agency that had conceived, negotiated, and paid for them. Concentration camp inmates were starving, and the Red Cross boxes contained the nutrients that might save them.

Sending food packages into concentration camps, the WRB's final major project, also proved one of its largest bureaucratic and logistical challenges. The board's duty to provide relief without hampering the Allied military effort posed an enormous philosophical challenge to many outside the Treasury Department's walls. While helping refugees escape and dropping leaflets could not aid the enemy, sending much-needed food, clothing, and medicine for distribution to prisoners—without Allied or neutral supervision—might.

In mid-March 1944, when the War Refugee Board was only two months old, its new relief specialist, Paul McCormack, had reminded his boss, "Appreciating that we must and should continue to think and act in terms of actual release and rescue, it will become necessary, at one time or another, to actually engage in a program of some form of feeding to insure the availability of people to release and rescue." John

Pehle agreed with McCormack and didn't believe that small amounts of humanitarian relief material would delay Allied victory. He approved many projects proposed by private organizations—sending medical supplies to French refugee camps and aid to resistance fighters' families, supporting rescuers hiding Jews—writing licenses totaling nearly $6 million for twenty groups in 1944. They already had underground supply chains and weren't obligated to put up with the vast number of meetings and paperwork involved in WRB's direct relief work. But they also rarely managed to get packages into concentration camps.

The bureaucratic challenges to large-scale relief were vast. Throughout the spring of 1944, the International Red Cross struggled to spend the $100,000 from the JDC at its disposal. Many products simply weren't available in neutral countries, and Allied blockade authorities wouldn't allow imports from elsewhere. Distribution channels could appear and disappear suddenly, based on the whim of a camp commandant or the movement of an army, so the Red Cross asked the WRB to establish stockpiles of food, clothing, and medical supplies in Geneva, which would allow it to move quickly if new opportunities arose. Paul McCormack, who joined the WRB from the American Red Cross, shepherded the request along, and by June Pehle had secured permission from the State Department and the Foreign Economic Administration for stockpiles. The British government was the last hurdle.

In a series of interminable meetings over two warm June days less than a week after D-day, British officials summarily rejected the idea of stockpiles. The parliamentary secretary of the ministry of economic warfare, the Honorable (and fantastically named) Dingle M. Foot, claimed not to have the authority to approve such things, and with Joel Brand waiting in Istanbul to discuss ransom, the British were particularly sensitive to the idea of sending goods anywhere near enemy territory. On the second day, Pehle broke through with another plan: 300,000 food packages, given to the Red Cross to send to concentration camps, 100,000 per month, for a three-month trial. The Red Cross, which could only officially visit camps imprisoning Allied or neutral citizens, couldn't supervise the package distribution in person but, after a trial mailing a few months earlier, had received signed receipt cards from prisoners. The British wanted similar evidence of receipt before expanding the program. Pehle proudly updated Roosevelt on the relief agreement, writing, "At this stage, sustaining the lives of these unfortunate people may be quite as important as attempting to rescue them from enemy territory."

Pehle already knew of available food inside Europe that the Red Cross could distribute while he worked out the details for the 300,000 food packages. The SS *Christina,* a cargo ship carrying 315,120 relief packages originally intended for French and Belgian prisoners of war, was attacked on May 6, 1944, and beached near Sète, France. The cardboard boxes were waterlogged and no longer fit for POW distribution but could be dried out and mined for any food suitable for concentration camp prisoners. The WRB paid a reduced price for the remnants and transferred ownership to the International Red Cross in Geneva. Among the wreckage, Red Cross workers salvaged powdered milk, margarine, tinned meat, corned beef, salmon, pâté, jam, coffee, soap, sugar, and cheese.

The Red Cross repackaged the *Christina* goods into 25,600 fresh boxes and sent them into concentration camps, including 7,273 to Sachsenhausen, 7,694 to Buchenwald, and 3,799 to Dachau. With the WRB support, it also routed 250 tons of canned goods from the *Christina* along with food, clothing, soap, and medical supplies from Sweden to Pruszków, in Nazi-occupied Poland, which served as a way station for Poles fleeing the Warsaw uprising. By September, more than fifteen hundred signed package receipt cards from Dachau prisoners, each bearing between one and fifteen signatures, had arrived in Geneva. With the names of twenty thousand Dachau prisoners, the Red Cross could inform families of new evidence their loved ones were still alive.

Bolstered by these successes, the Red Cross and the WRB collaborated on other relief projects. Roswell McClelland learned 260,000 boxes, designated for North African POWs imprisoned in Germany, sat unused in the Red Cross's warehouses. With the blessing of Allied officials, the Red Cross distributed 40,000 of them into concentration camps. A few weeks later, McClelland's Red Cross contacts alerted him to a harrowing report from Ravensbrück. As many as thirty thousand women were malnourished, crammed into thirty-two barracks,

and dependent on a few female prisoner physicians who had no supplies. Using his discretionary fund, McClelland purchased antibiotics,
vitamins, cleansers, Vaseline, and bandages for five hundred packages
the Red Cross sent into Ravensbrück.

All the while, Pehle struggled through the red tape entangling his
trial shipment. Despite the agreement at the June meetings, British
blockade authorities took nearly two months to finally grant official
permission for the WRB to send the 300,000 relief packages—almost
two million pounds of food—from the United States, through
Gothenburg, Sweden, into Nazi territory. As soon as he received the
final authorization from London, Pehle insisted on shipping the first
batch of packages immediately. He persuaded the American Red Cross
to donate space for 15,000 packages on the next available ship, the
Gripsholm, a Swedish humanitarian ship scheduled to leave New York
at the end of August, only a few weeks later. None were ready, so the
WRB had to buy the first 15,000 from commercial companies that
sold packages to Americans for loved ones overseas.

Ten days before the boxes were due on the dock, Macy's and Gim-
bels canceled the WRB's orders, claiming to lack the manpower to
process such a large order on deadline. McCormack raced to New
York and, with the help of the JDC, selected two new companies.
Wallace, Burton & Davis Co. packed cheese, Kraft whole milk powder,
sugar, dehydrated soup, raisins, and prune butter into 10,000 packages, while Prince Company prepared 5,000 parcels of tinned meat
and meat spread, cookies, fruitcakes, dehydrated soup, marmalade,
tea, and processed cheese. The War Refugee Board staff frantically
obtained the necessary export license and the large number of ration
points—seventy-five thousand red ration points, and two thousand
sugar coupons—necessary for wartime food purchases. Government
money transfers weren't fast enough and the JDC stepped in to loan
$41,475. On August 23, the *Gripsholm* left for Sweden, carrying 15,002
WRB relief packages. At a meeting with Morgenthau, Pehle boasted,
"We had to beat the British down on it. We had to talk the Red Cross
out of space on the ship. We had to buy the food in New York. We did
the whole thing."

The packages arrived in Gothenburg in mid-September 1944
after a rough voyage. The contents had shifted in the large crates, and

almost all the sugar had been lost. All the boxes needed to be re-taped, the telltale English words on the outsides blacked out, and the correct receipt cards included before the Red Cross could ship them. It was good the WRB had started with a small trial.

Due to prior commitments, the American Red Cross, which agreed to pack the remaining 285,000 WRB packages, couldn't begin work until October 26. When it did, the staff averaged 14,000 packages a day working six days a week; within a month, 224,328 packages were ready, containing cigarettes, biscuits, cheese, powdered milk, salmon or tuna, margarine, sugar, chocolate bars, dehydrated soup, meat, vitamin C, and a bar of soap. The Feinberg Kosher Sausage Company of Minneapolis sold the WRB canned kosher meat, which the company had to drive to Washington to make the shipment deadline. A third of the WRB packages were kosher, marked with a *K,* while the rest included pork. At the WRB's request, Roosevelt authorized the transfer of $1,068,750 from the Department of Agriculture's and Treasury's Foreign War Relief accounts to pay the American Red Cross for the contents and for its packing work. The *Saivo,* carrying the readied parcels in 37,388 shipping cartons, sailed with the tide on December 1 toward Gothenburg.

In the meantime, the 15,002 *Gripsholm* boxes were repackaged and set for distribution in various camps. The World Jewish Congress criticized the Red Cross's lists in advance (though it had not seen them), writing to the WRB to "express our deep concern over the probability that the camps specified by the ICRC are not likely to benefit any substantial number of Jews" and implying to James Mann in London that Red Cross officials might be antisemitic. It submitted its own list of distribution sites, which McClelland believed were "largely misspelled and garbled" names, possibly referring to camps in Poland. Even if the locations could be deciphered, they were likely out of reach. The Red Cross "would not be able to enforce even remotely the minimum necessary control as to allocation and reception of parcels," McClelland told the WRB. The Red Cross, concerned that any publicity would endanger its ability to successfully distribute packages, reminded McClelland to ensure the WRB kept the camp names confidential, a decision that added to the World Jewish Congress's frustration.

This first shipment of packages didn't reach their destinations until February 1945. After being loaded onto freight cars, they had gotten stuck for nearly two months in Warnemünde, Germany, due to an overall halt in cargo shipping. The Nazis were using all available rail transport to bring men and supplies to the western front and had no interest in sending packages to concentration camps. The Red Cross told McClelland the *Gripsholm* boxes were finally en route on January 25.

By that time, the *Saivo* cartons had arrived and were waiting in Sweden. Everyone hoped this much larger distribution would go more smoothly. The 39,324 kosher packages would be reserved for Jewish prisoners, and the remaining 185,004 sent to the larger German camps where both Jews and non-Jews were imprisoned. The final 60,672 boxes of the WRB's trial sailed from Philadelphia on the *Caritas II* toward Toulon, France, in mid-December.

The 300,000-package trial had taken so long—more than six months for the last packages to leave the United States—that Pehle didn't want to wait to send more. At the beginning of November, even though none had been successfully delivered yet, British blockade authorities consented to an additional 300,000 packages. The American Red Cross offered to ship the crates but couldn't pack the individual boxes this time, because it was already responsible for packing over 1.3 million per month for Allied prisoners of war. The WRB would need to purchase all 300,000 from commercial package companies.

At the end of January 1945, Roosevelt authorized an additional $1.125 million from the Treasury Department's unobligated Foreign War Relief funds for the project. Florence Hodel and Paul McCormack, two of the only WRB staff members left, got to work on the new batch. This time, half the parcels would be kosher. Due to wartime regulations, McCormack had to send detailed instructions to the Treasury procurement officer, down to the size of the cracker (whole wheat, square, in packages 4" x 2¾" x 2¾"). The board obtained ration coupons and filled out forms to avoid cigarette taxes but by the end of March was still awaiting bids from three companies. Meanwhile, the WRB obtained permission from blockade authorities for a third set of parcels if it finished the second one. While the bureaucratic details were tedious, the WRB was determined to have everything ready in case an emergency or opportunity arose.

The International Red Cross struggled to distribute the first 300,000 packages. Due to the "rapid deterioration [of] internal rail transport," Roswell McClelland asked the WRB on January 22 for permission to obtain four or five large trucks, each five to seven tons, to lend to the Red Cross for deliveries. As "Germany internally becomes more disorganized, transportation breaks down, but also camp commanders and isolated SS groups become increasingly independent and open to making of valuable local working arrangements." Trucks would give the Red Cross flexibility to capitalize on opportunities.

The War Refugee Board drafted a cable granting McClelland permission to find the trucks, but the War Department balked at the plan. McClelland's idea would set a "precedent which would have an adverse effect . . . This Government has taken the firm view that the Germans should provide transportation for the distribution of these packages." But while the Geneva Convention made Nazi Germany responsible for shipping POW packages to captured Allied soldiers, there were no stipulations for Axis or stateless civilian prisoners. In mid-February 1945, the War Department launched Operation Clarion, an Allied bombing offensive targeting railways, bridges, and roads. The War Department's position, placing the onus on the Germans for delivering packages while eliminating their ability to transport anything, jeopardized the WRB's entire relief program.

On February 20, William O'Dwyer convened Morgenthau, Stimson, and the new State Department undersecretary, Joseph Grew. The intelligence he received from McClelland and others indicated the Nazis had abandoned wholesale extermination, but prisoners were threatened by starvation, exposure, and deliberate neglect. By the end of the meeting, the War Department agreed the WRB could source trucks for the Red Cross.

In Switzerland, the Red Cross was growing desperate trying to secure not only trucks but gasoline and tires, all incredibly valuable in a country surrounded by war for nearly six years. In meetings with McClelland, representatives stressed the need for packages in the Neuengamme and Dachau camps, where they (correctly) believed the Nazis were centralizing prisoners: again and again, they reminded him,

"Invaluable aid could be rendered to at least some thousands if a few trucks were on hand."

O'Dwyer ordered McClelland to procure anything he could from inside Switzerland and promise the United States would replace it after the war. Frustrated by the days passing by, O'Dwyer updated Morgenthau in early March: "We have untold numbers of people dying over there. There isn't any way in the world that I can get a pound of that food in to these people. The Army won't release gasoline and the Swiss government won't release gasoline. We have all the money in the world to buy trucks but we can't get trucks, and if we get trucks, we can't get gasoline because the Army won't release it."

Finally, after Morgenthau intervened and O'Dwyer and Hodel took a quick trip to the Pentagon, John McCloy sent a cable to General Eisenhower instructing the military to provide ten five-ton trucks and between fifteen hundred and two thousand gallons of gas weekly for the use of the International Red Cross. War Refugee Board staff would work out the details once they arrived at Allied headquarters in Paris.

Roswell McClelland, laid up by a flu that took him out of commission for the first two weeks of March, tried to monitor package distribution. The Red Cross used its few trucks to transport packages, but tracking was almost impossible. Convoys were diverted and delivered packages in alternate locations, and headquarters in Geneva would sometimes lose contact with staff for weeks at a time. Some War Refugee Board packages, rather than being distributed in camps, were being handed out to prisoners on roadsides, the surviving remnants of forced marches. On March 16, railcars containing 10,800 WRB packages left for Ravensbrück; the next day 9,600 headed toward Neuengamme. Approximately 1,170 left for Theresienstadt on March 23, and 4,900 more toward Jews doing forced labor near Vienna. The Red Cross found and rented six twelve-ton trucks, but tires and gasoline were the only way to guarantee all the War Refugee Board packages would reach their intended destinations.

Before he left for Paris, McClelland sent a cable to quietly update the WRB about ongoing negotiations between the Red Cross and the Nazis. McClelland had a good relationship with Carl Burckhardt, president of the International Red Cross, who, at a meeting with

SS-Obergruppenführer Ernst Kaltenbrunner in Berlin, obtained permission for Red Cross representatives to be stationed in the larger concentration camps to oversee the distribution of relief supplies. Once in the camps, they would be forbidden to leave until the end of the war. Kaltenbrunner agreed that all camps could receive packages, provided delivery remained discreet because German civilians were suffering from food shortages. He also informed the Red Cross it might be permitted to evacuate some prisoners on the empty trucks, but only women, children, the elderly, and the sick.

Burckhardt's conversation with Kaltenbrunner built upon Saly Mayer's masterful negotiations with Kurt Becher, which had stalled after the WRB granted the JDC a license for 20 million Swiss francs in January. Throughout the winter, Mayer had slowly turned the talks toward purchasing food and material goods for prisoners in concentration camps—effectively offering to supply the Red Cross with enough funds to care for them. By mid-March, with the Red Cross now negotiating directly with the Nazis to allow more relief workers and increased aid, Mayer finally declared his "commission as executed and his trust fulfilled." He had successfully strung Becher along for seven months.

Three War Refugee Board representatives—Katzki from the United States, Mann from London, and McClelland from Switzerland—converged on Paris on March 27, 1945. It was the first time in two and a half years that Roswell McClelland had been able to leave Switzerland, and the very first time he met another War Refugee Board employee. McClelland also spoke to William O'Dwyer and Florence Hodel for the first time, placing several calls to Washington that week. At meetings with military personnel, the WRB staff "stressed the urgency" and finally secured a promise of two thousand gallons of gasoline per week, including oil and grease, and thirty truck tires. They could only obtain six army trucks, but because the Red Cross had recently commandeered some French trucks, this wasn't as imperative. After almost a week, McClelland returned to Switzerland to shepherd the tires across the border. In his last phone call to O'Dwyer, McClelland confided, "I hope we can keep it up, especially at this critical moment, because this is sort of the last lap now. I hope that the Army really finishes it off for us, because that's the only final solution, but if we can get in behind there and save a few of these people, why that's what we are really interested in doing now."

The military delivered thirty truck tires to the Pontarlier border station on Monday, April 2, but despite the WRB's instructions the French refused to let the tires cross without customs paperwork. Mann and Katzki, still in Paris, had to intervene. The Red Cross enthusiastically welcomed the trucks, gasoline, and tires, and McClelland cabled Paris that five trucks full of food packages would leave for Germany that Saturday, and ten more the week after, "though geographic area still accessible is rapidly shrinking."

Considering the desperate need, when Isaac Sternbuch asked to buy food using 500,000 Swiss francs from his Musy account, McClelland approved. Sternbuch rented four trucks, filled them with twenty thousand pounds of matzo flour, and sent them to Bergen-Belsen in time for Passover. He loaded additional trucks with condensed milk, cheese, and canned fish for Theresienstadt.

McClelland appeased the World Jewish Congress's continued concerns about package distribution by allowing it to decide that the 39,324 kosher War Refugee Board boxes should go to Bergen-Belsen and Theresienstadt, as majority-Jewish camps. On April 9, however, McClelland learned that while the Red Cross had transported 18,000 of the kosher packages, the World Jewish Congress had unilaterally kept 20,000 in Stockholm as a reserve of kosher food for rabbinical groups after liberation. The WJC's representatives requested the WRB give them 30,000 additional packages to distribute, which McClelland immediately rejected, annotating the letter with "They have a lot of nerve!" All packages needed to be sent into Germany right away.

With Red Cross trucks moving toward concentration camps—or at least disappearing into Nazi Germany—the War Refugee Board staff in Washington worked to find more food packages. The second group of 300,000 wasn't remotely ready, and O'Dwyer finally asked Pehle to help cancel the order. With no time to ship from overseas, on April 5 O'Dwyer negotiated with the War Department to purchase 206,000 of its 7 million POW packages in Switzerland (though the War Department originally refused, claiming that the United States controlled only 2 million). The American Red Cross insisted that all 206,000 needed to be repackaged in Switzerland to remove the markings designating the packages as former Red Cross POW shipments. The WRB needed to purchase new boxes and maintain constant security on the old ones until they could be destroyed, to prevent them from being illegally repurposed.

The news that the WRB was purchasing POW packages arrived just as the International Red Cross calculated that the remaining sixty thousand WRB parcels would be distributed within the next two weeks. When McClelland inquired about repackaging, the International Red Cross thought that in light of the urgent need perhaps just blacking out the insignia on the boxes would suffice. But the War Department and the American Red Cross insisted on complete re-boxing, because "the Germans would then be encouraged to take prisoner of war packages destined for American and Allied prisoners of war, black out the symbols and labels and distribute the packages to German civilians." The next day, Buchenwald was liberated.

Time slipped through their fingers. No more than three thousand packages could be re-boxed per day. The War Department also insisted on an official payment of $762,200 before the boxes could be turned over to McClelland. On April 20, after the War Refugee Board filled out the proper forms and mailed the check, the American Red Cross instructed its representatives to transfer the boxes to McClelland. Three days later, the International Red Cross informed McClelland that war conditions forced it to cancel all convoys into Germany.

There is no final accounting of the WRB's packages. Some disappeared, no doubt stolen by German civilians or Nazi guards, but clearly many arrived at Neuengamme, Ravensbrück, Mauthausen, Landsberg, Theresienstadt, Salzburg, and Linz. More than 140,000 were listed solely as having been distributed to "civilian internees." Some were handed out to former Oranienburg prisoners, possibly the same prisoners Masur saw, who were discovered and liberated by the Red Cross on the side of the road.

Survivors remembered clutching their packages, hauling them onto bunks. Some decided to eat only a little and risk the rest being stolen, while others gorged themselves to illness and sometimes to death, because their bodies couldn't handle the sudden influx of calories. Those who survived to liberation remembered the Red Cross packages as a sign the Allies were coming soon for those who could hold out. None of them knew the American government had anything to do with it.

23

Liberation

ON APRIL 12, 1945, GENERALS Eisenhower, Patton, and Montgomery toured the newly liberated Ohrdruf concentration camp. Eisenhower later wrote to General George Marshall at the Pentagon, "The visual evidence and the verbal testimony of starvation, cruelty and bestiality were so overpowering as to leave me a bit sick. In one room, where they were piled up twenty or thirty naked men, killed by starvation, George Patton would not even enter. He said he would get sick if he did so. I made the visit deliberately, in order to be in position to give first-hand evidence of these things if ever, in the future, there develops the tendency to charge these allegations merely to 'propaganda.'" Eisenhower urged all soldiers in the proximity of a camp to become eyewitnesses and called for press and congressional delegations to fly to Germany immediately to document the crimes.

Once Allied soldiers liberated a concentration camp, the prisoners were the military's responsibility. In short order, the WRB staff went from being among the best informed in the United States about Nazi crimes to seeing the same press reports and newsreels as other Americans. When Roswell McClelland cabled asking whether specific camps had been liberated, the board directed him to Allied headquarters in Paris.

The images of liberation provided devastating public evidence of what the board had been fighting against. *Life* magazine published a multipage photo spread of Buchenwald and Bergen-Belsen. Newsreels like "Nazi Murder Mills" were in American theaters less than two weeks after Eisenhower toured the Ohrdruf camp. James Mann, closing the WRB's London offices and preparing to tackle Treasury Department work in Switzerland, told Florence Hodel he had obtained OWI photographs of the camps, adding, "You may care to get these pictures and see the indescribable brutality of the Germans." It's likely she had already seen them.

On April 24, after Ohrdruf, Buchenwald, and Bergen-Belsen were liberated but before Dachau and Mauthausen were, the United States, Great Britain, the Soviet Union, and France dropped leaflets printed with one final joint warning against any further atrocities, one the WRB hadn't authored. Hodel knew it was coming, because in late March she had attended an exasperating meeting at the Pentagon. She sat stunned by the draft text, which promised special treatment to any German who assisted prisoners, and listened to Pentagon officials argue that "war criminals must be appeased ... the whole program on war criminals was stupid and unrealistic." They had deliberately excluded any reference to Jewish prisoners, who were supposedly able "to get a great deal of help from people on the scene ... asking for humanitarian treatment for them would serve no useful purpose at all." Hodel, the lone woman in the meeting, spoke up to insist the phrase "persons detained by reasons of race, religion, or political belief" be added; the military had absolutely forbidden the word "Jew." The final text, scattered in the thousands from the skies over the remaining fragments of Nazi Germany, dropped the appeasing language and became a straightforward warning. Any person "guilty of maltreating or allowing any Allied prisoner of war, internee, or deported citizen to be maltreated, whether in battle zone, on lines of communication, in a camp, hospital, prison, or elsewhere, will be ruthlessly pursued and brought to punishment."

The War Refugee Board offices fell quiet. The final projects—the re-boxing of POW packages, the refugees fighting removal from Switzerland, the final ransom offers—all took place far from Washington. Still, some bureaucratic ruts were hard to escape. Until the end of April, the board staff continued forwarding names of rumored Bergen-Belsen prisoners to Bern for Swiss protection, even after the camp was liberated. Finally, in mid-May, O'Dwyer told the INS to stop sending the names of family members for the WRB's visa program.

In Washington, the professional, nonclerical staff of the board consisted only of O'Dwyer, Hodel, McCormack, and David White, who handled the board's administration. At the end of March, they moved from the main Treasury building to the fifth floor of the Sloane building, above the furniture store, where Pehle had met with Bernard Meltzer about the Riegner license nearly two years earlier.

William O'Dwyer steadfastly refused to announce his mayoral candidacy but, after a few weeks of rumors, stopped denying it too. The War Refugee Board proved a bigger job than he had assumed, but he still regarded it as part-time. He agreed to give two speeches in California in early May for the United Jewish Appeal, figuring he would spend a month on his brother's ranch afterward, and persuaded Florence Hodel to join him for the events. Morgenthau complained out loud about the absence of WRB leadership: "Suppose something breaks, what do I do? I'm carrying the ball. I have enough to do." Yet he didn't rescind an order, kicking John Pehle out of the office for two weeks on vacation: "You never had a chance to recover from your brother and everything. You have had a bad time. You have done a swell job, so get a little rest, a little sunshine, and come back."

After assisting with O'Dwyer's speeches and lecturing to a Jewish women's group, Hodel flew back to Washington alone to resume her wartime work and arrived to discover the war was over. In a letter to his sons, Henry Morgenthau described the subdued reaction to Nazi surrender at Treasury: "V-E Day has come and gone, and it is hard to realize it here in Washington. When the announcement finally came, everybody took it very quietly here. Nobody left their desks, and there was no celebration in the streets at night. It really was quite an amazing performance. The people here in Washington seem to realize what a big task we have ahead of us in the Pacific."

The War Refugee Board, as an emergency agency authorized to work only in enemy-occupied areas, no longer had a jurisdiction. On May 12, Hodel called the State and War Departments to inform them the War Refugee Board would close down as soon as possible after July 1, 1945. In the meantime, she planned to seek a small extension to the board's congressional appropriation.

With Morgenthau opening the seventh war bond drive in Buffalo,

New York, his staff took advantage of the quiet time to discuss the WRB's future among themselves. Despite Hodel's calls, she felt uneasy about closing down. Ansel Luxford, who had been deeply involved in the WRB's creation before Bretton Woods planning dominated his time, called her into his office to say he "felt very strongly that a separate government agency was necessary to handle the problems of the displaced persons in Europe and other oppressed people." Josiah DuBois vowed to "knife" any plans to disband the WRB, despite the emergency nature of its charge.

When Morgenthau returned a few days later, he called a meeting to discuss revising the WRB's mandate so the agency could continue in peacetime. Luxford and DuBois argued that "one of the greatest achievements of the War Refugee Board was to lift this problem of what to do with the refugees in Europe out of the realm of clerks over in the State Department into a Cabinet level where you could force decisions, where you could get some action on important problems . . . We weren't interested in doing this job and then folding our hands and quitting." Herbert Gaston, one of Morgenthau's assistant secretaries, added that liberated prisoners were still war refugees, after all.

John Pehle stayed silent. Finally, when Morgenthau commanded him to speak, he was noncommittal: "Our job was rescuing human lives while the war was going on, and we always cut our pattern to that end." But newspapers reported millions of displaced persons, and while the problem should probably revert to the State Department, where it (in theory) belonged, "the thing everybody is fearful of and with good reason is that the State Department isn't going to do any-thing." A new war refugee board could tackle the complicated issues of repatriation and Palestine. As with most of his meetings, Morgenthau had the last word: "I don't want this thing wound up until I have more time to look at it. Once this thing is killed, you can never reconsecrate it."

Florence Hodel, who Morgenthau teased had "gone Hollywood," joined a meeting the next afternoon, May 16. O'Dwyer, still in California, had resigned by phone and officially entered the Democratic primary race. With the War Refugee Board's work winding down—or, if it continued, in need of a fully committed director—Morgenthau accepted O'Dwyer's resignation. Pehle, in the midst of turning Surplus Property over to the Department of Commerce, happily agreed to "pinch-hit" as acting director but did not want to head a postwar agency. Florence Hodel glared disapprovingly at him, and Morgenthau joked he'd be stuck with it.

Florence Hodel then brought up the "trouble brewing in Oswego." It's "bad business," Pehle announced. The fate of the Fort Ontario refugees—who had no legal status as "guests of the President"—loomed unanswered. Some Yugoslav refugees wanted to voluntarily repatriate to Europe to rebuild and search for family, but the vast majority of the group, especially those with family in the United States, wanted to remain. They were still not allowed to spend a night outside the camp, and the attorney general shot down any proposal that differed from Roosevelt's June 1944 assurances to Congress and to the public. At the beginning of May, Fort Ontario's director, Joseph Smart, suddenly resigned from government service to lead a lobbying campaign for the refugees to remain, and Congressman Samuel Dickstein started an official investigation to devise a fair solution.

After he'd had a long weekend to think about the War Refugee Board as a permanent agency, the tired secretary of the Treasury decided he was done.

The previous month had taken a toll. On April 11, while on his way back to Washington after visiting his wife, who was recovering from a heart attack at a Florida hospital, Morgenthau had stopped in Warm Springs to see Roosevelt for dinner. As was his habit, Morgenthau dictated his recollections after dinner: "I was terribly shocked when I saw him, and I found that he had aged terrifically and looked very haggard. His hands shook so that he started to knock the glasses over, and I had to hold each glass as he poured out the cocktail . . . I found his memory bad, and he was constantly confusing names . . . I was in agony watching him." The next afternoon—the same day as Eisenhower's Ohrdruf tour—Morgenthau got the call that the president had died.

In a statement to the press, Morgenthau wrote, "I spent last evening with President Roosevelt, and he was in the best of spirits, and took a keen interest in discussing world affairs . . . It is a tragedy he did not live to see the unconditional surrender of Germany and Japan. He more than any one person is responsible, in my opinion, for the successful conduct of this terrible war against the aggressor nations. I am confident that history will recognize in him a great force for democracy and human rights." He then added, "I have lost my best friend."

Morgenthau offered to send President Truman a few suggestions, but none of them would involve his continued membership on the War Refugee Board, or whatever this new board would be. Two days later, Treasury staff presented a proposal of the new War Refugee Board's mandate and structure, recommending "the establishment of a Cabinet Committee to deal specifically with the problem of the permanently displaced and non-repatriable groups in Europe and to handle the relations of this Government with the Inter-governmental Committee on Refugees and the UNRRA. Such a Committee might consist of the Secretaries of State, Interior, and Commerce."

Truman considered the idea but on June 2 sent his response: "Dear Henry: I have been thinking about your suggestion of May twenty-third about the Refugee program and I have about made up my mind not to appoint any committee."

With that, the War Refugee Board's days were numbered. Because Hodel could handle all the details and the board would close before the November elections, O'Dwyer agreed to remain as nominal executive director instead of Pehle.

It was up to Florence Hodel to appear before the House Committee on Appropriations to request to use $16,000 to wind down WRB operations. The board's congressional appropriation was set to expire on June 30, and without Congress's approval the WRB would have to return the unused money from the $150,000 it had been allocated six months earlier. Though this should have been easy—the WRB had a balance of $64,674 and planned to return all but the $16,000—Hodel was sharply questioned about the WRB's work. One congressman told her he'd never understood what the board did, thought that UNRRA had responsibility for all refugees (it did, but only after they were in liberated territory), and did not understand why the board still required a staff of eleven (mostly messengers and secretarial staff). Hodel explained that the war crimes prosecutorial team had been borrowing the WRB's files for research, while secretaries tried to organize them for final transfer to the National Archives.

The Appropriations Committee added language into the authorization requiring that the $16,000 could only be used to close the War Refugee Board.

As the Treasury Department staff had predicted, the congressmen also asked about Fort Ontario. Hodel explained that the camp would belong to the Department of the Interior. (Truman signed the transfer two days later.) The fate of the Fort Ontario refugees remained in limbo until December 1945, when Truman finally announced they could enter the United States. In January and February 1946, groups of refugees boarded buses for the long trek to Canada, where they turned around and reentered as legal immigrants.

A week after President Truman rejected extending the board into the postwar world, Henry Morgenthau made a series of calls to the State and War Departments. Over dinner, some friends had alerted him to rumors of deplorable conditions for Jews in displaced persons camps. "They say they are being treated just as badly as they were before we defeated Germany." Morgenthau thought Earl Harrison, the new American representative to the Intergovernmental Committee (and the former commissioner of the Immigration and Naturalization Service), should survey the camps. Both departments supported the idea.

Everything came together very quickly. Harrison visited Pehle at the Treasury Department the next day and within two weeks had his orders and boarded a plane to Europe. Eager for the assignment, Harrison welcomed Pehle's suggestion that Roswell McClelland accompany him.

From Bern, McClelland apologetically explained he could not travel with Harrison. With the board's permission, he and Herbert Katzki, who moved to Geneva to assist McClelland, had just returned from a trip to Germany and Austria, where they toured the Mauthausen concentration camp. McClelland stood solemnly in the middle of the stone quarry, where prisoners had been forced to carry fifty-pound blocks of granite up the 186 "stairs of death." They visited Dachau and Hitler's home in Berchtesgaden, where they saw "Max Cohen, Bronx, NY" graffiti from a Jewish American GI painted on a wall. At thirty-one years old, McClelland had witnessed the deportations from

France, was likely the first American to read the Auschwitz escapees' report, and now had seen the remnants of concentration camps. He was ready to finish his work, resign from the War Refugee Board, and take a vacation with his family.

McClelland also rejected one last request from Isaac Sternbuch—to write a recommendation for "some German(?) factory director from Cracow who treated the Jews well." Because McClelland knew nothing personally about Oskar Schindler, he told Sternbuch that Schindler should explain his story to the Allied occupying forces directly.

At the end of July, McClelland submitted a detailed final report, describing all his confidential expenditures and the projects he couldn't share with the WRB during the war, even in coded communication. He neglected to include his November 1944 meeting with Kurt Becher.

Through McClelland, the WRB had paid for the creation of thousands of false identity cards in France and helped the Oeuvre de Secours aux Enfants smuggle Jewish children over the border to Switzerland. The board had donated to partisan groups in northern Italy, supported a courier service, and aided clandestine relief work. McClelland tasked informants with investigating the location, demographics, and details of various concentration camps, including whether the commandant or guards were easily bribed. He purchased small trinkets in Switzerland—watches and razors and the like—to be secreted across the German border to pay off Germans hiding Jews in their homes. McClelland also contributed money to the Central Jewish Office in Bratislava and the Czech underground, supporting the partisan liberation of camps in Nováky and Sered, adding, "I should estimate it saved the lives of close to 1500 people although it is hard to know how many of them later fell into German hands." He placed newspaper articles condemning the atrocities; he paid *passeurs* to help people cross borders and paid the Spanish and Communist undergrounds to use their channels for rescue; he helped fund the resistance in southern France. The effort was collective, McClelland reminded the War Refugee Board in Washington. "I did my best to contribute to this larger endeavor in which all of us, both in the United States and abroad, shared."

The day after he submitted his report, McClelland and his family

left on a month's vacation, a break before he joined the Bern legation as
a foreign auxiliary specialist. Having accidentally stumbled into relief
work five years earlier, the McClellands looked forward to more stabil-
ity and to a job better suited to Roswell's training. He would spend the
rest of his career in the Foreign Service, including several years as an
American ambassador. There is no record of whether he ever met John
Pehle in person.

Ten days after McClelland left on vacation, the *Skagerack,* a
twenty-six-foot speedboat, arrived in New York and was soon shipped
to Iver Olsen's mother's home in New Hampshire. The Treasury
Department had transferred Olsen from Stockholm to The Hague
after the war ended, but before leaving, he spent his own money to
raise and repair the *Skagerack,* which sank in the Stockholm harbor
after a rescue mission across the Baltic Sea. He sent it home as a present to his sons. It was, of course, not his boat, and Washington eventually made him return it to the federal government. Yet Iver Olsen's son
Jerry still remembers racing down the lake in New Hampshire in the
speedboat that had saved lives in the summer of 1944.

At the beginning of July, Henry Morgenthau Jr. had an awkward
conversation with President Truman, who was preparing for the
Potsdam Conference. There had been many cabinet resignations and
appointments in the previous weeks; Truman accepted Secretary of
Labor Frances Perkins, Secretary of Agriculture Claude Wickard, and
Attorney General Francis Biddle's resignations on May 23. On June 27,
Edward Stettinius also left. Morgenthau assumed he would eventually
be replaced, too, and what with the cabinet turnover and his own con-
troversial projects—particularly Bretton Woods and the Morgenthau
Plan—he wanted a public show of support for his remaining days.

When Truman hesitated and refused to commit to keeping Morgenthau through the end of the war, the secretary of the Treasury
submitted his resignation after more than eleven years of service. Truman originally asked Morgenthau to remain until after Potsdam, but
so much staff upheaval had placed Morgenthau next in the order of
presidential succession if something happened to Truman on the trip.
Truman had already selected his longtime friend Fred Vinson to take
over at Treasury and Morgenthau saw no need to delay the inevitable.

His resignation already accepted, he asked Truman to submit Vinson's name to Congress for a confirmation hearing.

Morgenthau's resignation took effect on Monday, July 23, 1945. He was in a cheerful mood and kept a commitment that afternoon to appear at a New York State Finance Commission luncheon, telling attendees he "felt ... that I was once more a free man." He left the Treasury Department with more than eight hundred volumes of documents and meeting transcripts. Morgenthau later became the head of United Jewish Appeal. A group of Holocaust survivors who immigrated to Israel named their agricultural settlement after him.

Earl Harrison spent July 1945 touring former concentration camps, some of which had morphed into makeshift displaced persons centers. He was shocked at what he found, as was Herbert Katzki, who accompanied him for part of the tour. Harrison sent cables along the way listing the immediate needs of displaced persons in Germany and Austria, missives so dire the new secretary of the Treasury, Fred Vinson, alerted the State Department for immediate intervention. Harrison urged separate camps for Jewish survivors being victimized by the Allied military's unwillingness to inconvenience the German civilian population. UNRRA, which had "rehabilitation" in its name, needed to take over as soon as possible.

Harrison addressed his final report to Truman, reiterating his discoveries. Many Jewish displaced persons still lived under guard in former concentration camps with no communication with the outside world. Some only had their old uniforms to wear, while others, due to lack of clothing, had to wear Nazi uniforms. There had been no repatriation efforts and no way to reunite with loved ones or to trace their fates. Winter would soon compound a serious food and housing shortage. Jews were suffering more than other prisoners. The "plain truth," Harrison explained, was that the Nazis singled out this group for special treatment, and the Allied occupying forces should too. "In the days immediately ahead, the Jews in Germany and Austria should have the first claim upon the conscience of the people of the United States and Great Britain and the military and other personnel who represent them in work being done in Germany and Austria." Displaced persons should be assisted with repatriation if desired, though many wished to go to the United States or other destinations, and "it is nothing short of calamitous to contemplate that the gates of Palestine should soon be closed." The situation was dire: "As matters now stand, we appear to be treating the Jews as the Nazis treated them except that we do not exterminate them." Harrison's report, released to the press on September 30, 1945, is responsible for radically changing American policy in favor of treating displaced persons, especially Jewish survivors, more humanely. Jewish displaced persons were soon transferred to their own separate camps, and later that year Truman issued a directive granting priority to displaced persons within the existing U.S. immigration quotas.

On September 14, 1945, President Truman signed Executive Order 9614, which took effect the next day, formally dissolving the War Refugee Board. In a press release, the White House stated that "the War Refugee Board . . . had succeeded in saving the lives of hundreds of thousands of innocent victims of Nazi oppression . . . the tremendous effort which went into the saving of these lives will have been in vain unless steps are taken for the immediate rehabilitation of these survivors of Nazi savagery, as well as for a humane, international solution to the problem of their ultimate resettlement."

Six days later, the War Refugee Board released a seventy-six-page final summary of its work to the press. Though the report came out under O'Dwyer's signature, Florence Hodel, the only board staff member working full-time in September 1945, almost certainly wrote it. (Paul McCormack had snuck out in early July for an UNRRA job, leaving Hodel a note to say good-bye and promising to duck the next time he saw her.)

The final report described the board's functions, personnel, and activities fairly accurately. It was organized by location or project— Turkey, Sweden, psychological warfare—which correctly emphasized the volume of the WRB's work but minimized the effect the military war and other external factors had on its decision making. The report overly praised the Vatican for assisting the WRB; O'Dwyer was in the midst of an active political campaign, and openly criticizing the

Roman Catholic Church wouldn't have been a smart move. But it also rightfully noted British obstruction, summarized the difficulties with Red Cross package distribution, provided some financial details, and described a few of McClelland's clandestine rescue efforts.

Most of the subsequent press, though, focused on Palestine. The final section of the report, titled "The Remaining Problem," included Harrison's suggestions regarding refugees and displaced persons. It also issued a public appeal, in O'Dwyer's voice: "I am of the firm conviction, based on my experience with the War Refugee Board, the deep personal concern of large elements of our population and the ideals of the American people, that the United States Government, as a matter of national policy, should initiate aggressive action at once for a United Nations solution of this international humanitarian problem." The focus of articles about the board's report were split between "War Refugee Board Saved Thousands" and "O'Dwyer Urges US Action to Open Palestine."

Two months later, O'Dwyer, whose political ads included Yiddish-language ones touting his work rescuing Jews, won the mayoral election with the largest plurality in the history of New York City.

With that, the War Refugee Board closed, its staff forever connected by their experiences fighting a different war from most of the country, battlefield comrades without a battlefield. To a person, the last messages in the War Refugee Board's files expressed how privileged and honored they felt to have had the opportunity and means to save lives.

John Pehle resigned from the Treasury Department in 1946 and opened a law firm in Washington, D.C. Pehle, Lesser, Mann, Riemer & Luxford specialized in international commercial law, though it also took cases for the JDC and, at least in one instance, prosecuted a suspected Yugoslav war criminal. Four of the five lawyers had been associated with the War Refugee Board, though the war was rarely a topic of conversation. They all kept in touch with Florence Hodel, who spent the rest of her career at the International Monetary Fund.

In his final report, Ross McClelland summarized the War Refugee Board: "Such was the fight . . . with its sorties and skirmishes, its trenches stormed and its ground gained—and lost—in the uneven struggle to succor and to save some of the victims of the Nazi assault on human decency. Its successes were slight in relation to the frightful casualties sustained; yet it is sincerely felt that its accomplishments constitute a victory, small in comparison to that far greater one carried by force of arms, but which nevertheless adds a measure of particularly precious strength to our cause."

THE WAR REFUGEE BOARD'S creation was—and remains—the only time in American history that the U.S. government founded a government agency to save the lives of non-Americans being murdered by a wartime enemy.

The WRB's existence is an anomaly, an unexpected deviation, a sudden and surprising altruistic moment at a time when the world war was all-consuming and official American efforts to assist persecuted European Jews had been halfhearted or nonexistent for a long time. People who point to the 1930s and 1940s with outrage that the United States did not do more to save the Jews of Europe neglect the context of the period. The uncomfortable truth is that the United States could have "saved" the most Jews only by preemptively loosening immigration restrictions—by enlarging and filling the quotas when Nazi persecution became clear but before the murders began. And for myriad reasons, that was unlikely to happen.

The United States in the 1930s was rife with racism and antisemitism and suffering the devastating effects of the Great Depression. Americans warily looked across the ocean at a worsening international situation and grew concerned about national security. Similar economic and security concerns—valid or not—have echoed throughout the decades in the face of most refugee crises since the Holocaust. No one knew the word "genocide" until 1944, and few could imagine that a civilized country would systematically murder millions of people based on race or religion. If we don't have a solution to a refugee crisis or genocide today, when the world is far more interconnected and we have the Holocaust and other genocides as precedents, why should it surprise us that Americans didn't do more in the face of the Nazi threat? And indeed, when the war ended and the WRB dissolved, any lessons learned were promptly forgotten. The United States did not change the immigration laws or substantively address the issue of refugees for another twenty years.

The twenty months between the board's creation in January 1944 and its closure September 1945 represent a moment in history when American action matched American rhetoric about democratic values. In contrast to many subsequent American human rights efforts, the War Refugee Board had no secondary, cynical motive. It was not part of a larger program to gain overseas prestige or power, nor was it driven by the desire for political favor or influence over a minority group. The refugees in peril were not and were never intended to become Americans, nor would most ever know the United States had any interest in their survival. The historian Yehuda Bauer wrote, "What made the WRB such a unique body is that it was officially permitted to break practically every important law of a nation at war in the name of outraged humanity." That the United States would devote any resources toward a humanitarian crisis abroad while fighting an all-out, two-front war, with sons and daughters, brothers and sisters, dying daily, is illogical. But it happened, and it saved thousands of lives.

Most people have never heard of the War Refugee Board. Its efforts are glossed over or written out of many histories of the United States and the Holocaust. Perhaps this is because the sheer existence of the WRB disrupts the popular narrative that the United States was indifferent or even callous toward the fate of the Jews. Some even claim that Roosevelt and his administration were complicit in their murders. This, of course, is preposterous. Nazi Germany and its collaborators, not the United States, murdered European Jews, and diluting guilt absolves the real perpetrators of these atrocities.

None of the staff members of the War Refugee Board, save for Ira Hirschmann, wrote memoirs or kept daily diaries. By the 1970s, the narrative of an indifferent America, an antisemitic State Department, and a refusal to bomb Auschwitz had taken hold with the American public. The former WRB staff sat for few interviews, and when

they did, most questions centered almost exclusively on these topics. Roswell McClelland had no personal knowledge of the wartime
State Department's obstruction or the War Department's decision
making, yet the documentarian Claude Lanzmann grilled him for
details in an interview for his documentary *Shoah*. John Pehle seemed
annoyed when asked about the proposal to bomb Auschwitz, a part of
the WRB history he barely remembered until aerial photography of
the camp was discovered in the late 1970s and interviewers came calling. A popular perception of American abandonment of the Jews,
selectively featuring the pieces of the WRB's work that reinforce this
narrative, has proven remarkably resilient, robbing us of a more complicated, nuanced, yet ultimately hopeful history.

It is absolutely true, however, that the War Refugee Board had no
impact on the lives or deaths of the vast majority of Jews in Europe,
and the WRB is frequently dismissed as "too little and too late." Historians often quote John Pehle himself, who used this phrase in a 1978
interview while answering a question about how he felt about the
WRB's work after seeing images of liberation. Yet after the first victim was murdered, wasn't the United States already too late, and what,
except somehow preventing the Holocaust entirely, would not have
been too little? The fact remains that the mass murder of European
Jewry began after American diplomatic and journalistic observers
were cut off from Nazi-occupied territory. Mass rescue was never possible, especially after the United States entered the war in December
1941. The Allied armies invaded North Africa in 1942, Italy in 1943,
and France in 1944. All along, they were thousands of miles away from
the Nazi killing centers where millions were murdered.

The War Refugee Board was created out of the convergence
between the State and the Treasury Departments' battle over licenses
and the popular support spearheaded by the Bergson group. The particular circumstances of the winter of 1943–1944 meant that Morgenthau and his staff could successfully convince FDR of the need for
radical change. The new agency had teeth because it sat outside the
State Department and operated in 1944, when the Allies knew more,
were clearly winning, and had begun making plans for the postwar
world. In February 1944, a CBS radio broadcast similarly argued, "A
year or two ago, a War Refugee Board could have accomplished little

or nothing. We did not have the power then to bring any pressure to bear on Romania, Hungary, Spain, and other countries more or less in the Axis camp. But the approach of victory changes all that."

The establishment of the War Refugee Board—a purely American program—in January 1944 fundamentally improved the possibilities for relief and rescue in Europe. It is difficult to separate the impact of the WRB's work from Allied military victories, but the United States dedicated many more resources toward humanitarian efforts during 1944–1945 than at any other point during the war.

The War Refugee Board saved lives, though the exact number can never be known. The staff did not publicly attempt to count the number of those "saved" and only produced one internal report on the matter. In February 1945, Paul McCormack sent the newly appointed director, William O'Dwyer, a memo titled "Number of Persons Rescued Since the Establishment of the War Refugee Board." McCormack's estimate was 126,604, but this number included all refugees known to have escaped enemy territory, with or without the WRB's help. In the board's final report, Florence Hodel wrote, "The accomplishments of the Board cannot be evaluated in terms of exact statistics, but it is clear, however, that hundreds of thousands of persons as well as the tens of thousands who were rescued through activities organized by the Board, continued to live and resist as a result of its vigorous and unremitting efforts, until the might of the Allied armies finally saved them and the millions of others who survived the Nazi holocaust."

The War Refugee Board's importance cannot be measured in the number of people it "saved." While murder is definitive—victims can only be killed once—most Holocaust survivors were "saved" many times, sometimes proactively, but often by accident. Some received visas, safe-conduct passes, or protective papers at the right moment; others found a kind neighbor who hid them; still others survived due to the support of prisoner comrades. Beyond these singular acts are thousands of small graces: every time a false identity paper was acknowledged, a nosy villager purposely ignored a strange new visitor, or a laborer managed to satisfy the capricious whim of a German guard, the person was saved again. Many small "rescue" efforts were needed to save one person.

We know now that many people the WRB assisted were already "saved." The Fort Ontario refugees, for example, were in Allied-occupied southern Italy in 1944. But what if the Allies lost that territory and the Axis deported the Jewish refugees who had managed to flee there? In this counterfactual, the War Refugee Board would have "saved" these 982 (and indeed, McCormack's list includes this group). Rescue is often only evident in retrospect.

Likewise, a person could be saved and later still be murdered in the Holocaust. Slovak Jews saw their protective papers torn up prior to deportation; does this invalidate the WRB's efforts to persuade Latin American countries to recognize those papers? The passengers on the *Mefkure* perhaps perished as a result of the board's work, as did emaciated prisoners who fatally gorged themselves on food from WRB packages. Should these tragedies be weighed in an examination of the board's merit?

So much of the WRB's work was intangible. It shot arrows into the dark, hoping to have an impact but rarely knowing if a particular project succeeded. The board was usually at least twice removed from any work in enemy territory, because license money funneled through private relief agencies to workers in the underground. Do their successes, so far from Washington, count as WRB successes? Leaflets or radio broadcasts warning would-be war criminals of postwar punishment were widely disseminated, and reports from enemy territory noted their impact. There is no way to quantify how many people survived because of the board's psychological warfare campaign, though it clearly played a role in Admiral Horthy's decision to spare Budapest's Jews from deportation. Does this mean that the board can claim credit for their survival? Does the prevention of atrocities mean that people were "saved" from an act that never happened?

The War Refugee Board's importance is in its sheer existence and its actions, not in pithy summaries of quantifiable "results." There were clearly people alive in 1945 thanks to the board's efforts. We just do not know exactly who they were.

Yet when we forget the War Refugee Board existed, reduce its work to statistics, or treat it merely as an inconvenient afterword to a story of American apathy, indifference, or complicity, we lose the ability to learn from its work.

When today's State Department or Treasury Department officials debate humanitarian questions about money or goods falling into enemy hands, ransom, or collaboration with nongovernmental organizations, they should look to the War Refugee Board and examine how the staff dealt with similar challenges.

When today's private citizens question whether their voices count, they should be inspired by the creation of the WRB, born in part out of public pressure and fueled by idealism.

When today's federal workers wonder if government service can make a difference, the War Refugee Board should demonstrate that bureaucratic tools can be used to cut red tape rather than create it. Henry Morgenthau, John Pehle, Florence Hodel, and the other staff were proud and patriotic members of the Roosevelt administration who saw their country as a force for good in the world, yet recognized the importance of international cooperation.

The American responses to Nazi genocide—and there were many, not just one—are complicated and nuanced, but the period should not be dismissed solely as a stain on American history. The Holocaust did not occur because the United States stayed silent; rather, the Holocaust happened because the Nazis wanted to kill Jews and had more access, control, and will over and against them than the Allied nations had to protect them. The War Refugee Board tried everything in its power to prevent atrocities, provide relief, and rescue potential victims. The staff worked ceaselessly to save lives during the final months of the Holocaust.

May we come to resemble them.

ACKNOWLEDGMENTS

I have been researching and writing about the War Refugee Board for nearly a decade, which means there is a decade's worth of people who have helped along the way. First, I want to thank all of the families of the WRB and WRB-adjacent figures, all listed in the Note on Sources, for their time, patience, and willingness to engage with me. I particularly want to thank Henry Morgenthau III, George Lesser, Jerry Olsen, and Kirk McClelland. These men have shared an extraordinary amount of time, documents, and memories with me. I hope they—and all the WRB families—feel I have done justice to the lives and work of their loved ones.

This story touches on so many physical locations and complicated stories, and I'm grateful to the historians who have helped me with contextual questions: Charles King, Corry Guttstadt, Tuvia Friling, László Csősz, Rebecca Clifford, Irene Pimentel, Karin Kvist Geverts, Pontus Rudberg, Pedro Correa Martín-Arroyo, Clarence Ashley, Waitman Beorn, Meredith Hindley, Peter Samson, Gerald Steinacher, Barry Trachtenberg, Marion Kaplan, and Melissa Jane Taylor. The International Holocaust Remembrance Alliance's November 2014 conference in Madrid on "Perpetrators, Bystanders, Victims? The Neutral Countries and the Shoah" gave me the opportunity to present some of this work to scholars I've admired for years—particularly Yehuda Bauer—and I am grateful to Corry Guttstadt and Yessica San Román for the invitation. I would also like to single out Abby Gilbert and the members of the Treasury Historical Association for providing additional documents and answering questions about life inside the Treasury Department during the war. Dr. Friedrich Schreiber described his experience as a young teenager in wartime Germany discovering Allied propaganda, including Roosevelt's March 1944 statement, proof that the WRB's psychological warfare campaign had an effect. I'm so grateful he was willing to share his story.

I could not have written a book based almost solely on original sources without the passionate, hardworking, and helpful archivists who protect and promote these sources for all of us. The staff of the Franklin Delano Roosevelt Library, particularly Kirsten Carter, Sarah Malcolm, and Patrick Fahy; Don Davis at the American Friends Service Committee in Philadelphia; the staff of the Library of Congress's Manuscript Division and of the National Archives in College Park; the wonderful volunteers at the Safehaven Museum and Education Center at Fort Ontario in Oswego, New York; the staff of the Harry Ransom Center, particularly Michael Gilmore; and Tamar Zeffren at the American Jewish Joint Distribution Committee Archives all made the research possible.

I am fortunate enough to work at the best museum in the world, the United States Holocaust Memorial Museum. The museum's unparalleled collections and library made research much easier, but the support and assistance of my colleagues made it better. They provided constant encouragement, alerted me to new materials, answered questions, and kept me from becoming overwhelmed: Mike Abramowitz, Brad Bauer, Peter Black, Belinda Blomberg, Jeff Carter, Judy Cohen, Clare Cronin, Dr. Sidney Davidson, Jo-Ellyn Decker, Michael Dobbs, Adam Fielding, Jason Fields, Peggy Frankston, Grace Cohen Grossman, Nancy Hartman, Michelle King, Jane Klinger, Caroline Waddell Koehler, Megan Lewis, Steve Luckert, Scott Miller, Ann Millin, Greg Naranjo, David Neumann, Ted Phillips, Anna Rennich, Diane Saltzman, Kristin Scalzo, Jenn Schmidt, Julie Schweitzer, Vincent Slatt, Suzy Snyder, Rachel Wimberley, and Lindsay Zarwell. Kyra Schuster, Mike and Avi Scheinberg, Joan Suttin, and Jon Fee deserve special mention for housing me during the difficult early research, a debt I'll pay forward. I hope Danny Greene and Gretchen Skidmore know how absolutely vital their feedback and friendship has been to me.

Beyond my work family, I need to thank John Lillard and Tracy

Fisher, who got me through grad school; Jeff McClurken, who has always been an enthusiastic supporter of my work; and my George Mason University professors and the members of my dissertation committee—Dr. Marion Deshmukh and Dr. Martin Sherwin of George Mason, and Dr. Joseph Bendersky of Virginia Commonwealth University—who advised me. It's important to have friends who are inspirations, and I strive to be as good—as a writer and as a human being—as Emily Langer Scott, Rachel Vorona Cote, and Meredith Hindley are. Meredith, in particular, guided me through the logistics of writing a book; I'm not sure it would exist without her.

My agent, Anna Sproul-Latimer, is one of the coolest people I know and has made this process as easy as it could possibly be. Kris Puopolo, my fantastic editor, understood this story from the start, shepherding me out of the fog and onto the right path. Dan Meyer patiently answered all my questions.

My family might not have always known what to do with such a history-obsessed kid, one with her own lending library and set of First Lady flash cards, but they never discouraged me. The Coleman, Boyd, and Petry families have welcomed me, and haven't judged me for always working during family holidays. My parents, Bruce and Beth Erbelding, listened patiently and edited chapters; their pride made me work even harder. Andy, Debbie, Madison, and Carter Erbelding, and Laura, Matt, and Colton Bechtler gave me lots of love, even when they could not understand how a book could possibly take this long.

Most important, more than anything, I want to thank my best friend and husband, Ron Coleman. He helped immeasurably—with the research, with daily life, with keeping me happy, safe, sane, and loved. While all mistakes are mine, all the best parts of this book—and all the best parts of my life—are thanks to him.

A Note on Sources

When I set out to find a topic for my doctoral dissertation—something that would combine my planned degree in American history with my intimate knowledge of the United States Holocaust Memorial Museum's collections—I went to the best source: my colleagues at the USHMM. They all suggested I write about the War Refugee Board.

At that time, sixty-five years after the end of World War II, the WRB—the only official American response to the Nazi massacre of Jews—had never received book-length treatment. Literature on the United States' relationship to the Holocaust can be divided into two categories, which emerged in the 1970s and have remained unchanged. Scholars like Henry Feingold and Richard Breitman sought to examine the context of American society during World War II, acknowledging the limited possibilities for wartime rescue efforts. Other historians, like David Wyman and Rafael Medoff, saw excuses in such contextualization, arguing that much more could have been done to save Jews during the war. Both categories of historians have generally positioned the WRB as the afterword in longer works about the American response, the one bright spot, however "little and late." No one had studied it in depth. Breitman and Wyman have separately called for an examination of the War Refugee Board's work, and I hope my scholarship will answer some of the long-standing questions on both sides of the scholarly divide.

I relied almost exclusively on archival research for this book. The War Refugee Board's administrative records comprise 120 boxes at the FDR Library in Hyde Park, still in their original 1944–1945 order. The records are split into a few different groupings, including two main series: an alphabetical correspondence series, and a topically arranged "projects" series. The WRB's secretaries were not consistent in their filing. For example, the subject "Evacuation to and Through Turkey" consists of thousands of unarranged documents in four boxes, with hundreds of relevant papers scattered elsewhere. A clerk in 1945 might have filed letters alphabetically by author or organization or could have chosen to file by topic, seemingly without instruction. As a result, the historians who have written about the WRB have described a series of isolated stories—the WRB's efforts in Sweden, in Turkey, in Hungary—eliminating crucial context and chronology. (This segmentation echoes the organization of the WRB's 1945 published history.)

To reconstruct events as they occurred, I needed to put the records in chronological order. I spent 2011 and 2012 photographing the entirety of the WRB's records, digitizing the folders that had already been microfilmed, and using a handheld camera to capture the rest. After deleting duplicates, I had nearly nineteen thousand unique documents.

I doubled my count with images from dozens of other collections in the FDR Library, Library of Congress, National Archives, Harry Ransom Center, Bowdoin College, American Friends Service Committee Archives, American Jewish Joint Distribution Committee Archives, and, the best Holocaust archive in the world, the United States Holocaust Memorial Museum. I added Roswell McClelland's papers, Ira Hirschmann's papers, hundreds of transcripts and documents from Morgenthau's diaries, State and Treasury Department records, relief organization papers, newspaper clippings, and more.

After converting my images into PDFs, I assigned each a unique and intricate title, including the date of the original document's creation and current location—collection, box, and folder. With the date at the beginning of each title, all the PDFs, when placed in a single folder, sorted chronologically. The Papers database software—which cost all of $50—ingested all my PDFs, allowing me to see the images, take searchable notes, and add authors, titles, and keywords. This book would not have been possible without the database.

After two years of collecting and manipulating the scans, I finally began reading the WRB's documents. Multipart cables, split by file clerks in 1944 and placed in multiple folders, had reassembled themselves, and query letters in one box had rediscovered their answers from another. I learned that the WRB staff drafted requests for relief organization representatives to pass along to foreign governments in secret—the proof of which was spread dozens of boxes apart. I could tell how much time the WRB staff spent on various projects, could see whether they were ever successful, and could study the WRB's decisions as they were made, avoiding the historian's trap of hindsight.

The chronological organization allowed me to disprove some myths about the WRB and to be definitive about my arguments. Josiah DuBois, as it turns out, did not author the "Acquiescence of This Government in the Murder of the Jews" report on Christmas Day 1943, as evidenced by the newly discovered drafts of the memo and by the chronology of events made clear in the Morgenthau diaries. The agency was not understaffed—a common historian criticism—because many employees (including John Pehle) were detailed to the WRB's efforts rather than counted in the official tally. Despite some historians' desire to use the WRB's funding as an opportunity to attack Roosevelt, the documents show the staff was not underfunded, returning $635,939.55 to the federal government and never once, in any of the records, complaining about a lack of financial resources.

After two more years, when I had finally almost finished taking notes and felt confident in my knowledge, I contacted the families of the staff I had come to know so well. Many were kind enough to share additional documents and photographs with me, and all answered my sometimes intrusive questions: Bennett Boskey (friend of Leonard Ackermann); George Naughton (son of Mary Harriet Bixler); Reid Blickenstaff (nephew of David Blickenstaff); Selma Milchen (daughter of Emanuel Borenstein); Robert DuBois (son of Josiah DuBois); Jay Weber, and the Weber and Thron families (nephew and relatives of Florence Hodel); Louise Korn Waldron (daughter of Lewis Korn); George Lesser (son of Lawrence Lesser); Henry Morgenthau III (son of Henry Morgenthau Jr.); Iver "Jerry" Olsen Jr. (son of Iver Olsen); Judy Mann (daughter of James Mann); Kirk McClelland (son of Roswell McClelland); Irene McCormack Weinrot (daughter of Paul McCormack); Cecilia Pehle (daughter-in-law of John Pehle); Annie Herr McClintock (granddaughter of Daniel Reagan); Dr. James Saxon and Lucy Neher (children of James Saxon); Kenneth Sargoy (son of Milton Sargoy); and Phil Stewart (son of Ward Stewart).

Over the years I have been working on this project, the FDR Library has taken my digital copies of the WRB papers and placed them online, alongside the newly digitized Morgenthau Diaries and a curated collection of Holocaust-related archival material. Future scholars would be wise to mine these collections further, because I'm sure there are many more stories to tell.

Notes

List of Abbreviations

AFSC: American Friends Service Committee Archives, Philadelphia

BLP: Breckinridge Long Papers, LOC

CDF: Central Decimal File (RG 59, NACP)

FDRL: Franklin Delano Roosevelt Presidential Library and Museum, Hyde Park, N.Y.

GVC: General Visa Correspondence (RG 59, 811.111, NACP)

HRFDRWH: Holocaust Refugees and the FDR White House (originals at FDRL; microfilm at USHMM)

IHP: Ira Hirschmann Papers, FDRL

JDC-NY: American Jewish Joint Distribution Committee Archives, New York

LM0305: Call number for the USHMM microfilm copy of PWRB, Correspondence and Reports files

LM0306: Call number for the USHMM microfilm copy of PWRB, Project and Documents files

LOC: Library of Congress, Washington, D.C.

NACP: National Archives, College Park, Md.

PSC: Palestine Statehood Committee (originals at Yale University; microfilm at USHMM)

PWRB: Papers of the War Refugee Board (originals at FDRL; microfilm at USHMM)

SMP: Saly Mayer Papers, JDC-NY

TMD: The Morgenthau Diaries, FDRL

USHMM: United States Holocaust Memorial Museum, Washington, D.C.

WJC-NY: World Jewish Congress, New York Office

PROLOGUE

3 At least seventeen: Benton, Marseille consular report, Nov. 4, 1942, GVC, 1940–1944, box 224, W.R./1110½. I compared the list enclosed in the report with the list in Serge Klarsfeld, *Les transferts de juifs de la région de Marseille vers les camps de Drancy ou de Compiègne en vue de leur déportation 11 août 1942–24 juillet 1944* (Paris: Association Les Fils et Filles des Déportés Juifs de France, 1992), 3–8.

6 At 6:30 sharp: Details about this deportation are found in Roswell McClelland's 1942 notes, which he later expanded and edited into "An Unpublished Chapter in the History of the Deportation of Foreign Jews from France in 1942" (1986), found in the Roswell and Marjorie McClelland Collection, 2014.500, USHMM. Raymond-Raoul Lambert, the head of the Jewish council in Vichy (the Union Générale des Israélites), corroborated McClelland's descriptions in his diary, published as *Diary of a Witness, 1940–1943*, ed. Richard I. Cohen, trans. Isabel Best (Chicago: Ivan R. Dee, 2007). Lambert would later be deported to Auschwitz with his family. Details about the prisoners were found by comparing the deportation list with the AFSC case files at the USHMM (2002.296). These twenty thousand files hold the correspondence, photographs, and paperwork collected by the AFSC to track its work on behalf of each person or family. There are nearly fifty case files for people deported from Les Milles in the early morning hours of August 11, 1942.

CHAPTER 1: TWO WARS

8 The president felt: Morgenthau and Rosenman, phone conversation, Jan. 15, 1944, TMD, vol. 694, 126–28.

9 Most Americans: The word "refugees" was used at the time both to mean persecuted people trying to get out of Europe and as a catchall term for victims of Nazi oppression in need of assistance. Concentration camp prisoners and Jewish immigrants coming to America were both referred to as "refugees." In light of this, I will use the term "refugees" to generally mean persecuted people whom the War Refugee Board was interested in assisting.

9 The Johnson-Reed Act: In 1924, quota immigration was capped at 164,667; after 1929, it was readjusted to 153,879.

9 The act also: One of the main authors, John Bond Trevor, was the head of the American Coalition of Patriotic Societies. At their 1936 annual conference, participants debated whether to protest the Emma Lazarus poem on the Statue of Liberty. Proceedings, Annual Meeting of the

American Coalition, Nov. 20, 1936, John Bond Trevor Papers, Bentley Historical Library, University of Michigan, 68.

9   Great Britain had: The quotas were recalculated in 1929; this is the post-1929 number. There were two types of immigration: quota and non-quota. Quota visas were given to regular applicants from Europe, Africa, and Asia (though some countries were entirely barred and others had a token quota of 100 persons). Non-quota visas were given to religious leaders, students, teachers, intellectuals, and immigrants from the Western Hemisphere. These visas had no numeric limitation, so long as the applicant met the necessary qualifications. Numbers here relate to quota immigration unless otherwise specified.

10   "is one of the most": Messersmith, letter, July 27, 1933, RG 59, Records Related to Immigration, 1910–1939, 150.626J/14, box 148, NACP.

10   In the first full year: These numbers are calculated using the German consulate visa reports, issued monthly, for February 1933–June 1934. Some Germans were on the waiting list voluntarily. They knew they would be rejected as "likely to become a public charge" but wanted to reserve a place in line in case they could scrape together enough money to qualify for a visa. Visa years ran from July 1 to June 30, so this number is for the end of visa year 1934. Note, Sept. 10, 1934, GVC, 1914–1940, Quota/456.

11   The desperate Jews: Wiley, report, July 27, 1938, CDF, 1930–1939, 862.4016/1772.

11   In the spring of 1938: Dickstein's and Celler's bills (HJ Res. 637 and HR 10013) were both submitted in March 1938. O'Toole's bill (HR 6245) had been submitted in April 1937 but was still in committee, so the hearings were bundled together. Copies of Bills Sent to State, March 31, 1938, RG 59, Records Related to Immigration, 1910–1939, 150.01/Bills/26, box 17, NACP.

11   After the hearings: Richard Breitman and Alan Kraut, *American Refugee Policy and European Jewry, 1933–1945* (Bloomington: Indiana University Press, 1987), 101.

12   The congressmen listened: Messersmith, memo, April 7, 1938, CDF, 1930–1939, 150.01 Bills/34.

12   The Jewish members: Celler did resubmit his bill for consideration in January 1939 but pulled it again soon afterward.

12   To most Americans: Survey by *Fortune*. Methodology: Conducted by Roper Organization during May 1938 and based on 5,151 personal interviews. Sample: National adult. Roper Center for Public Opinion database, George Mason University, USROPER.3801.Q07.

12   "With the exception": Kennedy, report, Nov. 14, 1938, CDF, 1930–1939, 840.48/Refugees/896.

13 "could scarcely believe": FDR, draft statement, Nov. 15, 1938, President's Secretary's Files, Diplomatic Correspondence: Germany, 1933–1938, FDRL.

13 But while a Gallup: Gallup poll, Nov. 25–29, based on fifteen hundred personal interviews. Sample: National adult. Roper Center for Public Opinion database, George Mason University, USGALLUP.120938. R01A.

14 Others, like the Unitarian: The American Unitarian Association created the Unitarian Service Committee in May 1940.

15 "Continuing examination": Davis, cable from Warsaw, Sept. 6, 1939, GVC, 1914–1940, Quota/60C/369.

15 "Day after day": Pickett, letter, Sept. 23, 1940, "American Friends Service Committee," National Refugee Service Records, I-92, box 1, Center for Jewish History.

15 Of the 54,740: The consular offices were also issuing the maximum allotment per month, indicating that the fifteen unissued quota numbers in 1940 might have been a clerical error.

15 From 1938 to 1940: See the *American Jewish Yearbook* for 1938–1940 and subsequent years.

16 The American army: This is the number used by the National World War II Museum.

16 "Now, of course": Transcript, June 5, 1940, Press Conferences of FDR, FDRL.

16 "All applications": On June 26, 1940, Assistant Secretary of State Breckinridge Long responded to a colleague's memo about the State Department's options in case of a national emergency. In an oft-quoted paragraph, Long wrote, "We can delay and effectively stop for a temporary period of indefinite length the number of immigrants coming into the United States. We could do this by simply advising our consuls to put every obstacle in the way and to require additional evidence and to resort to various administrative advices which would postpone and postpone and postpone the granting of visas." Some historians use this as evidence that Long and the State Department cruelly and unilaterally attempted to completely end refugee immigration. They also quote this memo as if Long's scenario actually happened. To be sure, immigration fell from 1940 to 1941, in large part because of the onerous State Department scrutiny and the difficulties inherent in wartime immigration. But immigration did not end. The 26,490 quota immigrants from Nazi-occupied and collaborationist countries who arrived between July 1, 1940, and June 30, 1941, represented 73 percent of all immigration to the United States that year. See Long's memo in context in GVC, 1940–1944, W.R./107;

Hull, cable to diplomatic missions, June 29, 1940, GVC, 1940–1944, W.R./108A.

16 Immigration under: INS monthly review, Sept. 1946.

17 "All immigration": Marjorie McClelland, letter to family, July 15, 1941, McClelland Papers, 2014.500, USHMM.

18 Fewer and fewer: These numbers were calculated from the *New York Times*'s daily "Shipping and Mails" column.

CHAPTER 2: REVELATION

19 "in great agitation": Elting, report, Aug. 10, 1942, CDF, 1940–1944, 862.4016/2233.

20 After spending: See Walter Laqueur and Richard Breitman, *Breaking the Silence: The German Who Exposed the Final Solution* (Hanover, N.H.: University Press of New England, 1994), for more details about Eduard Schulte, the German industrialist.

20 "permanently settle": Elting, report, Aug. 10, 1942, CDF, 1940–1944, 862.4016/2233.

20 "My personal opinion": Ibid.

20 "The report has": Harrison, cable 3697, Aug. 11, 1942, CDF, 862.4016/2233.

20 "see any justification": Culbertson, note attached to cable 3697, Aug. 13, 1942, ibid.

21 "the impossibility": Durbrow, memo regarding cable 3697, Aug. 13, 1942, CDF, 862.4016/2235.

21 "unsubstantiated character": Squire, letter, Aug. 24, 1942, D-Series (Rescue and Relief), WJC-NY-D, 107–16, USHMM.

22 "Gentlemen": Stephen Wise, *Challenging Years: The Autobiography of Stephen Wise* (New York: Putnam and Sons, 1949), 275–76.

22 "severe measures": Translation of Vatican report, Nov. 23, 1942, CDF, 1940–1944, 740.00116 European War/1939/726; and Welles to Taylor, Oct. 21, 1942, Myron C. Taylor Papers, box 1, "1942," LOC.

22 Harrison, initially: Gerhart Riegner, *Never Despair: Sixty Years in the Service of the Jewish People and the Cause of Human Rights* (Chicago: Ivan R. Dee, 2006), 49–50.

22 Consul General: Squire, letter, Sept. 25, 1942, CDF, 1940–1944, 862.4016/2242.

23 Wise announced: See, for example, "2 Million Jews Slain by Nazis, Dr. Wise Avers," *Chicago Daily Tribune*, Nov. 25, 1942, 4.

23 "take such action": Petition to Roosevelt, Dec. 8, 1942, Official File 76-Church Matters: 76c-Jewish, Oct.–Dec. 1942, FDRL.

23 "call off": Memo regarding "Dr. Wise mail," Dec. 9, 1942, CDF, 1940–1944, 862.4016/2251.

23 "governments": Reams, memo, Dec. 10, 1942, CDF, 1940–1944, 740.0116/694.

24 "bloody cruelties": United Nations Declaration on Atrocities, Dec. 17, 1942, PWRB, LM0305, reel 28, 835.

CHAPTER 3: JOHN PEHLE

25 The Treasury Department staff: Thompson, directive related to correspondence, Nov. 26, 1941, RG 56, Office Files of Secretaries, Records of Assistant Secretary John W. Pehle, entry 190, box 206, "Green Slip Letters," NACP.

25 "influencing his": William O. Player, "John W. Pehle—Refugee Board's Chief," *New York Post*, March 11, 1944, PWRB, box 61, folder 2, FDRL.

26 There John planted: Ibid.

26 He and his staff: In 2017, this is the equivalent of about $140 billion.

26 Sometimes the job: There isn't a lot written about the important work of Foreign Funds Control. The best summaries and statistics exist in the staff's yearly congressional testimony surrounding approval of the Treasury Department's Appropriation Bill. There is a five-hundred-page unpublished history of Foreign Funds Control located in RG 56, entry 66A-816, box 47, NACP.

27 Riegner thought: I have standardized "Rumania" to "Romania" throughout this book. Meltzer to Pehle, June 25, 1943, CDF, 1940–1944, 862.4016/2274.

27 It's hard to say: Conducted by Gallup Organization, Jan. 9–14, 1943, and based on fifteen hundred personal interviews. Sample: National adult. Sample size is approximate. Roper Center for Public Opinion database, George Mason University, USGALLUP.43287.QKT12.

27 "similar proposals": Pehle, letter, June 21, 1943, LM0305, reel 1, 980–81.

28 Riegner also realized: In Riegner's first proposal, he did not believe that it would be necessary to send currency into France, but by the time his request reached Pehle's desk, Riegner had changed his mind. See Daniel Reagan's notes of his conversation with Riegner for a detailed summary of the proposal as of early June 1943. June 4, 1943, RG 84, General Records, Bern embassy, box 14, "World Jewish Congress," NACP.

28 "Current prohibitions": Pehle, letter, June 21, 1943, LM0305, reel 1, 980–81.

28 "very troublesome": The idea of paying ransom for Romanian Jews stemmed in part from a *New York Times* article in February 1943 in which the reporter indicated that the Nazi-collaborating Romanian government would release internees in exchange for a per-person payment. The State Department investigated and decided it was a

Nazi trick. Still, the Committee for a Jewish Army (Peter Bergson's advocacy group) took out a full-page ad, also in the *Times,* advocating for a ransom payment and proclaiming, "If the refugees were British, American, or Russian, the United Nations would be up and doing something despite all difficulties." Committee for a Jewish Army, "For Sale to Humanity" advertisement, *New York Times,* Feb. 16, 1943; Pehle and O'Connell, memo to Morgenthau, July 1, 1943, TMD, vol. 645, 68.

28 After Meltzer shared: Meltzer to Pehle, July 14, 1943, CDF, 1940–1944, 862.4016/2278.

28 "Treasury's approval": Memo of conversation, July 16, 1943, CDF, 1940–1944, 840.48/Refugees/4074.

29 "This can undoubtedly": Ibid.

29 "too independent": Press release announcing the passing of Professor Emeritus Bernard D. Meltzer, issued by the University of Chicago News Office, Jan. 4, 2007, www-news.uchicago.edu.

29 "faded and moth-eaten": Robert Bendiner, *The Riddle of the State Department* (New York: Farrar and Rinehart, 1942), 143.

30 He raised funds: Ibid., 179.

30 "tricky, deceitful": "Introduction to Report on Various Organizations and Individuals Engaged in Refugee Migration Activities," Sept. 26, 1942, CDF, 1940–1944, 840.48/Refugees/3479.

30 "fantastic[al]": Reams, memo, Aug. 26, 1942, CDF, 1940–1944, 862.4016/2234.

30 "call off": Memo regarding "Dr. Wise mail," Dec. 9, 1942, CDF, 1940–1944, 862.4016/2251.

30 "negotiations with the various": Ibid.

31 "the most liberal": State Department staff, Memorandum: Views of the Government of the United States Regarding Topics Included in the Agenda for Discussion with the British Government, April 19, 1943, in *Intergovernmental Committee on Refugees: The West's Response to Jewish Emigration* (Farmington Hills, Mich.: Gale, 2010).

31 "nothing but a series": Freda Kirchwey, "A Program of Inaction," *Nation,* June 5, 1943, 366–67.

31 "Hitler's mass executioners": "Bermuda Parley," *Washington Post,* April 20, 1943, 12.

32 On the last full day: Dodds, cable to State, April 28, 1943, in *Intergovernmental Committee on Refugees.*

32 "To 5,000,000": Committee for a Jewish Army, "For 5,000,000 Jews in Nazi Death-Trap," *New York Times,* May 4, 1943.

32 If these Jewish groups: Long, letter, May 15, 1943, BLP, "Refugee Hearings . . . 1939–1944," box 203.

32 Riegner had seen: Harrison, cable 4558, July 29, 1943, CDF, 1940–1944, 862.4016/2280.

33 "without, I repeat": Wise to FDR, July 23, 1943, TMD, vol. 652, 230–31.

33 "It would appear": Meltzer, "Proposed Arrangement for Relief and Evacuation of Refugees in Romania and France," July 30, 1943, CDF, 1940–1944, 840.48/Refugees/4211.

33 "There are certain": "Group" meeting, Aug. 5, 1943, TMD, vol. 654, 5–12.

33 "discourteous": Phone conversation, Sept. 20, 1943, TMD, vol. 6881, 81–84.

33 "Any view": Hull, memo for the secretary of the Treasury, Aug. 7, 1943, TMD, vol. 6881, 10.

33 Hull's note: Brandt, memo to Feis, Aug. 3, 1943, CDF, 1940–1944, 840.48/Refugees/4212.

34 "best get away": Berle, diary, Sept. 1, 1943, Adolf Berle Papers, box 215, "Diaries," FDRL.

34 Welles's sudden: Hull had never gotten along with the genial diplomat Welles. Roosevelt preferred to conduct his own foreign policy, using Welles when he needed a surrogate—a choice that Hull correctly interpreted as a deliberate personal slight. In August 1943, Hull and Welles were barely speaking. The incident at the root of Welles's resignation is recounted in many places including a biography written by Sumner Welles's son Benjamin. Benjamin Welles, *Sumner Welles: FDR's Global Strategist* (New York: St. Martin's Press, 1997), 273–74.

34 Long struggled: Long, diary, Aug. 29–Sept. 27, 1943, BLP, box 5, "Diaries."

34 Meanwhile, Pehle was: Paul, memo to Morgenthau, Aug. 12, 1943, TMD, vol. 6881, 12.

35 "Nearly 4000": Harrison, cable 3465, June 9, 1943, ibid., 29–30.

Chapter 4: State Department Hubris

36 On Wednesday: After the march, Eri Jabotinsky summarized the day's events in a letter sent to Emergency Committee supporters. He wrote that Congressman Sol Bloom had tried to dissuade the marchers, but "the Jewish Congressmen had held a meeting and decided that we had licked them and that they would appear in a body to greet the Rabbis." Jabotinsky accused Bloom of having "spoiled the soup by telling one of the Rabbis, as an additional inducement for not going, that it would be very undignified for a group of such un-American looking people to appear in Washington." In Jabotinsky's telling, this made the rabbis even more eager to march in Washington. Multiple historians, including David Wyman in *The Abandonment of the Jews: America and the*

Holocaust, 1941–1945 (New York: Pantheon Books, 1984), have taken this anecdote as fact, even though Jabotinsky's letter was clearly meant to drum up support and is filled with demonstrable exaggerations and inaccuracies. The historian Theodore Hamerow, in *Why We Watched* (New York: W. W. Norton, 2008), wrote that it had been *Roosevelt* who felt the rabbis were "unmistakably Jewish. They had long beards and earlocks, they wore black coats and hats, and many of them spoke English with a pronounced Old World accent. Quite a few, in fact, resembled the antisemitic caricatures that the *Stürmer* was circulating" (346). Hamerow cited Wyman as his source, who cited a propaganda letter. Jabotinsky, letter to supporters, Oct. 12, 1943, PSC, LM0399, reel 1, folder 10, USHMM.

36 "save the remnant": A week after the march, Senator William Barbour of New Jersey introduced a resolution, SJ Res. 85, calling for the admission of up to 100,000 refugees into the United States for the duration of the war. Barbour had stood on the Senate steps listening to the rabbis' pleas and, obviously moved by the experience, decided to act. He passed away a month later, on November 22, and his resolution was tabled permanently. Petition, Oct. 8, 1944, CDF, 1940–1944, 840.48/Refugees/4745.

36 A small delegation: For more details about the context of the rabbis' march and the attempted meeting with Roosevelt in particular, see Rebecca Erbelding, "About Time: The History of the War Refugee Board" (PhD diss., George Mason University, 2015), 94–97.

37 In fact, as: Long, memo of conversation, Oct. 6, 1943, BLP, box 202, "Refugees 2."

37 He believed: Bergson to Hershey, Selective Service, June 18, 1943, PSC, LM0399, reel 1, folder 9, USHMM.

38 "Refer to Committee": Cartoon attached to "Washington Pilgrimage," *Answer,* Nov. 1, 1943, 6, PSC, reel 3, USHMM. The cartoon, drawn by Eric Godal, himself a German Jewish refugee, originally appeared in *PM,* Oct. 3, 1943.

38 "nothing special": "Group" meeting, Aug. 5, 1943, TMD, vol. 654, 5–12.

38 "the Government's blanket": Paul, memo to Morgenthau, Aug. 26, 1943, LM0305, reel 1, 1063–66.

38 "we have now had": Ibid.

38 Pehle authorized: Morgenthau to Hull, Sept. 16, 1943, LM0305, reel 1, 1048–50.

39 Within two weeks: In Bern, Daniel Reagan (the legation's financial attaché) reminded Mayer that the "telegram in itself does not constitute the authority to carry out the operations proposed therein" and that he would still need a license. The JDC did not apply for one, and the Treasury Department did not follow up about it. In its correspondence

with Mayer, the JDC referenced payments of $100,000 per month for six months beginning in September 1943. Reagan, letter, Sept. 21, 1943, RG 84, General Records, Bern legation, box 14, "Joint," NACP.

39 "Are we now": Keeley, memo, Sept. 14, 1943, CDF, 1940–1944, 840.48/Refugees/4502.

39 Morgenthau spoke: Morgenthau learned the license had not been sent in a phone conversation with Herbert Lehman on September 15; after he complained, the State Department promised to send it that day. It was actually sent September 28. Phone conversations, Sept. 15 and 20, 1943, TMD, vol. 688I, 79–84; Berle, cable 2373, Sept. 28, 1943, RG 84, General Records, Bern legation, box 14, 848, "World Jewish Congress," NACP.

39 "type of adventurers": British commercial secretary, note about Riegner plan, Oct. 2, 1943, RG 84, General Records, Bern legation, box 14, "World Jewish Congress," NACP.

40 "not believe": Reams, memo, Oct. 25, 1943, CDF, 1940–1944, 862.4016/2292.

40 "in accordance": Henderson, memo, Oct. 26, 1943, ibid.

40 Breckinridge Long: Long, memo, Oct. 26, 1943, BLP, box 209, "Riegner."

40 Stettinius prized: Martin Weil, *A Pretty Good Club* (New York: W. W. Norton, 1978), 142–43.

41 The two men: Peter Cox, *Journalism Matters* (Gardiner, Maine: Tilbury House, 2005), 28, quoting Drew Pearson.

41 "resettlement": Cox, letter, June 16, 1943, TMD, vol. 642, 210–13.

41 One of Morgenthau's: Kades, memo, June 21, 1943, TMD, vol. 643, 278–80.

41 "extreme measures": Reams, memo, Oct. 8, 1943, BLP, box 202, "Refugees 2."

42 "You should": Stettinius, cable 2626, Oct. 25, 1943, CDF, 1940–1944, 862.4016/2292.

42 "Enthusiastically": *New York Post,* Nov. 21, 1935.

43 At 2:45 p.m.: In this and the many Treasury Department meetings held in November, December, and January about the Riegner plan, the "staff" in question refers to Randolph Paul, John Pehle, Josiah DuBois, and Ansel Luxford.

43 "Gentlemen, I can say": "Jewish Evacuation" meeting, Nov. 23, 1943, TMD, vol. 688I, 111–18.

43 "I fully appreciate": Morgenthau, letter, Nov. 24, 1943, CDF, 1940–1944, 862.4016/2297.

44 "nobody's fool": "Jewish Evacuation" meeting, Dec. 13, 1943, TMD, vol. 688II, 1–19.

44 "the Department": Hull, letter, Dec. 6, 1943, ibid., 20–23.

44 "conclusions": Paul, memo, Dec. 14, 1943, ibid., 25–34.

44 "a commission": In the Senate, Guy Gillette (D-Iowa) introduced SR 203 with eleven co-sponsors: Robert Taft (R-Ohio); Elbert Thomas (D-Utah); George Radcliffe (D-Md.); James Murray (D-Mont.); Edwin Johnson (D-Colo.); Joseph Guffey (D-Pa.); Homer Ferguson (R-Mich.); Bennett Clark (D-Mo.); Frederick Van Nuys (D-Ind.); Sheridan Downey (D-Calif.); Allen Ellender (D-La.). In the House of Representatives, Will Rogers Jr. (D-Calif.) and Joseph Clark Baldwin (R-N.Y.) introduced HR 350 and 352. *Congressional Record* introducing House Resolutions 350 and 352, Nov. 9, 1943, LM0305, reel 24, 915–18.

45 The day after: *Problems of World War II and Its Aftermath, Part 2: The Palestine Question, Problems of Postwar Europe,* Selected Executive Session Hearings of the Committee, 1943–1950 (Washington, D.C.: U.S. Government Printing Office, 1976).

45 "an excellent record": Ibid.

45 It's hard to understand: *PM* criticized Long's testimony in its "Bunk . . . Because" column, calculating a total of 476,930 immigrants who had entered the United States between 1933 and June 1943—certainly not all of them Jews and not all of them refugees. Jewish refugees made up 209,932 of the immigrants. The World Jewish Congress investigated *PM*'s statistics and found that the number was closer to 190,000. Accounting for refugees who did not self-identify as Jewish and those who escaped prior to their countries' being overrun by the Nazis, a figure of 190,000 refugees is not unreasonable, but probably low. After the war, a group of Jewish organizations hired a sociologist, Maurice Davie, to study exactly how many refugees entered the United States between 1933 and 1945. His final figure was approximately 260,000, accounting for all Jews coming from Europe in 1933–1945, and all immigrants from Nazi-occupied and collaborationist territories. The real number is probably somewhere in between, but certainly nowhere near 580,000.

45 "His statement": Celler, press release, Dec. 11, 1943, GVC, 1940–1944, W.R./1560.

45 "They ask": Long, memo, Dec. 16, 1943, BLP, box 202, "Refugees 2."

45 State Department officials: In May 1943, Long proposed a *Collier's* article about the work of the State Department as an attempt to silence critics. In his draft to Sumner Welles, meant to convince Welles of the feasibility of the piece, Long guessed the consulates issued a staggering 340,000 visas for Germans between 1933 and 1939—a number more than twice the amount legally allowed under the quota and more than four times the actual number, about 78,000. Long, memo, May 15, 1943, BLP, box 203, "Refugee Hearings."

45 "The radical press": Long, diary, Jan. 1, 1944, BLP, box 5, "Diaries."

46 "strong, shocking": "Jewish Evacuation" meeting, Dec. 17, 1943, TMD, vol. 688II, 50–62.

46 "concerned with": Winant, cable 8717, Dec. 15, 1943, ibid., 48–49.

46 "away from all": "Jewish Evacuation" meeting, Dec. 18, 1943, ibid., 82–94.

47 "a straw man": "Jewish Evacuation" meeting, Dec. 19, 1943, ibid., 103–30.

47 On Saturday: Hull, cable 3168, Dec. 18, 1943, CDF, 1940–1944, 862.4016/2295.

47 "astonishment": Hull, cable 7969, Dec. 18, 1943, ibid., 97.

47 "From the time": "Jewish Evacuation" meeting, Dec. 20, 1943, TMD, vol. 688II, 148–71.

48 "Excuse me": Ibid.

CHAPTER 5: ON THE ACQUIESCENCE OF THIS GOVERNMENT

49 "not (repeat not)": Harrison, cable 2450, April 20, 1943, CDF, 1940–1944, 860.4016/2268.

50 "With regard": Welles, cable 354, Feb. 10, 1943, RG 84, General Records, Bern legation, box 4, 840.1 "Jews," NACP.

50 "6000 Jews": DuBois, copy of index card, Dec. 20, 1943, William Spiegler papers related to Josiah E. DuBois Jr., box 1, 2014.115.1, USHMM.

51 "In the first place": "Jewish Evacuation" meeting, Dec. 21, 1943, TMD, vol. 688II, 201–18.

51 "cheap trick": "Jewish Evacuation" meeting, Dec. 20, 1943, ibid., 172–85.

51 The paraphrased: Long, paraphrase of 354, Dec. 20, 1943, BLP, box 209, "Riegner."

51 "Acheson's assistant": Luxford, memo, Dec. 21, 1943, TMD, vol. 688II, 99.

52 "To put it bluntly": This paragraph was a last-minute addition to the memo. DuBois's draft from December 22 does not include this paragraph, but his draft dated December 23 (edited with the assistance of Pehle, Luxford, and Orvis Schmidt) includes a handwritten addition of this paragraph to the main text. It must have been added that day. "Memorandum: For Secretary Morgenthau's Information Only," Dec. 23, 1943, ibid., 223J–223X.

52 DuBois had tried: Later in his life, DuBois claimed to have drafted the memo titled "A Report to the Secretary on the Acquiescence of This Government in the Murder of the Jews" on Christmas Day 1943. Various historians and authors—most prominently Rafael Medoff, who based the main premise of his book *Blowing the Whistle on Genocide: Josiah E. DuBois Jr. and the Struggle for a U.S. Response to the Holocaust* (West Lafayette, Ind.: Purdue University, 2009) on the heroism of DuBois's authorship—have taken this claim at face value and ascribed the entire authorship of the memo to DuBois. Based

on his own drafts, it is clear that DuBois played a large role, but others, including Pehle, Luxford, and Schmidt, were active collaborators. On December 25, the Treasury staff was still planning a detailed memo for Hull—taking verbatim language from their December 23 memo to Morgenthau and inserting a new introduction, transitions, and conclusion. If DuBois did draft anything on December 25, it was likely this language, which was written sometime between December 23 and December 28 (the draft is undated). Very little of this new language was incorporated into the eventual "Acquiescence" memo. The drafts are located in 2014.115.1, Spiegler papers related to DuBois, box 1, USHMM.

52 "and no damn fooling": Morgenthau and Pehle, phone conversation, Jan. 4, 1944, TMD, vol. 690, 92–94.

53 "State felt": Hodel, memo, Jan. 5, 1944, LM0305, reel 1, 992–93.

53 "very, very disturbed": Pehle and Riegelman meeting, Jan. 6, 1944, TMD, vol. 691, 175–80.

53 "Unless remedial": "Report to the Secretary on the Acquiescence of This Government in the Murder of the Jews," Jan. 13, 1944, TMD, vol. 693, 212–29.

54 When Morgenthau called: Oscar Cox was Jewish, but did not practice, and concealed his religious upbringing from his sons. "Jewish Evacuation" meeting, Jan. 13, 1944, ibid., 187–211.

54 Cox and several: I use "agency" for the WRB because it appeared in the annual digest of federal agencies, though governmental definitions of what constitutes an agency versus a task force versus an organization and so on vary.

54 Promptly: Sam Rosenman never made it: the president had the flu and had slept in, so Rosenman was stuck at the White House waiting for the morning briefing.

54 William Riegelman had spoken: "Jewish Evacuation" meeting, Jan. 15, 1944, TMD, vol. 694, 59–110.

54 "One of the greatest": Ibid., 59–110.

55 "I dreamed": Ibid.

55 "the time to act": Ibid.

55 They assembled: In an *American Experience* interview Pehle gave at least forty years later, he remembered the meeting took place in the Oval Office. The memo he wrote at the time is not specific. In 1946–1947, Randolph Paul gave a detailed recollection of the meeting, which he remembered as taking place in the Oval Study. Due to the details he remembered (which echo the contemporary meeting transcripts) and the date of Paul's recollections, I am inclined to believe Paul. Pehle later had several meetings with FDR in the Oval Office and might have conflated these.

56 "There are the facts": "Jewish Evacuation" meeting, Jan. 15, 1944, TMD, vol. 694, 59–110.

56 He, too, believed: Stettinius, memo, Nov. 11, 1943, CDF 1940–1944, 840.48/Refugees/4843.

57 "The President seemed": Roosevelt was referencing the President's Advisory Committee on Political Refugees, which was most active from 1938 to 1941 and submitted lists of supposedly prominent political, cultural, and religious figures for preferential State Department consideration for immigration. Long felt the President's Advisory Committee was distracting an overtaxed State Department and complained that the political figures in particular were leftists, Communists, or spies.

57 The meeting: Pehle, memo for the secretary's files, Jan. 16, 1944, RG 56, Records of the Secretary, Undersecretary, Assistant Secretaries (entry 193B), box 171, NACP. After the war, when Morgenthau was preparing an article for *Collier's,* his ghostwriter interviewed Randolph Paul, who recalled additional details. The interview notes are located in 2015.255.1, Morgenthau Family Papers, USHMM.

Chapter 6: A War Refugee Board

58 Henry Morgenthau didn't: Oscar Cox was out of town that Sunday and, upon learning that his War Refugee Board plan would become a reality, wrote a beautiful handwritten note to Morgenthau. It reads, in its entirety, "Thousands upon thousands will have the cruel hand of suffering and death lifted from them by what you have done. To feel with and as humans whom you haven't seen in the lands of persecution is one of the marks of your human depth and greatness. Deep in my heart I am warmed. Rare individuals like you are what give me, at least, the driving hope to carry on with the war and what comes after." Cox, letter, Jan. 17, 1944, TMD, vol. 694, 212.

58 After more than four years: Prior to Stettinius's appointment and before his congressional testimony, Long had requested a transfer out of the Visa Division, which Hull had granted.

59 Pehle left Morgenthau's: Pehle, memo for the secretary's files, Jan. 16, 1944, RG 56, Records of the Secretary, Undersecretary, Assistant Secretaries (entry 193B), box 171, NACP.

59 "left no unfavorable": Morgenthau, memo, Jan. 17, 1944, Morgenthau Presidential Diaries, vol. 5, FDRL.

59 "and I'm not going": Morgenthau, phone conversation, Jan. 17, 1944, TMD, vol. 694, 186–89.

60 "Pehle's girl Friday": Akzin to Lawrence Lesser, Jan. 12, 1976, in private collection. My thanks to George Lesser for sharing it with me.

61 Pehle persuaded: Armour, cable, Feb. 16, 1944, PWRB, box 60, "James Mann," FDRL.

62 Pehle cobbled: A staffing breakdown as of March 1944 lists fifty-three staff members, most detailed from various departments within Treasury, though this number does not include overseas personnel (or Pehle, for that matter). A recurrent myth about the War Refugee Board is that it was "understaffed." Historians who make this claim never provide evidence of what this means, show any evidence of Pehle's requesting staff he did not receive, or any projects that suffered for lack of personnel. Documentary evidence indicates staffing was never a problem. Staff list, March 22, 1944, PWRB, box 60, folder 9, FDRL.

62 "You can't have": "Jewish Evacuation" meeting, Jan. 26, 1944, TMD, vol. 696, 193–228.

62 "has a foot": "Jewish Evacuation" meeting, Jan. 18, 1944, TMD, vol. 695, 38–47; "Jewish Evacuation" meeting, Jan. 26, 1944, TMD, vol. 696, 193–228; Morgenthau, phone calls, Jan. 27, 1944, TMD, vol. 697, 79–86.

62 "too emotional": Morgenthau and Paul, phone call, Jan. 31, 1944, TMD, vol. 698, 130–31.

62 "Thanks": "Jewish Evacuation" meeting, Jan. 26, 1944, TMD, vol. 696, 193–228; "Jewish Evacuation" meeting, Jan. 27, 1944, TMD, vol. 697, 12–46.

62 Even Roosevelt's: "Group" meeting, Feb. 3, 1944, TMD, vol. 700, 12–46.

62 "It really gets": "Jewish Evacuation" meeting, Jan. 26, 1944, TMD, vol. 696, 127–49.

63 "tough son": "Jewish Evacuation" meeting, Jan. 18, 1944, vol. 695, 38–47.

63 On January 22: The joint congressional resolutions calling for an agency were both permanently tabled after the announcement of the WRB.

63 "Whereas it is": Executive Order 9417, Jan. 22, 1944, LM0306, reel 1, 2–3.

63 "Rarely has": "Rescue the Refugees!" editorial, *El Paso Herald-Post*, Jan. 25, 1944, 4.

63 "Three years": Bergson, telegram, Jan. 23, 1944, LM0305, reel 25, 67.

63 "among those fortunate": Werner, letter, Jan. 23, 1944, PWRB, box 60, folder 5, FDRL.

64 "It is not": Pell, letter, Jan. 22, 1944, HRFDRWH, reel 14, folder 6, 705, USHMM.

64 "singling out": Pell, letter, Jan. 25, 1944, ibid., 708–9.

64 Herbert Emerson: Winant, cable 656, Jan. 24, 1944, CDF, 1940–1944, 840.48/5041.

64 "American, British": Helen Kirkpatrick, "Naming of Refugee Board Complicates Allied Relief Picture," Jan. 28, 1944, LM0305, reel 25, 49. After agreeing that they needed to keep the British informed of their actions,

Morgenthau joked with Pehle in a British accent, "Well, somebody had better prepare an extra scotch and soda for the whole foreign office." Pehle and Morgenthau, conversation, Jan. 27, 1944, TMD, vol. 697, 87–89.

64 "I cannot see": Gerhardt, memo, Feb. 11, 1944, RG 107, entry 183, box 63, "War Refugee Board," NACP.

64 "The Pres't": Long, diary, Jan. 24, 1944, BLP, box 5.

65 "Now where does that": Rosenman and Morgenthau, phone call, Jan. 18, 1944, TMD, vol. 695, 31–37.

65 In fact, few: Hull, cable 634, Jan. 25, 1944, LM0306, reel 23, 900–901.

66 "terrible headache": Friedman, memo, Jan. 26, 1944, LM0306, reel 1, 710–13.

66 "as a Christian": Morgenthau and Stettinius, phone call, Jan. 25, 1944, TMD, vol. 696, 75–90.

66 Hull complained: "Jewish Evacuation" meeting, Jan. 26, 1944, ibid., 193–228.

67 "a resentment": Woodward, cable 3122, Feb. 10, 1944, LM0306, reel 3, 940–41.

67 "It is unlikely": Facci, cable from Tegucigalpa, Feb. 4, 1944, LM0305, reel 23, 385–86.

67 The impoverished: White, cable 2521, Jan. 31, 1944, LM0306, reel 4, 141–42.

67 Eleven days: In early April, Lescot clarified that the $500 was meant for the U.S. National War Fund, but the future lottery proceeds would be for the WRB. White, cable 2559, Feb. 10, 1944, ibid., 143–44. White, cable 2710, April 3, 1944, ibid., 149–51.

67 "in the past two": Moose, cable from Jidda, Feb. 16, 1944, ibid., 442.

67 Baghdad refused: Henderson, cable from Baghdad, Feb. 28, 1944, LM0306, reel 2, 155–57.

67 Egypt was: Kirk, cable 1621, Feb. 26, 1944, LM0306, reel 4, 401–2.

68 "is not interested": Johnson, cable from Canberra, Feb. 24, 1944, LM0306, reel 1, 739–42.

68 Recent epidemics: Patton, cable from Calcutta, Feb. 23, 1944, LM0306, reel 2, 151.

68 "The willingness": Engers, cable 405, March 5, 1944, LM0306, reel 4, 368–69.

68 The American consulate: The State Department was aware that thousands of Jewish refugees were in Shanghai, which was an open city for which no entry permits were needed, but this was in Japanese-occupied territory, and there was no official American presence.

68 Yunnan reported: Gauss, cable 2245, March 22, 1944, LM0306, reel 1, 786–96.

68 "there are no special": Schoenfeld, cable, March 3, 1944, LM0306, reel 2, 218–20.

68 Ireland thought: Gray, cable from Dublin, Feb. 10, 1944, ibid., 400–402.

68 "since Iceland": Morris, cable from Reykjavík, Feb. 19, 1944, LM0306, reel 4, 426–27.

69 "the Board is not": Pehle, WRB asks for suggestions, Feb. 8, 1944, LM0305, reel 1, 333–34.

69 Some of the relief: Lesser, list of organizations, Feb. 10, 1944, LM0306, reel 24, 448–68.

69 In case they missed: To keep the responses organized, one staff member wrote an extensively indexed report clearly demonstrating the overlap of the various ideas. WRB staff, Digest of Suggestions Submitted to the War Refugee Board by Various Private Organizations in Response to Circular Letter, n.d., ibid., 427–46.

70 "all possible relief": Executive Order 9417, Jan. 22, 1944, LM0306, reel 1, 2–3.

CHAPTER 7: GETTING STARTED

72 John Pehle arrived: Pehle, transcript, *American Experience* oral history interview, n.d. He repeated the story to the Treasury Historical Association, interview with Dorothy Daly and Abby Gilbert, Aug. 19, 1997. My thanks to the Treasury Historical Association for providing me with the transcript.

74 "I appreciate": Riegner, letter, Feb. 17, 1944, PWRB, box 70, folder 9, FDRL.

74 "run-arounds": "Jewish Evacuation" meeting, Jan. 13, 1944, TMD, vol. 693, 187–211.

75 By early January: Getsinger, memo, Jan. 6, 1944, PWRB, box 70, folder 9, 13–16.

75 Long finally: Hodel, memo, Jan. 12, 1944, TMD, vol. 693, 223–36.

75 The Treasury staff: Luxford, memo, Jan. 13, 1944, ibid., 292.

75 "could get it": "Jewish Evacuation" meeting, Jan. 13, 1944, ibid., 187–211.

75 "Greece": Hodel, memo, Jan. 19, 1944, LM0305, reel 24, 965–69.

75 "with the changing": Ibid.

76 "We are prepared": Pehle, cable to Bern, Jan. 27, 1944, LM0306, reel 9, 668–70.

76 Pehle trusted: Meeting transcript, Jan. 10, 1944, Florence Hodel Papers, 2014.300.1, USHMM.

76 "The necessary funds": Hull, cable 437, Feb. 9, 1944, LM0305, reel 28, 929.

76 "convey": Huber, letter, Feb. 17, 1944, LM0306, reel 20, 638–39.

76 With the War: Emerson, letter, Feb. 21, 1944, ibid., 655.

77 At Roosevelt's: Keith Pomakoy, in his book *Helping Humanity: American Policy and Genocide Rescue* (Lanham, Md.: Lexington Books, 2011),

argued that Roosevelt's decision to only provide the War Refugee Board with administrative funds was in keeping with the tradition of American philanthropic organizations. Both Roosevelt and Morgenthau had been involved in the Near East Relief (NER) organization during World War I, which collected aid for Armenians in the Ottoman Empire and funneled this aid through American governmental channels. Unlike the WRB, the NER—though it enjoyed vast governmental support—was a private organization.

77 "this might cause": Leavitt, meeting, Feb. 10, 1944, AR 45-54, 00193-1264, JDC-NY.

77 Pehle's staff would: Ibid.

77 "was at the moment": Ernst, letter, March 8, 1944, Morris Leopold Ernst Papers, box 35, folder 2, Harry Ransom Center, University of Texas at Austin.

78 Pehle got: Raynor, memo, Feb. 4, 1944, RG 59, War Refugee Board, box 1, "Misc. 1944 Jan.–March," NACP.

78 The IGC's money: In May, Roosevelt reimbursed the WRB $200,000 from the Emergency Fund. The additional $9,811.93 and a later grant of $8,061.92 were never reimbursed.

78 Out of the president's: Stewart, WRB Financial Obligations for February 1944, March 19, 1944, PWRB, box 60, folder 3, FDRL.

79 "in no way": Murphy, note, March 1, 1944, ibid., 388; Russell, cable 44, Feb. 21, 1944, ibid., 389–92.

79 "I can see": Ackermann, V-mail, Feb. 29, 1944, Lesser Family Papers, private collection.

79 Beckelman even: Beckelman, report, Jan. 23, 1944, LM0305, reel 1, 248–54.

80 John Pehle sent: Pehle, letter, March 13, 1944, LM0305, reel 8, 703.

80 The former chairman: Myron Taylor deserves a good biography and doesn't have one yet. The best summary of his life was written for the *Cornell Law Forum* alumni magazine in 2006–2007. W. David Curtiss and C. Evan Stewart, "Myron C. Taylor: Cornell Benefactor, Industrial Czar, and FDR's 'Ambassador Extraordinary,'" *Cornell Law Forum,* Summer/Fall 2006, Winter 2007.

81 "make the other": DuBois, memo, March 2, 1944, LM0305, reel 24, 947–51.

81 "There followed": Ibid.

81 "to clear up": Taylor, memo, March 3, 1944, BLP, box 202, "Refugees 2."

82 "I don't—no": Morgenthau and Stettinius, phone call, March 9, 1944, TMD, vol. 708, 30–34.

82 "Now, you didn't": "Jewish Evacuation" meeting, March 11, 1944, TMD, vol. 709, 16–22.

82 "the full co-operation": Emerson, letter, Feb. 25, 1944, LM0306, reel 21, 772–73.

82 "The two groups": Taylor, letter, May 25, 1944, HRFDRWH, LM0255, reel 14, 747–48, USHMM.

84 "It is still": Hayes, cable 683, March 1, 1944, LM0305, reel 7, 488.

84 "It has not yet": Hayes, cable 974, March 20, 1944, PWRB, box 46, "Evacuation Through Spain," FDRL.

84 "the War Refugee Board's efforts": Hayes, cable 1195, April 6, 1944, LM0306, reel 2, 655–56.

84 "Hayes has made": Pehle, memo, March 27, 1944, TMD, vol. 714, 217–18.

84 Morgenthau began: "The Ambassador is the personal representative of the President. How can the Ambassador be there if he doesn't carry out the President's wishes?" "Jewish Evacuation" meeting, April 10, 1944, TMD, vol. 719, 179–86.

85 At the end of April: Pickett, letter to Spanish ambassador, April 28, 1944, AFSC Refugee Section, box 5, "Spanish Embassy," AFSC.

CHAPTER 8: HIRSCHMANN IN TURKEY

86 "I may have": Hirschmann, letter, Feb. 18, 1944, IHP, box 2, "Correspondence."

87 His noncombatant: Certificate of identity, Jan. 27, 1944, IHP, box 2, "ID."

87 "he sounded": Morgenthau and Pehle, phone call, Jan. 25, 1944, TMD, vol. 696, 87.

87 "clothed": Hodel, memo, Jan. 24, 1944, PWRB, box 60, folder 18, FDRL.

88 "the first and only": Joseph Levy, "Refugee Aid Chief at Work in Turkey," *New York Times,* Feb. 20, 1944, 11.

88 "See possibilities": Hirschmann, cable, Feb. 12, 1944, LM0305, reel 23, 781.

88 The late president: Post report, Jan. 2, 1945, RG 84, Ankara embassy, General Records 1943–1949, 1945, box 88, "Ankara," NACP; Edwin Wilson, History of the Ankara Embassy, Jan. 31, 1946, RG 59, War History Branch, entry A1-716, box 29, "Ankara," NACP.

89 In April 1943: Steinhardt, cable 574, Feb. 20, 1944, LM0305, reel 23, 764–76.

90 Hirschmann met: Hirschmann, memo, Feb. 18, 1944, HRFDRWH, reel 7, folder 6, 2–3; Steinhardt, cable 314, Feb. 22, 1944, LM0306, reel 12, 978–80.

91 Hirschmann approached: Hirschmann, memo, Feb. 25, 1944, LM0306, reel 8, 741–46.

91 "secrecy": Campbell, letter, Sept. 9, 1943, LM0306, reel 1, 982–84.

92 Ninety other: Fredka Mazia, oral history, Feb. 28, 1991, RG 50. 120*0102, USHMM.

92 "I really broke": Hirschmann, diary, March 4, 1944, IHP, box 1.

92 "It seems desirable": Hirschmann, cable 345, Feb. 26, 1944, TMD, vol. 704, 45–48.

92 "Palestine Door": "Palestine Door Opens to 5,000 Balkan Children," *New York Post,* March 13, 1944, LM0306, reel 15, 588.

93 "The point": Hirschmann, cable 282, Feb. 18, 1944, HRFDRWH, LM0255, reel 6, 428–29, USHMM.

93 Pehle received: Pehle, letter, Feb. 26, 1944, LM0306, reel 12, 312.

93 "The tone": Hirschmann, diary, Feb. 28, 1944, IHP, box 1, "Typed Diaries."

93 "Water vivid": Hirschmann, diary, Feb. 27, 1944, ibid.

94 "It was fascinating": Hirschmann, diary, Feb. 29, 1944, ibid.

94 "their cooperation": Steinhardt, cable 465, March 16, 1944, LM0305, reel 24, 722–23; Hirschmann, letter, March 16, 1944, IHP, box 2, "Correspondence."

94 "I was clear": Hirschmann, diary, March 23, 1944, IHP, box 1, "Typed Diaries."

94 "All clarinets": Ibid.

95 "What a race": Hirschmann, diary, March 21, 1944, ibid.

95 "even down": Hirschmann, diary, March 25, 1944, IHP, box 1.

95 "The Board": WRB, cable 298, April 5, 1944, LM0306, reel 12, 251–54.

96 "tired of the noisy": Steinhardt, cable 657, April 12, 1944, ibid., 221–27.

96 The final outstanding: Dalia Ofer, *Escaping the Holocaust: Illegal Immigration to the Land of Israel* (Oxford: Oxford University Press, 1991), 194–95.

97 "This is Transnistria": Ira Hirschmann, *Life Line to a Promised Land* (New York: Jewish Book Guild, 1946), 46.

97 "The advance": The text of the cable states that there were 150,000, but the "1" is crossed off. Hirschmann, cable from Ankara, March 9, 1944, IHP, box 2, "Correspondence."

98 "This is a monumental": Hirschmann, diary, March 18, 1944, IHP, box 1, "Typed Diaries."

98 The bribery: Hirschmann, interview with Laurence Jarvik, Jan. 20, 1979, Morgenthau Family Papers.

98 But in subsequent: Cretzianu's papers, at the Hoover Institution at Stanford, are sealed until 2020. Hirschmann, memo, March 11, 1944, IHP, box 1, "Miscellaneous Official"; Ira Hirschmann, *Caution to the Winds* (New York: D. McKay, 1962); Ira Hirschmann, *Obligato: Untold Tales from a Life with Music* (New York: Fromm International, 1994); Alexandru Cretzianu, *Relapse into Bondage: Political Memoirs of a Roma-*

nian Diplomat, 1918–1947, ed. Sherman David Spector (Iaşi: Center for Romanian Studies, 1998).

99 "of the category": Barlas, letter, March 20, 1944, IHP, box 2, "Correspondence."

99 "open the flood gates": Steinhardt, cable 573, March 30, 1944, LM0306, reel 12, 266–70.

99 "It is the intention": Steinhardt, cable 564, March 29, 1944, ibid., 384.

99 "In this manner": Barlas, report, April 24, 1944, LM0306, reel 14, 780–85.

100 "Steinh. saved": Hirschmann, diary, March 30, 1944, IHP, box 1, "Typed Diaries."

100 "undulating": Hirschmann, diary, April 8, 1944, ibid.

100 Even without: Steinhardt, cable 986, May 31, 1944, LM0306, reel 12, 344.

101 "refrain": Steinhardt, cable 788, May 2, 1944, ibid., 350–51.

101 "it would be possible": "Steinhardt Helps 254 More Exiles," *New York Times,* April 11, 1944, 2.

CHAPTER 9: WARNINGS

102 "There has been": It's unclear whether Pehle handed this statement out or if Morgenthau's warnings stopped him from doing so. Newspaper articles do not quote from the statement, but Pehle's oral remarks were similar. Pehle, statement, Feb. 4, 1944, LM0305, reel 25, 609.

102 "A lot of agencies": "Group" meeting, Feb. 4, 1944, TMD, vol. 700, 106–13.

103 "in view": Ibid.

104 "hopes": British Foreign Office, copy of Jan. 25 telegram, Feb. 5, 1944, LM0306, reel 1, 1014–15.

104 "we mean business": Pehle, letter, Feb. 11, 1944, TMD, vol. 701, 66–71.

104 "Whether": Ibid.

105 "friendly": Raynor, memo to Reams, note from EUR Division, Feb. 12, 1944, RG 59, "War Refugee Board," box 1, "Misc. 1944 Jan.–March," NACP.

105 "One of the blackest": WRB staff, draft declaration, Feb. 19, 1944, TMD, vol. 702, 148–49.

105 "a world based": Ibid.

106 The Geneva Convention: Jean-Claude Favez, *The Red Cross and the Holocaust* (Cambridge, U.K.: Cambridge University Press, 1999); Arieh Kochavi, *Prelude to Nuremberg: Allied War Crimes Policy and the Question of Punishment* (Chapel Hill: University of North Carolina Press, 2000).

106 "hinted": Morgenthau, memo, March 6, 1944, TMD, vol. 706, 168–71.

106 When he visited: Morgenthau, memo, March 7, 1944, Morgenthau Presidential Diaries, 1337–44.

107 "too much for the Jews": Pehle: "Did Rosenman indicate when you said the President had asked to have the resolution broadened—I take it that means he doesn't want it aimed just—" Morgenthau: "What happened is this: Rosenman didn't see the President direct. His message came to him from Stettinius, but Stettinius told me that the President said this was too much for the Jews. Wasn't that the language?" Mrs. Klotz: "It was too something." "Jewish Evacuation" meeting, March 8, 1944, TMD, vol. 707, 219–34.

107 "The declaration isn't": Ibid.

107 "explained": Pehle, memo, March 8, 1944, TMD, vol. 707, 242–43.

108 "very reluctantly": Ibid.

108 "I read it": Meeting, March 9, 1944, TMD, vol. 708, 1–3.

108 "In one of the blackest": Draft, March 9, 1944, ibid., 5–7.

108 "would be delighted": Meeting, March 9, 1944, ibid., 1–3.

109 "and he was not": Pehle, memo, March 9, 1944, LM0305, reel 4, 551–53.

109 Pehle also: "Jewish Evacuation" meeting, March 9, 1944, TMD, vol. 708, 42–47.

109 "although some": Pehle, memo, March 18, 1944, LM0306, reel 4, 549.

109 "I'll ask Sam": Conversation with the president, March 18, 1944, TMD, vol. 711, 208–10.

109 "Well, my God": Morgenthau and Rosenman, phone call, March 18, 1944, ibid., 211–14.

109 Beginning that night: Joseph Lelyveld, *His Final Battle: The Last Months of Franklin Roosevelt* (New York: Alfred A. Knopf, 2016), 90, 102–24.

110 "All communications": Dulles, cable, March 21, 1944, RG 266, entry 190C, box 6, "Dulles, Hungary," NACP.

110 "There is nothing": News stories received from McNulty, March 21, 1944, RG 84, Lisbon General Records, box 92, 800/Hungary, NACP.

110 "will remain safe": Hodel, memo, Jan. 19, 1944, LM0305, reel 24, 965–69.

111 "will be looked": Lesser, proposed cable, March 21, 1944, TMD, vol. 709, 53.

111 "the military events": Many believed Nazi Germany would invade Romania next. While the Nazis did plan an invasion, they never carried it out. Pehle, memo, March 22, 1944, LM0306, reel 4, 545–46.

111 "As a result": FDR, statement, March 24, 1944, LM0305, reel 17, 1001–2.

111 "Roosevelt Warns": John Crider, "Roosevelt Warns Germans on Jews," *New York Times*, March 25, 1944, A1.

111 "earnestly": "Germans Warned Not to Persecute," *Stars and Stripes Weekly*, March 25, 1944, LM0305, reel 1, 216–17.

112 "fully in all": Hull, cable 2273, March 24, 1944, LM0306, reel 4, 526–27.

112 "whether ... he has": Winant, cable 2647, March 31, 1944, LM0306, reel 1, 872–73.

112 "Let the people": Pehle, statement, March 24, 1944, LM0306, reel 4, 640–43.

CHAPTER 10: PROTECTIVE PAPERS

113 "Over one million": Dr. Samuel Braun, letter, March 25, 1944, LM0305, reel 21, 250.

113 "I am an American": Lillian Ringler-Young, letter, March 27, 1944, LM0305, reel 22, 76–77.

113 "I am turning": Margaret Zikeli, letter, March 29, 1944, ibid., 409.

114 "I am sure": Pehle, letter, March 30, 1944, LM0305, reel 21, 249.

114 As one staff: Herbert Katzki, comparing the JDC and the HIAS (but it works for the WRB, too). Katzki, oral history interview, June 2, 1995, RG 50.030*0337, USHMM.

114 Physical rescue: WRB, memo, March 20, 1944, LM0306, reel 5, 7–12.

114 It played: OWI, memo, March 27, 1944, LM0306, reel 4, 511–13.

114 "An Emotional": "An Emotional Explosion in the White House [translation]," *Berliner Börsen-Zeitung*, March 31, 1944, ibid., 501–2.

114 But the WRB's: Ackermann, letter, April 14, 1944, LM0305, reel 1, 158–65.

115 "The Failure": "The Failure of the Office for European Refugees," *Új Magyarság*, March 23, 1944, PWRB, box 72, folder 1, FDRL.

115 "backsliding Presbyterian": Kirk McClelland, interview with author, Feb. 2, 2014.

116 The head of the AFSC: Hodel, memo, Feb. 10, 1944, LM0306, reel 1, 270.

116 Because the Quakers: "Jewish Evacuation" meeting, Feb. 13, 1944, TMD, vol. 701, 165–78.

116 Florence Hodel asked: Noble, letter, May 3, 1944, LM0305, reel 1, 670.

116 "This appointment": McClelland, letter, March 21, 1944, AFSC Foreign Service, box 1944, Switzerland-NY, "Switzerland," AFSC.

117 Due to some missing: McClelland's cable asking about his appointment sat, lost on George Warren's desk at the State Department, for over a month. Warren had been worried that the WRB had never answered the cable, only to realize he had never forwarded it. Mann, memo, April 20, 1944, LM0306, reel 1, 542.

117 Because the American: Ross's former office in Bern, at Elfenstrasse 6, is now the Iraqi embassy.

118 Sternbuch knew this: Sternbuch, letter, May 4, 1944, PWRB, box 70, folder 2, FDRL.

118 "an affront": McClelland, memo, May 5, 1944, PWRB, box 71, folder 7, FDRL.

118 Within a few weeks: Mayer, report, June 12, 1944, ibid.; McClelland, notes, June 7, 1944, ibid.

119 "punishment of traitors": Riegner, report, April 28, 1944, PWRB, box 70, folder 9, FDRL.

119 "endangers": DeCourey, memo, May 8, 1944, LM0306, reel 23, 197–99.

119 Gerhart Riegner: Riegner, letter, April 3, 1944, PWRB, box 66, folder 1, FDRL.

119 In early May: They actually began in earnest in mid-May. Winant, cable 3642, May 4, 1944, LM0306, reel 4, 853.

119 Allen Dulles: Baron Bakach-Bessenyey opposed the new regime and was known to the OSS as "684" or "BB." Dulles reported BB "learned that negotiations were being concluded for the deportation to Poland, and presumably to their deaths, of approximately 300,000 Jews ... BB suggested that publicity be given to this fact over the radio in America and England, and that notice be given that all those who had any part in planning or carrying out this deportation would be included among the war criminals." Dulles, memo, May 18, 1944, PWRB, box 66, folder 2, FDRL.

119 At the end of May: Israel Gutman, ed., *The Auschwitz Album: The Story of a Transport* (Jerusalem: Yad Vashem, 2002).

120 The World Jewish Congress: Kubowitzki to Pehle, May 10, 1944, LM0306, reel 6, 484; Hull, cable 1631, May 10, 1944, LM0306, reel 20, 42–43.

120 In late June: Hamori's parents were deported to Auschwitz in the spring of 1944 and perished. "Laszlo Hamori," in Refugee Services, box 10, AFSC.

120 "Oswierzim": Kubowitzki, letter, June 1, 1944, LM0305, reel 27, 66–67.

120 "Dost or Tost": Akzin, draft cable, May 30, 1944, TMD, vol. 737, 75.

120 "Dostortost": McClelland, memo, June 9, 1944, PWRB, box 64, folder 2, FDRL.

121 "Assistance": Sternbuch, letter, May 2, 1944, PWRB, box 70, folder 2, FDRL.

121 On a windy day: John Pehle detested Baruch Korff. In his 1952 memoir, *Flight from Fear,* Korff described himself as one of the board's "unofficial consultants." He supposedly purchased twenty-two hundred Latin American protective papers; proposed the "free port" idea; suggested a psychological warfare campaign; persuaded McCloy to bomb the rail lines surrounding Auschwitz, which halted deportations; and personally bullied Morgenthau into issuing a license for the Musy negotiations. There is no archival evidence that any of these things are true and plenty

of evidence that they are not. Korff later became famous as "Nixon's rabbi." Baruch Korff, *Flight from Fear* (New York: Elmar, 1953), 41–86.

121 Located in: Harrison, transmission of YMCA report on Vittel by the Andermos, March 31, 1944, RG 59, Special War Problems Subject Files, box 92, "Vittel Internment Camp," NACP.

122 "punished": Lesser, "Poles and Jews with Latin-American Passports," Feb. 12, 1944, LM0306, reel 27, 111–18.

122 Switzerland, too: Ibid.

122 On February 21: Pehle, cable to Bern, Feb. 21, 1944, LM0306, reel 19, 107–10.

122 In light: Lesser, cable to Harrison, March 25, 1944, ibid., 63–64.

123 Pehle immediately: Akzin, memo, April 5, 1944, ibid., 68–72.

123 "Now, look": "Jewish Evacuation" meeting, April 6, 1944, TMD, vol. 718, 2–25.

123 "pretty well force": Cabot, memo, April 12, 1944, RG 59, "War Refugee Board," box 1, "Misc. 1944 April–May," NACP. Pehle's confidence was not misplaced, but the spring of 1944 was full of cables to Latin American countries, explaining and reiterating what was being asked of them. The board received universal support for a request to confirm the validity of protective papers in Vittel with the exception of Peru, which had already invalidated the papers but promised to be more sympathetic with any requests in the future. When the board asked Latin American countries to recognize protective papers in general—at least until the end of the war or until the holder was removed to safety—and to allow the holders of these papers to be eligible for prisoner exchanges, this was a bit of a harder sell. After the War Refugee Board confirmed that none of the holders of protective papers would ever arrive on their shores, some Latin American countries issued new instructions, validating the papers to their protecting powers.

124 "told them": "Jewish Evacuation" meeting, April 6, 1944, TMD, vol. 718, 2–25.

124 "The poor fellows": Morgenthau and Brown, phone call, April 6, 1944, ibid., 111–13.

124 "So right": "Jewish Evacuation" meeting, April 7, 1944, ibid., 168–70.

125 At 11:30: Morgenthau's fear that the cable would be further delayed if it were not dispatched until Friday was justified. The cable did not arrive in Bern until Monday, April 10. Hull, cable 1221, April 10, 1944, LM0306, reel 20, 97–99.

125 "Nothing has pleased": "Jewish Evacuation" meeting, April 7, 1944, TMD, vol. 718, 221–22.

125 The board staff: The WRB ultimately learned that the group had been sent to Drancy and from there to Auschwitz.

125 "There is no": Pehle, memo, April 19, 1944, TMD, vol. 722, 341.

125 Pehle wrote: State Department staff disagreed with the board's desperate tactics. In response to the War Refugee Board's request for Switzerland to approach the German government regarding prisoner exchanges, J. H. Keeley wrote, "This Division has itself been working on the problem for some time, believing that if the matter were properly presented the German Government would of its own accord cease persecuting these unfortunate people upon learning that a possibility exists for their exchange for German nationals in this hemisphere. We were given to understand that the War Refugee Board was not interested in our views ... the War Refugee Board's course of action has appreciably decreased, if not wholly eliminated, the chances of success for this humanitarian project." Keeley, memo, April 12, 1944, RG 59, "War Refugee Board," box 1, "Misc. 1944 April–May," NACP.

126 There was an easy: Mantello was born near the present-day town of Iclânzel. A balanced scholarly account of Mantello's work has yet to be written. Currently, the only book on Mantello purports to be a scholarly account, but is riddled with un-cited claims, blatant factual errors, and unfounded disdain for Roswell McClelland. In one chapter "McClelland—a Silent Antagonist," the author, David Kranzler, wrote McClelland "took an even harsher stand than the State Department, which was not especially known for its sympathy toward the Jewish plight." David Kranzler, *The Man Who Stopped the Trains to Auschwitz: George Mantello, El Salvador, and Switzerland's Finest Hour* (Syracuse, N.Y.: Syracuse University Press, 2000), 216.

126 Jews in Switzerland: McClelland, letter, June 21, 1944, PWRB, box 64, folder 2, FDRL.

126 McClelland feared: Ibid.

126 Though the War: In July 1944, the Salvadoran government informed Spain, which acted as its protecting power in Germany, that it wished to change its position regarding protecting papers. In April, the Salvadoran foreign minister had requested Spain extend protection to all who bear Salvadoran passports or claim Salvadoran citizenship. Now a new foreign minister requested the phrase "claim Salvadoran citizenship" be changed to "prove Salvadoran citizenship." The Spanish ambassador in El Salvador confidentially told the American embassy that he felt the two words so similar he did not transmit the request to Madrid. Gade, cable A-288, July 14, 1944, LM0306, reel 19, 296–97.

126 In Bern: Banyai, letter, Aug. 9, 1944, PWRB, box 68, folder 1, FDRL.

126 They compiled: Joel Teitelbaum escaped on the Kasztner train. For more about Gertrude van Tijn, see Bernard Wasserstein, *The Ambiguity of Virtue: Gertrude van Tijn and the Fate of the Dutch Jews* (Cambridge, Mass.: Harvard University Press, 2014). Emanuel Ringelblum founded

the Oneg Shabbat Archive in the Warsaw ghetto, collecting and burying artwork, poetry, and documentation about his vibrant community. Pehle, memo, May 27, 1944, LM0306, reel 28, 201–5.

127 For their plan: Lesser, memo, May 1944, LM0306, reel 28, 910.

127 If this experiment: Pehle, memo, June 1, 1944, LM0306, reel 28, 193.

127 "the most wishful": Pehle, memo, June 3, 1944, ibid., 194–95.

127 The State Department: Duggan, memo, June 16, 1944, RG 59, "War Refugee Board," box 2, "Misc. July," NACP; Berle, memo, Aug. 5, 1944, RG 59, "War Refugee Board," box 2, "Misc. Aug–Dec," NACP.

128 Finally, after: Berle, memo, July 20, 1944, LM0305, reel 9, 543–44.

128 Soon after: Berle, memo, Aug. 5, 1944, ibid., 536–42.

128 "I will chop": Grossman, memo, Aug. 30, 1944, WJC-NY-D, 108–18, USHMM.

128 The American Friends: Gallagher, memo, Aug. 28, 1944, AFSC Refugee Section, box 12, "War Refugee Board," AFSC; Gallagher, instructions regarding visa program, Sept. 4, 1944, AFSC Refugee Section, box 12, "War Refugee Board," AFSC.

129 "last known address": The letters from the INS are found in LM0305, reels 9–13.

CHAPTER 11: BLOOD FOR GOODS

130 In the evening: "Double Rainbow over Capitol Seen as a 'Good Omen,' " *Washington Post*, June 7, 1944, 25.

130 "our Allied forces": "Text of President Roosevelt's Address on the Fall of Rome," *Washington Post*, June 6, 1944, 2.

131 "I got the word": "Group" meeting, June 6, 1944, TMD, vol. 740, 1–15.

131 "on the sorry": Ibid.

131 A fat-cheeked: Brand traveled with Andrea Gyorgy, known as Bandi Grosz, a smuggler and double agent who later claimed to be sent by the Nazis—possibly by Himmler—to negotiate a separate peace between Nazi Germany and the Western Allies against the Soviet Union. Because the WRB knows little of Grosz, I'm not including him here so readers don't get confused in an already complicated story.

131 The Nazis had: Much has been written about Joel Brand and ransom negotiations in 1944–1945, with many opinions but few agreed-upon facts. For a summary of the historical debates and major works on the topic, see Richard Breitman and Shlomo Aronson, "The End of the 'Final Solution'? Nazi Plans to Ransom Jews in 1944," *Central European History* 25, no. 2 (1992): 177–203. For a more recent account—though one that takes Hirschmann's later memoirs as truthful—see Ronald Florence, *Emissary of the Doomed: Bargaining for Lives in the Holocaust* (New York: Viking, 2010).

131 Adolf Eichmann: Steinhardt, cable 950, May 25, 1944, LM0305, reel 28, 544.

132 "The Jewish Agency": Jewish Agency, memo, May 26, 1944, LM0306, reel 26, 464–65.

132 At Steinhardt's request: Resnik, memo, June 4, 1944, ibid., 328–33.

132 "Everyone with": Ibid. Leslie Squires, the American vice-consul in Istanbul, wrote a similar report. Squires, memo, June 8, 1944, ibid., 434–45.

133 Pehle knew: Goldmann, letter, April 13, 1944, LM0306, reel 6, 524–27.

133 "sheer case": British embassy staff, aide-mémoire, June 5, 1944, TMD, vol. 739, 242–46.

133 "The best thing": "Group" meeting, June 6, 1944, TMD, vol. 740, 1–15.

133 "Turkish cognac": Hirschmann, letter, April 18, 1944, IHP, box 2, "Correspondence."

134 "I have spoken": Hirschmann, letter, June 10, 1944, Laurence Steinhardt Papers, box 43, "Correspondence G–I," LOC.

134 "observation tower": Hirschmann, speech, May 4, 1944, ibid.

134 Hirschmann, in Ohio: *Billboard* magazine wrote about Hirschmann's interest in "tele." Hirschmann "also said that he hopes that the stores will not use tele as a 'cheap shoddy device' to sell their merchandise. 'Broadcasters,' he stated, 'will have to learn that you do not have to visually hit people over the head to sell them something.'" "Tele Has a Great Selling Future, Says Hirschmann," *Billboard,* May 20, 1944, 10.

134 Pehle also: In 1944, $1,500 was half of an average worker's yearly salary. Pehle, letter, Oct. 19, 1944, Ernst Papers, container 35.2, "War Refugee Board."

135 "there are disturbing": "War Refugee Board" meeting, June 7, 1944, TMD, vol. 740, 231–36.

135 "will learn": Goldmann, letter, June 7, 1944, LM0305, reel 14, 632–33.

135 "convince": Pehle, draft cable, June 7, 1944, LM0306, reel 26, 432.

135 Ten thousand: "Perez," letter, June 10, 1944, PWRB, box 66, folder 3, FDRL.

135 Hirschmann spent: Hirschmann frequently alluded to his loneliness and wrote of "hysterical dreams in thoughts of New York." His personal troubles were apparent, and during a meeting Pehle told Morgenthau, "I think there is some trouble on the home front." Hirschmann, diary, June 27, 1944, IHP, box 1, "Typed Diaries"; "Group" meeting, June 20, 1944, TMD, vol. 745, 113–39.

136 "did not want": Hirschmann, diary, June 19, 1944, IHP, box 1, "Typed Diaries."

136 "has worked": Hirschmann, diary, June 18–20, 1944, ibid. Outwardly, Hirschmann seems to have displayed no malice toward Resnik and the

day after deciding Resnik was "obviously my enemy" wrote a friendly note: "Dear Rube, Greetings from America! I had hoped to see you in the next few days, but am rushing back to Cairo ... I hope you have been well." Resnik extended "warm greetings of welcome and hope that too much time will not elapse before we see each other." If there was a rivalry other than in Hirschmann's perception, it was a strange one. Hirschmann, letter, June 21, 1944, 1937–1949: Istanbul Records of the American Jewish Joint Distribution Committee-IST 37–49, Administration-IST 37-49/1, file 108_00904, JDC-NY; Resnik to Hirschmann, June 22, 1944, ibid., file 108_00902.

136 "Neither British": Steinhardt, cable 1055, June 13, 1944, LM0306, reel 26, 423–24.

136 By June 19: Hull, cable 546, June 19, 1944, ibid., 402.

136 "I have the inside": Hirschmann, diary, June 20, 1944, IHP, box 1, "Typed Diaries."

136 "any conversations": Harriman, cable 2184, June 19, 1944, LM0306, reel 27, 698.

137 "Please take no": Pehle, memo, June 21, 1944, LM0306, reel 26, 394.

137 "a somewhat": Alex Weissberg, *Desperate Mission: Joel Brand's Story as Told by Alex Weissberg* (New York: Criterion Books, 1958), 184; Hirschmann, *Caution to the Winds,* 175.

137 Brand was also: This was a valid fear: that very day, the Jewish Agency told Steinhardt it had received a message from Budapest that the Germans were furious Brand had yet to return, and "unless Brand and Georgy return immediately to Budapest, 'all efforts are useless.'" Steinhardt, cable 1131, June 22, 1944, LM0306, reel 26, 390.

137 "always take": Hirschmann, interrogation, June 22, 1944, IHP, box 3, "Joel Brand."

137 "some big propaganda": Ibid.

137 In his report: Hirschmann, memo, June 22, 1944, ibid.

138 Though Hirschmann wrote: Hirschmann, diary, June 25, 1944, IHP, box 1, "Handwritten Diaries."

138 "trading in concert": WRB, text from Eden, July 1, 1944, LM0306, reel 26, 375.

139 "The fate": "Nazis Reported in Bid to 'Spare' 400,000 Jews," *New York Herald Tribune,* July 19, 1944.

139 "fresh evidence": On July 13, Whitehall received a transcript of Bandi Grosz's interrogation, where he admitted he had been sent to negotiate a separate peace. Yehuda Bauer, *Jews for Sale: Nazi-Jewish Negotiations, 1933–1945* (New Haven, Conn.: Yale University Press, 1994), 191–92; Poate, letter, July 18, 1944, LM0306, reel 26, 290–91; British Foreign Office, cable, July 19, 1944, PWRB, ibid., 292–93; "Group" meeting, July 27, 1944, TMD, vol. 759, 1–13.

CHAPTER 12: FREE PORTS

141 "because of its": The report is undated. The date June 17 is assumed from the average time it took to compile the report prior to distribution and the date that Hodel drafted the Brand cover letter. Pehle, letter, June 17, 1944, LM0306, reel 26, 406. The report itself is located at LM0305, reel 25, 931–49.

141 "upon the free": DuBois and Friedman, report, March 6, 1944, TMD, vol. 707, 235–44.

141 "permit the entry": Stewart, cable A-55, Feb. 25, 1944, LM0306, reel 4, 211.

141 "must not be given": In the prewar years, the Nazis had excitedly pointed out how "astounding" it was that countries condemning the persecution of the Jews as "wholly incomprehensible . . . seemed in no way particularly anxious" to open their own borders. "Germans Belittle Results," *New York Times,* July 13, 1938, 12; DuBois and Friedman, report, March 6, 1944, TMD, vol. 707, 235–44.

142 "There will be": FBL, letter, Feb. 10, 1944, LM0305, reel 2, 463–64.

142 "treating them as": DuBois and Friedman, report to the War Refugee Board, March 6, 1944, TMD, vol. 707, 235–44.

142 "I am convinced": "Jewish Evacuation" meeting, March 8, 1944, ibid., 219–32.

142 Stettinius liked: "Jewish Evacuation" meeting, March 9, 1944, TMD, vol. 708, 42–47.

142 "like ham": Morgenthau and Rosenman, phone call, March 8, 1944, TMD, vol. 707, 211–13.

142 At a formal: WRB, minutes, March 21, 1944, LM0305, reel 25, 510–12.

143 "proportion": Stimson, letters, March 31, 1944, TMD, vol. 717, 34–37.

143 "this Board": Pehle, "We, Too, Are Impatient," April 2, 1944, LM0305, reel 2, 252–56.

143 "If we set up": Grafton, "I'd Rather Be Right," *New York Post,* April 5, 1944, TMD, vol. 717, 187.

143 "A reporter": The reporter was Al Gregory of United Press. Hirschmann, letter, June 10, 1944, Steinhardt Papers, box 43, "Correspondence G–I."

144 "America can heave": Jay, transcript, April 25, 1944, TMD, vol. 724, 108–12.

144 "I am for": "Jewish Evacuation" meeting, May 2, 1944, TMD, vol. 726, 146–64.

144 Pehle drafted: WRB, memo, May 18, 1944, TMD, vol. 733, 10–17.

144 In a meeting: In April 1944, Anne Laughlin of the WRB toured several Japanese internment camps, reporting back that "the job accomplished is so superior to the impression held by the public due to newspaper publicity." Laughlin, letter, May 6, 1944, LM0306, reel 22, 704.

144 The president also: Pehle, memo, May 20, 1944, HRFDRWH, LM0255, reel 4, 24–25, USHMM.

144 "very, very": "War Refugee Board" meeting, May 16, 1944, TMD, vol. 731, 62–66.

145 "a real emergency": Ibid.

145 "discourage": Murphy, memo, April 29, 1944, LM0306, reel 26, 737.

145 Ackermann protested: Ackermann, memo, May 5, 1944, LM0306, reel 1, 117–20.

145 "since it only": Ackermann, letter, May 11, 1944, ibid., 111–15.

145 In 1942: Navy personnel information bulletin, June 1942, vol. 303, 41.

146 "congenital liars": Saxon, report, April 10, 1944, LM0306, reel 26, 812–29.

146 The Yugoslav: Stern, letter, May 31, 1944, LM0306, reel 28, 703–4.

146 "the important thing": WRB meeting, May 18, 1944, TMD, vol. 733, 1–8.

146 "The facilities": Pehle, "To the President," May 18, 1944, ibid., 10–17.

147 To push: DuBois, memo, May 26, 1944, TMD, vol. 736, 73–74.

147 "You people give": "Re: Cabinet" meeting, May 26, 1944, ibid., 67–72.

147 Unbeknownst: FDR, cover note, May 20, 1944, RG 59, "War Refugee Board," box 1, "Fort Ontario," NACP.

147 "As the hour": Stettinius, draft, June 8, 1944, HRFDRWH, LM0255, reel 4, 2–13, USHMM.

147 Tuesday: Decoration Day became Memorial Day after World War II and was always May 30 until 1971, when it became the last Monday in May.

148 "he clearly": Morgenthau and Pehle, phone conversation, May 31, 1944, TMD, vol. 737, 85.

148 Pehle presented: In addition to those mentioned in the text, the list included War-Time Refugee Haven, War Refugee Center, War Rescue Shelter, International Transient Center, War Victim Shelter.

148 "it connoted": Pehle, memo, June 1, 1944, TMD, vol. 738, 39–51.

148 "revealed that": Morgenthau and McCloy, phone conversation, June 2, 1944, ibid., 225–31.

148 "twenty-four": Ibid.

148 "a good climate": "War Refugee Board" meeting, June 2, 1944, ibid., 240–48.

149 "I just wanted": Ibid.

149 "Fort Ontario": Pehle, memo, June 8, 1944, TMD, vol. 741, 47–50.

149 "I can't let": Pehle, letter, June 9, 1944, LM0305, reel 20, 689–95.

150 "In the face": FDR, "Message from the President," June 12, 1944, LM0305, reel 8, 984–85.

150 "flying motor tour": Ackermann, letter, June 22, 1944, LM0305, reel 1, 90–94.

150 "one of the most": Ackermann, letter, July 30, 1944, Lesser Family Papers.

150 Ackermann and Korn: Ackermann, letter, July 12, 1944, LM0305, reel 1, 74–81.

151 While examining: Ackermann, letter, July 30, 1944, Lesser Family Papers.

151 "It has been": Ackermann, letter, July 12, 1944, LM0305, reel 1, 74–81.

CHAPTER 13: WHETHER TO BOMB, WHETHER TO RANSOM

153 Like all Americans: McClelland, letter to family, Oct. 8, 1944, 2014.500, McClelland Papers, USHMM.

154 In the middle: Now Mukachevo and Košice.

154 "It is urgently": Harrison, cable 3506, June 2, 1944, LM0306, reel 6, 428–31.

154 "the necessary steps": Sternbuch, letter, May 26, 1944, PWRB, box 70, folder 2, FDRL.

154 "De Jonge tells": McClelland, handwritten notes, June 8, 1944, ibid.

154 "paralyzing": Rosenheim, letter, June 18, 1944, LM0306, reel 6, 734.

155 "I had several": Pehle, memo, June 24, 1944, ibid., 722.

155 To visualize the proposal: McClelland had the map made for his own use; it was not transmitted to Washington. Map of Transcarpathia, June 15, 1944, PWRB, box 66, folder 1, FDRL; McClelland, letter, July 4, 1944, PWRB, box 72, folder 6, FDRL.

155 "No doubt exists": Harrison, cable 4041, June 24, 1944, PWRB, box 66, folder 3, FDRL.

155 When he received: Pehle, memo to McCloy, June 29, 1944, LM0306, reel 6, 717–20.

156 "such Jews": Akzin, memo, June 29, 1944, ibid., 713–14.

156 "the first victims": Kubowitzki, letter, July 1, 1944, ibid., 715–16; Kubowitzki, letter, July 1, 1944, ibid., 712.

156 "impracticable": McCloy, letter, July 4, 1944, ibid., 711.

156 "Anachitz": McClelland, cable copy, June 24, 1944, PWRB, box 66, folder 3, FDRL; Harrison, cable 4041, June 24, 1944, LM0305, reel 25, 818–20.

157 "shocked": Kubowitzki, letter, July 5, 1944, LM0305, reel 20, 555.

157 "Treblinski": Sternbuch, letter, June 27, 1944, PWRB, box 70, folder 2, FDRL.

157 In late June: The WRB never learned the prisoners' names during the war. Rudolf Vrba (born Walter Rosenberg) and Alfred Wetzler were the Slovak Jews, and Jerzy Tabeau wrote the Polish major's report (though he was not actually a Polish officer). George Mandel-Mantello also circulated copies of the report around Switzerland with minor variations

to Kopecký's. Allen Dulles sent McClelland a copy of Mantello's version on July 10, but McClelland already had the full text from Kopecký. Dulles, memo, July 10, 1944, 2014.500, McClelland Papers, USHMM.

158 He checked: McClelland, drafts, July–Oct. 1944, ibid.

158 "For whatever": Harrison, cable 4303, July 6, 1944, LM0306, reel 5, 824–29.

158 By the time: Johnson's version originated with the Swedish legation in Budapest and listed the full reports as enclosures, but Johnson either never received or just never forwarded them to Washington. Schoenfeld, dispatch 142, July 5, 1944, TMD, vol. 750, 184–88; Johnson, cable 2510, July 7, 1944, LM0306, reel 5, 625–27.

158 At first: Luftman, letter, June 16, 1944, WJC-NY-D, 107-06, USHMM; Hull, cable 2077, June 16, 1944, LM0306, reel 27, 695–96.

158 "request your Board": Kalmanowitz, letter, June 23, 1944, ibid., 710.

158 But despite: Harrison, cable 4258, July 5, 1944, ibid., 720–23.

158 In his cable: Hamori, notes, June 3–6, 1944, PWRB, box 68, folder 1, FDRL; McClelland, notes, June 7, 1944, PWRB, box 71, folder 7, FDRL.

159 "over-zealous": McClelland, notes, July 5, 1944, PWRB, box 70, folder 3, FDRL.

159 Because no one: Harrison, cable 4258, July 5, 1944, LM0306, reel 27, 720–23.

159 McClelland thought: Mayer, list of proposals, June 29, 1944, PWRB, box 66, folder 4, FDRL; Harrison, cable 4170, June 30, 1944, LM0306, reel 27, 677–79; Harrison, cable 4802, July 26, 1944, ibid., 767–70.

159 "First time": Sternbuch, letter, July 17, 1944, PWRB, box 66, folder 5, FDRL.

159 Apparently, twelve hundred: McClelland tried to calculate the length of the train trip but ultimately assumed that the train must already be waiting in Vienna. Ibid.

159 Sternbuch had already: HIJEFS, letter, July 18, 1944, PWRB, box 66, folder 6, FDRL.

160 "1,200 holy men": The JDC finally allocated 200,000 Hungarian pengö for Sternbuch's plan. Saly Mayer also provided Sternbuch with 69,200 Swiss francs for forty tractors, shipped to Germany in September 1944. This secret agreement did not change German policy and was conducted entirely without McClelland's knowledge. Mayer, letter, July 19, 1944, PWRB, box 66, folder 6, FDRL; Bauer, *Jews for Sale,* 223; minutes of Emergency Administration Committee of the JDC, Aug. 8, 1944, SMP, reel 6.

160 "Are shaken": McClelland, memo, July 22, 1944, PWRB, box 66, folder 6, FDRL.

160 In a telegram: JDC and Vaad meeting minutes, July 25, 1944, SMP, reel 6.

160 "Sternbuch decided": Harrison, cable 4802, July 26, 1944, LM0306, reel 27, 767–70.

160 "Sternbuch claims": Stettinius, cable 2614, July 30, 1944, PWRB, box 71, folder 8, FDRL.

161 "Neither Saly Mayer": Harrison, cable 5023, Aug. 5, 1944, LM0306, reel 27, 791.

161 In early August: Johnson, cable 2975, Aug. 6, 1944, LM0306, reel 28, 178–79.

161 "to pump out": Harrison, cable 5197, Aug. 11, 1944, PWRB, box 66, folder 7, FDRL.

161 On July 15: Hirschmann, cable to WRB, July 19, 1944, LM0306, reel 26, 279–83.

162 Schwartz was: Kelley, cable 1320, July 20, 1944, ibid., 256–59.

162 "reluctantly": Norweb, cable 2374, Aug. 1, 1944, ibid., 222–23.

162 On this basis: Harrison, cable 5197, Aug. 11, 1944, PWRB, box 66, folder 7, FDRL.

162 "Saly Mayer should": Ibid.

CHAPTER 14: THE HORTHY OFFER

163 "Admiral Nicholas": Nicholas is the Anglicized version of Miklos. "Horthy Promises Not to Oust Jews," *New York Times,* July 19, 1944, LM0306, reel 6, 824.

163 In Bern: Phone message, July 18, 1944, PWRB, box 66, folder 6, FDRL.

164 Admiral Horthy also: Norweb, cable 2222, July 19, 1944, LM0306, reel 5, 435–36.

164 "the whole thing": Mannon, memo, Aug. 1, 1944, ibid., 207–9.

164 Bergson's committee: Emergency Committee, "A Year in the Service of Humanity," Aug. 7, 1944, PSC, LM0399, reel 5, folder 22, USHMM.

164 Nearly fifty thousand: Office of the Adjutant General, "Army Battle Casualties and Nonbattle Deaths in World War II: Final Report, 7 December 1941–31 December 1946."

165 "big guns": Marks, memo, May 29, 1944, LM0306, reel 7, 115.

165 "that a people": Spellman explicitly instructed the WRB to transmit his message with no edits, but when the statement reached Turkey, Ambassador Steinhardt deleted a reference to Turkish attacks on Hungarian Catholics. Lesser, draft cable, June 28, 1944, TMD, vol. 747, 280–81; Steinhardt, cable to WRB, July 3, 1944, LM0306, reel 7, 72.

165 The First Magyar: "Service Here Asks Aid for Hungary's Jews," *New York Herald Tribune,* July 10, 1944, LM0306, reel 6, 844.

166 Both the Senate: Pehle, memo, June 6, 1944, TMD, vol. 740, 133.

166 "by its servile": "Hull Again Scores Nazi Massacres," *New York Times,* July 15, 1944, LM0306, reel 6, 829.

166 "dare not": "Churches Protest," *Christian Science Monitor,* July 10, 1944, LM0306, reel 6, 840.

166 "all neutrality": Johnson, cable 2503, July 6, 1944, LM0306, reel 7, 181.

166 "many unfortunate": Cicognani, letter, July 7, 1944, LM0306, reel 6, 968–69.

166 Dr. Robert Dexter: Friedman, meeting, Feb. 26, 1944, LM0305, reel 8, 55–96. For Dexter's disagreeableness, see James Mann, Report on visit to Portugal and Spain, Aug. 30, 1944, LM0306, reel 28, 208–97.

166 Dexter had been: The conflict between the JDC and the World Jewish Congress over the credit, monetary needs, and fate of several dozen children who escaped France in 1944 finally resulted in a written truce agreement, which the WJC violated less than a week later. See Erbelding, "About Time."

167 "the lives": Hull, cable 1479, May 25, 1944, LM0306, reel 4, 822.

167 But Ambassador: Norweb, cable 1671, June 1, 1944, LM0306, reel 5, 441–42.

167 three other options: James G. McDonald, James Saxon, and James Mann.

167 "happily far": Hayes, cable 1943, June 1, 1944, LM0306, reel 5, 522–23.

167 Pehle, fed up: Pehle, memo, May 17, 1944, LM0306, reel 1, 458–60.

167 There's no direct: In Pehle's complaint to Hull, he noted Hayes was not scheduled to return to the United States. Hayes was recalled for consultation very soon thereafter, and the WRB prepared a five-page report of its problems with Hayes right before he returned.

168 A wealthy: Mann, "Report of James H. Mann on Trip to Portugal and Spain," Aug. 30, 1944, LM0306, reel 28, 208–97.

168 After the British: Hayes, cable 1931, May 31, 1944, LM0306, reel 11, 171.

168 The real reason: British representative, memo, June 1, 1944, ibid., 541–42.

168 Blickenstaff, forced: Jessup, letter, Aug. 11, 1944, AFSC Refugee Section, box 5, "Spanish Refugees," AFSC.

169 Within weeks: UNRRA staff, cable A-5, July 22, 1944, LM0306, reel 20, 846–48.

169 "indicates that he": Hull, cable 7017, Aug. 31, 1944, LM0306, reel 11, 130–31.

169 After Hayes's return: In the fall of 1944, Foreign Funds Control focused on preventing the Axis from using the neutral countries as a safe haven for currency that could be used by escaping Nazis after the war. Hayes tried to obstruct the project, repeating, in Pehle's eyes, his reaction to the WRB. The Madrid embassy, under his direction, did not like outsid-

ers. Memo, Nov. 30, 1944, RG 56, entry 66A-816, box 47, "Flight of Axis Capital," NACP.

169   "that every Jew": Steinhardt, cable 794, May 2, 1944, LM0306, reel 4, 854.

169   After the War: On April 20, Turkey, succumbing to Allied pressure, agreed to reduce its sale of chrome from ninety thousand tons per year to forty-five hundred tons. Steinhardt, cable 795, May 2, 1944, LM0306, reel 12, 162–63.

170   The United States: Tait, memo, June 12, 1944, PWRB, box 66, folder 3, FDRL.

170   Per Anger: Anger is not named as the source in either of Johnson's cables to the WRB, but Anger was visiting Stockholm and is most likely the witness. Johnson, cable 3242, Aug. 22, 1944, LM0306, reel 5, 576.

170   The board even: The suggestion came from a messenger traveling through Ankara from Budapest and purportedly came from the Swedish legation staff. Ankara embassy, memo, June 12, 1944, LM0306, reel 8, 432.

171   "In making": Johnson, cable 2360, June 29, 1944, LM0305, reel 29, 257–58.

172   "since money": Hull, cable 1353, July 7, 1944, LM0306, reel 5, 617–20.

172   The Intergovernmental: Winant, cable 5811, July 22, 1944, LM0306, reel 27, 155–56.

172   On July 26: Poate, letter, July 26, 1944, ibid., 143–44.

173   The International: Stettinius, cable 2657, Aug. 3, 1944, PWRB, box 66, folder 7, FDRL.

173   "accept completely": Pehle, memo, July 29, 1944, LM0306, reel 27, folder 3, 128–34.

173   The State Department: Friedman, memo, July 31, 1944, ibid., 120.

173   The United States: Friedman, memo, Aug. 3, 1944, ibid., 100.

173   "a plot": Winant, cable 6293, Aug. 5, 1944, ibid., 75.

174   "It is not thought": Russell, letter, Aug. 10, 1944, ibid., 67–68.

174   "The Government": Harrison, letter, Aug. 11, 1944, PWRB, box 66, folder 7, FDRL.

174   Portugal, too: Norweb, cable 2594, Aug. 22, 1944, TMD, vol. 764, 250.

174   In July 1944: LM0305, reel 8, 164–80.

175   "I do not": McClelland, memo, Oct. 20, 1944, PWRB, box 65, folder 8, FDRL.

175   "Swedish Legation": Johnson, cable 5043, Dec. 9, 1944, LM0305, reel 29, 790–91.

175   "The United States": Friedman, memo, Aug. 11, 1944, LM0306, reel 27, 62–64.

175   "arrangements for": The British originally proposed, "The United States Government, with whom his Majesty's Government in the United

Kingdom will cooperate to the extent of their resources, will arrange for the care of all Jews leaving Hungary." "Group" meeting, Aug. 17, 1944, TMD, vol. 763, 62–85; British staff, draft statement, Aug. 12, 1944, LM0306, reel 27, 40–42.

175 DuBois finally: Winant, cable 6608, Aug. 16, 1944, LM0306, reel 6, 34–36.

176 "in spite": Harrison, cable 5197, Aug. 11, 1944, PWRB, box 66, folder 7, FDRL.

176 "Information received": Kelley, cable 1479, Aug. 12, 1944, LM0306, reel 27, 57–58.

176 "would depend": "Jews of Hungary," *New Republic,* Sept. 4, 1944, LM0306, reel 6, 756.

CHAPTER 15: ADRIFT

177 In *Survey Graphic:* Blair Bolles, "Millions to Rescue," *Survey Graphic,* Sept. 1944.

177 "the Zionists": Pehle also used David's story on an NBC radio broadcast. William O. Player, "Encounter with a Citizen of Tomorrow on the Road to Palestine," *New York Post,* April 17, 1944; WRB, press release 11, May 14, 1944, LM0305, reel 20, 721–26.

177 "We invented": "Secretary's Address on War Refugee Board" meeting, Sept. 19, 1944, TMD, vol. 772, 82–91.

178 So to publicly: WRB, press release 11, May 14, 1944, LM0305, reel 20, 721–26.

178 Finally recovered: Hirschmann, diary, July 5, 1944, IHP, box 1.

178 "The enormous": Hirschmann, diary, June 20, 1944, ibid.

178 "grossly": Steinhardt, cable 991, June 1, 1944, PWRB, box 48, "Turkey, Volume 5-AF1-10A," FDRL.

179 Eri Jabotinsky: The WRB did assist with his travel priorities but quickly confirmed to Ankara that Jabotinsky was not a WRB staff member. Translation from *Mitteilungsblatt,* May 26, 1944, LM0305, reel 6, 109–12; Pehle, cable 577, June 27, 1944, LM0306, reel 27, 261–62.

179 To deal with: Hirschmann, minutes, July 11, 1944, LM0306, reel 14, 600–605.

179 On Saturday, July 8: Norweb, cable 2120, July 11, 1944, LM0306, reel 12, 597.

179 "258 children": Hirschmann, diary, July 10, 1944, IHP, box 1.

179 "Germans consider": Harrison, cable 3421, May 29, 1944, LM0305, reel 12, 145.

179 "a hemorrhage": Steinhardt, cable 941, May 23, 1944, ibid., 150–51.

180 "doomed": Pinkerton, cable 74, June 2, 1944, LM0306, reel 6, 91–92; Kolb, letter, May 31, 1944, LM0306, reel 13, 471.

180 The War Refugee Board: In November, when Eri Jabotinsky tried to charter the *Tari,* he reminded the Turkish government that the United States had never paid for the time the ship sat waiting. Steinhardt, livid, raged that if he received a bill, he would "be obliged to deposit the same in [Jabotinsky's] lap." There is no evidence anyone ever paid the *Tari*'s charter in 1944. Steinhardt, letter, Dec. 18, 1944, LM0306, reel 12, 127–29.

180 "a beauty": Hirschmann, diary, April 7, 1944, IHP, box 1.

180 The *Bardaland* waited: Johnson, cable to the WRB about the *Bardaland,* May 16, 1944, LM0306, reel 12, 82–83.

180 "even expressed": Johnson, cable 1744, June 5, 1944, ibid., 55.

180 The *Bardaland* was: Stettinius, cable 4594, June 9, 1944, ibid., 42–44.

180 A trio: Steinhardt, cable 848, May 10, 1944, LM0306, reel 13, 596–97.

180 Hirschmann gave: Hirschmann, meeting, July 31, 1944, PWRB, box 49, "Turkey-9-1," FDRL; Griffel, cable, Aug. 4, 1944, Steinhardt Papers, box 43, Correspondence J–L.

180 "sinister fool": Hirschmann, diary, July 13, 1944, IHP, box 1; Hirschmann, letter, July 29, 1944, LM0306, reel 12, 846–48; Jabotinsky, letter, July 31, 1944, LM0306, reel 13, 785–86.

180 On August 1: Hirschmann, diary, Aug. 1, 1944, IHP, box 1.

181 Amid the drama: Kelley, cable 1346, July 22, 1944, RG 84, Turkey General Records, box 81, 711.1, NACP.

181 After the *Kazbek*'s: Hirschmann, memo, July 3, 1944, PWRB, box 49, "Turkey, Volume 8-4," FDRL; Hirschmann, memo, July 12, 1944, LM0306, reel 15, 207.

181 Chartered: In cables, the names of the ships vary widely, so I am using the most common postwar spellings. The JDC also paid for the two voyages each of the *Milka* and the *Maritza* in the spring. The four total voyages of those ships brought 1,074 passengers at a cost of $453,220. The JDC estimated the four Turkish boats and one Greek boat would bring 3,700 passengers at a cost of $752,720. Schwartz, cable, July 19, 1944, LM0306, reel 13, 733–34.

181 On August 2: Hirschmann, memo, Aug. 2, 1944, LM0306, reel 12, 582–83.

181 "largest number": Kelley, cable 1429, Aug. 5, 1944, LM0306, reel 12, 580–81.

181 It was nearly midnight: Hirschmann, memo, Aug. 6, 1944, ibid., 573.

182 The three boats: Hirschmann, diary, Aug. 6, 1944, IHP, box 1.

182 Upon leaving: Turan, statement of the captain, Aug. 24, 1944, LM0306, reel 12, 466–71; Katzki, memo, Aug. 14, 1944, LM0306, reel 12, 508–12; "Jewish Woman Rescued from the 'Mefkure' Tells How Germans Shelled Ship," *Jewish Telegraphic Agency,* Aug. 22, 1944; Chaim Barlas, final

report on the *Mefkure*, Sept. 10, 1944, LM0306, reel 14, 33–38; Joseph Levy, "Nazis Blamed by Refugee for Sinking Turkish Boat," *Louisville (Ky.) Courier Journal*, Aug. 17, 1944; Leon Dennon, *Trouble Zone: Brewing Point of World War III?* (New York: Ziff-Davis, 1945), 4–5.

183 For several days: Hirschmann, memo, Aug. 11, 1944, LM0306, reel 12, 520.

183 Katzki, however: Turan, statement, Aug. 24, 1944, LM0306, reel 12, 466–71; Katzki, memo, Aug. 14, 1944, LM0306, reel 12, 508–12.

183 "We know that": Stettinius, cable 694, Aug. 10, 1944, LM0306, reel 12, 527–29.

183 "If anyone had": WRB staff, press release 13, Aug. 22, 1944, ibid., 492.

183 Pehle had no idea: The attack on the *Mefkure* was carried out by Soviet submarine Shch-215. After the war, the Soviet captain stated that he had intercepted the ship, but the *Mefkure* failed to identify itself and kept sailing. When the Soviets saw what they believed to be armed men on the ship, they attacked. The *Bülbül* was also likewise intercepted but identified itself and was unmolested. Jürgen Rohwer and Gerhard Hümmelchen, *Chronology of the War at Sea, 1939–1945* (New York: Arco, 1972), 347.

184 "scandalous": Hirschmann, cable 1414, Aug. 2, 1944, LM0306, reel 9, folder 1, 21–23.

184 "stinger": Hirschmann, diary, Aug. 15, 1944, IHP, box 1.

184 "It is assumed": Stettinius, cable 697, Aug. 12, 1944, LM0306, reel 9, 9–10.

184 "leave much unsaid": Pehle, letter, Aug. 18, 1944, LM0306, reel 9, 946–49.

184 "I get off": Hirschmann, diary, Aug. 29, 1944, IHP, box 1.

184 "and by quick": Hirschmann, diary, Aug. 10–14, 1944, ibid.

185 He did, however: Hirschmann, diary, Aug. 24, 1944, ibid.

185 "Ambass. Steinh": Hirschmann, diary, Aug. 29, 1944, ibid.

185 On September 1: Hirschmann, memo, Sept. 1, 1944, LM0306, reel 8, 351–53.

185 Upon receiving: Friedman, draft cable, Sept. 8, 1944, TMD, vol. 770, 251.

185 "broader questions": Friedman, draft cable, Sept. 19, 1944, TMD, vol. 772, 296.

185 "As the policy": Steinhardt, cable 1767, Sept. 20, 1944, LM0306, reel 11, 861–63.

186 "lacking": Hirschmann, diary, Oct. 6 and 7, 1944, IHP, box 1, "Typed Diaries."

186 "since he is a marked": Hirschmann, diary, Oct. 7, 1944, IHP, box 3, "Joel Brand."

186 Hirschmann spoke: Brown, transcript, Oct. 17, 1944, LM0306, reel 13, 320–37.

186 "In time of war": Hirschmann, letter of resignation, Oct. 17, 1944, PWRB, box 60, folder 18, FDRL.

CHAPTER 16: MIDNIGHT SUN

188 "the most skillfully": Johnson, cable 1952, June 1, 1944, LM0306, reel 17, 718–19.

188 After a confidential: Johnson, cable 1820, May 22, 1944, TMD, vol. 734, 92.

189 "very interested": Olsen also observed that Swedish Jews had been "most apathetic" to the 1943 rescue of eight thousand Danish Jews. Olsen, letter, Aug. 10, 1944, LM0305, reel 29, 355–60.

189 "This arrangement": Johnson, cable 2037, June 7, 1944, TMD, vol. 740, 352.

189 By June 1944: Olsen, letter, June 12, 1944, LM0306, reel 28, 457–60.

189 "Wolbe's comprehension": Olsen, letter, Aug. 10, 1944, LM0305, reel 29, 355–60; Johnson, cable 2915, Aug. 3, 1944, LM0305, reel 20, 256.

190 "Practically nothing": Stettinius, cable 268, Nov. 15, 1944, PWRB, box 70, folder 4, FDRL.

190 The Nazis guaranteed: Johnson, cable 2362, June 28, 1944, LM0306, reel 26, 1016–19; Lesser, draft cable, July 5, 1944, ibid., 1011.

190 "This chap": Olsen, letter, Aug. 10, 1944, LM0305, reel 29, 355–60.

191 The Latvian group's: Salnais and Cielens, report, Aug. 1944, LM0306, reel 28, 562–66.

191 "most refugees": Latvian group, report, Oct. 1944, ibid., 556–60.

192 "everything is": Olsen, letter, July 3, 1944, LM0306, reel 30, 21–24.

192 "a few score": Olsen, letter, Aug. 10, 1944, LM0305, reel 29, 355–60.

192 Olsen excitedly: Ibid.

192 "war whores": Olsen, final report, Nov. 22, 1944, ibid., 364–91.

192 Many of those: Olsen, letter, Aug. 10, 1944, ibid., 355–60.

192 "most certainly": Olsen, letter, July 3, 1944, LM0306, reel 30, 21–24.

192 "my man": Olsen, letter, Aug. 10, 1944, LM0305, reel 29, 355–60; Johnson, cable 3046, Aug. 11, 1944, LM0306, reel 17, 707.

192 "Consequently": Olsen, final report, Nov. 22, 1944, LM0305, reel 29, 364–91.

193 On September 29: Johnson, cable 3955, Sept. 29, 1944, LM0306, reel 27, 771–75.

193 "charge that": Johnson, letter, Nov. 27, 1944, LM0306, reel 28, 650–60.

193 "most happy": Sejr, letter, Nov. 22, 1944, LM0306, reel 30, 59.

193 They mostly carried: Despite my best efforts, I have been unable to find a copy of *Occupation Humor*. However, Kathleen Stokker, in her book *Folklore Fights the Nazis: Humor in Occupied Norway, 1940–1945* (Mad-

ison: University of Wisconsin Press, 1997), 24, gives a typical joke: "Do you know the difference between the Nazis and a bucket of manure? The bucket." Sejr, statement of activities, Nov. 3, 1944, LM0306, reel 30, 52–58.

193 They supported: Tranmael and Evensen, report, Aug. 9, 1944, PWRB, box 53, "Rescue, Norway, Volume 1, Folder 1(2)," FDRL.

194 American Relief: Johnson, cable 4800, Nov. 22, 1944, ibid.

194 Pehle never had: Ingrid Carlberg, *Raoul Wallenberg: The Biography* (New York: MacLehose Press, 2015), 101.

194 By the end: Johnson, cable 2779, July 25, 1944, LM0305, reel 29, folder 3, 276–78.

194 The board staff: Stettinius, cable 1551, Aug. 3, 1944, ibid., 282–83.

194 "jumped in": Olsen, letter, Aug. 10, 1944, ibid., 355–60.

195 By September: A few weeks earlier, the board had issued a license for $100,000 for Wallenberg, but this wasn't included in these calculations.

195 While he had: Johnson, cable from Stockholm with report from Wallenberg, Sept. 22, 1944, LM0305, reel 29, folder 3, 290–93.

195 The board made: McClelland also spent quite a bit of time investigating the Leopold Aschner case. See RG 84, Bern Records, box 75, folder "Aschner," NACP.

195 "When I arrived": Olsen, letter to Pehle enclosing letter from Wallenberg, Nov. 14, 1944, LM0305, reel 29, folder 3, 297–99.

195 Wallenberg obtained: Carlberg, *Raoul Wallenberg,* 282.

195 Olsen excitedly: Johnson, cable 4639, Nov. 9, 1944, LM0306, reel 17, 979–82.

CHAPTER 17: WHAT KIND OF PEACE

196 "John, you are": "Army Directive" meeting, Aug. 23, 1944, TMD, vol. 765, 39–43.

196 If Berlin: In June 1944, after the D-day invasion, the Gestapo seized the Bayeux Tapestry from its hiding place and moved it to the Louvre's basement. In August, Morgenthau's visit and the anticipated battle over Paris reminded Himmler to order the tapestry's removal to Berlin. The Gestapo was unable to retrieve it before the liberation of the city. Carola Hicks, *The Bayeux Tapestry: The Life Story of a Masterpiece* (New York: Random House, 2011), 232–47; *Time,* Aug. 21, 1944.

196 "treat them rough": "Group" meeting, Aug. 17, 1944, TMD, vol. 763, 82–115.

197 "I have asked": Morgenthau, memo, Aug. 18, 1944, ibid., 202–5.

197 A week later: Morgenthau and Stimson, phone call, Aug. 22, 1944, TMD, vol. 764, 171–73.

198 "Well, that is": Morgenthau, notes, Aug. 23, 1944, TMD, vol. 765, 14–16.

198 "the kind of peace": Pehle, memo, Aug. 21, 1944, TMD, vol. 764, 120.

198 "just has a normal": "Army Directive" meeting, Aug. 23, 1944, TMD, vol. 765, 39–43.

198 As summer turned: "Revision of German Surrender Document" meeting, Sept. 7, 1944, TMD, vol. 770, 17–39; "Material for Quebec Conference" meeting, Sept. 9, 1944, TMD, vol. 771, 6–16; "Proposed Book on German De-militarization" meeting, Nov. 3, 1944, TMD, vol. 791, 5–27.

198 "The President seemed": Morgenthau, dictation, Aug. 25, 1944, Morgenthau Presidential Diaries, reel 2, 1389–92.

199 International law: DuBois, memo, Aug. 17, 1944, LM0305, reel 17, 984–87.

199 "Needless to say": Pehle, memo, Aug. 28, 1944, ibid., 962–70.

199 "very much": Stettinius, memo, Sept. 4, 1944, ibid., 958.

199 "State and War": Friedman, memo, Dec. 16, 1944, LM0305, reel 17, 886.

199 Pehle received: Stettinius, letter, Dec. 14, 1944, ibid., 891.

200 Mann was now: Olsen, diary, Dec. 1, 1943, Iver Olsen Papers, in the collection of Iver Olsen Jr. My thanks to Jerry Olsen for sharing his father's writings from 1943 with me.

200 "to undertake": Mann, cable 7637, Sept. 16, 1944, LM0306, reel 1, 119–21.

200 In October: Winant, cable 8414, Oct. 6, 1944, ibid., 108–9.

200 "It is clear": WRB staff, draft cable, Oct. 6, 1944, ibid., 80–81.

200 The WRB received: Hodel, letter, Nov. 2, 1944, ibid., 94–96.

201 "savage": Stettinius, cable 3618, Oct. 24, 1944, RG 84, Bern legation, American Interests Section, 840.1-Jews-Europe, box 41, NACP.

201 "Instead": "WRB Says Bricker Signed Refugee Appeal and Now Assails the President's Haven Action," *New York Times,* Oct. 25, 1944, 13.

201 In response: WRB staff, press release 16, Oct. 25, 1944, 1945–1954: New York Records of the American Jewish Joint Distribution Committee-NY 45–54, Administration-NY 45–54/1, file 00193_1077, JDC-NY.

201 "just what": Gamble, press release, Nov. 6, 1944, TMD, vol. 792, 29–30.

201 After both: Ibid.

202 "Germans!": WRB, draft leaflet, Sept. 28, 1944, LM0306, reel 28, 409.

202 Eisenhower had approved: McCloy, memo, Oct. 20, 1944, ibid., 423–24.

202 Pehle, having: Pehle, memo, Oct. 30, 1944, ibid., 418.

203 In mid-September: Marks, draft executive order, Sept. 12, 1944, LM0305, reel 25, 457–58; Sargoy, memo, Sept. 23, 1944, LM0305, reel 1, 16–17.

203 The WRB had: Friedman, memo, Nov. 24, 1944, PWRB, box 60, folder 1, FDRL.

203 "As a matter": Appropriations Committee testimony, Nov. 20, 1944, ibid.

203 In New York: Hirschmann, letter, Nov. 1944, HRFDRWH, reel 6, 122–25, FDRL.

CHAPTER 18: A COUP IN HUNGARY

204 Mayer had: McClelland, letter, March 8, 1969, included in McClelland, interview with Yehuda Bauer, July 13, 1967, Hebrew University, Jerusalem; Bauer, letter, May 19, 1968, 2014.500, McClelland Papers.

204 "any goods": Wyler, notes, Aug. 13, 1944, PWRB, box 66, folder 7, FDRL.

205 "Ransom transactions": Hull, cable 2867, Aug. 21, 1944, LMo306, reel 27, 641–42.

205 In late June: This was an astronomical sum, equivalent to $23 million in 2017. Bauer, *Jews for Sale,* 198.

205 "to show": Mayer, notes, Aug. 14, 1944, PWRB, box 66, folder 7, FDRL.

205 As proof: The released group was 182 prisoners shy of the promised 500.

205 "There is no other": Translation from the original German. Mayer, notes, Aug. 21, 1944, SMP, reel 6.

206 Notably: For more information on Kurt Becher and these negotiations, see Gábor Kádár and Zoltán Vági, *Self-Financing Genocide: The Gold Train, the Becher Case, and the Wealth of Hungarian Jews* (Budapest: Central European University Press, 2004), esp. pt. 2.

206 "visibly annoyed": Both McClelland and Wyler, writing separately, reference Mayer's use of "Menschenhandel." Wyler, notes, Aug. 23, 1944, PWRB, box 66, folder 8, FDRL; McClelland, notes, Aug. 23, 1944, ibid.; Mayer, notes, Aug. 14, 1944, PWRB, box 66, folder 7, FDRL.

206 "If we lose war": Mayer, notes, Aug. 21, 1944, SMP, reel 6.

206 McClelland sent: Though this copy says $2,000, that's clearly a transcription error. Harrison, cable 5588, Aug. 26, 1944, LMo306, reel 27, 625–30.

206 The board agreed: Hull, cable 2990, Aug. 30, 1944, ibid., 615–17.

206 On the first day: McClelland, notes, Sept. 3, 1944, PWRB, box 65, folder 7, FDRL.

206 Around this time: Virginia Mannon asked the photo editor at *Life* if it would send the WRB a print of that particular photograph. Pehle, letter, Sept. 28, 1944, LMo306, reel 26, 574–75.

206 "US to be held": McClelland, notes, Sept. 4, 1944, PWRB, box 65, folder 7, FDRL.

206 "What will ARBA": McClelland, notes, Sept. 5, 1944, ibid.

207 "all time possible": Harrison, cable 6110, Sept. 16, 1944, LMo306, reel 27, 563–64.

207 It pressured: Pehle and Cicognani, letters, Sept. 21–Oct. 2, 1944, LMo306, reel 9, 144–45.

207 From Switzerland: The funds were broken down as follows: 95,000 to Czech resistance for Slovakia by Riegner and McClelland; 50,000 through Hechaluz to Bratislava; 500,000 to Bratislava by Saly Mayer;

305,000 to Neutra by Sternbuch. Harrison, cable 6252, Sept. 21, 1944, LM0306, reel 27, 552–53.

207 Mayer complained: McClelland, notes, Sept. 29, 1944, PWRB, box 65, folder 7, FDRL.

208 "By bluffing": Harrison, cable 6619, Oct. 5, 1944, LM0306, reel 5, 728–31.

208 The rabbi: Rabbi Samuel David Ungar, the rabbi of Neutra, was the father-in-law of Michael Dov Weissmandl, who led the Slovak "Working Group," a Jewish rescue group that helped thousands of Jews to escape over the border of Slovakia to Hungary. After the uprising began, Ungar escaped into the forest and remained in hiding over the winter. He starved to death in February 1945 after refusing to eat food left for him by Christian locals because it could not be cleansed according to Jewish law.

208 "does not": Harrison, cable 7542, Nov. 15, 1944, PWRB, box 67, folder 7, FDRL.

208 Within a day: Maria Madi, diary, vol. 12, Oct. 15–17, 1944, Maria Madi Collection, 2013.264.1, USHMM.

208 Raoul Wallenberg: Johnson, cable 4416, Oct. 30, 1944, LM0305, reel 29, 297–99.

209 "messages which": Pehle, letter, Oct. 20, 1944, LM0306, reel 6, 946; Stettinius, cable 55, Oct. 25, 1944, ibid., 906–7; Harrison, cable 7049, Oct. 24, 1944, LM0306, reel 5, 717–19.

209 It had reason: "War News Summarized," *New York Times,* Nov. 1, 1944, 1.

209 "not directly": Harrison, cable 7565, Nov. 16, 1944, ibid., 512–16.

209 "It is my considered": Ibid.

209 "I was at Savoy": McClelland, notes, Nov. 9, 1944, PWRB, box 65, folder 6, FDRL.

210 "a tremendous talker": McClelland told two different interviewers—Yehuda Bauer in 1967 and Claude Lanzmann in the late 1970s—about the Thompson article, though I have not been able to locate the piece. McClelland, interview with Bauer, July 13, 1967.

210 In the midst: Bauer, *Jews for Sale,* 226.

210 "With all happenings": Mayer, letter, Nov. 12, 1944, PWRB, box 71, folder 8, FDRL.

210 "cannot (repeat not)": Stettinius, cable 3932, Nov. 18, 1944, LM0306, reel 27, 509–10.

210–11 "Without funds": McClelland, cable 3932, Nov. 19, 1944, PWRB, box 65, folder 6, FDRL.

211 In the early morning: Due to births, deaths, and the continued imprisonment of a few passengers on the original Kasztner train, the numbers

do not add up to the 1,684 passengers who were processed as "arriving" in Bergen-Belsen in July 1944.

211 In effect: Huddle, cable 8118, Dec. 13, 1944, LM0306, reel 27, 495–98.

211 "personally skeptical": Ibid.

211 But the board: Stettinius, cable to Bern about change in ransom negotiations, Dec. 19, 1944, ibid., 491.

211 "There are two": Mayer, memo, Dec. 28, 1944, PWRB, box 65, folder 9, FDRL.

212 McClelland sent: Huddle, cable 8390, Dec. 28, 1944, LM0306, reel 27, 482–85.

212 After informing: Kennan, cable A-27, Jan. 29, 1945, ibid., 552–53.

212 "pretty binding": McClelland, letter, Jan. 26, 1945, PWRB, box 71, folder 9, FDRL.

CHAPTER 19: MCCLELLAND'S REPORT

213 He spent much: Pehle and White, memo, Nov. 1, 1944, TMD, vol. 790, 5–9, 21–25.

213 Morgenthau was busily: "Treasury Department Reorganization" meeting, Nov. 2, 1944, ibid., 153–82.

213 A secret courier: Harrison, report, Feb. 8, 1946, RG 59, Histories of Embassies, A1-716, box 29, NACP.

213 Allen Dulles: See NACP, RG 226, entry 190C, box 3 for 1944 phone transcripts. See also Allen Dulles, *From Hitler's Doorstep: The Wartime Intelligence Reports of Allen Dulles, 1942–1945,* ed. Neal H. Petersen (University Park: Pennsylvania State University Press, 1996).

213 Any time-sensitive: Harrison, report, Feb. 8, 1946, RG 59, Histories of Embassies, A1-716, box 29, NACP.

214 He covered: The handwritten drafts and notes on the Auschwitz reports are located in 2014.500.1, Roswell and Marjorie McClelland Papers. My thanks to Kirk McClelland for locating them, sending them to me, then agreeing to donate them to the USHMM.

214 "While it is": McClelland, cover letter and "The German Extermination Camps" report, Oct. 12, 1944, LM0305, reel 5, 309–64.

214 "devoid": Harrison, cable 6818, Oct. 12, 1944, ibid., 592.

214 At daybreak: Marjorie McClelland, letter, Dec. 7, 1944, McClelland Collection, 2014.500.1.

214 The envelope: McClelland, cover letter and "The German Extermination Camps" report, Oct. 12, 1944, LM0305, reel 5, 309–64.

215 "because this ought": "Group" meeting, Nov. 2, 1944, TMD, vol. 790, 122–38.

215 While awaiting: Hodel, memo, Nov. 2, 1944, LM0305, reel 5, 380–81.

215   He had remained neutral: Throughout the summer and early fall, a hand-
      ful of requests to bomb—or undertake some other operation to destroy
      gas chambers, crematoriums, rail lines, or the entire camp—reached
      the WRB. A. Leon Kubowitzki of the World Jewish Congress, by far
      the most persistent correspondent on the subject, pressed the idea that
      instead of aerial bombing, Russian paratroopers or Polish partisans
      should destroy the gas chambers from the ground. Lawrence Lesser
      cautioned him not to "expect much from the Russians who had writ-
      ten off their [own] war prisoners in German camps." On September 2,
      after the Vaad Hatzalah's Abraham Kalmanowitz called him at home,
      the WRB researcher Benjamin Akzin urged Pehle to approach the War
      Department again. Kalmanowitz was desperate, because Sternbuch
      (erroneously) reported from Switzerland that deportations from Buda-
      pest had begun again, at a rate of twelve thousand people a day. Akzin
      reminded Pehle that McCloy's rejection "quite likely stems from the
      habitual reluctance of the military to act upon civilian suggestions. It
      is submitted, however, that the WRB was created precisely in order to
      overcome the inertia and—in some cases—the insufficient interest of
      the old-established agencies." But when Kalmanowitz visited Washing-
      ton to make his demands in person, he focused on getting Sternbuch
      ransom money rather than bombing. In London, James Mann received
      bombing requests from members of the Polish government in exile and
      various relief agency representatives, which Pehle dutifully forwarded
      to McCloy, who didn't respond. Kubowitzki, memo, July 21, 1944,
      WJC-NY-D, 107-03, USHMM; Akzin, memo, Sept. 2, 1944, LM0306,
      reel 6, 694–95.

215   "Until now": Pehle, letter, Nov. 8, 1944, LM0305, reel 5, 388–89; Kal-
      manowitz, letter, Sept. 8, 1944, LM0305, reel 24, 517–19; Pehle, memo,
      Oct. 3, 1944, LM0306, reel 6, 691.

216   "given careful consideration": McCloy, letter, Nov. 18, 1944, LM0305,
      reel 5, 386–87.

216   Neither man knew: Danuta Czech, *Auschwitz Chronicle, 1939–1945*
      (New York: Henry Holt, 1989), 743.

216   "We on the": Paul, draft article, Nov. 7, 1944, LM0305, reel 5, 398–99.

217   "Our reports were": Mannon, memo, Nov. 16, 1944, ibid., 396–97.

217   "'a hell of a hot story'": Ibid.

217   It had just published: Scherman, letter, Dec. 13, 1944, ibid., 532–33.

217   Pehle also provided: Pehle, letters, Nov. 20, 1944, ibid., 480–503.

217   "It is a fact": WRB staff, "German Extermination Camps," Nov. 26,
      1944, ibid., 413–75.

218   "We did run": Pehle, letter, Nov. 28, 1944, RG 56, Records of the Assis-
      tant Secretaries, John Pehle, box 210, NACP.

218 "concerned with": Mannon, memo, Nov. 22, 1944, LM0305, reel 5, 405–6.

218 "the whole meeting": Ibid.

218 After the meeting: Davis, letter, Nov. 23, 1944, ibid., 407–8; Pehle, draft, Nov. 25, 1944, ibid., 410–11.

219 The ten million: The shoes on display at the United States Holocaust Memorial Museum are borrowed from Majdanek. Richard Lauterbach, "Sunday in Poland," *Life,* Sept. 18, 1944, 17–18; Raymond Davies, "A Scrap of Paper Carries the Odor of Death from Maidanek Across the World to U.S.A.," *PM,* Nov. 12, 1944.

219 The *New York Times:* "Harriman Confirms German Atrocities," *New York Times,* Oct. 27, 1944, 8.

219 "the most incredibly": Hugh Morrow, "1,765,000 Jews Killed with Gas at German Camp," *Philadelphia Inquirer,* Nov. 26, 1944, LM0305, reel 4, 405–6.

219 Larger newspapers: WRB staff, list of newspaper and press coverage, Nov. 28, 1944, TMD, vol. 799, 231–36.

219 "This time": "Nazi Brutality," *Topeka Capital,* Nov. 29, 1944, LM0305, reel 4, 372.

220 "Many Germans": "German Culture," *Fall River (Mass.) Herald News,* Nov. 27, 1944, ibid., 378.

220 "war guilty": "War Crimes," *New York World-Telegram,* Nov. 30, 1944, ibid., 365.

220 "It is time to silence": "Evidence Now Released Exposing Criminals We Fight," *Salt Lake Tribune,* Dec. 2, 1944, PWRB, ibid., 356.

220 An editorial cartoon: Justus, "The Weight of Evidence," *Minneapolis Star-Journal,* Dec. 1, 1944, ibid., 363.

221 "I am almost": Mannon, memos, Nov. 27, 1944, ibid., 567–72.

221 The army requested: Ibid.

221 The France Forever: Weill, letter, Nov. 27, 1944, LM0305, reel 5, 133.

221 "many of my relatives": Hecht, letter, Nov. 26, 1944, LM0305, reel 4, 462.

221 "underestimated": "Gallup Finds Most Believe Atrocity Tales," *Washington Post,* Dec. 3, 1944, ibid., 331–32.

222 "systematic": "Genocide," *Washington Post,* Dec. 3, 1944, ibid., 333.

CHAPTER 20: WAR AT CHRISTMAS

223 "served the useful": Pehle, letter, Oct. 26, 1944, RG 59, Secretary of the Treasury, Assistant Secretaries, Pehle, box 210, NACP.

223 "If 'their skirts' ": Reilly, letter, Oct. 21, 1944, ibid.

223 "Maybe it is": Pehle, letter, Oct. 26, 1944, ibid.

225 He had argued: Morgenthau, memo to the president, Nov. 27, 1944, TMD, vol. 799, 100–102.

225 "Pehle has run": "Surplus Property Disposal" meeting, Nov. 28, 1944, ibid., 168–81.

225 Henry Stimson: Transcript, Nov. 27, 1944, ibid., 19–22.

226 Now tasked: Ibid.

227 On October 26: "Zionist Dinner Tonight," *PM,* Oct. 26, 1944, PWRB, box 60, folder 18, FDRL.

227 In October: Stettinius, cable 8925, Oct. 26, 1944, LM0306, reel 28, 152–53.

227 Once the quota: Steinhardt, cable 2178, Nov. 15, 1944, LM0305, reel 17, 24–26.

227 "while the bookkeeping": Friedman, memo, Nov. 18, 1944, LM0305, reel 17, 29–30.

228 The new restrictions: Katzki, letter, Nov. 8, 1944, LM0306, reel 13, 442–49.

228 The Turkish Foreign Office: Packer, letter, Oct. 26, 1944, LM0306, reel 15, 67–68.

228 The day before: Steinhardt, cable 2070, Oct. 28, 1944, LM0306, reel 11, 849–50; Katzki, letter, Oct. 31, 1944, LM0306, reel 8, 245–57.

228 "indicated clearly": Steinhardt, letter, Nov. 11, 1944, LM0306, reel 11, 842–43.

229 The other group: Steinhardt, cable 2226, Nov. 21, 1944, ibid., 835–36.

229 Though the group: Steinhardt, cable 2256, Nov. 28, 1944, ibid., 824–26.

229 "energetic interventions": Steinhardt, cable 2438, Dec. 31, 1944, ibid. 782–83.

229 Katzki believed: Steinhardt, cable 31, Jan. 6, 1945, ibid., 777–78.

229 On New Year's Day: Hodel, memo, Jan. 1, 1945, LM0306, reel 7, 839.

229 On January 19: Stettinius, cable 95, Jan. 19, 1945, LM0306, reel 13, 25–26.

229 The Istanbul consulate: Metcalf, inventory, Feb. 12, 1945, LM0306, reel 30, 641–42.

229 In all of 1944: Goldin, statistics, Jan. 2, 1945, LM0306, reel 15, 242–43.

230 "I think that no one": Pehle, letter, Dec. 6, 1944, LM0305, reel 29, 399–400.

230 On December 22: Johnson, cable 5235, Dec. 22, 1944, LM0306, reel 5, 537–41.

230 The Spanish: Stettinius, cable 2566, Dec. 21, 1944, ibid., 534–36.

230 Before the end: Johnson, cable 5293, Dec. 29, 1944, ibid., 533.

230 "Wallenberg is safe": Johnson, cable 246, Jan. 20, 1945, LM0305, reel 29, 307.

231 "men and women": "Christmas in Freedom," Dec. 23, 1944, Refugee Services 1944, box 5, "Internees—Fort Ontario," AFSC. The recording is part of the NBC collection at the Library of Congress, RWA 7601 B1.

231 "In view": Pehle, letter, Dec. 23, 1944, LM0305, reel 17, 867.

231 "inadvisable": Stettinius, letter, Jan. 10, 1945, ibid., 876.

232 The commission's: John MacCormac, "Britain Ignores War-Crime Plans," *New York Times,* Jan. 11, 1945.

232 Two weeks later: Bertrand Hulem, "Pell Leaves War Crimes Board; He Favored Wider Punishments," *New York Times,* Jan. 27, 1945.

232 "a cornerstone": "Group" meeting, Jan. 12, 1945, TMD, vol. 809, 68–102.

232 "will have to act": DuBois and Luxford, memo, Jan. 12, 1945, ibid., 149.

232 Pehle thought: Pehle, memo, Jan. 17, 1944, TMD, vol. 810, 140.

232 The nudge worked: Morgenthau and McCloy, phone call, Jan. 26, 1945, TMD, vol. 812, 282–83.

232 Morgenthau explained: Morgenthau, letter, Jan. 27, 1945, TMD, vol. 813, 59.

232 "I cannot": Pehle, letter, Jan. 27, 1945, PWRB, box 60, folder 7, FDRL.

Chapter 21: Prisoner Exchanges

234 His name had first: "Jewish Evacuation" meeting, Jan. 26, 1944, TMD, vol. 696, 193–228.

234 O'Dwyer had emigrated: In 1986, Paul O'Dwyer published *Beyond the Golden Door,* purportedly his brother William's autobiography, compiled from notes and drafts. The WRB section of the book is both short and incorrect. According to the book, the White House contacted O'Dwyer in December 1943, claiming the WRB wasn't making sufficient progress and needed a new director. The fact that the WRB wasn't created until January 1944 seems entirely lost on the author. The book also includes a segment on the initial meetings with the Vaad about Vittel, which occurred seven months before O'Dwyer took over.

234 After working: "Former Mayor O'Dwyer Dead; Prosecuted Murder, Inc., Gang," *New York Times,* Nov. 25, 1961. See also Meyer Berger, "Murder, Inc.," *Life,* Sept. 30, 1940, 86–96.

235 "We were both": "Personnel" meeting, March 3, 1945, TMD, vol. 825, 129–34.

235 Carefully noting: Pehle, memo, Feb. 3, 1945, TMD, vol. 816, 12–16.

235 "the Refugee Board": "O'Dwyer to Return to Office in Kings," *Sun,* Jan. 29, 1945, LM0305, reel 24, 989.

235 By early February: "O'Dwyer Bobs Up in Mayoralty Pot," *New York Times,* Feb. 6, 1944, 21.

235 "there can be no": O'Dwyer, memo, Jan. 31, 1945, LM0305, reel 22, 947.

235 "beautiful blonde": "O'Dwyer Shocks Capital by Modest Demeanor," *Philadelphia Inquirer,* Feb. 2, 1945, LM0305, reel 24, 977.

235 Florence Hodel: Press conference, Jan. 31, 1945, LM0305, reel 25, 401–21.

236 Jacob Hodel: Jerry Kluttz and Electa Kluttz, "She's Uncle Sam's Wallet Watchdog," *Washington Post,* March 27, 1955, F11.

236 "I didn't have to": "War Refugee Board" meeting, March 7, 1945, TMD, vol. 826, 9–19.

236 "Miss Hodel": Morgenthau, "Procurement—Personnel—Bretton Woods," Feb. 17, 1945, TMD, vol. 820, 155–76.

236 "take up the cudgels": Press conference, Jan. 31, 1945, LM0305, reel 25, 401–21.

237 "I declare now": Winchell, transcript, Jan. 28, 1945, TMD, vol. 813, 95–103.

237 "crimes against": DuBois, memo, Jan. 29, 1945, LM0305, reel 17, 849–54.

237 "persistent": Grew, press release, Feb. 1, 1945, ibid., 839–40; "War Crimes," *Washington Post,* Feb. 3, 1945, 4.

237 "those responsible": "US Defines War Criminals to Include Jews' Persecutors," *New York Post,* Feb. 27, 1945, LM0305, reel 17, 826.

237 "sadistic orgy": Smertenko, letter, March 31, 1945, LM0306, reel 4, 935.

237 In Bern: McClelland, notes, Feb. 3, 1945, PWRB, box 79, "Negotiations in Switzerland," FDRL.

238 The Nazis identified: Swiss Foreign Office, verbal note, Dec. 22, 1944, PWRB, box 64, folder 7, FDRL.

238 With the support: Hadraba, message to Swiss Foreign Office, Dec. 28, 1944, PWRB, box 64, folder 6, FDRL.

239 The JDC agreed: Pehle, memo, Jan. 3, 1945, LM0306, reel 16, 179–80.

239 On January 30: The exchangees included the wife and children of Alfred Wiener, a refugee in London and the founder of the Wiener Library, the oldest Holocaust archive in the world. They had been in Bergen-Belsen, on Paraguayan papers. Wiener's wife, Margarethe, died almost immediately after her release from Belsen. State Department, press release, Feb. 5, 1945, LM0305, reel 6, 265–91.

239 On February 8: List of exchangees sent to Philippeville, March 2, 1945, PWRB, box 64, folder 8, FDRL.

239 A Swiss inspection: Tait, letter, March 23, 1945, ibid.

239 In the fall of 1944: Sternbuch, letter, Oct. 19, 1944, PWRB, box 70, folder 4, FDRL.

240 Sternbuch reassured: Ibid.; McClelland, notes, Jan. 19, 1945, PWRB, box 70, folder 5, FDRL.

240 "highly doubtful": McClelland, notes, Feb. 6, 1945, ibid.

240 The 1,210 prisoners: McClelland, notes, Feb. 13, 1945, ibid.; McClelland, list to Frischer, March 1, 1945, PWRB, box 69, folder 2, FDRL.

240 The Vaad held: "1200 Jews Safe in Switzerland," *PM,* Feb. 8, 1945, LM0306, reel 27, 901.

240 Sternbuch touted: "Grâce à M. Musy," *Tribune de Genève,* Feb. 8, 1945, PWRB, box 70, folder 5, FDRL; "Merci, M.," *Servir,* Feb. 11, 1945, ibid.

241   "Musy would be": McClelland, notes, Feb. 11, 1945, ibid.

241   "there had been": Harrison, cable 1069, Feb. 17, 1945, ibid.

241   "has been charged": Maher, notes, Feb. 10, 1945, ibid.

241   O'Dwyer grew: Hodel, memo, Feb. 21, 1945, ibid., 957.

242   "under the circumstances": Kalmanowitz, note, Feb. 21, 1945, ibid., 959.

242   "Henry Morgenthau, the Jew": "War Refugee Board" meeting, Feb. 27, 1945, TMD, vol. 823, 80–113.

242   "unanimous decision": O'Dwyer, letter, Feb. 28, 1945, LM0306, reel 28, 13–14.

242   Two weeks later: Hodel, memo, March 13, 1945, ibid., 41–42.

242   The next day: "War Refugee Board" meeting, March 14, 1945, TMD, vol. 828, 99–105.

242   "One of the Rabbis": "Group" meeting, Jan. 12, 1945, TMD, vol. 809, 68–102.

243   In Switzerland: McClelland, notes, March 2, 1945, PWRB, box 70, folder 6, FDRL; Sternbuch, letter, March 5, 1945, ibid.; Leavitt, letter, May 2, 1945, LM0306, reel 28, 105–8.

243   "Sternbuch, rather": Harrison, cable 1069, Feb. 17, 1945, PWRB, box 70, folder 5, FDRL.

243   "you saboteur": McClelland, letter, Feb. 28, 1945, PWRB, box 71, folder 9, FDRL.

243   "grossly": McClelland, letter, April 6, 1945, LM0306, reel 27, 434–36.

243   Musy returned: McClelland, notes, April 10, 1945, PWRB, box 70, folder 6, FDRL.

243   "Negro occupation troops": Ibid.

243   After assuring: In reality, some American soldiers did shoot German guards after liberation, notably in Dachau. See Jürgen Zarusky, " 'That Is Not the American Way of Fighting': The Shooting of Captured SS-Men During the Liberation of Dachau," in *Dachau and the Nazi Terror, 1933–1945,* ed. Wolfgang Benz (Dachau: Dachauer Hefte, 2004).

243   The War Refugee Board had promised: Rothmund, letter, Dec. 22, 1944, PWRB, box 65, folder 2, FDRL.

244   Though the largely: Huddle, cable 881, Feb. 8, 1945, LM0306, reel 16, 154–59.

244   "stunning shock": "We Appeal to the War Refugee Board Not to Transfer Refugees to Africa," *Egyleti Élet,* March 15, 1945, LM0305, reel 15, 783–84.

244   Josef Fischer: Fischer, letter, April 12, 1945, PWRB, box 65, folder 2, FDRL; McClelland, cable 44, June 1, 1945, PWRB, box 65, folder 4, FDRL.

244   "thoroughly hysterical": Desider, letter, April 18, 1945, PWRB, box 65, folder 3, FDRL.

244 "I wish": McClelland, letter, March 8, 1945, PWRB, box 65, folder 2, FDRL.

244 "personally": McClelland, letter, April 17, 1945, ibid.

244 "I do not imagine": McClelland, letter, May 29, 1945, ibid.

245 Iver Olsen had returned: Grew, cable 193, Feb. 2, 1945, LM0305, reel 1, 489–90.

245 The Lithuanian: Vokietaitis died in California in 1994. Olsen, receipt, March 17, 1945, LM0306, reel 30, 46.

245 In March: Johnson, cable 891, March 7, 1945, LM0305, reel 29, 308–9.

245 Finally, Olsen: Johnson, cable 1251, April 4, 1945, ibid., 334.

246 The spring brought: Johnson, cable 932, March 12, 1945, TMD, vol. 827, 107–14.

246 Kersten, whose: Johnson, cable 1186, March 29, 1945, LM0306, reel 26, 942–48.

246 "appeared in top form": Johnson, cable 1547, April 26, 1945, ibid., 899–903.

247 Musy, reporting: McClelland, notes, April 10, 1945, PWRB, box 70, folder 6, FDRL.

Chapter 22: Packages

248 "Appreciating": McCormack, memo, March 13, 1944, LM0306, reel 1, 262–63.

249 They already: Some organizations, including the JDC and the World Jewish Congress, sent packages into Theresienstadt (Terezin), a ghetto/camp populated by German World War I veterans, their families, and other "privileged" prisoners. The Nazis continued to maintain that Terezin was a "model city" and allowed the International Red Cross to visit in June 1944, entirely staging the experience. When McClelland transmitted a positive Red Cross report on Terezin, known as the Rossel report, to Washington, he explained that the picture presented "can unfortunately not be taken at its face value." McClelland, Rossel report, Oct. 26, 1944, LM0306, reel 9, 369–89.

249 Distribution channels: Burckhardt, letter to WRB, Feb. 29, 1944, PWRB, box 68, folder 2, FDRL.

249 The Red Cross: James, letters, April 14, 1944, PWRB, box 68, folder 4, FDRL.

250 The British wanted: Kuppinger, memos, June 17, 1944, LM0306, reel 24, 519–32; Foot, letter, June 13, 1944, LM0306, reel 1, 210–12.

250 "At this stage": Pehle, memo, June 22, 1944, LM0305, reel 1, 185–86.

250 The SS *Christina*: The Red Cross spelled the ship "Cristina." Stettinius, cable 4505, June 7, 1944, LM0306, reel 1, 223–24.

250 The WRB paid: Stettinius, cable 2769, Aug. 11, 1944, LM0306, reel 24, 639–41.

250 Among the wreckage: Squire, cable 223, July 7, 1944, ibid., 490–91.

250 The Red Cross repackaged: Schwarzenberg, letter, Dec. 4, 1944, PWRB, box 68, folder 5, FDRL.

250 With the WRB support: Johnson, cable 4440, Nov. 1, 1944, LM0306, reel 24, 795.

250 By September: The cards are located in RG 58.002M, USHMM. Harrison, cable 6263, Sept. 21, 1944, ibid., 919–21; Harrison, cable 7366, Nov. 8, 1944, ibid., 963–64; Schwarzenberg, letter, Sept. 21, 1944, PWRB, box 68, folder 4, FDRL.

250 Roswell McClelland learned: Cipher cable to MEW, Oct. 13, 1944, PWRB, box 68, folder 5, FDRL.

251 As many as thirty thousand: McClelland, memo, Nov. 17, 1944, PWRB, box 68, folder 5, FDRL.

251 Using his discretionary fund: ICRC, letter, Nov. 24, 1944, ibid.

251 Despite the agreement: McCormack, memo, Aug. 14, 1944, LM0306, reel 24, 632–37; Livingston, letter, Aug. 9, 1944, PWRB, box 68, folder 4, FDRL.

251 Ten days: Buchman, memo, Aug. 11, 1944, 1945–1954: New York Records of the American Jewish Joint Distribution Committee-NY 45–54, Administration-NY 45–54/1, file 00193_1108, JDC-NY.

251 Wallace, Burton & Davis: Buchman, order, Aug. 14, 1944, LM0306, reel 24, 628–30.

251 The War Refugee Board staff frantically: Pehle, letter, Aug. 16, 1944, LM0305, reel 1, 161–62.

251 Government money: The JDC decided to donate $15,000, and the WRB reimbursed it for the remaining $26,475. Leavitt, letter, Sept. 7, 1944, LM0306, reel 24, 751–52.

251 "We had to beat": "Group" meeting, Aug. 22, 1944, TMD, vol. 764, 47–75.

252 When it did: McCormack, memo, Oct. 21, 1944, LM0306, reel 24, 828–29.

252 The Feinberg: Feinberg, letter, Jan. 23, 1945, LM0306, reel 25, 172.

252 A third: Stoddard, letter, Dec. 26, 1944, ibid., 18–19.

252 At the WRB's request: FDR, memo, Sept. 12, 1944, LM0306, reel 24, 772.

252 The *Saivo:* McCormack, memo, Nov. 27, 1944, LM0306, reel 25, 92.

252 "express our deep": Kubowitzki, letters, Aug. 9 and Oct. 24, 1944, LM0306, reel 24, 645–47, 823.

252 It submitted its own: McClelland, letter, Nov. 22, 1944, PWRB, box 68, folder 5, FDRL.

252 "would not be able": McClelland, cable 5971, Sept. 9, 1944, LM0306, reel 24, 776.

253 The final 60,672: McCormack, memo, Dec. 15, 1944, LM0306, reel 25, 43.

253 At the beginning: Stettinius, cable 9419, Nov. 10, 1944, LM0306, reel 24, 960–61.

253 The American Red Cross: O'Connor, letter, Dec. 8, 1944, LM0306, reel 25, 64–65.

253 At the end of January: Pehle, letter, Jan. 19, 1945, ibid., 180–81.

253 Florence Hodel: FDR, memo, Jan. 31, 1945, ibid., 150.

253 Due to wartime: Hodel, memo, Jan. 31, 1945, ibid., 143–48.

253 Meanwhile, the WRB: Grew, cable 1554, March 1, 1945, ibid., 399–400.

254 "rapid deterioration": Huddle, cable 455, Jan. 22, 1945, ibid., 174–76.

254 "precedent": Hodel, memo, Feb. 1, 1945, LM0306, reel 17, 194.

254 But while: McCormack and Akzin, memo, Feb. 10, 1945, ibid., 190–91.

254 In mid-February: Allied Air Forces, "Effect of Allied Bombings of German Transportation System," Feb. 27, 1945, TMD, vol. 823, 174–76.

254 On February 20: Grew, who had been U.S. ambassador to Japan from 1932 to 1941, was imprisoned after Pearl Harbor and exchanged in July 1942. He had the bushiest eyebrows you have ever seen.

254 The intelligence: O'Dwyer, minutes, Feb. 28, 1945, TMD, vol. 823, 233–34.

255 "Invaluable aid": Harrison, cable 1217, Feb. 24, 1945, LM0305, reel 23, 49–50.

255 O'Dwyer ordered: McClelland, letters, Feb. 28, 1945, PWRB, box 68, folder 6, FDRL.

255 "We have untold": "War Refugee Board" meeting, March 7, 1945, TMD, vol. 826, 9–19.

255 Finally, after: McCloy, cable, March 8, 1945, RG 107, Asst. Secretary of War John McCloy, Formerly Security Classified Correspondence, box 44, "400.38—Countries—Germany," NACP; Hodel, memo, March 9, 1945, LM0306, reel 17, folder 2, 134.

255 The Red Cross used: McClelland, notes, March 9, 1945, PWRB, box 68, folder 7, FDRL.

255 Some War Refugee Board packages: Harrison, cable 1765, March 24, 1945, LM0306, reel 17, 260–62.

255 The Red Cross found: McClelland, cable 1738, March 23, 1945, ibid., 268.

255 Before he left: Harrison, cable 1727, March 22, 1945, ibid., 275–77.

256 "commission": Wyler, letter, March 14, 1945, PWRB, box 71, folder 9, FDRL.

256 "stressed the urgency": Mann, letter, April 9, 1945, LM0306, reel 17, 403–10.

256 "I hope we can": Phone conversation, March 29, 1945, ibid., 229–36.

257 The military delivered: Harrison, cable 297, April 4, 1945, PWRB, box 68, folder 9, FDRL.

257 "though geographic area": Ibid.

257 Sternbuch rented: Harrison, cable 1740, March 23, 1945, LM0306, reel 17, 270–71.

257 McClelland appeased: Schwarzenberg, letter, March 16, 1945, PWRB, box 68, folder 7, FDRL.

257 "They have": Storch, cable copy, April 9, 1945, PWRB, box 68, folder 9, FDRL.

257 The second group: O'Dwyer, letter, April 6, 1945, LM0306, reel 25, 468.

257 With no time: Gerhardt, letter, March 30, 1945, LM0306, reel 25, 987–88.

258 The news: Hodel, memo, April 6, 1945, LM0306, reel 17, 199–200.

258 When McClelland: Harrison, cable 2009, April 6, 1945, LM0306, reel 25, 981.

258 "the Germans would": Hodel, memo, April 10, 1945, ibid., 961–62.

258 three thousand packages: Harrison, cable 2120, April 10, 1945, ibid., 964–65.

258 On April 20: O'Connor, letter, April 20, 1945, ibid., 942.

258 Three days later: In June 1945, the WRB arranged to resell the 206,000 POW packages to UNRRA. Harrison, cable 2421, April 25, 1945, ibid., 345–47; Weintraub, letter, Aug. 30, 1945, ibid., 929.

258 Some disappeared: Johnson, cable 2071, June 8, 1945, ibid., 548–49.

258 More than 140,000: McClelland, letter, June 20, 1945, ibid., 543–46.

258 Some were handed out: Images of this liberation are in the ICRC archives and described in Sébastien Farré, "The ICRC and the Detainees in Nazi Concentration Camps (1942–1945)," *International Review of the Red Cross* 94, no. 844 (Winter 2012): 1381–408.

Chapter 23: Liberation

260 "The visual evidence": Alfred D. Chandler, ed., *The Papers of Dwight David Eisenhower: The War Years* (Baltimore: Johns Hopkins Press, 1970), 4:2615–16.

260 When Roswell: Stettinius, cable 1485, April 17, 1945, LM0305, reel 4, 30–31.

261 "You may care": Mann, letter, May 10, 1945, LM0305, reel 15, 790–91.

261 "war criminals": Hodel, memo, March 20, 1945, LM0306, reel 4, 899–900.

261 "guilty of maltreating": "Big Three Warns Germany Against Maltreatment of POWs," *PM*, April 24, 1945, ibid., 916.

261 Finally, in mid-May: O'Dwyer, letter, May 18, 1944, LM0305, reel 12, 316.

262 "Suppose": "War Refugee Board" meeting, April 21, 1945, TMD, vol. 839, 124–26A.

262 "You never": "Group" meeting, April 21, 1945, ibid., 100–114.

262 "V-E Day": Morgenthau, letter, May 10, 1945, 2015.255.1, Morgenthau Family Papers.

262 On May 12: Warren, memo, May 12, 1945, RG 59, WRB records, box 1, "WRB 1945," NACP.

262 In the meantime: Hodel and Gerhardt, phone call, May 12, 1945, RG 107, entry 180, box 44, "WRB," NACP.

263 "felt very strongly": Hodel, memo, May 12, 1945, PWRB, box 60, folder 2, FDRL.

263 "one of the greatest": "War Refugee Board" meeting, May 15, 1945, TMD, vol. 847, 25–32.

263 "Our job": Ibid.

263 O'Dwyer, still: "O'Dwyer Hat Tossed in Ring," *Sun,* May 16, 1945, PWRB, box 61, folder 2, FDRL.

264 Pehle, in the midst: "War Refugee Board" meeting, May 16, 1945, TMD, vol. 847, 132–36.

264 "trouble brewing": Ibid.

264 They were still: Hodel, memo, March 19, 1945, TMD, vol. 829, 391.

264 "I was terribly": Morgenthau, diary entry on dinner with President Roosevelt, April 11, 1945, Morgenthau Presidential Diaries, reel 2.

264 "I spent last": Morgenthau, message for the press on Roosevelt's death, April 12, 1945, ibid.

265 "the establishment": Morgenthau, memo, May 23, 1945, TMD, vol. 848, 343–47.

265 "Dear Henry": Truman, letter, June 2, 1945, TMD, vol. 851, 147.

265 It was up to: Bernays, memo, June 2, 1945, RG 226, entry 146, box 39, "War Refugee Board," NACP; Hodel, transcript, June 4, 1945, PWRB, box 60, folder 2, FDRL.

266 As the Treasury: Morgenthau, memo, June 6, 1945, TMD, vol. 852, 149–50.

266 "They say": It seems the idea likely originated with Meyer Weisgal of the Jewish Agency. Weisgal, letter, June 14, 1945, TMD, vol. 855, 1; Morgenthau and Grew, phone call, June 11, 1945, TMD, vol. 854, 5–6.

266 Eager for the assignment: Hodel, memo, June 12, 1945, LM0305, reel 8, 827.

266 With the board's: Marjorie McClelland, letter, June 26, 1945, McClelland Papers, 2014.500.

267 "some German(?)": Sternbuch, letter, July 5, 1945, RG 84, Bern lega-

tion, American Interests Section, box 96, "Union of Orthodox Rabbis," NACP; McClelland, letter, July 13, 1945, ibid.

267 Through McClelland: McClelland, report, Aug. 2, 1945, LM0306, reel 15, 860–921.

267 "I should estimate": McClelland, report, Nov. 27, 1944, 1945–1954: New York Records of the American Jewish Joint Distribution Committee-NY 45–54, Administration-NY 45–54/1, file 00193_1063, JDC-NY.

267 "I did my best": McClelland, report, Aug. 2, 1945, LM0306, reel 15, 860–921.

268 Ten days: Olsen, affidavit, Dec. 13, 1945, LM0306, reel 29, 298–301.

269 "felt . . . that": Morgenthau, letter, July 26, 1945, 2015.255.1, Morgenthau Family Papers.

269 Harrison sent cables: Vinson, letter, Aug. 1, 1945, LM0305, reel 8, 783–84.

269 "plain truth": Harrison, report, Aug. 4, 1945, ibid., 739–58.

270 "the War Refugee Board": Latta, letter, Sept. 14, 1945, LM0305, reel 25, 752–53.

270 Paul McCormack: McCormack, letter, July 11, 1945, PWRB, box 60, folder 2, FDRL.

271 "I am of": O'Dwyer, report, Sept. 15, 1945, LM0305, reel 25, 275–351.

271 "Such was the fight": McClelland, report, Aug. 2, 1945, LM0306, reel 15, 860–921.

AFTERWORD

274 The United States did not change: The Hart-Celler Act of 1965; the United States finally signed the Protocol to the United Nations Refugee Convention in 1968.

274 "What made the WRB": Yehuda Bauer, *American Jewry and the Holocaust: The American Jewish Joint Distribution Committee, 1939–1945* (Detroit: Wayne State University Press, 1981), 403.

275 John Pehle seemed: Lawrence Lesser's son, George, remembers Pehle and Lesser on the phone together after reading about the photographs. Neither recalled the requests to bomb the camp at all. Interview with the author, May 21, 2017.

275 Historians often: Pehle, interview with Laurence Jarvik, Oct. 16, 1978, 2015.255.1, Morgenthau Family Papers.

275 "A year or two ago": Howe, broadcast, Feb. 21, 1944, LM0305, reel 20, 714–17.

276 The War Refugee Board saved: The historian David Wyman estimated the WRB saved 200,000 Jews and 20,000 non-Jews, and his calculations are frequently cited. Wyman credits the WRB with the lives of

all the surviving Jews of Budapest and Transnistria, a vast overestimation given the complicated political and military situation at the time. Wyman, *Abandonment of the Jews,* xiv and 405n129.

276 In February 1945: McCormack, memo, Feb. 19, 1945, LM0305, reel 25, 392–95.

276 "The accomplishments": WRB, "History of the War Refugee Board," vol. 1, 1945, LM0305, reel 27, 575.

ILLUSTRATION CREDITS

The views or opinions expressed in this book, and the context in which the images are used, do not necessarily reflect the views or policy of, nor imply approval or endorsement by, the United States Holocaust Memorial Museum.

INSERT

PAGE 1
Courtesy of the Franklin D. Roosevelt Presidential Library and Museum, Hyde Park, New York

PAGE 2
Top: Library of Congress
Bottom: Thomas D. McAvoy for *Life* magazine / Getty Images

PAGE 3
Top: Courtesy of the Franklin D. Roosevelt Presidential Library and Museum, Hyde Park, New York
Bottom: Library of Congress

PAGE 4
Top: Courtesy of the Spertus Institute for Jewish Learning and Leadership
Bottom left and right: USHMM

PAGE 5
Top left: Courtesy of the Franklin D. Roosevelt Presidential Library and Museum, Hyde Park, New York
Top right: American Jewish Joint Distribution Committee, New York
Bottom left and right: USHMM

PAGE 6
Top: American Jewish Joint Distribution Committee, New York
Bottom left and right: Courtesy of the Franklin D. Roosevelt Presidential
Library and Museum, Hyde Park, New York

PAGE 7
Top left and bottom: USHMM
Top right: Courtesy of the Riksarkivet, Stockholm, Sweden

PAGE 8
International Committee of the Red Cross

INDEX

Page numbers beginning with 289 refer to endnotes.

Auschwitz-Birkenau studied by,
156–58
and Auschwitz reports, 213–19
and "Blood for Goods," 133, 136–37,
138, 139, 141
British protest at licenses of,
200–201
budget of, 76, 77, 78, 203, 304
closing of, 202–3, 262–64, 265–66,
270, 271
creation of, 7–8, 55, 56, 57, 58,
59–60, 63, 64, 273, 275
Dewey's praise for, 201
in diplomatic conflicts, 83
estimate of refugees saved by, 276,
343–44
false identity cards paid for by, 267
final summary of work released by,
270–71
food packages sent to camps by,
248–59, 261, 271
Hayes vs., 83–85
Hirschmann's trips to Turkey for,
see Hirschmann, Ira
and Hungarian concessions on
Jews, 163
Hungarian newspaper's letter to,
on liberated prisoners, 244
information on Hungarian
deportations learned by, 120
international unwillingness to
work with, 65–66
Istanbul office closed by, 229
JDC trusted by, 118
letter from British embassy to, 104
license rules of, 117, 118
McClelland appointed to Swiss
post by, 117
McClelland's final summary of,
271–72
and Mayer's ransom negotiations,
176, 204–5, 239, 261
message to diplomats from, 65–68

and money for Neutra rabbi, 158,
160
Morgenthau's warning about
closing of, 102–3
negotiations over Hungary with,
166, 170, 175, 243–44
O'Dwyer put in charge of, 232, 233,
234–35
Pehle's resignation from, 232–33
and Pehle's statement on postwar
reckoning, 103–12, 113, 114, 115
Pehle's twofold strategy for, 105
plans for U.S. refugee camp of,
141–50
and plan to relocate Hungarian
Jews in Palestine, 164
prisoner exchange considered by,
123, 125–26
protective papers plan of, 125–29
psychological warfare by, 70, 81,
104, 114–15, 164, 199, 215
reaching out to neutral nations
over Hungary, 166–76
refugees saved at end of war by, 238
rescue money laundered through
Goodyear by, 188–89
revision of mandate of, 263, 265
staffing of, 60–62
Sternbuch's tractor scheme rejected
by, 160–61
Turkish aid considered by, 89
Turkish refugee ships and, 93, 96,
99, 101, 179–81, 324
Vaad's request of license from,
241–42
Vatican appealed to over Hungary
by, 208–9
violence at end of war as concern
of, 237–38
Vittel prisoners as concern of,
122–25
Wallenberg's work for, 194, 195,
208, 229–30, 246

About the Author

Rebecca Erbelding is an archivist, curator, and exhibition research historian at the United States Holocaust Memorial Museum in Washington, D.C. She has a PhD in American history from George Mason University. She and her work have been profiled in *The Washington Post, The New York Times,* and *The New Yorker,* and featured on the History Channel, NPR, and other media outlets.